PUBLIC SERVICE
IN TOUGH TIMES

PUBLIC SERVICE
IN TOUGH TIMES

Working Under Austerity in Manitoba

EDITED BY JESSE HAJER, IAN HUDSON, AND JENNIFER KEITH

ump
University of Manitoba Press

Public Service in Tough Times: Working Under Austerity in Manitoba
© The Authors 2025

29   28   27   26   25   1   2   3   4   5

University of Manitoba Press
Winnipeg, Manitoba, Canada
Treaty 1 Territory
uofmpress.ca

For EU product safety concerns please contact Mare Nostrum Group B.V., Mauritskade 21D, 1091 GC Amsterdam, The Netherlands, gpsr@mare-nostrum.co.uk.

Cataloguing data available from Library and Archives Canada
ISBN 978-177284-130-5 (PAPER)
ISBN 978-177284-132-9 (PDF)
ISBN 978-177284-133-6 (EPUB)
ISBN 978-177284-131-2 (BOUND)

Cover and Interior Design by Jess Koroscil

The University of Manitoba Press acknowledges the financial support for its publication program provided by the Government of Canada through the Canada Book Fund, the Canada Council for the Arts, the Manitoba Department of Sport, Culture, and Heritage, the Manitoba Arts Council, and the Manitoba Book Publishing Tax Credit.

Support for open access publication was provided by University of Manitoba Libraries.

Funded by the Government of Canada | Canadä

🍁 CERTIFIED CANADIAN PUBLISHER

IN MEMORY OF JOHN LOXLEY

CONTENTS

ILLUSTRATIONS

Tables

Figures

ACKNOWLEDGEMENTS

This work was supported by the generous funding of the Social Sciences and Humanities Research Council under Grant 895-2020-1005 awarded to the Manitoba Research Alliance, Community-Driven Solutions to Poverty: Challenges and Possibilities. Funding was also received from the University of Manitoba Graduate Enhancement of Tri-Agency Stipends (GETS) program.

We would like to thank the University of Manitoba Press for carefully seeing the manuscript though the publication process. Jill McConkey guided us through the whole process, which included organizing the encouraging and helpful comments of two anonymous reviewers. Barbara Romanik organized the copyedits and proofs. Finally, Rachel Taylor did the invaluable and careful work of copyediting.

We were very fortunate to have two amazing research assistants for this project. Jack MacAuley put in yeoman's work to collect much of the data on staffing and spending that was used in each chapter. Holly Scotland supported this project from start to finish, organizing chapter authors, processing and summarizing survey data, providing editorial suggestions, compiling the disparate chapter formats and styles into a single manuscript, and ensuring that deadlines were actually met. It is no exaggeration to say that the book would not have been possible without Jack and Holly's work.

We would also like to thank our labour and community partners who worked with the project team to promote worker participation in our research, review draft materials, and provide subject matter expertise in their areas of work, including the Association of Employees Supporting Education Services (AESES), the Brandon University Faculty Association, the Canadian Community Development Network–Manitoba, the Canadian Union of Public Employees–Manitoba and Locals 204, 500, 998, 1063, 1482, 2153, and 2348, We are grateful to Doctors Manitoba, the International Brotherhood of Electrical Workers Local 2034, the Manitoba Association of Newcomer Serving Organizations, the Manitoba Arts Network, the Manitoba Government and General Employees' Union, the Manitoba Association of Crown Attorneys, the Manitoba

Association of Health Care Professionals, the Manitoba Federation of Labour, the Manitoba Non-Profit Housing Association, the Manitoba Teachers' Society, Operating Engineers of Manitoba Local 987, United Food and Commercial Workers, UNIFOR, the Manitoba Association of Women's Shelters, the University of Manitoba Faculty Association, the University of Winnipeg Faculty Association, Winnipeg Association of Non-Teaching Employees, and the Winnipeg Association of Public Service Officers. Finally, we would like to thank the dedicated workers delivering publicly funded services in Manitoba who completed our research survey and trusted us to share their stories.

CONTRIBUTORS

Brenda Austin-Smith is a professor of English, Theatre, Film, and Media at the University of Manitoba.

Fletcher Baragar is an associate professor of Economics at the University of Manitoba.

Katherine Burley has a master's degree in Economics from the University of Manitoba.

Robert Chernomas is a professor of Economics at the University of Manitoba.

Elizabeth Comack is a distinguished professor emerita of Sociology and Criminology at the University of Manitoba.

Sarah Cooper is an associate professor of City Planning at the University of Manitoba.

Amelia Curran is an instructor of Criminal Justice at the University of Winnipeg.

Lynne Fernandez is a research associate for the Canadian Centre for Policy Alternatives–Manitoba and the Manitoba Research Alliance.

Scott Forbes is a professor of Biology at the University of Winnipeg.

Mara Fridell is an associate professor of Sociology and Criminology at the University of Manitoba.

Shreya Ghimire is a PhD candidate in Political Science at York University.

Julie Guard is a professor in Labour Studies and History at the University of Manitoba.

Jesse Hajer is an associate professor of Economics and Labour Studies at the University of Manitoba.

Niall Harney is a senior researcher for the Canadian Centre for Policy Alternatives–Manitoba where he holds the Errol Black Chair in Labour Issues.

Ian Hudson is a professor of Economics at the University of Manitoba.

Mark Hudson is a professor of Sociology and the coordinator of the Global Political Economy program at the University of Manitoba.

Jennifer Keith is a PhD graduate of Indigenous Studies at the University of Manitoba.

Karine Levasseur is a professor in Political Science at the University of Manitoba.

Orly Linovski is an associate professor of City Planning in the Faculty of Architecture at the University of Manitoba.

Shauna MacKinnon is a professor and chair of Urban and Inner-City Studies at the University of Winnipeg.

James P. Mulvale is a professor in the Faculty of Social Work at the University of Manitoba.

Susan Prentice is a professor of Sociology at the University of Manitoba.

Andrea Rounce is a professor in Political Science at the University of Manitoba.

Holly Scotland is a graduate student in Economics and Society at the University of Manitoba.

Jim Silver is professor emeritus in Urban and Inner-City Studies at the University of Winnipeg.

Niigaan Sinclair is a professor of Indigenous Studies at the University of Manitoba.

Ee-Seul Yoon is an associate professor of Educational Administration, Leadership, and Policy in the Faculty of Education at the University of Manitoba.

Sarah Zell is an assistant professor of Urban and Inner-City Studies at the University of Winnipeg.

PREFACE

Methodology and Methods

The research presented in this volume analyzes the degree and impact of the austerity policy implemented in Manitoba from 2016 to 2022, with a focus on profiling the views and experiences of the workers delivering provincially funded public services. The research methodology and methods are based on two earlier projects of a smaller but similar nature, in partnership with the Manitoba Government and General Employees' Union (Hajer and Keith 2018; Keith, Hajer, and Conway 2021). A participatory action research (PAR) methodology was utilized. MacKinnon (2018), drawing upon Green et al. (2003), describes a PAR methodology as "systematic inquiry, with the collaboration of those affected by the issue being studied, for purposes of education and taking action or affecting social change" and notes crucially that "PAR values engaging non-researchers in the research process" (4–5). A PAR methodology allowed us to build the level of trust necessary for workers to feel confident that their confidentiality would be protected and that their investments in the research process would be put toward making positive change, in hopes of improving public administration in Manitoba. This was particularly important given the suspicion shown by the 2016–2023 Progressive Conservative (PC) government toward public sector workers, in particular civil servants, and fear of reprisal. Transparency regarding our motivations and the connections we had and developed with worker and community organizations—many of whom already had a relationship with the Manitoba Research Alliance, the network of scholars sponsoring the research, and/or its host organization, the Canadian Centre for Policy Alternatives–Manitoba—helped facilitate worker participation in the project.

Within the PAR methodology, a mixed-methods approach was utilized, for several reasons. The first stems from a strong belief in the value of mixed-methods research, in particular the insightful findings that result from combining qualitative and quantitative research methods when undertaking applied public policy analysis of this nature. Many of the contributors to this volume are collaborators in the Manitoba Research Alliance, an organization that also supports and promotes a plurality of methods, in particular community-based participatory research. Second, based on experiences in the precursor projects noted above, there was an expectation that qualitative data from workers was necessary to produce a rich and informed research contribution. While public reporting of expenditures and staffing levels provides some insight and was utilized, the expertise and experience of the public sector workers delivering the services being studied was not only beneficial to the study but also necessary given the limited public disclosure of the actions of government and rationale for public policy changes. Partners who joined the project, along with the editorial team, helped shape the research and survey questions, with varied participation based on capacity and interest. The contributions of partners included providing background information on the issues facing their membership, informing the survey questions, promoting participation in the survey among their members, reviewing findings, and providing feedback. Partners were also encouraged and supported in sharing the key findings of the study most relevant to their membership, including brief plain language summaries written by chapter authors. The plain language chapter summaries are available on the Austerity in Manitoba project website (Hajer 2023).

Survey of Public Sector Workers

A survey of public sector workers was administered in partnership with worker and community organizations. The full set of survey questions can be found on our project website (Hajer 2023). Public sector unions and networks representing provincial workers who deliver provincially funded public services were contacted to partner in the study. Partners included: the Association of Employees Supporting Education Services (AESES), the Brandon University Faculty Association, the Canadian Community Economic Development Network, the Canadian Union of Public Employees–Manitoba and Locals 204, 500, 998, 1063, 1482, 2153, and 2348, Doctors Manitoba, the International Brotherhood of Electrical Workers Local 2034, the Manitoba Association of Newcomer

Service Organizations, the Manitoba Arts Network, the Manitoba Government and General Employees' Union (MGEU), the Manitoba Association of Crown Attorneys, the Manitoba Association of Health Care Professionals (MAHCP), the Manitoba Federation of Labour, the Manitoba Non-Profit Housing Association, the Manitoba Teachers' Society, Operating Engineers Local 987, United Food and Commercial Workers, UNIFOR, the Manitoba Association of Women's Shelters, the University of Manitoba Faculty Association (UMFA), the University of Winnipeg Faculty Association, Winnipeg Association of Non-Teaching Professionals, and the Winnipeg Association of Public Service Officers. Survey responses were collected between 15 November 2022 and 18 January 2023, with 96 percent of the surveys being completed by 15 December 2022.

To help ensure the integrity of data gathered through the survey, access was not public and required unique one-time use invitations sent to eligible participants. Participants gained access to the survey invitations in one of four ways. If the partner organization was able and willing to share email addresses of members, all members with emails provided were sent a link to access the survey. This was the preferred method and was used for all civil service bargaining units and other workers represented by MGEU. If sharing of email addresses was not possible, but the partner had the capacity to send out individualized links to members, the invitations were sent out by the partner. If neither of these options were possible, a general recruitment letter was sent by the partner organization to its membership, instructing them to contact the principal investigator for a link. In addition, participation was promoted though a social media campaign and by encouraging survey participants to refer colleagues.

Our total survey response of 2,078 workers is well above the number that would be required for a confidence interval of 95 percent with a 5 percent margin of error at the aggregate level if a random sample was used. In the two major subcategories of the sample, members of the civil service and those working for an arm's length provincial entity, such as a school division, health region, university, or Crown corporation, also independently had sufficient numbers to meet this threshold. However, given the partnership recruitment method, our sample participation across service areas was shaped by our ability to secure partner organizations and their ability and limitations to share member contact information and/ or deliver unique one-time use survey links to each member. While all public sector workers delivering provincially funded public services were eligible to participate, and a public recruitment process did take place, participation rates were higher when unions were able to share the email addresses of their members or send out a unique link to each member. Of particular note, nurses, teachers, and doctors are underrepresented in the sample, while civil service, Crown corporation, post-secondary education workers (especially UMFA and AESES members), and other healthcare professionals (especially MAHCP members) are strongly represented. This and the PAR model used for this study should be considered by readers when interpreting the statistical results presented in our study.

Financial and Staffing Data

The province of Manitoba publishes various reports including data on expenditure, revenue, the size of the provincial economy, population data, and government staffing levels, including data on full-time equivalent (FTE) positions (which may be filled or vacant), annual employee counts reported by the Public Service Commission, and vacancy rates in 2022. This data is published in its annual budget documents, departmental annual reports, and the government's annual *Report on the Estimates of Expenditure and Supplementary Information* published with the government's Annual Reports and Public Accounts (Government of Manitoba 2023). Our compiled data used throughout this report with detailed referencing and notes is available in our online data set on our project website (Hajer 2023). Of particular note: in order to present time series data of government expenditures and FTEs in specific program and policy areas, data decomposition and recompilation was required to account for the changes in departmental responsibilities over time. Given that the government does not explicitly or proactively report what units and staff are transferred when cabinet responsibilities are shuffled, this work required a careful review of departmental annual reports. Our online data set cites the source of each datapoint, allowing readers to retrace our steps. Given the complexity of this task and the incomplete data at our disposal, we welcome any feedback and look forward to building on these efforts in the future.

When it comes to announcing expenditure in popular policy areas such as health and education, governments of all stripes will often make reference to "record spending." On the surface, these claims are generally true: it is rare for spending in these areas, or overall government spending for that matter, to go down in any given year. However, there are at least two problems with relying on "dollars spent" as a measure of the support being dedicated to any given public service over time. The first is that the value of a dollar changes over time; due to inflation, a dollar today buys less than it has in the past. The second is that the population is growing over time, requiring greater investment to maintain service levels. To adjust for these factors, this volume primarily uses population and consumer price index data published by Statistics Canada to generate inflation-adjusted expenditure per resident. When examining the provincial government as a whole, revenue and debt statistics are presented in relation to the size of the economy, as measured by gross domestic product.

Jesse Hajer
University of Manitoba

References

Government of Manitoba. 2023. *Report on the Estimates of Expenditure and Supplementary Information*. Winnipeg: Government of Manitoba. https://manitoba.ca/asset_library/en/publicaccounts2023/REESI2022-2023.pdf.

Green, Lawrence, M. Anne George, Mark Daniel, C. James Frankish, Carol P. Herbert, William R. Bowie, Michel O'Neill, Meredith Minkler, and Nina Wallerstein. 2003. "Appendix C: Guidelines for Participatory Research in Health Promotion." In *Community-Based Participatory Research for Health*, edited by Nina Wallerstein, Bonnie Duran, John G. Oetzel, and Meredith Minkler. San Francisco: Jossey-Bass.

Hajer, Jesse. 2023. "Austerity in Manitoba." Manitoba Research Alliance. 29 August. https://mra-mb.ca/austerity-in-manitoba/.

Hajer, Jesse, and Jennifer Keith. 2018. *Air Services for All Manitobans: Assessing the Rationale for Privatizing Manitoba Government Air Services*. Breakwater Group Worker Cooperative. 26 July. https://www.mgeu.ca/uploads/ck/files/mgas_privatization_report_web.pdf.

Keith, Jennifer, Jesse Hajer, and Michael Conway. 2021. *Hard Infrastructure, Hard Times: Workers Perspectives on Privatization and Contracting Out of Manitoba Infrastructure*. Winnipeg: Canadian Centre for Policy Alternatives–Manitoba. https://www.policyalternatives.ca/publications/reports/hard-infrastructure-hard-times.

MacKinnon, Shauna. 2018. *Practising Community-Based Participatory Research: Stories of Engagement, Empowerment, and Mobilization*. Vancouver: University of British Columbia Press.

INTRODUCTION

Jesse Hajer with Katherine Burley and Ian Hudson

To save or to spend? Big or small government? These tend to be two of the central questions for governments at every level as they contemplate how best to generate economic growth and improve their citizens' overall health and welfare. Some economists and policy makers promote larger governments and deficit spending in areas such as infrastructure, education, healthcare, and social services as necessary investments in future growth and shared prosperity. Others emphasize the costs of "big government" and deficits, including higher interest payments and the potential to displace private sector spending and investment. They then may choose to advocate fiscal constraint or austerity, particularly if the size of the debt relative to the economy is increasing, in an effort to reduce the relative size of government, eliminate deficits, and decrease the burden of debt. The latter was the policy of the Progressive Conservative (PC) Party of Manitoba when first elected to replace the New Democratic Party (NDP) of Manitoba in April 2016, in stark contrast to the previous government's emphasis on economic stimulus and tolerance of deficits to support investments in infrastructure, education, and skills training.

By the time of the 2016 election, the provincial NDP had governed for over sixteen years. Departing from the NDP's long track record of balanced budgets, the new leader and premier, Greg Selinger, taking a stimulus approach, led the province relatively successfully out of the 2008/09 financial crisis, with above-average economic growth and lower unemployment (Scarth 2016). While deficit spending was initially accepted as necessary in the aftermath of the fiscal crisis and historic flooding in 2011, persistently high deficits and a surprise increase of the provincial sales tax

(PST) to 8 percent, led to the government falling out of favour with many Manitobans. While polling suggested that voters were open to the idea of the PST increase to fund public investments in critical infrastructure (Scarth 2016), the premier's unpopularity, the manner in which the PST was raised (without consultation, after public statements interpreted as promising not to do so), and internal party conflict led to the fall of the NDP government (Rounce and Levasseur 2016).

The PCs seized on Manitobans' discontent with Selinger and his NDP. Under the leadership of soon-to-be premier Brian Pallister, the PCs campaigned on a platform to reduce taxes, with an emphasis on returning the PST to its former 7 percent rate, cutting income taxes, and restoring a closer balance between revenues and spending. The campaign platform did not emphasize deep austerity. In the lead-up to the 2016 election, Pallister softened earlier calls for expenditure cuts, noting that a PC government would only seek to contain expenditure growth as opposed to making year-over-year reductions, and did not commit to balancing the budget in the first term (Lambert 2015).

Despite these commitments, through a combination of expenditure cuts and restraint, the PCs rapidly reduced and eliminated the budget deficit. In each of the three fiscal years following the 2016 election, the government underspent its budget, and the provincial deficit rapidly contracted from $932 million in 2015/16 to a $9 million surplus in 2018/19, according to the auditor general (the government disputed this).[1] This work was facilitated by the engagement of for-profit multinational business consulting and accounting firms, including PwC and KPMG, who were embedded in the public service to prepare detailed reports with recommendations on how to reduce expenditures and downsize government. Expenditures as a proportion of gross domestic product (GDP) were 24.4 percent in 2016/17, dropping a full percentage point—the equivalent of $734 million in spending—within two years.[2] Over this period of retrenchment, civil service wages were frozen, and the size of the civil service was reduced by 16 percent, resulting in the loss of over 2,000 workers.

On 1 July 2019, the PCs followed through with their PST promise, reducing the rate to 7 percent. Then Premier Pallister called an early election for September 2019 and campaigned on familiar themes of fiscal balance and tax cuts, including a commitment to eliminate the education property tax, at the time an $874 million revenue source. Following another majority victory, the PCs continued on the same path, generating a $5 million surplus in 2019/20, despite an estimated loss of $237 million in revenues from the PST cut.[3] In March 2020, Premier Pallister announced his party's intention to further reduce the PST rate to 6 percent on 1 July, and by March of 2021 he had reduced the civil service work force by more than 600 additional workers (Hajer 2025).

The onset of the COVID-19 pandemic, however, temporarily derailed plans for fiscal balance and further tax cuts. Although the PCs initially used the pandemic as an opportunity to pursue deep cuts to the broader public sector, popular backlash, including from the business sector, eventually led the party to relent and commit to significant spending for COVID-19 relief, more in line with the approach of other provinces (Hajer and Fernandez 2021). The government deferred a further PST reduction—which was never implemented—and ran a historically unprecedented deficit of $2.124 billion in 2020/21, and another $704 million deficit in 2021/22. The PCs, however, did make progress on their commitment to eliminate the education property tax, refunding 25 percent of the taxes at a cost of nearly $250 million in 2021/22, with the rebate increasing to 50 percent and estimated to cost $453 million in 2023/24 (Manitoba Finance 2022; Government of Manitoba 2023a). Despite these tax cuts, the province still ended up running a $373 million surplus in 2022/23, thanks to inflationary revenue windfalls, large federal transfers, and spending increases well below the rate of inflation.

Defining Austerity and Its Motives

Many have argued that the Manitoba government's policies from 2016 to 2022 represent an example of austerity (Brodbeck 2020; Evans et al. 2023, 149; Hajer and Fernandez 2021; Lett 2019; Wilt 2019). The most common definition of austerity, employed by proponents such as Alesina, Favero, and Giavazzi (2019), is a change in government fiscal policy aimed at reducing deficits, including expenditure cuts or tax increases. Rooted in conservative, supply-side economic theory, proponents of austerity suggest that balanced budgets will inspire private sector confidence, leading to greater investment and stronger economic growth (Whiteside et al. 2021). While the PC government clearly pursued expenditure restraint, a continuing commitment to tax cuts does not fit squarely with a deficit-focused definition of austerity, as tax cuts increase the deficit, all other things being equal.

However, other authors have challenged the deficit reduction definition of austerity, arguing that it misses the deeper motives operating behind this governance approach (Whiteside et al. 2021). While austerity using this definition can be pursued by cutting spending or increasing revenues, proponents do not see the two as equally effective. Alesina et al. (2019), for example, suggest that pursuing tax increases is costlier from an economic growth perspective compared to expenditure cuts. The logic is that higher taxes hurt investor confidence, create disincentives for economic activity, and in turn depress economic growth, while cutting government expenditures, especially social welfare benefits, increases the willingness of people to work and the overall labour supply available to the private sector. According to its proponents, then, austerity works best when focused on reducing the size of government. For supply-side economists, a reduction in the size of government also opens areas previously occupied by government to the benefits of competition between privately owned firms. Tax cuts, while on the surface at odds with austerity, if paired with continuing downsizing of government and balanced budgets, fit with this logic of downsizing government to increase economic growth.

This suggests a second definition of austerity based on a reduction in the size of the government. Yet this second definition is also incomplete because, in practice, austerity often prioritizes a decrease in certain kinds of expenditures while sparing other areas. Specifically, while publicly delivered services are often targeted for cuts, spending that supports corporate profits and capital accumulation is often spared or may even be enhanced, with "state support for capital . . . often extended in new and familiar ways" since there is "a lot of spending to account for in times of austerity" (Whiteside et al. 2021, 29). For example, the federal Conservative government led by Prime Minister Stephen Harper undertook deep civil service cuts alongside increased infrastructure spending that promoted private financing and ownership (Whiteside 2015).

Some prominent analysts then question both the claimed objective (smaller deficits), realized outcomes (strong economic growth), and beneficiaries (society broadly) of austerity as put forward by its proponents.

Instead, these critics suggest that austerity is not a technocratic exercise in good economic management to the benefit of common good; instead, it is aimed at shifting the composition of growth from wages to profits. Blyth (2015, 2), for example, notes that the goal of austerity is "the reduction of prices, wages and public expenditure to restore competitiveness," and that austerity is in practice growth reducing, increasing government's debt burden due to lack of revenues. This is due to the multiplier effect of government spending, a concept at the centre of Keynesian economic ideas emphasizing the importance of aggregate demand in determining employment and output levels in the economy. Health, education, housing, and social protection spending have some of the largest multipliers, and cuts to these services can not only negatively impact the macroeconomy but harm population health and well-being, especially among the already vulnerable, and have negative impacts on the quality and quantity of labour supply (Stuckler and Basu 2013). Instead of government spending crowding out private investment, this multiplier approach emphasizes the complementarities between government and private investment. Empirical evidence supports the case against austerity, showing reduced employment and economic growth (McBride 2017), yet the "expansionary austerity zombie" idea lives on (Krugman 2015).

Another critic of austerity, Mattei (2022, 128), speaks of *fiscal austerity*, the cutting of government expenditures and regressive tax changes, leading to "the transfer of resources from the majority of citizens to the minority—the saving-investing classes" to support growing profits and capital accumulation. She also includes the changing of production models and labour institutions through privatization and deregulation as *industrial austerity*, to undermine the ability of workers to challenge employers, disrupt production, and make wage gains. According to Mattei, fiscal and industrial austerity are mutually reinforcing, advancing a logic that "conflates the good of the whole with the good of the capitalist class" (131). McBride (2014, 13) makes a similar argument regarding class-based motivations, with austerity being in "the general interests of capital, although individual capitals may win or lose."

Evans and McBride (2017, 8) similarly and succinctly capture the critical conception of austerity as including: "(1) fiscal consolidation, (2) structural reforms of the public sector, and (3) flexibilization of the labour markets," a definition that has been usefully applied by several critical scholars (e.g., Evans et al. 2023; Evans and Fanelli 2018; Whiteside et al. 2021, 4), many of whom are associated with the New Canadian Political Economy tradition (Clement 2019; Whiteside 2020). In addition to cutting social benefits and public services, fiscal consolidation is often focused on reducing the wages, benefits, and staffing complement of the public service. For example, Manitoba Bill 28, the Public Sector Sustainability Act, bypassed the collective bargaining process with all public sector unions and imposed a four-year wage mandate of a two-year wage freeze, followed by a 0.75 percent increase in the third year and 1 percent in the fourth year. The structural reforms undertaken under austerity are diverse and wide-ranging, but are unified in making the government more responsive to corporations and reducing its capacity to regulate and monitor an increasingly privatized economy, while shifting and transforming government services to support corporate profitability and competitiveness (Evans and McBride 2017). An example of a structural reform in Manitoba under the PCs was the extensive contracting out and privatization that took place in areas such as "homecare, air ambulance services, road and bridge maintenance, conservation services, provincial park campgrounds, wildfire suppression, public housing, and social services more broadly through social impact bonds" (Keith, Hajer, and Conway 2021, 9). Flexibilization of the labour markets, overlapping with Mattei's idea of industrial austerity, involves reducing worker protections and the ability of workers to bargain collectively to secure improvement in wages and benefits. The Manitoba PCs, for example, engaged in industrial austerity by changing labour law to make it more difficult for workers to unionize and by reducing the capacity of the provincial government to enforce employment standards (see Chapter 17 in this volume).

Broadly speaking, these authors situate austerity as the neoliberal reform agenda for government, with neoliberalism defined as "an ideology and practice that ... stresses the priority of individualism, competitiveness, and entrepreneurship over collective interests and needs, including trade union rights and universal welfare programs" (Evans et al. 2023, 265). The "political practice" (Evans et al. 2023, 6) of neoliberalism is transforming the state to more deliberately tilt the economic policy environment in favour of business. This includes policies geared at "reducing public services and assets in order to open up the state sector to new profit-making opportunities; lowering wages, benefits, and working conditions for a more flexible and market-dependent workforce; and deploying the coercive capacities of the state to enforce these market measures" (Evans et al. 2023, 6). The definition of austerity in this book follows from that used by the above critical scholars: it is the application of neoliberal principles to the government, often with a focus on reducing expenditures, but with the larger aim of benefiting the private for-profit sector.

On the surface, the mainstream definition and its proponents paint austerity as in the best interests of society, while critical approaches, this book included, highlight how it is primarily about redistribution, with winners and losers. Digging deeper, however, shows that there is some consensus with respect to the impacts of austerity, with the leading academic economists who promote austerity acknowledging its redistributive mechanisms and consequences. As documented by Mattei (2022, 297), Alesina and his collaborators have candidly noted how cuts to government employment increase unemployment, reduce the bargaining power of labour, and lower average worker earnings, driving down private sector wages, leading to a fall in the labour (versus capital) share of total income, and increasing income inequality.

Changes in Manitoba's economic outcomes under recent austerity, compared to the rest of Canada, have been consistent with these predicted results. Before 2016, Manitoba had unemployment rates that were consistently below the rest of Canada. However, between 2016 and 2022 that gap decreased for all years except 2020, vanishing completely in 2018.[4] The gap between Canada's higher average hourly real wage and Manitoba's also increased by 52 percent between 2016 and 2022.[5] While the labour (versus capital and self-employment) income share of the economy fell in Canada from 2015 to 2021, the loss was 27 percent greater in Manitoba than nationally.[6] Manitoba, a province with traditionally lower inequality, has also seen income inequality worsen since 2015, both in absolute terms and relative to Canada as a whole (Hudson 2023).

Did Manitoba Experience "Austerity"?

Reflecting on the above, did Manitoba experience austerity under the PC government from 2016 to 2022? The main findings of this study suggest that yes, Manitoba did experience austerity, but with some important qualifications. First, Manitoba's austerity reduced government expenditures in relative, not absolute, terms. As a share of the economy, expenditure cuts of 1 percent of GDP by 2018/19 brought government expenditures, as a share of GDP, to their lowest level since at least 2006/07, the earliest year for which comparable expenditure statistics are available (Figure 0.1). But, unadjusted for inflation or population growth, government expenditures in dollars increased every year between 2016 and 2022.

The scale of expenditure austerity undertaken in Manitoba is not of the type seen in extreme examples, often triggered when debtholders and/ or multilateral organizations view fiscal discipline to be lacking, downgrade bond ratings, and demand austerity measures in exchange for refinancing. Austerity, then, may be forced upon governments, but in the Canadian context austerity has generally been voluntary (Baines and McBride 2014). Canada's federal austerity in the 1990s, for example, inspired by the general neoliberal ideas outlined earlier and some debt market pressure, saw spending in absolute terms reduced and maintained below previous levels for several years (OECD 2023; O'Brien and Zhang 2014; Russell 2014; Evans et al. 2023, 103). Other examples emerged after the 2008 crisis when many European governments slashed social spending, ostensibly to bring their budgets back in balance. The most draconian cuts were in the countries collectively known as the PIIGS (Portugal, Italy, Ireland, Greece, and Spain). For example, in Greece, public sector wages were cut by 20 percent, social security spending was slashed by €4 billion, and €50 billion was raised by selling government assets to the private sector. Spending was cut in absolute terms, and as of 2023 had yet to recover (for an excellent discussion of the differences between Canadian and Spanish austerity see Whiteside et al. 2021).

Manitoba's austerity was not of this severity. As illustrated in Figure 0.1, the relative expenditure changes that did take place with the change in government in 2016, while significant, were much less than the changes associated with the economic crises of the 2010s and were interrupted by the COVID-19 pandemic. Austerity in Manitoba from 2016 to 2022 was more akin to the PC provincial government between 1988 and 1999, led by Gary Filmon, which capped spending growth at 2 percent a year in 1993 while enacting balanced budget legislation that prohibited annual budget deficits. The Filmon government was also like the post-2016 PCs in the spending areas that they chose to constrain. Spending on the protective role of the state was particularly targeted. Hospital beds were closed, healthcare jobs eliminated, and payments to foster care cut. Consistent with our redistributional definition of austerity, spending was dramatically constrained in the area of social assistance; benefits were cut in Winnipeg, those who could not participate in their workfare program were penalized, and a "snitch line" to rat out welfare benefit "abusers" was opened (Loxley 2003, 110–14).

A second qualification is that increases in taxes, particularly regressive taxes aimed at reducing consumption by workers, are often part of intensive austerity packages and were not prominent in PC austerity. Manitoba did not, for example, follow Alberta's pre-2009 policy of levying a fixed $1,056 payment per family (the Alberta Health premium), which obviously represents a larger percentage of a poor person's income than a rich one. In the 2016 and 2017 budgets, a number of mostly boutique tax credits were reduced or eliminated, particularly those associated with the previous NDP government, restoring an estimated $126 million in annual revenues. Income tax cuts were, however, concurrently implemented through the indexation of tax brackets, costing $59 million over this two-year period. While the net impact of tax changes led to net revenue increases in the first two years of the PC government, tax cuts dominated in subsequent years. By 2023/24, the estimated net impact of tax changes led to a loss of nearly $1.6 billion in provincial revenues per year (Hajer et al. 2023). Like most tax cuts, the monetary benefits of these were greater for higher-income earners, so do not conflict with redistribution-focused definitions of austerity, particularly given that tax cuts were pursued after significant fiscal consolidation had occurred. Yet Manitoba did not move to obviously flatten the progressive tax rates which would have aligned more closely with other conservative (with the brief exception of the Notley government in Alberta from 2015 to 2019) prairie provinces. Until 2015, after oil revenues collapsed in the wake of the 2008 crisis, Alberta had a flat tax of 10 percent on incomes (Evans et al. 2021). Even after some progressivity was introduced in its desperation for revenue, Alberta, and its similarly austere neighbour Saskatchewan, had two of the three lowest marginal tax rates on their highest income earners in the country (the other was Ontario) in 2022.

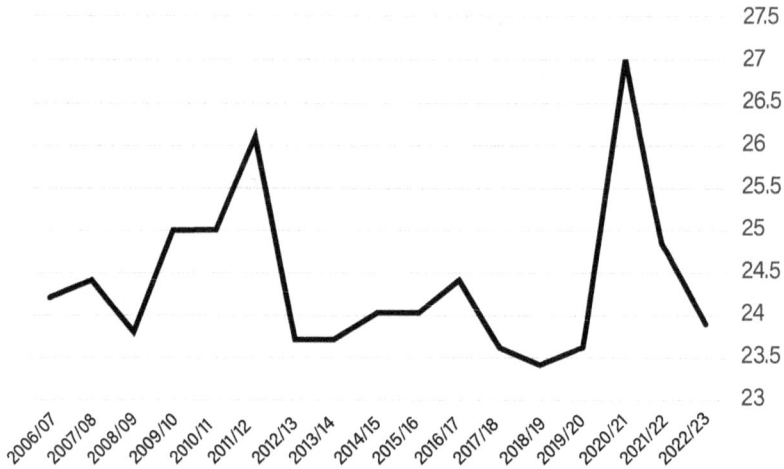

Figure 0.1. Manitoba government expenditures, as percentage of GDP, 2006/07 to 2022/23.

A third and final qualification is that the austerity of the PCs is more acute if seen in the broader frame of government reconfiguration to serve private sector for-profit interests. As detailed in the chapters of the volume, in addition to the privatization of government assets to raise revenue and the scaling back of entitlements, contracting out has taken place across multiple areas of government, particularly Crown corporations and infrastructure (Evans et al. 2023, 149). As clearly articulated in Chapters 15 and 16 on Crown corporations and infrastructure, contracting out, particularly to for-profit entities, has dubious cost-savings potential if quality is to be maintained, but fits solidly within the critical definition of austerity focused on reforming the state in favour of private corporations and businesses vis-à-vis workers. This PC approach aligned with conservative austerity in Saskatchewan, where Premier Brad Wall pursued "active incrementalism" (Smith 2018, 72) on expenditure and welfare state reductions, while more aggressively restructuring the state through privatization and attacks on unions.

As shown in Figure 0.2, there was a dramatic downsizing of the civil service between 2016 and 2021, one that continued during the pandemic

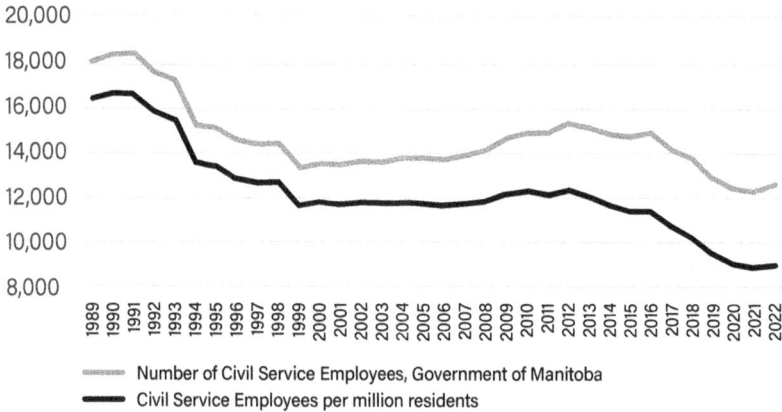

Figure 0.2. Number of civil service employees, Government of Manitoba, 1989 to 2022.

despite the surge of government spending. The reduction to 12,232 employees was a record low in recent decades, 1,000 fewer than the previous low in 1999. While the NDP left the civil service approximately 3 percent smaller on a per capita basis over sixteen years of governing, the PCs reduced the size of the civil service by 27 percent, in population-adjusted terms, over a six-year period.[7] On this score, Manitoba mirrored the record of the Saskatchewan Party, which slashed the public service by 15 percent in its first term in office after being elected in 2007 (Evans et al. 2023, 114).

Part of this reduction has been sustained by high job vacancy rates. Table 0.1 shows the calculated vacancy rates by department, based on data published in the 2022 Committee of Supply briefing binders (Government of Manitoba 2022b). Overall, the Manitoba civil service had a calculated vacancy rate of 21 percent in 2022.

Profiling the Experiences of Workers

Public sector workers, primarily through their unions, have been actively engaged in research and activism related to the impacts of austerity (Ross and Savage 2013). While the current volume presents financial data on government expenditures in Manitoba since 2016, the main focus of this research is to document the experiences of workers delivering provincially

Table 0.1. Manitoba civil service vacancy rates, 2022.

DEPARTMENT	VACANCY RATE (%)
Advanced Education, Skills and Training	18
Agriculture	20
Economic Development, Investment and Trade	23
Education	22
Environment, Climate and Parks	16
Families	19
Finance	28
Health	42
Indigenous Reconciliation and Northern Relations	21
Justice	8
Labour, Consumer Protection, and Government Services	27
Mental Health and Community Wellness	32
Municipal Relations	23
Infrastructure and Transportation	36
Natural Resources and Northern Development	27
Public Service Commission	11
Seniors and Long-Term Care	0
Sport, Culture and Heritage	25
Overall	**21**

funded public services in Manitoba in the context of austerity. While each chapter speaks to the insights of workers in specific areas of government, drawing on the qualitative data gathered, we present a summary of the survey results here, with illustrative quotes throughout.

In total, 2,078 workers participated in the survey. Forty-three percent were members of the civil service, with representation across all government departments and more participants from larger departments; and 46 percent identifying as working for an arm's length provincial entity, such as a school division, health region, university, or Crown corporation. Ten percent of respondents were with municipalities, nonprofit organizations, or other organizations who relied on provincial government funding. Most of the survey respondents (66 percent) identified as front-line workers, with 21 percent of the survey respondents identifying as working in management. Worker representation was also diverse with respect to geographic region of employment.

Impacts of Austerity on Working Conditions

When asked whether their work and work done by close coworkers in their area of work had been impacted by the Government of Manitoba's austerity measures aimed at reducing expenditures and balancing the budget since 2016, 85 percent said yes (58 percent greatly impacted, 17 percent moderately impacted). Table 0.2 presents a summary of the impacts reported by workers. A significant majority of workers (75 percent) listed increased workloads as a consequence, with 71 percent noting staffing shortages. Just over a quarter of workers noted work in their area had been privatized or contracted out to private companies or other nongovernment organizations. Several other negative impacts on job quality were also noted, with over 85 percent of respondents indicating that working conditions, job satisfaction, employee mental health, recruitment and retention, and worker safety had worsened.

Workers across sectors spoke of feeling undervalued and overwhelmed. One early learning and childcare worker commented, "I finally decided to resign. I was at the point of total burnout and my last day was in November 2022. No raises for years, continually feeling like this essential work with children is at the bottom of the rung of important work in our society. Staffing shortages have made things so stressful, so challenging to provide

Table 0.2. Worker-reported impacts of government austerity, 2016–2022.

	(%)
Impacts on individual respondents	
Intensified/increased workload	75
Increased number of tasks requested of worker	66
Led to considering jobs elsewhere or with other employers	70
Workplace impacts	
Staffing shortages	71
Other resource shortages (reduced budgets or limiting of spending to support work/tasks)	50
Hiring of more contract/casual staff (as opposed to permanent staff)	27
Privatization or contracting out of work	26
Led to considering jobs elsewhere or with other employers	70
Job quality outcomes	
Worsened working conditions and job satisfaction	87
Worsened employee mental health	88
Worsened employee recruitment and retention	85
Worsened worker safety	42
System outcomes	
Reduced quality of service for stakeholders/users of the service	77
Less value for money	74
Worsened public safety	34

a high level of quality for very vulnerable citizens. It was really hard to see so many amazing educators slowly leave the field, and now I'm one of them. I just had nothing left to give." As one employee in the Department of Environment, Climate and Parks noted, "More employees [are] going on stress leave, leaving fewer workers with increased workload, adversely affecting mental health of [those] remaining. Everyone is drowning and trying to grab for something to hold onto." As a support worker at St. Amant put it, "We, like those we support, feel voiceless and disrespected."

Austerity, Service Quality, and Value for Money

Workers also noted several negative system impacts. Seventy-seven percent indicated that quality of service for stakeholders or users of the service had been reduced by austerity measures. Examples of this, detailed in the chapters of this volume, are plentiful: Crown attorneys with "hundreds of files without being able to properly prosecute them"; Department of Health workers describing a "department wide backlog of work, resulting in longer wait time for services and programs being implemented ... Manitoba residents having to wait up to six months for a health card"; and a respiratory therapist noting that "with increased patient load, care has significantly reduced, and you can't spend the appropriate attention with patients."

The crises generated by austerity also prevented simple service improvements, with one worker describing how "a lot of improvements that people ask for and that are very doable sit on the back burner for years because we are too busy putting out fires." Over a third of respondents felt that public safety in their area of work had been compromised by austerity measures, and concerns regarding quality of work of contractors in a context of austerity were commonly expressed, with one public sector worker summarizing it as follows: "There's no one checking on contractors that do work. Issues are only identified after the work is done and nothing is done about it. [We are] forced to take the lowest bidder and we always have safety problems.... Everyone points blame but public sector employees are stuck with the result and contractors get paid." Nearly three-quarters felt that the austerity measures put in place would worsen value for money for taxpayers, and the majority of respondents were skeptical that any actual savings would be realized.

As shown in Table 0.3, 44 percent found that the austerity measures "ended up increasing costs in both my area of work and for the public sector as a whole" even in the short term, while 60 percent indicated they expected this to be the case in the long term. On top of this, a significant proportion of workers (16 percent in the short term, 12 percent in the long term) felt that savings were only being realized by transferring costs to other areas of the public sector. A Community Living disABILITY Services worker explained their perspective on costliness in the long term: "The government is spending less now, but it will only increase the costs in the future. Spending less on public services only serves to exacerbate societal issues. . . . Also these cuts increase worker burnout which affects quality of services. Austerity measures are causing more stress for staff and clients alike and end up causing more mental and physical health issues for all." As one family doctor put it, "When fee-for-service doctors have rising expenses and frozen fees they either work longer and see family less (burnout) or see more patients for shorter visits, more 1 problem per visit rules, etc. Public value and safety was affected. Also, it contributed to the massive burnout-retirement tsunami." Other workers noted how austerity is hindering necessary upkeep of provincial assets, leading to deterioration. As one Manitoba Hydro linesman noted, "Contracting out is more expensive than in house therefore less maintenance is being done," and "pushing off maintenance is going to cost more emergency work in the long run."

Despite a wealth of suggestions regarding cost savings from survey participants, with more than half having ideas for delivering better or more services at the same cost or a lower cost, workers were more likely to report that they were not meaningfully consulted by the government for ideas to reduce expenditures. A majority of workers strongly disagreed with the statement, "I feel the work-related experience, expertise and opinions of front-line workers in my area of work were reflected in the austerity measures implemented." As one environmental stewardship officer noted, "Under the former NDP government, internal consultation was common, including focus groups and department-focused working groups. These groups obtained feedback from all levels of government, and specifically front-line workers. Under the current administration, the collection of feedback, and round tables at which decisions are made are continually drifting up and away from the people their decisions affect and have

Table 0.3. Workers' perceptions of savings from austerity in the short and long term.

THINKING ABOUT COST SAVINGS, DO YOU BELIEVE THE AUSTERITY MEASURES IMPLEMENTED IN YOUR AREA OF WORK SAVE THE PUBLIC SECTOR MONEY?	IMMEDIATE OR SHORT-TERM IMPACT (WITHIN 1-2 YEARS)	LONG-TERM IMPACT (%)
Yes, they create savings for both my area and the public sector as a whole	7	5
They created savings for my area, but transferred costs to other areas of the public sector (other departments, areas, branches, levels of government etc.)	16	12
No, they ended up increasing costs in both my area of work and for the public sector as a whole	44	59
There were no austerity measures or efforts to reduce expenditures in my area	6	5
Other	9	5
Unsure/don't know	18	14

direction knowledge/solutions to offer. A lot could be accomplished if front-line workers were enabled to instigate and help develop/implement change." One Manitoba housing property manager shared, "There is no consultation with 'end-users' on the annual budgeting process. Unrealistic budgets are 'imposed' on end-users by government and rarely reflect actual expenses." Instead, the PC government relied on consultants, with concerns being raised by workers regarding the long-term consequences. One Manitoba Health policy analyst noted, "[It] feels like the administration does not trust its own civil service; [they] hire a bunch of mostly out of province consultants who don't know this work in MB and so need to consult with the civil servants to get the needed information, and then they package it for the government in the ways they want it—chunked out as largely siloed projects. . . . [It's] really frustrating, and having consolidated knowledge with the consultants, how does it live on in the civil service? They have undermined the professionalism and agency of the civil service."

Austerity in Manitoba over Time

Table 0.4 reviews the survey results for how the intensity of austerity has changed over time. Respondents were asked for feedback on three time comparisons: the NDP government prior to 2016 versus the PC government after 2016; before versus after the start of the COVID-19 pandemic; and the period under Premier Heather Stefanson (November 2021 to date of survey) versus the period under former premier Brian Pallister (April 2016 to October 2021). In the first instance, a large majority, 64 percent, indicate that austerity in their area of work has intensified under the PCs versus the previous NDP government. This is consistent with earlier assessments of the experience in Manitoba. Evans et al. (2023, 149) described the Pallister government as following an "aggressive austerity agenda." The Doer-Selinger NDP followed a "social-liberal" approach that "did relatively little to actively deepen neoliberalization in the province" (Camfield 2018, 106), despite social democratic parties more broadly aligning themselves with a broad austerity logic (Evans 2014). With respect to the pandemic, half the respondents noted that austerity intensified, consistent with findings elsewhere that Manitoba was an outlier relative to other provinces with respect to its attempt to implement large cuts ($1.25 billion) to the public sector in the early days of the pandemic (Hajer and Fernandez 2021, 31), while 30 percent felt the intensity of austerity remained the same before and after the pandemic. The majority of respondents indicate that the level of austerity remained about the same with the transition from Premier Pallister to Premier Stefanson, but more (20 percent) felt austerity had intensified compared to those who felt it had relaxed (9 percent) at the time of the survey, approximately thirteen months after the leadership change.

Table 0.4. Perceptions of austerity over time.

STATEMENT	% OF RESPONDENTS WHO AGREED WITH THE STATEMENT		
	Expenditure restraint under the NDP prior to 2016 vs. PC	Provincial austerity before and after the start of the COVID-19 pandemic (March 2020)	Provincial austerity under Stefanson (Nov. 2021 to date of survey) vs. Pallister
Provincial austerity in my area has been relaxed since 2016	2	5	9
The intensity of provincial austerity has remained about the same	12	30	53
Provincial austerity in my area of work has become more intense	64	50	20
Other	3	2	2
Unsure/don't know	18	13	16

Conclusion

Over the last forty years, in Canada and in the global North more broadly, austerity has gone together with neoliberal policy reforms, including increasing the private sector provision of public services, downsizing the public service, and deregulating labour markets. The consequences have clearly been greater inequality, a weakened labour movement, and increased precarity for working people (Peters 2014). As exemplified in the chapters of this volume, these impacts are also clear in the Manitoba case: compromised public services including healthcare, education, and other social programs; increased inequities in access to these services; and reduced capacity of the provincial government to promote Manitoba's collective social and economic interests. For public sector workers, austerity has created a vicious cycle of understaffing, burnout, and attrition, leading to despair. The question, then, is why has such action been voluntarily self-imposed by the government of Manitoba when the consequences appear so dire? In addition to summarizing the impact of austerity, this chapter has attempted to answer this question by highlighting not only the losers (who make up the vast majority of the population), but also the elite, small group of winners, and how austerity has been pursued in their interests.

Austerity and its consequences are increasingly pressing issues in our time, undermining our capacity to address existential threats such as global heating and biodiversity loss. Austerity has also been linked to the rise of extremist right-wing ethnonationalism (Crowley 2020; Fetzer 2019), generating political instability and increasingly organized hate and violence. The potential for these movements to seize governments—a threat many have thought was long confined to the history of advanced capitalist countries—is resurgent. We hope that this volume will help advance research on austerity through our case study of the Manitoba context, shining a light on how austerity operates and its consequences, and hopefully adding to the province's institutional memory, sustaining resistance to this "zombie ideology" (Kibasi 2020) that will inevitably be resurrected as recollections fade over time.

Notes

1   In 2018/19, the province reported a $149 million deficit, but according to the auditor general, the public accounts data was not reported according to public sector accounting conventions, and the province actually had run a surplus in 2018/19 of $9 million (Kusch and Botelho-Urbanski 2019). Data on provincial government expenditures and full-time equivalent (FTE) and actual employee counts in this and other chapters, if not otherwise noted, are from the annual reports published by the province of Manitoba. The primary source of expenditure data is the *Report on the Estimates of Expenditure and Supplementary Information* (Government of Manitoba 2022a). FTE staffing data and granular expenditure data not available in the *Estimates of Expenditure* reports were obtained from annual reports posted on departmental websites (Government of Manitoba 2023b), and actual employee count data was sourced from Public Service Commission annual reports (Government of Manitoba 2025). Past annual reports not available online were obtained through the Manitoba Legislative Library. See data appendix for details (Hajer 2025).

2   Authors' calculations based on actual expenditure and GDP data printed in Manitoba Budgets 2011 to 2023 in the five-year Manitoba Summary Financial Statistics. Data on expenditure and GDP are taken from the most current estimate available. For details on data sources used for provincial expenditures, employee staffing numbers, and FTE positions in this chapter, see data appendix (Hajer 2025).

3   Budget 2019 estimate. Revenue per percentage point of the PST in 2019/20 was $323 million.

4   Authors' calculation based on Statistics Canada (2023a).

5   Authors' calculations based on Statistics Canada (2023b, 2023c).

6   Authors' calculations based on Statistics Canada (2022).

7   Note that the data on civil service employment does not include special operating agencies and other arm's length public sector organizations. Structural changes such as the creation of the regional health authorities in the 1990s led to a drop in civil service counts as staff were transferred from the department of health. Similarly, during our period of study (2016–2022), a number of special operating agencies, including the Office of the Fire Commissioner and Manitoba Housing, were integrated into the civil service, resulting in an increase in the civil service employee count. While our FTE data used for each area of government was adjusted for these changes where possible. See online data appendix (Hajer 2025); data is not available to make similar adjustments to civil service counts.

References

Alesina, Alberto, Carlo Favero, and Francesco Giavazzi. 2019. *Austerity: When It Works and When It Doesn't*. Princeton: Princeton University Press.

Baines, Donna, and Stephen McBride. 2014. "Introduction: Context and Fight Back." In Baines and McBride, *Orchestrating Austerity*, 1–8.

Baines, Donna, and Stephen McBride, eds. 2014. *Orchestrating Austerity: Impacts and Resistance*. Halifax: Fernwood Publishing.

Blyth, Mark. 2015. *Austerity: The History of a Dangerous Idea*. 2nd ed. Oxford: Oxford University Press.

Brodbeck, Tom. 2020. "Dark Clouds of Austerity Chilling Forecast for Manitoba." *Winnipeg Free Press*, 27 April. https://www.winnipegfreepress.com/local/2020/04/27/dark-clouds-of-austerity-chilling-forecast-for-manitoba.

Camfield, David. 2018. "Manitoba: Fiscal Policy and the Public Sector under 'Today's NDP.'" In *The Public Sector in an Age of Austerity: Perspectives from Canada's Provinces and Territories*, edited by Bryan M. Evans and Carlo Fanelli. Kingston: McGill-Queen's University Press.

Clement, Wallace. 2019. "Locating the New Canadian Political Economy." In *Change and Continuity: Canadian Political Economy in the New Millennium*, edited by Mark P. Thomas, Leah F. Vosko, Carlo Fanelli, and Olena Lyubchenko, 25–40. Carleton Library Series 248. Kingston: McGill-Queen's University Press. https://doi.org/10.1515/9780773558441.

Crowley, Ned. 2020. "Austerity and Ethno-Nationalism: The Politics of Scarcity in Right-Wing Populism." In *Mapping Populism: Approaches and Methods*, edited by Majia Holmer Nadesan and Amit Ron, 134–45. Abingdon, UK: Routledge.

Evans, Bryan. 2014. "Social Democracy in a New Age of Austerity." In Baines and McBride, *Orchestrating Austerity*, 79–90.

Evans, Bryan M., and Carlo Fanelli, eds. 2018. *The Public Sector in an Age of Austerity: Perspectives from Canada's Provinces and Territories*. Kingston: McGill-Queen's University Press.

Evans, Bryan, Carlo Fanelli, Leo Panitch, and Donald Swartz. 2023. *From Consent to Coercion: The Continuing Assault on Labour*. 4th ed. Toronto: University of Toronto Press.

Evans, Bryan M., and Stephen McBride. 2017. "The Austerity State: An Introduction." In *The Austerity State*, edited by Stephen McBride and Bryan M. Evans, 3–24. Toronto: University of Toronto Press.

Fetzer, Thiemo. 2019. "Did Austerity Cause Brexit?" *American Economic Review* 109 (11): 3849–86. https://doi.org/10.1257/aer.20181164.

Government of Manitoba. 2019. "Governments of Canada and Manitoba Sign 10-Year Housing Agreement." News Release, 11 June.

———. 2020. "Governments to Invest More Than $17.5 Million to Connect Vulnerable Manitobans with Safe, Stable Housing." News Release, 17 December.

———. 2021. "Province Investing More Than $4 Million in Manitoba Housing Properties to Improve Tenant and Community Safety." News Release, 15 January.

———. 2022a. "Annual Reports and Public Accounts." Government Finances. https://www.gov.mb.ca/government/finances/annualreports-publicaccounts.html.

———. 2022b. "Departmental Information, Reports and Statistics." Info MB. https://www.gov.mb.ca/openmb/infomb/departments/index.html.

———. 2023a. *Historic Help for Manitobans Budget 2023*. www.gov.mb.ca/asset_library/en/budget2023/budget-2023.pdf.

———. 2023b. "Departments." https://www.gov.mb.ca/government/departments.html.

———. 2025. "Publications: Annual Reports." Public Service Commission. 2025. https://www.manitoba.ca/csc/publications/annrpt/index.html.

Hajer, Jesse. 2025. "Introduction to Data Appendix for Public Service in Tough Times: Working Under Austerity in Manitoba." Manitoba Research Alliance. 2025. https://mra-mb.ca/wp-content/uploads/Introduction-to-Data-Appendix.pdf.

Hajer, Jesse, Niall Harney, and David Macdonald. 2023. *Funding Our Way: Rebalancing Revenues and Spending for a Fair and Prosperous Manitoba*. Winnipeg: Canadian Centre for Policy Alternatives–Manitoba. https://policyalternatives.ca/publications/reports/funding-our-way.

Hajer, Jesse, and Lynne Fernandez. 2021. *COVID-19, Austerity and an Alternative Social and Economic Policy Path for Manitoba*. Winnipeg: Canadian Centre for Policy Alternatives–Manitoba. https://www.policyalternatives.ca/publications/reports/covid-19-austerity-and-alternative-social-and-economic-policy-path-manitoba.

Hudson, Ian. 2023. *Inequality in Manitoba*. Winnipeg: Canadian Centre for Policy Alternatives–Manitoba. https://mra-mb.ca/publication/the-chasm-widens-inequality-in-manitoba-update/.

Keith, Jennifer, Jesse Hajer, and Michael Conway. 2021. *Hard Infrastructure, Hard Times: Workers Perspectives on Privatization and Contracting Out of Manitoba Infrastructure*. Winnipeg: Canadian Centre for Policy Alternatives–Manitoba. https://www.policyalternatives.ca/publications/reports/hard-infrastructure-hard-times.

Kibasi, Tom. 2020. "Austerity Is a Zombie Ideology. It's Time to Bury It Once and for All." Opinion, *The Guardian*, 20 October. https://www.theguardian.com/commentisfree/2020/oct/20/austerity-zombie-imf-fiscal-restraint-not-right-pandemic-debt-uk.

Krugman, Paul. 2015. "The Expansionary Austerity Zombie." *The New York Times*, 20 November. https://archive.nytimes.com/krugman.blogs.nytimes.com/2015/11/20/the-expansionary-austerity-zombie/.

Kusch, Larry, and Jessica Botelho-Urbanski. 2019. "Manitoba Numbers Game: Province Announces $163-M Deficit; Auditor General Talks $9-M Surplus." *Winnipeg Free Press*, 26 September. https://www.winnipegfreepress.com/local/manitoba-numbers-game-561473592.html.

Lambert, Steve. 2015. "Conservatives Would Limit Growth in Spending, Avoid Cuts, Pallister Says." CBC Manitoba, 17 November. https://www.cbc.ca/news/canada/manitoba/manitoba-conservatives-say-they-would-limit-growth-in-spending-avoid-cuts-1.3323341.

Lett, Dan. 2019. "Austerity Working for Pallister, Why Won't He Brag about It?" *Winnipeg Free Press*, 19 August. https://www.winnipegfreepress.com/local/2019/08/19/austerity-working-for-pallister-why-wont-he-brag-about-it.

Loxley, John. 2003. *Alternative Budgets: Budgeting as if People Mattered.* Winnipeg: Fernwood Publishing.

Manitoba Finance. 2022. *Annual Report.* https://www.gov.mb.ca/finance/publications/pubs/annualrep/2021_22/finance_annual_report.pdf.

Mattei, Clara E. 2022. *The Capital Order: How Economists Invented Austerity and Paved the Way to Fascism.* Chicago: University of Chicago Press.

McBride, Stephen. 2014. "In Austerity We Trust." In Baines and McBride, *Orchestrating Austerity*, 10–20.

———. 2017. "The New Constitutionalism and Austerity." In *The Austerity State*, edited by Stephen McBride and Bryan M. Evans, 169–88. Toronto: University of Toronto Press.

O'Brien, Robert, and Falin Zhang. 2014. "Structural Adjustment for the North." In Baines and McBride, *Orchestrating Austerity*, 21–33.

OECD (Organisation for Economic Co-operation and Development). 2023. "OECD. Stat." https://stats.oecd.org/.

Peters, John. 2014. "Neoliberalism, Inequality, and Austerity in the Rich World Democracies." In Baines and McBride, *Orchestrating Austerity*, 50–64.

Ross, Stephanie, and Larry Savage, eds. 2013. *Public Sector Unions in the Age of Austerity.* Halifax: Fernwood Publishing.

Rounce, Andrea, and Karine Levasseur. 2016. "Introduction: Blue Manitoba 2016." In *Understanding the Manitoba Election 2016: Campaigns, Participation, Issues, Place*, edited by Karine Levasseur, Andrea Rounce, Barry Ferguson, and Royce Koop, 5–6. Winnipeg: University of Manitoba Press. https://uofmpress.ca/books/detail/understanding-the-manitoba-election-2016.

Russell, Ellen. 2014. "The Strategic Use of Budget Crises." In Baines and McBride, *Orchestrating Austerity*, 34–49.

Scarth, Todd. 2016. "The Economy and the 2016 Manitoba Election." In *Understanding the Manitoba Election 2016: Campaigns, Participation, Issues, Place*, edited by Karine Levasseur, Andrea Rounce, Barry Ferguson, and Royce Koop, 33–34. Winnipeg: University of Manitoba Press. https://uofmpress.ca/books/detail/understanding-the-manitoba-election-2016.

Smith, Charles. 2018. "Active Incrementalism and the Politics of Austerity in the 'New Saskatchewan.'" In *The Public Sector in an Age of Austerity: Perspectives From Canada's Provinces and Territories*, edited by Bryan M. Evans and Carlo Fanelli, 71–100. Kingston: McGill-Queen's University Press.

Statistics Canada. 2022. "Table 36-10-0221-01: Gross Domestic Product, Income-Based, Provincial and Territorial, Annual." 8 November. https://www150.statcan.gc.ca/t1/tbl1/en/tv.action?pid=3610022101.

———. 2023a. "Table 14-10-0020-01: Unemployment Rate, Participation Rate and Employment Rate by Educational Attainment, Annual." 6 January. https://www150.statcan.gc.ca/t1/tbl1/en/tv.action?pid=1410002001.

———. 2023b. "Table 14-10-0064-01: Employee Wages by Industry, Annual." 6 January. https://www150.statcan.gc.ca/t1/tbl1/en/tv.action?pid=1410006401.

———. 2023c. "Table 18-10-0005-01: Consumer Price Index, Annual Average, Not Seasonally Adjusted." 17 January. https://www150.statcan.gc.ca/t1/tbl1/en/tv.action?pid=1810000501.

Stuckler, David, and Sanjay Basu. 2013. *The Body Economic: Why Austerity Kills—Recessions, Budget Battles, and the Politics of Life and Death*. New York: Basic Books.

Whiteside, Heather. 2015. "Austerity Budgets and Public Sector Retrenchment: Crisis Era Policy Making in Canada, the United Kingdom, and Australia." In *After '08: Social Policy and the Global Financial Crisis*, edited by Stephen McBride, Rianne Mahon, and Gerard William Boychuk, 254–71. Vancouver: University of British Columbia Press.

———. 2020. "Introduction: Changes, Crises, and Conflicts in Canadian Political Economy." In *Canadian Political Economy*, 3–22. Toronto: University of Toronto Press.

Whiteside, Heather, Stephen McBride, and Bryan Evans. 2021. *Varieties of Austerity*. Bristol: Bristol University Press. https://doi.org/10.46692/9781529212259.001.

Wilt, James. 2019. "The Devastation of Manitoba: An Autopsy of Pallister's Austerity Regime." *Canadian Dimension*, 28 August. https://canadiandimension.com/articles/view/the-devastation-of-manitoba.

Chapter 1

CHILDCARE IN MANITOBA: AUSTERITY'S HARMS

Susan Prentice

Early learning and childcare in Manitoba has struggled through austerity under Premiers Brian Pallister and Heather Stefanson. As one experienced childcare educator told us, "The job has become more and more stressful and undervalued throughout the years"; another reported "continually feeling like this essential work with children is at the bottom of the rung." The harms of austerity have gone largely unrecognized as the political and public profile of childcare has recently soared, especially under the new and much publicized federal $10 a day plan. Nevertheless, a close look makes the scope of the struggle clear. While austerity in well-established sectors conventionally takes the form of spending cuts, in childcare, it can be seen in other policy choices: principally failing to invest and promoting privatization, with damaging effects on children and families, programs, and early childhood educators.

When Premier Pallister assumed office on 3 May 2016, there were 35,469 licensed childcare spaces in Manitoba, and 18.1 percent of youngsters under twelve had access to a licensed space.[1] While spaces have slowly increased, so too has the population of the province. Seven years later, the access rate is virtually identical at 19.6 percent, as most children continue to live in a childcare desert. Nearly one in two families report the cost of childcare was a barrier (Engage MB 2021, 2), even though parent fees remained unchanged since the 2016 election, before dropping to $10 a day on 1 April 2023. Today, there are fewer certified early childhood educators

(ECEs) working in the sector than there were in 2016. Despite provincial spending on early learning and childcare being higher than it was in 2016, federal funding accounts for all of the increase. Troublingly, the quality of care offered to children has been attenuated by the multiplied effects of the staffing crisis and funding decisions. As the *Winnipeg Free Press* has recently noted, "It didn't have to be this way. Years of austerity made this" (Editorial 2023).

Places Remain Scarce

Access to childcare is low in Manitoba, which scores near the bottom third of Canadian jurisdictions on availability (Macdonald and Friendly 2023). Growth in Manitoba's childcare supply has lagged behind other provinces over the past ten years. Where other provinces have averaged annual growth of 3.6 percent, Manitoba averaged 1.2 percent (KPMG 2020, 21). Licensed spaces are provided by centres and regulated family homes. Nearly all centres are owned and operated by not-for-profit or charitable organizations; a long-standing strength of Manitoba's policy architecture has been a funding model that prioritizes nonprofit delivery. Yet because the province relies on private actors to start up childcare facilities, there is little planning. Rural and northern families have particularly low access. In Winnipeg, more affluent areas have more access than lower-income (and often more racialized and Indigenous) neighbourhoods (Prentice 2007), a pattern that has not changed in years.

The Progressive Conservative (PC) government has consistently expressed a strong preference for family home childcare services over centre-based care. Their focus on family home care is misplaced, given that centres supply more than 90 percent of licensed spaces. The PC policy preference for homes has generated material inequities. From 2016 to 2021, operating grants for homes increased by 51 percent, even though centre-based funding was frozen. Despite attempts to incentivize family homes, home-based services make up a minuscule contribution to recent growth. While Manitoba grew 6,628 net new licensed spaces since 2016, family homes had a net loss of spaces. The policy preference for homes over centres is concerning for further reasons, given the current home care policy regime. Fewer than one in six family home caregivers has specialized early childhood education training. Manitoba family homes experience a high rate of closures, with half shutting within four years (Prentice, Sanscartier, and Peter 2016). About one in four family homes do not accept subsidized children (meaning they also will not participate in the $10 a day plan). At the end of 2022, just 20 of Manitoba's 404 family homes admitted children with additional support needs through the Inclusion Support Program.

Privatization Is Increasing

The long-standing tradition that prudently restricted public operating grants to nonprofit childcare centres was first challenged in 2018. That year, as minister of families, Heather Stefanson introduced the refundable Child Care Centre Development Tax Credit to "incentivize" private corporations to set up childcare centres (Manitoba Families 2019). A business could receive $740,000 if they established a new centre.[2] Once established, it could be operated as a nonprofit or for-profit business (although only nonprofits would be able to enrol subsidized children and receive provincial operating support). The initial tax credit total was $2 million, which more than doubled to $4.7 million by 2020.

The contrast with nonprofit and community groups is striking. In 2018, just $2.8 million was available to distribute to community-led childcare start-ups anywhere in the province. Nonprofit groups were eligible for no more than 40 percent of capital costs to a maximum of $600,000 per centre. While it was extremely challenging for community organizations to raise the remaining capital funds, there was fierce competition for the small pot of dollars. The province has maintained the business tax credit, today worth $12,000 per space. The updated Early Learning and Child Care Building Fund for nonprofits has become moderately more generous and now covers up to 60 percent of eligible construction costs (flipping the former ratio). But, then as now, funding for private business-led childcare start-ups was more generous.

In 2019, when she was still minister of families, Stefanson lamented that "the private sector is underrepresented" in Manitoba childcare compared to other provinces (Progressive Conservatives Manitoba 2019). In December 2019, she issued a twelve-point action plan that proposed another "private sector/for-profit capital grant to incentivize expansion or new development of for-profit childcare centres" (Minister of Families 2019).

More privatization is found in PC legislative proposals. In April 2021, the province introduced Bill 47, The Early Learning and Child Care Act. Among other provisions, Bill 47 would open for-profit childcare facilities to receive operating grants and enrol subsidized children. In their brief, the Manitoba Federation of Labour noted that "a privatization agenda runs throughout the bill," threatening quality (Manitoba Federation of Labour 2021). While Bill 47 passed third reading, it has not yet been proclaimed.

Manitoba already has a small supply of for-profit childcare centres. Fees in this "market" sector are high. One national study found that in Winnipeg, for-profit infant care costs $16,800 per year (compared to $7,800 in nonprofits), and fees for preschoolers are $11,784 (compared to $5,408 in nonprofits) (Macdonald and Friendly 2019, 6). For now, the new $10 a day plan does not apply in commercial facilities, which are currently not permitted to participate in the provincial operating funding system and so do not honour the provincial maximum fee. But, as one news report observed, "private daycares want [a] piece of [the] funding" (Abas 2023).

Privatization pressure finds a receptive milieu. Even though the commercial sector makes up just 5 percent of Manitoba's centres, the provincial government has assigned them a disproportionate role in policy development. One sign of this is the Minister's Consultation Table, which provides "direct information and feedback" to the minister, as required by the Canada-Wide Early Learning and Child Care Agreement. Manitoba stipulates that among the broad membership of the Table, there will be nine not-for-profit facilities and three for-profit providers, meaning that one-twentieth of centres enjoy one-quarter of centre voices (Canada and Manitoba 2021, 23).

Even $10 a Day Childcare Is Expensive

Fees for most parents fell to $10 a day on 1 April 2023 (Government of Manitoba 2023b), thanks to an influx of federal dollars. The $10 a day fee is a marquee feature of the national plan and has garnered extensive public and media attention. This extraordinarily welcome development means that one year of full-time care will cost most families $2,600. Parents of babies will no longer pay $7,800 per year for infant care; and parents of preschoolers will not face a $5,408 invoice for their two- to five-year-old.

What happens when even $10 a day is too expensive, as it is for low- and modest-income families? Manitoba has announced it will keep the subsidy system in parallel with the new $10 a day fee. Eligibility for a child-care fee subsidy varies by the number of adults and children in a family, and the parent(s) must demonstrate an acceptable reason for seeking childcare. For many years, the thresholds for subsidy have been brutally low; one national expert observed that Manitoba was among the "most stringent" in Canada (Beach 2022, 24). The level remained entirely unchanged from 2014 to 2021, meaning every year a family had be even more poor than the year below to qualify. Not surprisingly, the share of users who qualified fell precipitously. In 2014, just 24 percent of children received some subsidy; in 2021, the figure had fallen to 9 percent. In 2022, the province finally adjusted income levels for subsidy. After thresholds were boosted, the share of subsidized children rose to 11 percent; but the long-term trend of falling numbers signals systemic problems with the subsidy system, with its high administrative burdens and punitive surcharge of $2 a day per child for even the very poorest families.

Paradoxically, the new $10 a day price will have inequitable effects. First, a parent must already have secured a childcare spot—and these are scarce. Second, only middle-income or high-income families will have been able to afford the full fee. It is these lucky and well-off parents who are positioned to reap the full cost reductions introduced by Ottawa's plan. Meanwhile, the poorest subsidized Manitoba parents must continue to pay $520 per year per child (via the daily charge of $2 per child)—even as the cost for parents who pay full fees drops to $2,600 per year. Lamentably, the poorest families see no reduction in their childcare fees. Any parent who has not yet found a childcare space faces long waits for service.

Frozen Funding: Diminished Quality for Children, Staff, and Facilities

Provincial operating grants to centres were frozen for six consecutive fiscal years at 2016 levels, despite hefty increases to family homes (which rose by 51 percent in the same period). When centre operating grants finally rose by 12 percent in summer 2022, they still lagged well behind the cost of living in real dollars.

The choice to freeze funding to an already underfunded system was reprehensible. Moreover, it occurred just as Manitoba began to receive a steady stream of new federal dollars. The Canada-Manitoba Early Learning and Child Care Agreement was signed in 2017, initially for three years, yet has been renewed every year since. By the close of 2022, this agreement had transferred $75 million to Manitoba for childcare. Ottawa also began to roll out a second plan, the Canada-Wide Early Learning and Child Care Agreement. Manitoba signed on to this plan in August 2021, in order to receive $1.2 billion over five years (Canada and Manitoba 2017, 2021; Government of Canada and Government of Manitoba 2022). Manitoba's childcare spending in 2017 set the baseline: the deal stipulates that federal transfers are to be incremental and "will not displace existing Manitoba early learning and child care spending" (Government of Canada 2017, section 5.1.1[e]). While COVID-19 makes strict year-over-year comparisons complicated, data shows that Manitoba has cumulatively spent close to $21 million less on childcare than it would have if 2017 spending levels had simply remained constant, even before accounting for either inflation adjustments or increases in the number of spaces across the past five fiscal years. This is a clear demonstration of austerity in action.

As real revenue fell, childcare centres faced hard choices. Often this was aggravated by austerity in other sectors. A considerable number of programs are located in school buildings, and different schools and divisions negotiate varying lease terms and fees. All schools located in Winnipeg School Division began to be charged rent, as the division juggled its own finances. One centre in a Winnipeg school saw their rent go up by $16,812 per year as a direct result (Personal communication). That same centre formerly provided children with a hot lunch at a nominal $2 charge but had to abandon the program. Many programs stopped providing free snacks, asking parents instead to send food from home. Some began charging parents for supplies that were previously included—such as trips—or eliminating this programming altogether.

An ECE's working conditions are a child's learning conditions. Surveys done for this anthology project made damning findings about the effects of austerity on educators, and thus on program quality. Over three-quarters (77 percent) of respondents reported that the quality of childcare they offer has suffered. Over half agreed with "I am asked to provide the same

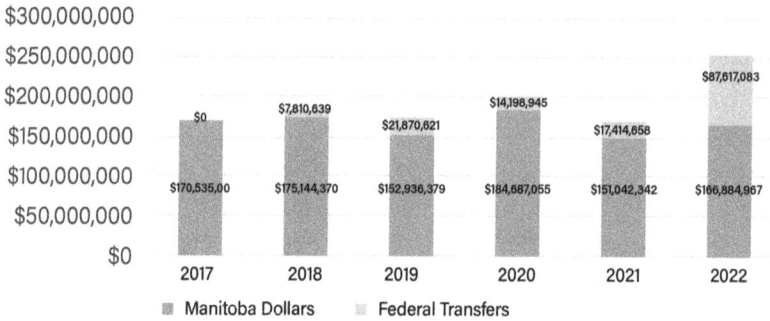

Figure 1.1. Manitoba total spending on early learning and childcare.

Note: Author's calculations using 31 March, from provincial annual reports and published federal agreements. CHST transfers are not included. The province managed to hold its own spending steady in several ways: by failing to index operating grants to inflation, by opting not to provide real increases, and by failing to extend operating funding to a sizable share of newly created spaces. Facilities responded by squeezing their already bare-bones budgets.

or increased service with fewer resources." Of a sample of ECE respondents, 96 percent said their work was impacted, with most of them saying it was "greatly" impacted. Frozen funding impaired the ability of facilities to expand or to innovate new programming. Building maintenance suffered and was deferred, and supply budgets were unchanged. Innovative programming could not be implemented if it had budget implications.

Heartbreakingly for young children with additional support needs, there have been funding cuts to the Inclusion Support Program. In 2015/16, 61 percent of centres participated in the program. By 2022/23, just half did. The number of children served fell from 1,541 to 1,242.

Personnel: ECE Workforce Crisis

For years, early childhood education professionals have been underpaid. Years of frozen funding aggravated this long-standing problem, and so facilities began to increasingly operate with fewer qualified educators to manage revenue shortfalls. When Premier Pallister was elected in 2016, there was one certified ECE II or III for every 11.3 licensed childcare spaces in Manitoba. By the end of 2022, there was one certified ECE II or III for every 14.3 licensed spaces. This is a precipitous decline in the number of children who can benefit from care offered by qualified educators.

Low wages are the central reason why Manitoba has fewer qualified ECEs today than in 2016, and this is the direct result of insufficient provincial operational funding. The 2022 average hourly wage for ECEs was 72 percent of the Manitoba Child Care Association's market competitive salary guidelines (Beach 2022, 33)—most staff would need wage increases of $7.50 to $7.92 per hour to meet the professional recommendations. Manitoba did not promise much remedy to ECE wages through the Canada-wide agreement, despite receiving millions of dollars in transfers. The initial provincial action plan suggested very modest targets, stressing that employers are responsible for establishing wages. In the 2022/23 fiscal year, the province finally increased provincial operating grants, ending the years-long freeze. Beginning July 2022, Manitoba used the increase primarily to promote what it called a "wage grid," but left significant ambiguity about whether the grid was required or merely recommended. Whichever is the case, most staff— those with Child Care Assistant (CCA) and ECE II qualifications—began with a starting hourly wage between $16.05 and $20.90 in 2022/23; such low entry wages basically reproduce the current status quo (Government of Manitoba 2023; Manitoba Early Learning and Child Care 2023).

Low pay is the clearest signal of disrespect to the important work of caring for young children. Manitoba reports that staffing costs make up 83 percent of a childcare centre's budget, meaning it is both the biggest and most elastic category (as cited in KPMG 2020, 34). As provincial funding was frozen at 2016 levels, programs had to find ways to manage budgets squeezed by the rising cost of living. One option was to run a deficit, something KPMG found 31 percent of centres in Manitoba did. As KPMG points out, when a facility is "operating at a deficit, even if revenue increases, they are unlikely to be in a position to improve staff pay" (35).

Early childhood educators earn high school wages, despite having post-secondary education. Manitoba recognizes three training levels, with different scopes of professional practice. An ECE II has a post-secondary degree (usually two years of community college) and an ECE III has the same training or better, plus post-graduate certification. A CCA has completed a forty-hour course. In family homes, there is no requirement for provider training beyond the forty-hour course. On paper, two-thirds of those working in Manitoba infant and preschool centres must be ECE II or III, and only an ECE III can be a director. In practice, however, many programs cannot meet these licensing requirements due to challenges with recruitment and retention. As far back as 2013, the auditor general noted that one-quarter of centres could not meet staffing requirements (Office of the Auditor General of Manitoba 2013, 119). This likely meant a shortfall of 250 or more ECEs that year.

Licensed childcare continues to operate without the required share of trained staff. The provincial *Annual Report* notes 3,040 ECE IIs and IIIs in the field in 2016, rising to 3,356 in 2019 (Government of Manitoba 2016, 2023a). Today, there are just 2,891 such professionals—a loss of more than 10 percent of the workforce from its peak. The drop is especially marked among senior leadership: there are about one-quarter fewer ECE IIIs now than there were three years ago. Moreover, since the number of spaces has risen during the same period, the losses are even more acute, as fewer credentialed educators care for a higher number of children. If funding had enabled facilities to maintain certified ECEs at the same ratio as in 2016 (albeit inadequate to meet regulations, even then), Manitoba today would have 750 more ECEs working in the field (in a field already short staffed, as noted by the auditor general). While families might be mollified to know that CCAs ensure basic health and safety, they should be very troubled by shortages of qualified ECE professionals.

The absolute lack of certified educators will worsen. By 2026, the 23,000 new spaces promised under Canada-Wide Early Learning and Child Care Agreements will require an estimated 5,000 new staff, of whom more than 3,000 will need to be certified ECEs II or III (Beach 2022, 32). It takes a minimum of two years full-time to obtain the credentials for an ECE II and even longer to qualify as an ECE III. Manitoba has to first recover from the current shortfall of an estimated 1,000 certified educators, then grow the professional corps at lightning speed. Few observers are confident this can happen in time.

Conclusion: Challenges to Austerity

This review has demonstrated multiple ways that austerity has harmed childcare in Manitoba. The supply of licensed childcare remains low: there are not enough places, and little planning for expansion. Privatization pressures are real and growing, and policy has been amended to incentivize for-profit childcare facilities and to amplify the voices of the commercial sector. On the parent fee front, there is positive news: fees held constant, and have dropped to $10 a day for many. Yet even $10 a day childcare is too expensive for modest-income households. The subsidy system entirely fails to create meaningful affordability for low- and modest-income children and their families—and subsidized families have not seen any reduction in their costs. Program funding freezes have cut quality for children, staff, and facilities, and these cuts have yet to be made up. There is a multifaceted workforce crisis; Manitoba is short an estimated 1,000 qualified ECEs today and is unlikely to find the 3,000 or more that will be needed if the system is to expand as promised. The provincial budget for childcare has increased, but since 2017 all funding increases are entirely due to transfers from the federal government.

This is a grim summary of the ways that austerity has been experienced by children, parents, and early childhood educators under PC governments since 2016. Yet there is reason for some optimism. First: the federal government is offering unprecedented support for childcare change. Thanks to Ottawa, childcare fees have dropped. The federal requirement that expansion spaces be primarily nonprofit and public tempers what might be a reflex by Premier Stefanson and her PC government to look to the private market to supply spaces. The national insistence on equity in access will ensure the province is required to introduce some planning measures. The workforce crisis is highlighting how much the quality of care for children depends on the quality of the educators who care for them—and we can predict this to generate improvements in their wages, benefits, and working conditions. Childcare professionals and advocates across the province collaborated on a *Roadmap to a Quality Early Learning and Child Care System in Manitoba* (Beach 2022) and are working to popularize its lessons.

There is one promising change to note. In 2022, childcare moved from Families (with a long legacy of welfare, targeting, and residual programs) to the newly renamed ministry of Education and Early Childhood Learning, finally affiliating childcare with rights and entitlements, purpose-built settings, and professional—and unionized—educators. While so far largely symbolic, this new institutional identity offers a promising foundation for continued childcare advocacy.

Notes

1   All data is drawn from provincial annual reports (Government of Manitoba 2016, 2023a), unless otherwise noted. When a single year is cited, I use 31 March (e.g., "in 2016" means at the end of the 2015/16 fiscal year). When I write "today," I mean as of 31 March 2023, the end of the 2022/23 fiscal year. This chapter was drafted in 2023, using 2023 as the most recent data year.

2   The tax credit, initially of $10,000 per space, would be claimed over five years.

References

Abas, Malak. 2023. "Private Daycares Want Piece of Funding." *Winnipeg Free Press*, 12 May. https://www.winnipegfreepress.com/breakingnews/2023/05/12/private-daycares-want-piece-of-funding.

Beach, Jane. 2022. *Roadmap to a Quality Early Learning and Child Care System in Manitoba*. Winnipeg: Manitoba Child Care Association.

Editorial. 2023. "Capacity Key for Working Daycare System." *Winnipeg Free Press*, 27 April. https://www.winnipegfreepress.com/opinion/editorials/2023/04/27/capacity-key-for-working-daycare-system.

Engage MB. 2021. "What We Heard: Early Learning and Child Care Modernization." Government of Manitoba. https://manitoba.ca/asset_library/en/proactive/20212022/what-we-heard-elcc.pdf.

Government of Canada. 2017. "Canada-Manitoba Early Learning and Child Care Agreement." https://www.canada.ca/en/early-learning-child-care-agreement/agreements-provinces-territories/manitoba-2017.html.

———. 2021. "Canada-Wide Early Learning and Child Care Agreement, 2021–2026." https://www.canada.ca/en/early-learning-child-care-agreement/agreements-provinces-territories/manitoba-canada-wide-2021.html.

Government of Manitoba. 2016. *Annual Report, 2015–2016*. Manitoba Families.

———. 2022. "Canada and Manitoba Make Child Care More Affordable for Low and Middle-Income Families—Province Triples the Number of Subsidized Spaces and Reduces Parent Fees by 30 Per Cent on Average for Families in Regulated Child Care." News Release, 3 February. https://news.gov.mb.ca/news/index.html?item=53259&posted=2022-02-03.

———. 2023a. *Annual Report, 2022–2023*. Manitoba Education and Early Childhood Learning. https://www.edu.gov.mb.ca/annualreports/index.html.

———. 2023b. "Manitoba Government Sets Stage for $10-A-Day Child Care, Prioritizing New Spaces, Training Early Learning and Child-Care Professionals, and Ensuring Access Across the Province." News Release, 3 March. https://news.gov.mb.ca/news/index.html?item=58353.

———. 2023c. "Early Learning and Child Care Wage Grid." Manitoba Early Learning and Child Care. https://www.manitoba.ca/education/childcare/students_workforce/wage_grid.html.

KPMG. 2020. *Early Learning and Child Care Transformation: Manitoba Department of Families, Final Report.* 31 August. https://manitoba.ca/asset_library/en/proactive/20212022/mb-families-elcc-review.pdf.

Macdonald, David, and Martha Friendly. 2019. *Developmental Milestones: Child Care Fees in Canada's Big Cities 2018.* Canadian Centre for Policy Alternatives. https://www.policyalternatives.ca/wp-content/uploads/attachments/Developmental%20milestones%20%284%29.pdf.

———. 2023. *Not Done Yet: $10/day Child Care Requires Addressing Canada's Child Care Deserts.* Canadian Centre for Policy Alternatives. https://policyalternatives.ca/sites/default/files/uploads/publications/National%20Office/2023/05/not-done-yet.pdf.

Manitoba Families. 2019. "A Guide to the Child Care Centre Development Tax Credit Program." Government of Manitoba. https://www.manitoba.ca/education/childcare/resources/centre_dev_tax_credit.html.

Manitoba Federation of Labour. 2021. Legislative Submission: Bill 47—The Early Learning and Child Care Act. https://mfl.ca/mflreports/.

Minister of Families. 2019. *Shared Priorities, Sustainable Progress: A 12-Month Action Plan for Manitoba Families.*

Office of the Auditor General of Manitoba. 2013. "Manitoba Early Learning and Child Care Program." https://www.oag.mb.ca/audit-reports/annual-report-to-the-legislature---chapter-4%3A-manitoba-early-learning-and-child-care-program-2013.

Prentice, Susan. 2007. "Childcare, Justice and the City: A Case Study of Planning Failure in Winnipeg." *Canadian Journal of Urban Research*, 16 (1): 92–108.

Prentice, Susan, Matthew Sanscartier, and Tracey Peter. 2016. *Home Sweet Home? An Evidence-Based Analysis of Family Home Childcare in Manitoba: Working Paper.*

Progressive Conservatives Manitoba. 2019. "PCs to Make Child Care More Affordable and Available." Press Release.

Chapter 2

SCHOOLING UNDER AUSTERITY: ERODING EQUITY AND WORSENING WORKLOADS IN K-12 EDUCATION

Ee-Seul Yoon

Introduction

Under a Progressive Conservative (PC) government (2026–2023), the provincial school system was subjected to cuts, cutbacks, and layoffs. Austerity directives imposed by the government led to a continuous stream of reductions or removals of educational programs, structures, resources, and supports across all school divisions and schools. Some school boards laid off staff, cut employee hours, and/or intensified workloads among workers and administrators at all levels. Some also eliminated their early years numeracy and literacy support programs and/or student services departments. Other boards eliminated bus services and cut programs related to the arts, vocational training, or university preparation. These cuts were mainly due to the government austerity policies but were particularly severe due to historic levels of inflation and the COVID-19 pandemic (and its lasting effects). Many school boards have struggled and continue to struggle to balance their budgets. Meanwhile, school divisions tried to meet the rising needs of students who experience poverty with staff who were overwhelmed with pandemic fatigue and declining resources. Some school trustees and superintendents expressed their concerns and raised awareness about schools' ongoing needs both in the print media (especially *Winnipeg Free Press*) and on social media (especially X, formerly known as Twitter). Nevertheless, little is known about how the austerity implemented by the PCs impacted workers in the education sector because workers were less likely to voice their views publicly.

This chapter aims to provide an in-depth look into the lived experiences and perspectives of workers in the public education sector, including teachers, principals, educational assistants, social workers, guidance counsellors, administrators, curriculum consultants, policy analysts, and bus drivers. The purpose is to raise awareness of the impact of austerity measures imposed by the PCs on the quality of education provided to various learners, especially those with additional needs, and among those who experience economic poverty and insecurity. It provides an overview of expenditure shortfalls and raises public awareness of the impact of funding cuts on the volume and intensity of work that was done by educators and others who worked in the education system. The perspectives of education workers, as reported here, provide critical insights into what happens when the government imposes expenditure constraints on the public education system with very little consultation or research. It is imperative to understand what happened to the public school system when austerity measures were rolled out with little to no consultation or assessment of the ongoing needs of the system. The chapter also sketches out alternative policy ideas.

This chapter is organized as follows. It begins with a brief overview of the role of the Manitoba government in the province's K–12 education and how the PC government made substantive changes in its approaches after coming to power. The chapter then provides a thematic summary and analysis of the results of surveys of public education sector workers from all regions of the province. The surveys were conducted in late 2022 and early 2023. The total number of participants is 109, including front-line workers (74 percent), management (16 percent), and others (10 percent). The major themes include: (1) the nature and trends of austerity in education; (2)

the impact of austerity on the quality of service provided; (3) the impact on working conditions; (4) an assessment of the short-term and long-term cost savings; and (5) considerations for future policy changes. The conclusion will discuss this study's significance in illuminating directions for future school finance.

The Role of the Provincial Government in the K–12 Education Sector: Vision Versus Ideology

A unique characteristic of Canada is that, unlike comparable countries (e.g., other Organisation for Economic Co-Operation and Development member countries), its provincial governments are responsible for the governance of the K–12 education sector. The provincial ministries of education set the priorities for all schools, with the exception of schools on reserves. In Manitoba, the education minister plays an important role in making key decisions on a range of educational policies and directives. These decisions include the level of annual school funding provided. Other decisions include curricular consultation and selection, teacher certification, high school graduation requirements, and modes of delivery (including distance education). Additional decisions include assessment, special education, language programs, and the renovation or construction of school buildings. The ministry also works closely with local school boards and superintendents in planning and managing schools and staff. Their decisions are supposed to be guided by the following statements on the ministry's website (Education and Early Childhood Learning n.d.):

> VISION: All Manitoba children and students succeed, no matter where they live, their backgrounds, or their individual circumstances.

> MISSION: To ensure responsive, equitable and high-quality childcare and learning from early childhood through to high school graduation to support all children and students to reach their full potential.

> MANDATE: The department's mandate is to set the overall strategic and operational policy direction, establish standards and allocate funding for childcare, early learning and K–12 education, ensuring accountability for outcomes.

Yet the ministry's annual agendas tend to be driven by "short-term political considerations at the expense of long-term educational needs" (Wallin et al. 2021, 75). The ministry's policy also tends to adhere to the governing party's political ideology and priorities, since the minister is an elected politician and a member of the party in power. Hence, the way the ministry ensures the "success" of all students is politically and ideologically driven. Austerity policy is a prime example of the advantages given to wealthy individuals by prioritizing greater tax cuts while lowering government spending on social and welfare programs, including education. Further austerity measures tend to reduce long-term investments in the public sector, which can further disadvantage future generations.

The PC Government's Austerity Agenda (2016–2023)

The PC government's political beliefs in fiscal conservatism were most notable in the education sector. Defined as deficit reduction primarily through expenditure reduction and restraint (Hajer and Fernandez 2021), the term *austerity* was a buzzword in the province while the PCs were in office. The list of cuts the government made was growing, and as such, it seemed to be departing drastically from its education mission, vision, and mandate, as stated above. The cuts threatened our school system as "the cornerstone of healthy, safe communities and of democracy" (McCracken 2019, sec. 1, para. 2).

As can be seen in Table 2.1[1] below, the share of provincial funding for public education declined according to the *Financial Reporting and Accounting in Manitoba Education and Early Childhood Learning (FRAME) Reports* (Government of Manitoba n.d.). The funding increase in 2020/21 was mostly to deal with the pandemic, including federal contributions. Nevertheless, the share of provincial funding continuously declined. In the meantime, inflation rose alongside student enrolment. These rising pressures led to a decline in funding for public education in real terms since 2016 (Ali 2021). In inflation-adjusted terms, funding fell every year from 2016/17 to 2019/20 and, despite a COVID-19 bump, was well below 2016/17 levels in 2020/21. Manitoba Education annual reports from 2015/16 to 2021/22 also show that provincial government full-time equivalent (FTE) staffing in the area of education declined from 373 to 317 FTEs from 2015/16 to 2021/22 (Hajer 2023).

Table 2.1. Share of provincial operating funding for public education, 2016–2020.[a]

YEAR	PROVINCIAL CONTRIBUTION AS % OF TOTAL FUNDING FOR PUBLIC EDUCATION	PROVINCIAL CONTRIBUTION (MILLIONS)	IN 2022 DOLLARS (MILLIONS)	POPULATION UNDER 18	PER MANITOBAN UNDER 18	IN 2022 DOLLARS
2016/17	62.5	$1,455	$1,610	300,410	$4,843	$5,592
2017/18	60.9	$1,488	$1,619	303,898	$4,896	$5,551
2018/19	60.4	$1,461	$1,551	306,460	$4,770	$5,342
2019/20	60.1	$1,461	$1,517	308,973	$4,728	$5,230
2020/21[b]	58.4	$1,512	$1,562	310,767	$4,865	$5,294

a   For details on data sources used for provincial expenditures, employee staffing numbers, and full-time equivalent (FTE) positions in this chapter, see Preface.
b   The funding increase in 2020/21 was mostly to deal with the pandemic, including federal contributions. Nevertheless, the share of provincial funding continuously declined.

The government also directed school divisions to cap their education property tax increases at 2 percent in 2019, and by 2019/20 had reduced the education budget by 7 percent in inflation-adjusted per child terms compared to 2015/16 levels. This directive limited school divisions' ability to raise tax-based funds to make up for funding shortfalls and meet their schooling needs. The divisions were told that they would face a 20 percent cut on administrative costs if they did not abide by the cap (Botelho-Urbanski 2019). At the same time, despite running a deficit, the PC government gave property tax rebates of $246 million in 2021 and $350 million in 2022, and $453 million in 2023 (Yoon 2022; Government of Manitoba 2022). Overall, the government underfunded public education by not keeping pace with inflation while rolling out property education tax rebates.

Provincially directed policy changes to manage funding shortfalls impacted classrooms negatively. Whereas the New Democratic Party (NDP), while in power from 1999 to 2016, capped K–12 class sizes at twenty students, the PCs removed the cap in 2017, and some classes were forced to accommodate as many as twenty-seven or twenty-eight children (according to one of the survey respondents). As a result, teachers had less time to identify the strengths and weaknesses of each student and provide additional support. These cuts disproportionately affected those who are from the most vulnerable groups. At the same time, the government-imposed wage freeze and interference in collective bargaining in the public sector severely undermined the bargaining power of unions representing the education sector. This led to worsening working conditions and additional stress on workers, and in some cases parents; for example, Winnipeg bus drivers had to strike for almost three months to secure minimal wage gains. The following sections provide further evidence of the impact of austerity from the perspectives of workers in the public education sector.

From Pallister to Stefanson: How Did Things Change over Time?

Most survey respondents noted that resource restraints became more intense over time. Comparing their experiences of the expenditure restraints to those of the NDP government prior to 2016, four out of five respondents (80 percent) reported that provincial austerity under the PC premier, Brian Pallister, was more intense, with increasing expenditure restraint/cuts and larger staff reductions. Three out of five (60 percent) respondents stated the intensity of provincial austerity measures actually increased after the COVID-19 pandemic began in March 2020, when even more support was needed in the school system.

Furthermore, while funding increased in 2020/21 and 2021/22, this was mostly to deal with the COVID-19 pandemic (including federal contributions), and the increase was primarily to fund negotiated and arbitrated wages settlements after years of real wage losses by teachers. As such, under Premier Heather Stefanson, education funding shortfalls continued across the province. Thus, one out of two survey respondents (54 percent) reported that the intensity of austerity has remained about the same, while one out of five (22 percent) felt there had been greater austerity. The education workers noted the impact of austerity measures in the following ways:

- 81 percent reported staffing shortages
- 73 percent reported an increased number of tasks
- 65 percent reported other resource shortages (reduced budgets or limiting of spending to support people's work/tasks)
- 40 percent reported shorter or missed breaks/meals

In other words, the system-wide cuts over several years have increased workloads. Three out of four education workers said that their workload has increased considerably. One out of four said their work has moderately increased. Five respondents reported having been laid off. Respondents elaborated on their experiences in the following ways:

- "Larger class sizes of more diverse student needs with fewer supports (both staff and resources). As well, dealing with greater mental and emotional needs within the classroom."
- "We are expected to fulfill tasks we did not have to do before—such as admin assistant duties, and EA [Educational Assistant] and support duties."
- "Needing to teach online, duplex [hybrid] teaching, larger class sizes, more meetings and training outside the school day, more supervision, less money to hire teachers, less money to buy supplies, etc. More special needs in classroom."
- "Students' needs in a post-pandemic world have increased. We are expected to meet greater needs, but using less money, in a

time when costs have only risen. This has become especially pronounced as of the start of the 2022–2023 school year."

These responses suggest increasing workload and growing staffing instability and shortages created an unnecessarily stressful work environment in the education sector, a problem unaddressed by the change from the Pallister government to the Stefanson government.

The Impact of Austerity on Service Quality: Worsening Inequality and Safety

The conditions for learning and teaching in Manitoba deteriorated under austerity. Education and teaching staff were not able to spend the necessary time with their students because they were tasked with doing more with fewer resources. In particular, teachers noted that they had less time to prepare for their lessons and were asked to cover more frequently for other teachers when there were not enough substitutes. As such, four out of five respondents (80 percent) noted that the quality of the service or education they provided declined. One staff person wrote, "We cannot meet the needs of our students . . . we are stretched so thin in elementary schools. Increased class sizes with fewer supports for growing exceptionalities."

School staff mentioned a notable reduction in service quality for low-income students. Three out of five respondents (63 percent) felt there was less support for students who were economically poor and insecure. One respondent wrote, "The people most affected by school cuts are low-income students who may need more services. Programs like free breakfast were the first to vanish, and family outreach programs they used were cancelled."

Furthermore, half of the respondents (53 percent) identified that the poor quality of education was in part due to a worsening sense of safety. Respondents pinpointed the short-term and long-term consequences of the effects of austerity as follows:

- "We have seen an increase in violent incidents and need for threat assessments in our school. I believe this to be due in part to a lack of resources that has led to larger class sizes, fewer course options, and general overcrowding in the building."
- "Effects of poor spending on education on public safety are most likely to be seen over a generation, not a couple of years."

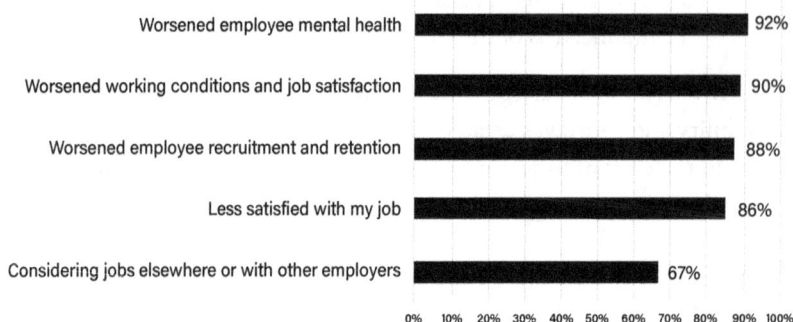

Figure 2.1. Survey responses: Impact of austerity on working conditions in K–12 education.

- "Important tasks were simply missed as the time did not allow. For example, proper police information and child abuse checks."

The Impact on Working Conditions and Job Satisfaction

One of the survey's key findings is the high levels of job dissatisfaction and worsening working conditions. Nine out of ten respondents (90 percent) mentioned that their working conditions worsened, and their job satisfaction plummeted (see Figure 2.1). Their mental health severely declined. These worsening working conditions became new challenges for the retention and recruitment of staff in the education sector. The following quotes illustrate growing frustration. Major themes include the challenges of teacher burnout, overstretched multitasking, work dissatisfaction, teacher attrition, economic insecurity, and a sense of despair:

- "I have 14 years teaching experience. I grew up in a home of educators. The amount of work, time and effort needed to do our jobs adequately is not feasible. Teacher burnout is real. Because of constant cuts, we are expected to be mental health experts, special needs interventionists, speech language pathologists, therapists, coaches, care providers, etc."
- "Retirements and resignations are on the rise, as are medical (stress) leaves. Teachers are very frustrated that the demands on

them are increasing, with less support, and they are unable to do the job to the level of quality that they used to be able [to].”

- “Throw in a completely irresponsible laissez-faire approach to managing the effects of a global pandemic at the provincial level, including diverting funds for COVID safety and mitigation to reduce the deficit . . . the result is exhausted, disenfranchised professionals.”
- “Class size makes a huge difference in a student’s success . . . I often feel guilty and feel like I am failing my students even though class size is not within my control. This makes me like my career choice less.”

Austerity: Cost Saving?

When asked whether they felt that austerity measures could lead to cost saving, an overwhelming majority of the respondents said that it would not. Four out of five said that Manitobans were getting less value for their money. The main reason to question the connection between austerity measures and cost saving seems to be that public education is both a long-term and interconnected investment. Education cuts will have an impact in the foreseeable future in the form of achievement and job readiness, as well as on other services, including the welfare and justice systems. One out of three respondents said that the austerity measures would end up costing the province more over time. Some were especially concerned about the lack of resources for those who need extra support, which is especially critical in the early years and throughout high school. Some respondents elaborated on their concerns:

- “I think the lack of commitment to understand how classrooms work, alongside a refusal to engage with research on which interventions have the best outcomes for learning (smaller class sizes, equitable access to technology, etc.) has led to cuts that don’t correlate with efficiency.”
- “We are not intervening early, and students/families/teachers/ staff are left to flounder. Which will increase the level of need/ concern in the long term.”

- "Children with special needs are especially affected and this can cost taxpayers in the long run if schools are not able to help them become independent."

Policy Alternatives?

When asked whether they had any suggestions for policy alternatives to austerity, the respondents noted first and foremost that they wanted the government to consult more thoroughly with workers in education. Many respondents expressed disappointment regarding the government imposing cuts without meaningful or systematic research. The ideological approach to cost cutting was conducted without understanding what current needs were and where cuts could have been made responsibly. The government directives to cut budgets without making any real assessment of the needs of schools was a source of hardship for many school divisions. As such, any policy alternatives would need to come with increased consultation with those who work in the education sector.

Most respondents said they were not consulted, and, as reflected in the comments below, expressed disappointment in not having been consulted as part of the policy change process:

- "They explained the government required cuts of 15 percent of management. . . . We were also told that budgets were cut a certain percentage."
- "Money and budget cuts are the only consideration, with no thought or consultation as to the real, severe impact on our children and future generations."
- "Staff are almost never surveyed for their opinion or ideas . . . you don't get a good understanding of what is actually happening."

This survey tells us that it is important to collaborate with those who work on the front lines, directly with students, staff, and administrators. Creating a collaborative culture can go far in terms of making the education system work for students and the wider society. Most respondents also disagreed with the notion that privatization efforts were an effective way to deal with expenditure reductions. Three out of four respondents doubted that privatization of education would provide more efficiency, effectiveness, or safety. These concerns echo the well-known problem of market failures in education, thereby making it the role of government to provide adequate and equitable education (see Stiglitz and Rosengard 2015). High-quality education for all citizens, especially those who experience economic poverty and insecurity, will not be equally accessible unless it is provided by the government as a public good. Some respondents made the following comments, raising important questions about equity:

- "No, I think the private sector would not take into account the diverse needs of students and communities in the education system."
- "Only the affluent can afford services, therefore our population will become divided."
- "Public education *cannot* be driven by private, corporate interests, who will inevitably become fixated on the bottom line at the expense of what is best for students."
- "Public education needs to remain exactly that, public and for the people."
- "Privatizing clinicians and services leads to reports and recommendations by people who don't know the students or the school culture, and costs three times as much for the same assessment/report."

The respondents provided some insights that can be summarized in the following areas and considered for alternative approaches, while being sensitive to institutional contexts and differences across localities:

- Invest more in human resources, since education is really about people.
- More teachers are needed to work with students to improve educational outcomes.
- There should be greater focus on recovery learning for students who have fallen behind academically.
- We need trained adults and professionals who can support students with profound needs.
- Invest in education and an educated workforce in order to grow the economy.
- To attract the highest quality of workers, pay wages that are competitive and comparable to private sector jobs for those with similar qualifications and experiences.

- Decrease funding for independent schools and reallocate it to public schools.
- Early intervention is key: keep class sizes small and provide support up front.
- Provide social services that improve the lives of low-income and impoverished families.
- More tax money should be raised from exceptionally wealthy citizens and businesses.
- Hire superintendents and bureaucrats who have a background in education.

Conclusion: Takeaways and Looking Ahead

Workers in the K–12 education sector indicate that funding shortfalls and austerity measures have negatively impacted the work they do and the children they serve, noting that the cuts and cutbacks were inefficient and ineffective. The austerity measures underserved the most vulnerable populations. Austerity measures were short-sighted and will undermine public confidence in the education system as a whole in the decades to come. Education workers who participated in the study echoed the challenges faced by other public service units that were under severe pressure, including healthcare workers and other emergency services units (Hajer and Fernandez 2021). The respondents in this survey suggested alternative approaches to providing equitable education with long-term societal goals in mind. More immediately, they called for engagement and consultation with front-line workers and teachers. The respondents suggested that top-down policy-making processes, especially cost cutting without consultation, is ineffective in education. Going forward, it will be important to listen to those who work in education and can offer their professional experiences and knowledge to inform and improve the education system.

Discussing the results of this study could be a good starting point for resetting future policy making in line with the education ministry's mandate, mission, and vision, as noted on its website and mentioned earlier in this chapter. The ministry needs to work to achieve its vision that "all Manitoba children and students succeed, no matter where they live, their backgrounds, or their individual circumstances" (Education and Early Childhood Learning n.d.). The government needs to recognize that schooling under austerity severely undermines the system's ability to meet the needs of all students and staff. Under-investing in the system will deteriorate the role education plays as a great equalizer of our society in the decades to come.

Notes

1   For details on data sources used for provincial expenditures, employee staffing numbers, and full-time equivalent (FTE) positions in this chapter, see Preface.

References

Ali, Amin. 2021. *K–12 Education, Funding and Equity in Manitoba*. Winnipeg: Canadian Centre for Policy Alternatives–Manitoba.

Botelho-Urbanski, Jessica. 2019. "Stray from Tax Cap, Get Cut: Minister. Province Promises to Punish Defiant School Divisions." *Winnipeg Free Press*, 6 March.

Government of Manitoba. 2022. *Budget 2022*. https://www.gov.mb.ca/budget2022/tax-and-fee-measures.html.

———. n.d. "About Us." Education and Early Childhood Learning. Accessed on 28 January 2023. https://www.edu.gov.mb.ca/aboutus.html.

———. n.d. "FRAME [Financial Reporting and Accounting in Manitoba Education and Early Childhood Learning] Reports." https://www.edu.gov.mb.ca/k12/finance/frame_report/index.html.

Hajer, Jesse. 2023. "Austerity in Manitoba." Manitoba Research Alliance. 29 August. https://mra-mb.ca/austerity-in-manitoba/.

Hajer, Jesse, and Lynne Fernandez. 2021. *COVID-19, Austerity and an Alternative Social and Economic Policy Path for Manitoba*. Winnipeg: Canadian Centre for Policy Alternatives–Manitoba. https://www.policyalternatives.ca/publications/reports/covid-19-austerity-and-alternative-social-and-economic-policy-path-manitoba.

McCracken, Molly. 2019. "What Is Happening to Public Education in Manitoba?" Winnipeg: Canadian Centre for Policy Alternatives–Manitoba. https://policy-alternatives.ca/wp-content/uploads/attachments/What is happening in public education in MB%3F.pdf.

Stiglitz, Joseph E., and Jay K. Rosengard. 2015. "Market Failure." In *Economics of the Public Sector*, edited by Joseph E. Stiglitz and Jay K. Rosengard, 81–100. New York: W.W. Norton.

Wallin, Dawn, Jonathan Young, and Benjamin Levin. 2021. *Understanding Canadian Schools: An Introduction to Educational Administration*. 6th ed. Saskatoon:

University of Saskatchewan Open Press. https://openpress.usask.ca/understandingcanadianschools/.

Yoon, Ee-Seul. 2022. "Stop the Education Property Tax Cut until We Have a Better Plan." Winnipeg: Canadian Centre for Policy Alternatives–Manitoba. https://policyfix.ca/2022/11/15/stop-the-education-property-tax-cut-until-we-have-a-better-plan/.

Chapter 3

AUSTERITY AND ADVANCED EDUCATION IN MANITOBA

Scott Forbes

Introduction

In April 2016, the Progressive Conservative (PC) government of Brian Pallister was elected to office in Manitoba. He had promised to reduce the budget deficit, lower taxes, and rein in public sector unions. Immediately upon taking office, he implemented austerity measures that were intended to reduce—quite dramatically—the size of the public sector, and curb wage settlements with public sector unions. One of his first targets was post-secondary education.

The coming years were to feature interference with collective bargaining, reduced public funding to our colleges and universities, and steadily rising tuitions fees, such that students paid more to get less. Workers across the sector were asked increasingly to do more with less, increasing workloads and stress levels and eroding morale. Then, in the spring of 2020 a system already financially strained was hit with a new, unexpected, and devastating challenge: the COVID-19 pandemic. Again, the Pallister government chose to make an example of our colleges and universities, giving them five days to prepare for immediate cuts of up to 30 percent of public funding. The Pallister government saw an opportunity to fast-track its austerity program and took it.

This chapter chronicles the era of austerity in post-secondary education under the Pallister government. It examines the changing finances, political interference in labour relations, and the impacts on students, faculty, administrators, and support staff at our colleges and universities. Among the data used here were the responses of staff and faculty to a survey conducted in 2022 (Hajer 2023). Although similar impacts occurred at our colleges, I use financial data from the four public universities that are more detailed and publicly accessible than for the colleges.

Background

The Manitoba public post-secondary system consists of four universities and four colleges: Brandon University, Université de Saint-Boniface, University of Manitoba, University of Winnipeg, Assiniboine Community College, Red River College Polytechnic, University College of the North, and Manitoba Institute of Trade and Technology. Funding for Manitoba's universities and colleges comes from three main sources: provincial funding for operating grants and capital projects, tuition fee revenue, and "other," which includes parking, residence fees, bookstore and food store revenue, federal grants, etc. (Figure 3.1). Different universities have different blends of revenue sources: the two smallest universities, Brandon and St. Boniface, rely most heavily on the provincial grant, while the University of Winnipeg has the highest reliance on tuition revenue (Figure 3.1).

Trends in Provincial Funding

The provincial government supports higher education through the provision of grants for both capital projects and operating expenditures. In real 2016 dollars, public funding for universities and colleges declined steadily from just over $675 million 2016 to under $600 million in 2022 (Figure 3.2a). To compensate, the province permitted universities to increase tuition fees, which had different effects on the four universities. Fees at St. Boniface remained relatively static while those at the other three universities increased substantially (Figure 3.1). As a result of the decreasing grants and increasing fees, the ratio of provincial grants to tuition revenue dropped steadily from 2016 to 2022. Again, there were differential impacts on the four universities. Brandon saw this ratio decline most steeply, but at all universities, students were contributing a higher share of total university budgets (Figure 3.2b).

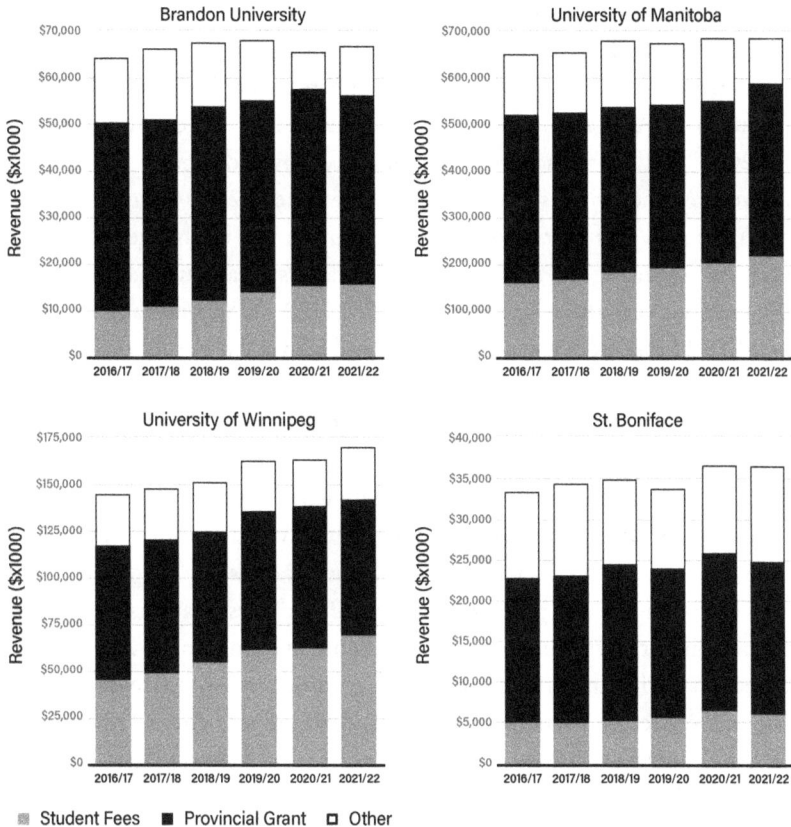

Figure 3.1. Revenue reported by Manitoba universities, budget years 2016/17 to 2021/22.

Sources: Audited annual financial statements on university websites: Brandon University, Audited Financial Report for the years 2017 to 2022; University of Manitoba, Annual Financial Statements for the years 2017 to 2022; University of Winnipeg, Consolidated Financial Statements for the years 2017 to 2022.

Note: Revenue is broken down into Student Fees, Provincial Grants, and Other. Height of the columns represents total reported revenue. Data for the University of Manitoba is for the operating budget.

The Effect of the Pandemic on University Budgets

The pandemic descended in early 2020 and began to affect university budgets in the 2020/21 fiscal year. The effects differed across universities (Figure 3.1). At Brandon, overall revenue in the first year of the pandemic (2020/21) fell from the previous year and recovered slightly the following year. At the University of Manitoba, revenue in 2020/21 rose slightly from the previous year, and remained more or less unchanged the next year. At Winnipeg, revenue in 2020/21 was essentially unchanged from the previous year and rose markedly in 2021/22. At St. Boniface, revenue in 2020/21 rose from the previous year and held stable the following year.

The Treasury Board Ultimatum to Universities and Colleges in April 2020

As the pandemic descended in early 2020, with its widespread economic effects, the Pallister government moved quickly to reduce expenditures. Universities and colleges were among the first targets.

Following hastily prepared Treasury Board presentations to university administrators, Finance Minister Scott Fielding on 16 April 2020 called upon the universities and colleges to prepare—in five days—for budgets reflecting immediate 10, 20, and 30 percent cuts to provincial funding. University administrators were explicitly told to cut salary budgets (Treasury Board Secretariat 2020).

The presentation was notable in several respects. First, unlike K–12 education and healthcare, post-secondary education (PSE) was *not* considered an essential service. PSE would take their lumps. Second, the Treasury Board presentation was based upon wildly exaggerated deficit projections. As *Winnipeg Free Press* columnist Dan Lett noted, "Clearly, the 30 per cent figure was a bluff designed to spook unions, school divisions, Crown corporations and post-secondary schools into accepting smaller cuts with no protest" (2020). Lett described the budget statements as "a level of dishonesty rarely seen in Manitoba politics." Claims of a $5 billion budget deficit indeed proved to be wild exaggeration. The Royal Bank of Canada estimated the projected Manitoba budget deficit at just $1.5 billion (cited in Lett 2020), almost exactly the actual budget deficit ($1.597 billion) reported in the 2021/22 fiscal year. The government's own forecast of the 2021/22 budget deficit was lower still, at just $1.393 billion.

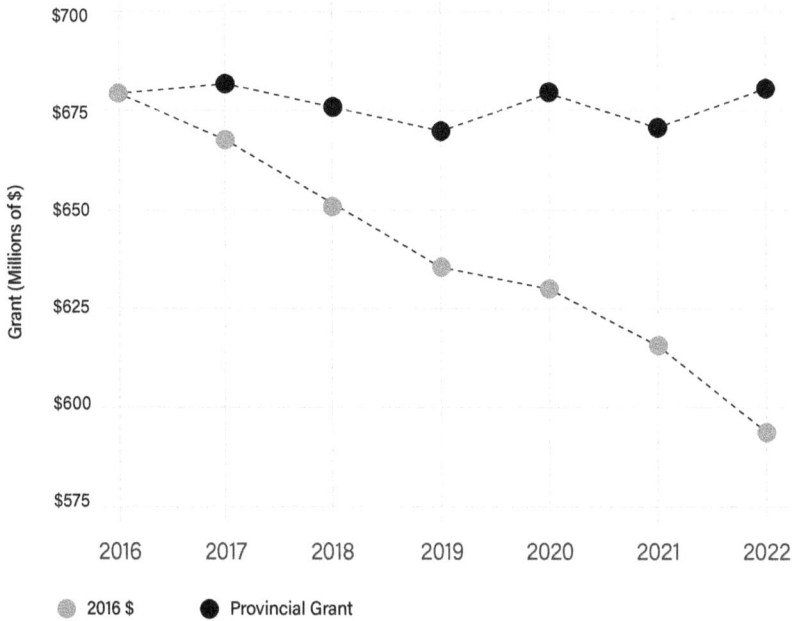

Figure 3.2a. Provincial funding for Manitoba colleges and universities, 2016–2022.

Under public pressure, the Pallister government ultimately backed down from the planned cuts; but in April 2020, the government's proposed plans created unnecessary fear, anxiety, and chaos within the post-secondary community.

Part of the justification for cutting PSE during the pandemic was that fewer students would enrol in college and university courses, as campuses closed to in-person instruction. But, except at Brandon, amid a long-term decline, enrolments did not fall (Figure 3.3). Perhaps better than any other sector of the economy, after a short hiatus, our colleges and universities shifted to an online environment to allow students to continue their studies more or less uninterrupted, and enrolment held steady in the first full year of the pandemic.

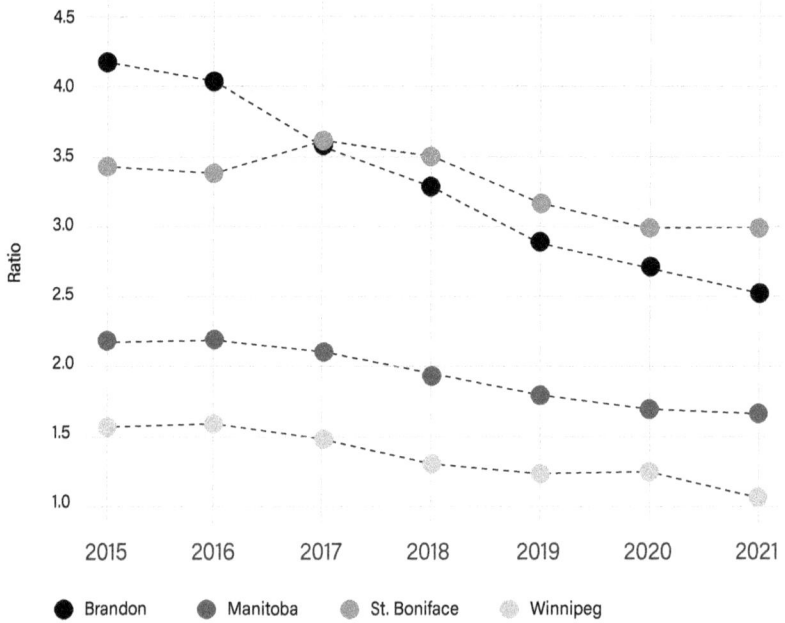

Figure 3.2b. Ratio of provincial grant revenue to tuition and student fee revenue (as reported in annual audited financial statements).

Sources: Government of Manitoba Estimates of Expenditure and Revenue for fiscal years ending 31 March 2017 (Fiscal 2016/17) through 2023 (Fiscal 2022/23), Support for Universities and Colleges, Operating Grants and Strategic Initiatives/Grant Assistance.

Note: Nominal funding and funding in constant 2016 dollars are shown. Funding in 2016 dollars calculated using the Bank of Canada Inflation Calculator: https://www.bankofcanada.ca/rates/related/inflation-calculator/.

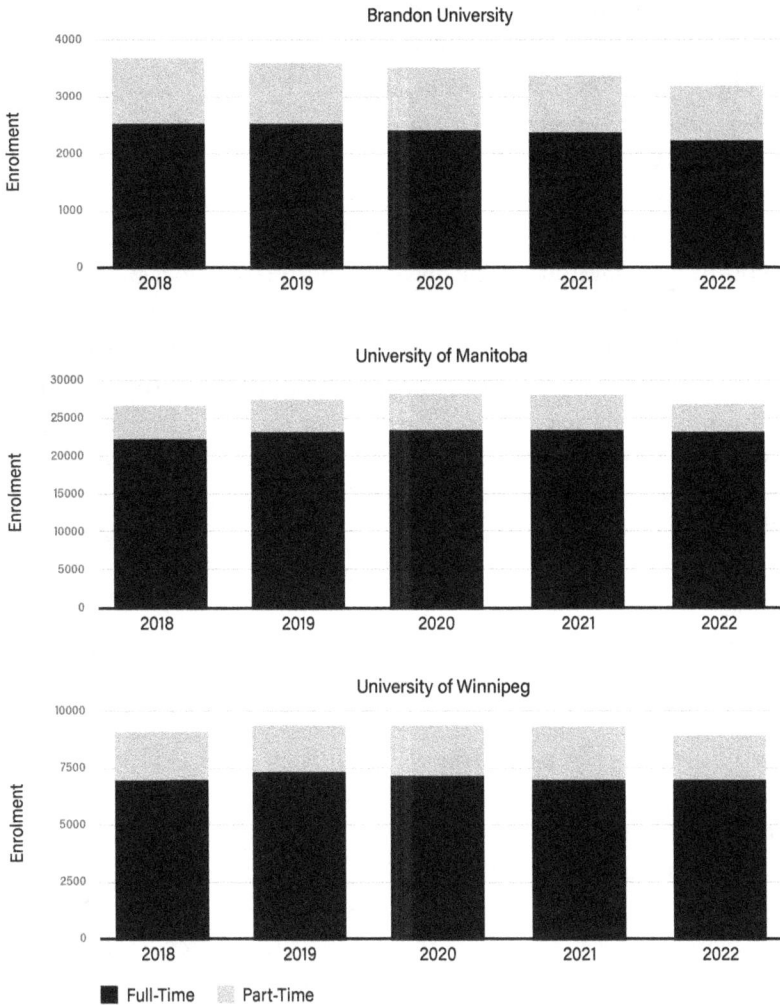

Figure 3.3. Annual enrolment of full-time and part-time students by Manitoba university, 2018–2022.

Sources: Audited annual financial statements of Brandon University (see Brandon University, Annual Financial Statements 2018–2022); the University of Manitoba (see the University of Manitoba, Annual Financial Statements, 2018–2022), and the University of Winnipeg (see University of Winnipeg, Consolidated Financial Statements, 2018–2022).

Collective Bargaining in the Era of Austerity

As the Pallister PCs had run on an election platform of fiscal restraint, public sector unions anticipated some belt tightening after they took office. Both the University of Manitoba Faculty Association (UMFA) and the University of Winnipeg Faculty Association (UWFA) were either already bargaining (UMFA) or set to begin bargaining (UWFA) in the summer of 2016. UWFA anticipated the forthcoming austerity program of the Pallister government and opted to quickly settle a four-year contract without entering into formal bargaining. In a letter to regular academic staff, Acting UWFA President Jacqueline Romanow remarked, "The risks associated with protracted bargaining into Fall or worse, Winter, are significant. As austerity measures proliferate, we can anticipate being offered a freeze in one or more years (almost certainly in the first)." This was prescient, as a two-year wage freeze and two further years of below-inflation increases were coming.

At the University of Manitoba, bargaining had already commenced before the Pallister government took office in the spring of 2016. It continued through the summer and early fall when the University of Manitoba tabled a salary offer that was similar to that obtained by UWFA: a 7 percent increase to base salaries over four years. The administration bargaining team described the offer as "fair and reasonable" (UMFA 2016). In October 2016, however, the university pulled its offer from the table without explanation (UMFA Bargaining Update #10). Behind the scenes, the Pallister government—without informing UMFA—instructed the university to offer a nonnegotiable one-year wage freeze (CBC Manitoba 2016). UMFA was forced to accept that wage freeze and focused bargaining on nonmonetary issues: workload, assessment using performance indicators, and job security. Normally salary and nonsalary issues are part of the overall bargaining matrix, and concessions in one area are traded against gains elsewhere. As salary was no longer on the table, the university could hold the line on nonmonetary issues. Ultimately, government interference in bargaining led to a three-week strike in the fall of 2016 (CBC Manitoba 2016). During the first week of the strike, UMFA filed an unfair labour practice complaint with the Manitoba Labour Board (CBC Manitoba 2018) and, along with the Brandon, University of Winnipeg, and St. Boniface faculty associations, and numerous other public sector unions, joined a lawsuit with the

Manitoba Federation of Labour at the Court of Queen's Bench (*Manitoba Federation of Labour et al. v. The Government of Manitoba* 2020).

The Manitoba Labour Board upheld UMFA's claim of bad faith bargaining, acknowledging that the university administration should not have kept the province's orders a secret from UMFA, and the university paid a $2.4 million penalty to UMFA and its members (Pursaga 2018). As well, the Manitoba Court of Queen's Bench ruled the Pallister government interference in collective bargaining a violation of Section 2(d) of the charter guaranteeing freedom of association. In February of 2022 the Court ordered the government of Manitoba to pay $19.4 million in damages, concluding that "there was a serious and substantial undermining and interference with what had been a meaningful and productive process of collective bargaining" by the province (CBC Manitoba 2022).

After contract negotiations in 2017, the 2016 wage freeze became the first of the provisions for all public sector workers under Bill 28, the Public Services Sustainability Act (PSSA): 0 percent increases in years one and two followed by 0.75 percent and 1 percent in years three and four. Bill 28 was introduced into the legislature in March 2017, and received royal assent but was never proclaimed. After the introduction of the bill, as it came time for universities and colleges to negotiate their next collective agreements, many faculty associations and public sector unions were bullied into accepting the Bill 28 provisions even though the legislation was never proclaimed: faculty at the University of Manitoba, Brandon University, Assiniboine Community College, and Red River Polytechnic all negotiated four-year collective agreements under the Bill 28 provisions.

Support staff were under even heavier pressure, facing the threat of furloughs and layoffs, especially for those with the misfortune to be bargaining during the pandemic. Space precludes a comprehensive review, but an example illustrates the challenges faced by support staff. On the University of Manitoba campus, the Association of Employees Supporting Education Services (AESES) faced temporary layoffs during the pandemic. In 2020, 200 AESES members were issued with temporary layoff notices by the University of Manitoba, which was responding to the austerity directives of the provincial government. AESES launched a grievance, claiming that the layoffs were in contravention of their collective agreement. And in 2021, after protracted hearings, the arbitrator agreed, and awarded AESES with a final settlement of $1.5 million—the largest in AESES history—that was distributed to 195 members. In addition, pension benefits, seniority, vacation, and benefits premiums were restored (AESES 2021). Again, the university was driven to take these measures at the behest of a government obsessed with austerity.

The Effects of Austerity on Students

Austerity cuts eventually get passed onto students.
—Associate professor

Cuts to public funding for higher education were accompanied by increases to tuition fees that ran far ahead of inflation. With overall budgets squeezed by ongoing reductions to public funding of PSE, students were paying more to get less. And then the pandemic arrived.

For students, the pandemic created a disruption unlike any other to normal college and university operations. After campuses closed in March of 2020, it was more than two years before in-person classes started to return to normal. The entire university experience for students was transformed. A tremendous component of the university experience relies on in-person interaction; on-campus extracurricular activities, conversations with professors and classmates, convocation ceremonies, even the opportunity to meet fellow students were all impossible. To consider a more important example, travel restrictions meant that some international students were unable to come to Canada for the fall 2020 term and had to continue studies online—sometimes joining classes in the middle of the night from other countries.

There was, however, no fall in demand for college and university education in 2021/22 as the government had—incorrectly—assumed when proposing deep cuts to PSE funding. Youth faced record levels of unemployment as the service sector and retail industry, primary sources of employment for youth, were almost entirely shuttered. For students, universities and colleges provided shelter from the economic storm in 2021/22. However, the move to remote learning disproportionately impacted lower-income students, who had less access to fast internet, acceptable computer hardware, and sufficient quiet spaces to study. Just as these students needed more supports, fewer were offered. As an associate professor pointed out, "Students from low-income households often have greater needs for student services including counselling. Our university was not adequately staffed to provide the needed services and so it would be a fair assessment to say that lower-income students were disproportionately affected." Another associate professor confirmed that grad students were another group hit hard as austerity measures increased, saying, "We also saw our graduate scholarship vanish, making it more difficult for low-income students to attend grad school. In addition, with less teaching assistant hours in courses, there is less support available for students struggling."

The Effects of Austerity on Faculty and Administrators

Budget cuts to every area of my teaching.
—Professor

Even prior to the pandemic, the effects of austerity on faculty and admin-istration were broad and deep. The ability to mount programs and provide services to students was adversely affected. A University of Manitoba employee commented, "There are now 3 people ... doing the work of 9 previ-ously. . . . We don't have enough people to accomplish what was previously done in our department, so we have had to modify services and reduce the level of service we provide." One associate professor respondent detailed the effects of the unfortunate decision to cut IT support prior to the pandemic: "Support mechanisms were completely eliminated. Most notably our entire online education advisory department (who advise faculty about best prac-tices and provide practical support for online course development) was let go due to budget constraints—about a year before the pandemic hit. As a result, we had zero support for the pandemic driven transition to online courses. It was chaotic and stressful. Other support roles have also been eliminated . . . we have one department assistant for over 30 faculty members."

Budget cuts have also made it difficult to attract and retain talented faculty. A University of Manitoba psychology professor commented, "My department has had extreme difficulty recruiting new hires, while we have lost long-term employees to universities in other provinces. I have no doubts that the cuts to our already tight budgets will continue to lead my department to lose talented employees." Another assistant professor commented on the adverse effects austerity has on research and tenure:

"Our workloads are increasing because we are unable to successfully recruit additional faculty. . . . In my department of seven, I believe I am the only one not teaching overload this year . . . this detracts from the time available to do research, which can make it more difficult for untenured faculty to meet the requirements for tenure." Furthermore, faculty are shouldering a greater burden of administrative and clerical tasks as support staff are trimmed. "The open and stealthy decreases to university funding have resulted in ongoing staff cuts that resulted in downloading of administrative tasks on an ongoing basis, resulting in a steady workload increase," said one University of Manitoba professor.

Other instructors did not face cuts, but rather struggled with funding that was insufficient in the face of increasing demand as class sizes and workloads increased. One educational assistant reported, "Our program doubled in student numbers, causing student lab hours requiring direct supervision to increase from approximately 16 hrs/week to 35 hrs/week. No pay increase or accommodation was given to compensate for this massive increase in workload. No office hours were given to allow for other duties required." The austerity-driven combination of increasing workload and decreasing resources predictably corresponds with rising stress levels and falling morale among faculty. One Red River College employee noted, "Morale at Red River College is the lowest I've seen in 22 years. We will go on strike soon, unless the college miraculously comes up with a fantastic offer. This won't happen. With the horrible morale a strike is inevitable."

And then the pandemic arrived. Universities were closed near the end of the winter semester in March 2020; were primarily online for the 2020/21 academic year; and slowly began to transition back to in-person classes in the fall of 2021. The abrupt cessation of classes was a shock to the system. Classes were briefly suspended while rapid preparations were made for online course delivery, followed by online exams. Post-secondary institutions responded impressively to the challenge of COVID-19 and its accompanying public health orders. Nearly all students were able to complete their studies that year without delay. However, the effort to maintain college and university operations as close to normal as possible during the pandemic resulted in unsustainable workloads and soaring stress levels, as both faculty and staff reported in the public sector survey results.

Survey respondents noted that austerity measures also meant there was increased reliance on precarious and sometimes less qualified personnel to deliver programs. One instructor commented that "more sessional instructors have been hired to fill in teaching gaps." An associate professor foresaw generational problems: "Everyone is exhausted with being asked to do more with less and the expectations keep increasing. There is also a move to hire more contract instructors and less tenure track faculty as they can more easily be fired or not rehired. As a consequence, we are hindering our ability to create new knowledge for future generations to save a few dollars." Another University of Manitoba professor voiced similar concerns regarding the overreliance on precarious faculty: "The shift from tenured and tenure-track faculty to precariously employed faculty has continued, resulting in more overworked course instructors who have less time to spend on preparing their courses and staying up to date on the latest research, who have no time to do their own research, and who undoubtedly struggle to be properly available and responsive to their ever-growing list of students."

The Effects of Austerity on Support Staff

We are bleeding staff, especially people under the age of 40. No one wants to work somewhere that refuses to negotiate a contract in good faith and refuses to replace lost staff. You can only increase the workload for someone with no support for so long before they quit or retire.
—University of Manitoba employee

Perhaps no group was more severely affected by the twin effects of austerity and the pandemic than support staff. With the onset of the pandemic, widespread temporary layoffs occurred in food services, bookstores, parking services, residences, and cleaning staff as cost-cutting measures. To take an example from one union, in 2017, UNIFOR represented about 500 members in operating services (power engineers, caretakers, groundskeepers, residence maintenance, dining services) on the campus of the University of Manitoba. At the height of the pandemic, that unit was reduced to about 300 members, as many jobs were eliminated when on-campus classes were cancelled. In November 2022, as the pandemic was receding, there were just 363 members in the unit. Vacancies were slow to be filled, if at all, and recruitment and retention was a problem for skilled workers (Paul McKie, UNIFOR, personal communication). The effects on the workplace environment were uniformly negative according to the survey results for post-secondary education (Figure 3.4).

Workers reported that the quality of service declined. One University of Manitoba technologist commented that "reduced expenditure are not 'savings.' It means improper funding to do the same work, or the work is incomplete or reduced. That is a decline in service." A systems analyst at the University of Manitoba stated that working conditions deteriorated with austerity: "The technical debt of not properly maintaining and replacing IT infrastructure to 'save money' is very expensive and will be paid for in future years at an increased rate from what was 'saved.'" Similarly, an office assistant pointed out that so-called savings as a result of austerity were elusive: "More time spent on trying to hire people because salaries are not competitive, and people accept an offer but then get a better offer and go elsewhere so we start the process all over again."

Respondents also reported overwhelmingly that austerity impacted mental health negatively. A Red River College employee stated, "57 percent of our department have been on extended stress leaves. Due to layoffs and job cuts we have 55 percent of the staff doing the duties of the full complement and the work of another entire department that was eliminated." An administrator in the Faculty of Health Science at the University of Manitoba noted, "I have employees that seek mental services, who started to drink more or show signs of depression. The ones who care the most to serve students and the public feel like they are letting them down due to the lack of support. Minimum wage in Manitoba goes up in the fall of 2023 to $15. Some of our employees are close to that already. I [have] considered finding jobs elsewhere already." Many post-secondary education support staff responded that there has been a marked decrease in job satisfaction over the years. One remarked that when they started twenty years ago, it was their "dream job." But austerity cuts have placed so much additional work and stress on individuals that it led—unfortunately—to some feeling suicidal ideations being reported in the survey results, and in conversations with individual employees.

Anxiety and stress permeated the working environment during the era of austerity especially after the Treasury Board ultimatum to prepare for severe budget cuts. Many workers, justifiably, feared for the loss of

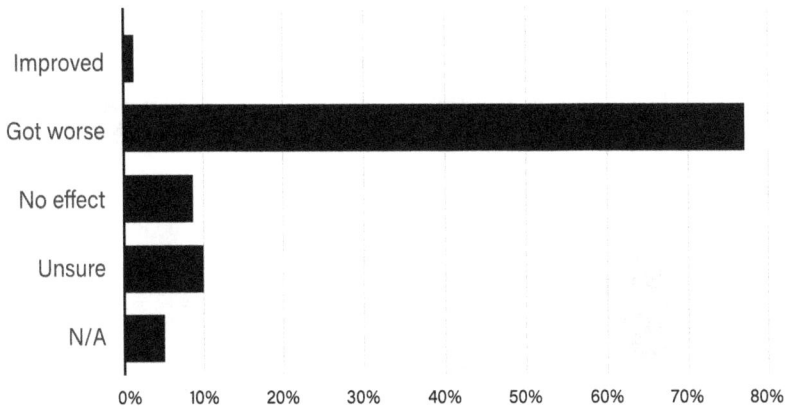

Figure 3.4a. Survey responses: Effects of austerity on the quality of service in post-secondary education.

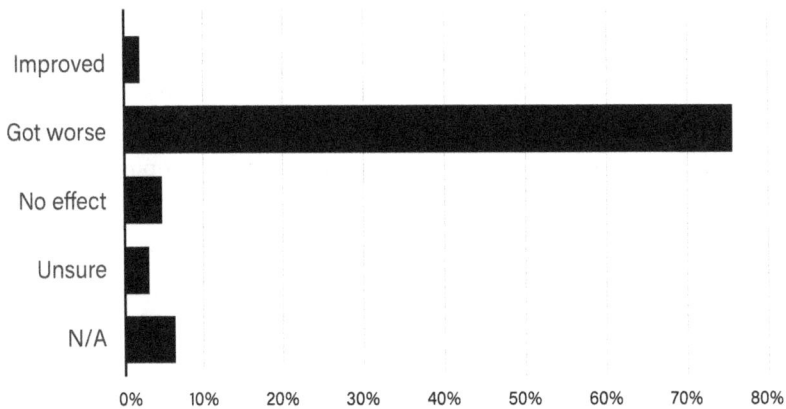

Figure 3.4b. Survey responses: Impact of austerity on working conditions in post-secondary education.

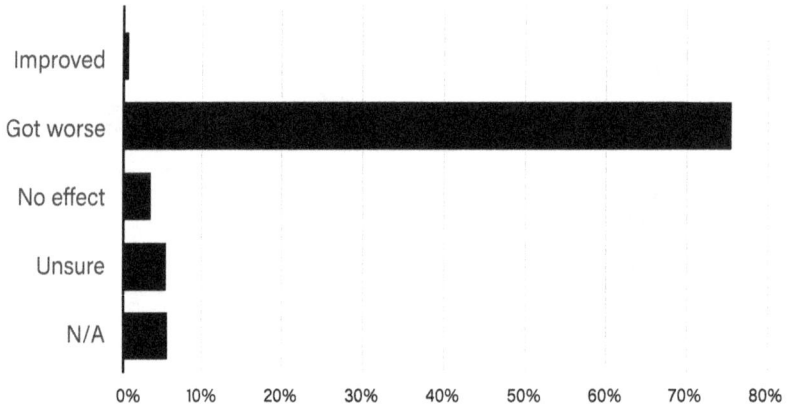

Figure 3.4c. Survey responses: Effects of austerity on mental health in post-secondary education.

their job at a time of unprecedented uncertainty. And many were laid off. Universities and colleges were under heavy pressure from government to cut budgets, thus many residences, food services, bookstores, and parking services were shuttered during the pandemic. The need for custodial staff for buildings under lockdown and grounds crews for campuses that did not have staff or students was greatly reduced.

Conclusions

The Pallister government, already engaged in an aggressive program of austerity, attempted to use the pandemic as cover for dramatic cuts to the public sector in general, and post-secondary education in particular. But it did not work. Once their proposed cuts became public, and the public outcry grew, they were forced to back down. The Pallister government had overplayed its hand. As the unpopular leader of an unpopular government with unpopular policies, he resigned as premier in the fall of 2021.

But his legacy of austerity still remains. For students, the steady decline in public funding for post-secondary education has meant fewer course offerings and longer lineups, larger classes, and higher tuition. Students now pay more to get less. Faculty, staff, and administrators have seen growing workloads with fewer resources. The far-ranging effects of an overzealous policy of austerity during the pandemic are only now coming into focus.

What is clear is that the damage inflicted on post-secondary education in Manitoba will take years to repair.

References

AESES (Association of Employees Supporting Education Services). 2021. "AESES Temporary Layoff and Recall Grievances." *InsideAESES Newsletter* 44 (5): 3.

Bernhardt, Darren. 2022. "Manitoba Government Appeals Order to Compensate U of M Union Members $19.3M." CBC Manitoba, 19 May. https://www.cbc.ca/news/canada/manitoba/manitoba-appeal-umfa-ruling-compensation-contract-interference-1.6459194.

Brandon University. 2017. *Annual Financial Report for the Year Ended March 31, 2017.* https://www.brandonu.ca/vp-finance/files/Brandon-University-Annual-Financial-Report-for-year-ended-March-31-2017-for-web-1.pdf.

———. 2018. *Annual Financial Report for the Year Ended March 31, 2018.* https://www.brandonu.ca/vp-finance/files/BU-Financial-Statements-e-version.pdf.

———. 2019. *Annual Financial Report for the Year Ended March 31, 2019.* https://www.brandonu.ca/vp-finance/files/BU-Financial-Statements-e-version-1.pdf.

———. 2020. *Annual Financial Report for the Year Ended March 31, 2020.* https://www.brandonu.ca/vp-finance/files/Brandon-University-Annual-Financial-Report-March-31-2020_Website.pdf.

———. 2021. *Annual Financial Report for the Year Ended March 31, 2021.* https://www.brandonu.ca/vp-finance/files/BU-Annual-Report_Final_website.pdf.

———. 2022. *Annual Financial Report for the Year Ended March 31, 2022.* https://www.brandonu.ca/vp-finance/files/BU-Annual-Financial-Report_final.pdf.

CBC News. 2016. "U of M Strike: President Aims to End Dispute 'as Soon as Possible.'" CBC Manitoba, 9 November. https://www.cbc.ca/news/canada/manitoba/pallister-university-of-manitoba-strike-negotiations-1.3844040.

———. 2018. "U of Manitoba Violated Bargaining Law During Faculty Strike, Labour Board Rules." CBC Manitoba, 31 January. https://www.cbc.ca/news/canada/manitoba/unfair-labour-practice-ruling-university-manitoba-1.4511802.

———. 2022. "Manitoba Government Must Pay U of M Union $19.3M for Interfering in 2016 Contract Negotiations: Judge." CBC Manitoba, 24 February. https://www.cbc.ca/news/canada/manitoba/university-manitoba-union-wins-legal-decision-1.6362857.

Government of Manitoba. 2017. *Manitoba Estimates of Expenditure and Revenue, 2017.* https://www.gov.mb.ca/finance/budget17/papers/r_and_e.pdf.

———. 2018. *Manitoba Estimates of Expenditure and Revenue, 2018.* https://www.gov.mb.ca/finance/budget18/papers/r_and_e.pdf.

———. n.d. "Provincial Budgets." Finance. https://www.gov.mb.ca/finance/budgets/provincialbudgets.html.

Hajer, Jesse. 2023. "Austerity in Manitoba." Manitoba Research Alliance. 29 August. https://mra-mb.ca/austerity-in-manitoba/.

Lett, Dan. 2020. "48 Hours of Deception: Premier Engages in Political Pandering as Questions Arise on Deficit Estimate." *Winnipeg Free Press*, 5 May. https://www.winnipegfreepress.com/breakingnews/2020/05/05/48-hours-of-deceit.

Manitoba Federation of Labour et al. v. The Government of Manitoba. 2020 MBQB 92 (CanLII).

Press Progress. 2020. "Brian Pallister's Government Demanded University of Manitoba Freeze Wages and Make Cuts, Letter Shows." *Press Progress*, 6 November. https://pressprogress.ca/brian-pallisters-government-demanded-university-of-manitfreeze-wages-and-make-cuts-letter-shows/.

Pursaga, Joyanne. 2018. "'SORRY': U of M Will Pay \$2.4M for Error in Judgement during Bargaining with UMFA." *Winnipeg Sun*, 11 May. https://winnipegsun.com/news/provincial/sorry-u-of-m-will-pay-2-4m-for-error-in-judgement-during-bargaining-with-umfa.

Treasury Board Secretariat. 2020. COVID-19, Financial and Workforce Impacts.

University of Manitoba. 2017. *Annual Financial Report, 2017.*

———. 2018. *Annual Financial Report, 2018.*

———. 2019. *Annual Financial Report, 2019.* https://umanitoba.ca/finance/sites/finance/files/2022-05/2019-um-annual-financial-report.pdf.

———. 2020. *Annual Financial Report, 2020.* https://umanitoba.ca/finance/sites/finance/files/2022-05/2020-um-annual-financial-report.pdf.

———. 2021. *Annual Financial Report, 2021.* https://umanitoba.ca/finance/sites/finance/files/2022-05/2021-um-annual-financial-report.pdf.

———. 2022. *Annual Financial Report, 2022.* https://umanitoba.ca/finance/sites/finance/files/2022-07/2022-um-annual-financial-report.pdf.

UMFA Bargaining Update #10. 2016. "Administration Refuses to Make Real Movement: Strike Deadline Looms." 24 October. https://www.umfa.ca/images/pdfs/members/Administration_Refuses_to_Make_Real_Movement-Strike_Deadline_Looms_Oct242016.pdf.

UMFA. 2016. "Update from Strike HQ: November 9 Morning Update." https://www.umfa.ca/images/pdfs/members/UpdateFromStrikeHQ_Nov92016.pdf.

University of Winnipeg. 2017. *Consolidated Financial Statements for the Year Ended March 31, 2017.* https://www.uwinnipeg.ca/financial-services/docs/2017-Consolidated-Financial-Statements.pdf.

———. 2018. *Consolidated Financial Statements for the Year Ended March 31, 2018.* https://www.uwinnipeg.ca/financial-services/docs/uw-consolidated-financial-statements-2018-web.pdf.

———. 2019. *Consolidated Financial Statements for the Year Ended March 31, 2019.* https://www.uwinnipeg.ca/financial-services/docs/uw-consolidated-financial-statements-2019-web.pdf.

———. 2020. *Consolidated Financial Statements for the Year Ended March 31, 2020.* https://www.uwinnipeg.ca/financial-services/docs/uw-consolidated-financial-statements-2020-web.pdf.

———. 2021. *Consolidated Financial Statements for the Year Ended March 31, 2021.* https://www.uwinnipeg.ca/financial-services/docs/uw-consolidated-financial-statements-2021-web.pdf.

———. 2022. *President's Report to the Board of Regents 2021–2022 and The University of Winnipeg Consolidated Financial Statements for the Year Ended March 31, 2022.* https://www.uwinnipeg.ca/financial-services/docs/uw-consolidated-financial-statements-2022-web.pdf.

Chapter 4

AUSTERITY AND ADULT BASIC EDUCATION

Jim Silver

Austerity has hit Manitoba's adult education system hard, especially in terms of the large opportunity cost. By opportunity cost I mean the value of what is given up by choosing one alternative rather than another. Maintaining a policy of austerity rather than investing in an enhanced and expanded adult education system has imposed a heavy price on Manitobans in terms of lost opportunities.

By Manitoba's adult education system, I mean the system of adult basic education in this province. It includes Adult Learning Centres (ALCs) that offer the mature high school diploma (adult students take eight high school credits, including grade 12 math and English, to earn this), and Adult Literacy Programs (ALPs) that improve adults' literacy and numeracy skills to a level sufficient to enable them to succeed in the mature high school program.

Adult basic education is transformative. It changes people's lives, as has repeatedly been shown (Silver 2022a, 15, 17–18, 26; Silver et al. 2016, 153–73; Silver 2013). It produces positive effects not only for individual adult learners, but also for their families and for society generally, in ways described below. Yet adult basic education has long been starved of the investment needed to produce all the many benefits that are possible. This was the case when the New Democratic Party was in office; it has worsened significantly since 2016 when the Progressive Conservatives (PCs) were elected. Austerity in adult basic education has served Manitoba poorly. That needs to change.

Austerity in Adult Education

An earlier study, titled *Unearth This Buried Treasure: Adult Education in Manitoba* (Silver 2022a), found that over the most recent decade for which information was then available, adult education had been "abysmally underfunded." Citing the Province of Manitoba's *Adult Learning and Literacy Annual Reports* published from 2009/10 to 2019/20, the report stated, "Combined investment in adult literacy programs and ALCs (Adult Learning Centres) remained effectively flat over the last decade, inching up from $19.15 million in 2009/10, to $19.92 million in 2019/20. . . . This was a total increase in nominal terms of less than half of one percent over ten years, which represents a decline in real terms" (Silver 2022a, 7–8).

Data prepared for this volume[1] show that when adjusted for inflation, total actual expenditures for adult basic education in Manitoba dropped from $26.55 million in 2015/16, to $20.3 million in 2021/22, a decline in real terms of 23 percent. Total actual expenditures per Manitoban over the age of seventeen declined sharply from $26 in 2015/16 to $19 in 2021/22.

These data make clear why one of the adult educators quoted in *Unearth This Buried Treasure* described the overall level of funding as "really, really pathetic" (Silver 2022a, 8). One respondent to the survey undertaken for this volume said, "Our funding is barebones," and another that the system has been "stripped to the bone in terms of funding."

As a result, the numbers of ALCs and ALPs have declined. In 2009/10 there were forty-two ALPs in Manitoba; in 2019/20 there were thirty ALPs—a decline of 28.6 percent. This is even though a 2013/14 study found that there were approximately 192,600 adults in Manitoba with literacy levels so low they could not fully participate in society (Silver 2022b, 5).

Numbers of adults enrolled in and graduating from ALCs and ALPs have declined. Enrolments in ALCs offering the mature high school diploma dropped from "approximately 9700 in 2003/04 to 7100 in 2019/20. The numbers of graduates of ALCs dropped from approximately 1200 in 2003/04 to 900 in 2019/20" (Silver 2022b, 5).

Adult basic education is simply not taken seriously in Manitoba: "Adult education is treated as an afterthought, as the 'poor cousin' of education. The total budget of adult education is two-thirds of 1% of the provincial education budget. The amount allocated per learner is less than the amount spent per inmate in provincial and federal penal institutions, and less than the per student amount spent on the K–12 component of our educational system" (Silver 2022b, 5).

The cost of keeping an inmate in a federal penal institution in 2016 was $115,000; the cost in a provincial institution was $69,000 (Silver 2022a, 9–10). According to the 2018/19 Manitoba budget, the operating cost per student in Manitoba's K–12 education system was $13,284, while the cost per adult learner in ALCs and ALPs in 2019/20 was $2,240. Manitoba invests in adult education at a rate of one-sixth what it invests in K–12 education (Silver 2022a, 9), and at a rate far less than the per-prisoner cost of incarceration.

Opportunity Costs

The opportunity costs resulting from this austerity can be thought of in terms of its effects on poverty, reconciliation, family health, and labour supply.

Poverty

Manitoba has long suffered from a particularly high rate of poverty, and especially child poverty—although child poverty really refers to families who have children and are living in poverty. In Winnipeg in 2020, 64,670 children were growing up in families living in poverty (SPCW 2023). In Manitoba as a whole, 76 percent of First Nations children living on-reserve and 42 percent living in Winnipeg were growing up in families living in poverty (Macdonald and Wilson 2016, 6), and Manitoba is the province with the highest rate of child poverty in Canada (SPCW 2023). Churchill-Keewatinook Aski in Northern Manitoba is the federal riding with the second highest rate of child poverty in Canada (SPCW 2023). As the director of one northern adult education program put it, "Poverty rates up here are atrocious" (Silver 2022a, 20).

Poverty produces enormous costs, not just to those living in poverty but to society generally. Poverty correlates strongly with poor health outcomes and lowered educational outcomes, as evidenced by the vast literature on the social determinants of health (for Manitoba, see Fernandez, MacKinnon, and Silver 2015). Children growing up in poor families are less likely to do well in school, and thus more likely to experience poverty as adults, thus reproducing poverty across the generations (Brownell 2013; Brownell et al. 2012; Brownell et al. 2010). The Manitoba Centre for Health Policy has found that the incidence of every type of health problem is higher in the province's lowest-income quintile than in higher-income quintiles and has found dramatically reduced longevity in the lowest-income quintile (Brownell, Fransoo, and Martens 2015). We are seeing today the extent to which our health system is overburdened, and poverty is an important part of the reason. Lowered levels of poverty would reduce the pressure on our healthcare system and produce improved K–12 educational outcomes.

A strong adult education system reduces poverty, and thus reduces poverty's damaging effects, in two ways. First, those adults who earn the mature high school diploma have a much improved likelihood of securing a job that will pay enough to pull them and their families out of poverty. Second, we know that when a parent or parents are pursuing adult education, their children are more likely to succeed in school, thus reducing the likelihood that the poverty will be reproduced across the generations. We all benefit when that is the case; we are all hurt when austerity limits the contribution that adult basic education makes to poverty reduction. As one of the respondents to the survey undertaken as part of the preparation of this volume wrote, "The cost of not being able to provide adult education is piled up elsewhere through unemployment, underemployment, poverty, child welfare."

Reconciliation

Adult basic education plays an important role in reconciliation. Justice Murray Sinclair has said on numerous occasions that "education got us into this mess, and education will get us out of it." Adult basic education has an especially important part to play in this. The higher incidence of poverty among Indigenous people, and the ongoing effects of colonialism and especially residential schools, has resulted in Indigenous youth being, on average, less likely to graduate high school on time than the population at large. However, Indigenous adults are turning to adult basic education in large numbers. According to Adult Learning and Literacy Annual Reports, while approximately 18 percent of Manitoba's population is Indigenous, 45 percent of students in ALCs and 38 percent in ALPs are Indigenous (Silver 2022b, 23). Adult basic education can be a major means of combatting the past and current failures of education systems that have caused so much harm to Indigenous people (TRC 2015). One northern adult educator whose program is 90 percent Indigenous described their work as "reconciliation in action," adding, "We are the boots on the ground for reconciliation" (quoted in Silver 2022a, 14).

Our failure to invest adequately in adult education—that is, the continued application of a policy of austerity to adult basic education—is therefore a failure to promote the reconciliation that is so crucial to Manitoba's future.

Stronger and Healthier Families

An enhanced and expanded adult basic education system would also produce many intangible benefits that would have the effect of strengthening families. For adults embarking upon adult basic education, the challenges are substantial. In many cases this is, in part, because of the low levels of self-esteem and self-confidence that many adults experience. Adult educators repeatedly told me that "low levels of self-confidence and self-esteem are major barriers to success for many adult learners" (Silver 2022a, 23). This is, in many cases, a product of the complex poverty that is so prevalent in Manitoba, and the many adverse effects of colonialism and racism. However, adult educators are skillful in working with adult learners in a slow and patient manner, building trusting relationships that can be the basis for educational gains: "Out of this often long, slow process can come the building of a sense of hope for a better future, for adult learners themselves, and for their families and communities" (Silver 2022a, 23). Stronger and healthier families produce multiple benefits, primarily to the members of those families but also to the future of Manitoba, because stronger and healthier families are likely to produce children and youth who are physically and emotionally healthy, and willing and able to contribute to the collective undertaking of building a better society. Austerity limits the extent to which adult basic education can contribute to building stronger and healthier families.

Meeting Labour Supply Needs

Finally, adult basic education can be a major factor in meeting the labour supply problems made so evident by the pandemic. There is a shortage of workers in a great many industries. Yet there are almost 200,000 adults in Manitoba with literacy levels sufficiently low—along with the related low levels of self-esteem and self-confidence—that they are unable to enter the labour force. There are many people on Employment and Income Assistance (EIA) who would like to improve their education and are capable of doing so, if only the EIA system would continue to support them financially while they study. With improved levels of education, they too would enter the labour force and contribute to our collective well-being. An enhanced and expanded adult basic education system will produce growing numbers of people capable of entering the labour force and contributing to the health and prosperity of all of us in Manitoba.

Building an Enhanced and Expanded Adult Basic Education System in Manitoba

In earlier publications (Silver 2022a, 2022b), I set out how the adult basic education system in Manitoba works and what steps need to be taken to build in Manitoba the best adult education system in Canada. This was based on two rounds of interviews and focus groups with first thirty, and then thirty-six directors of ALCs and ALPs. Based on the detailed, hands-on knowledge these adult educators gained over many years and even decades of work in adult education, I made a number of recommendations. These recommendations are supported by a great majority of those who work in adult basic education in Manitoba.

Key perhaps among these were the following: that the annual amount allocated to adult basic education—ALCs and ALPs—should be doubled; that the wages and benefits of all teachers and instructors in ALCs and ALPS should be brought up to the level of similarly qualified K–12 teachers; and that the school divisions or other educational partners with which ALCs and ALPs are affiliated should provide to them expanded administrative and financial support. Other important recommendations included that those on EIA who want to improve their level of education and are capable of doing so should continue to receive EIA payments while attending an ALC or ALP, subject to satisfactory attendance and performance; that adult learning hubs, where ALCs, ALPs, and childcare centres are colocated, should be promoted; and that the Adult Learning and Literacy branch should be housed in a permanent provincial department, rather than being pushed from one department to another and then another. With respect to the latter recommendation, one respondent to the current survey wrote, "The constant shuffle from one government department to another and then back to something else entirely is a real disgrace and has not done anything to improve the low literacy rates in Manitoba. These kinds of ill thought out and inept policies are the real money wasters and until governments start listening to those on the front lines and those who have done recent research on the state of adult education in Manitoba, more time and money will be wasted."

Results of the Survey of Adult Educators on the Effects of Austerity

Twenty-seven adult basic education workers responded to the survey conducted in the preparation of this volume, some of them in considerable detail. The twenty-seven adult educators work in all parts of Manitoba—slightly more of the respondents are from outside Winnipeg than in Winnipeg. Most have many years of experience in adult education—the mean number of years of experience is twenty-three. The respondents represent a sample that is large, geographically spread across the province, and very experienced.

When asked if their work has been affected by austerity, 85 percent of respondents said their work had been "greatly" or "moderately" impacted. Half of them said their "workload has intensified/increased." Three others said that their hours had been reduced. One respondent reported that s/he "very often worked extra days for free" to meet needs that would otherwise have been cut. Another respondent said that s/he had been hired to replace a director who retired, and that the previous director had worked forty hours per week: "When I was hired for the same role, I was expected to do the same work, but for 15–20 hours." Yet another respondent wrote, "A freeze in funding for our organization meant that we were unable to keep up with the demand, and we were unable to pay appropriate staff. We lost a number of staff members over the last three years, many who left due to poor wages and therefore, those of us left have had to pick up the slack with more hours and more workload."

Seventy-four percent of respondents reported that austerity measures had resulted in "a reduction in the quality of service for stakeholders/users." In some cases, fewer courses have been offered; in other cases, evening classes have had to be cut, thus eliminating access for some potential adult learners. One respondent wrote that their centre could no longer afford to hire substitute teachers when regular teachers were sick or at workshops: "We have cancelled classes. This is just a practice in the last two years." Another wrote that for their classes, "the number of students went from a manageable 17 or so per class to over 30," and added that this has been an important factor in "the drastic change in enrollment of adults seeking or continuing their education." Yet another respondent expressed frustration at the fact that "as our funding is frozen, we are not able to expand our program to meet the increasing need for adult education in our community." In an earlier study (Silver 2022a, 11–12), a Winnipeg-based adult educator said, "We do zero advertising and we are flooded" with applicants, while a northern director said, "We fill up as soon as the school opens" at the beginning of the academic year, and there are 2,000 people in her region wanting to get into the program. The unmet demand for adult education is huge; austerity prevents adult educators from meeting that demand.

Seventy-eight percent of respondents reported that austerity measures created "worse working conditions and job satisfaction." For example, one respondent described the personal impact of austerity: "I personally retired early because the increased pressure caused me to go on stress leave. . . . Today others of my colleagues say they don't think they can make it to retirement." Several respondents referred to the mental health challenges that staff experienced because of the impact of austerity. One elaborated: "I did feel very frustrated at work at the unrealistic and seemingly unconcerned attitude of the Province with regard to our issues." Another respondent simply said, "I felt overworked and underpaid."

Eighty-five percent of respondents said that they could provide value for money if budgets were to be increased, and many specified exactly what they would do with an expanded budget. What they said was virtually identical to the responses to the same question in late 2022 (Silver 2022b, 15–18). For example, they described the importance of wrap-around services to support adult learners, including counselling, childcare, and related supports, and they identified the importance of moving to a hub model where ALCs, ALPs, and childcare centres are colocated. There is a huge level of frustration among adult educators in Manitoba. They know in precise detail how they would use much needed additional funding, yet they are stymied by continued austerity.

Conclusions

On three separate occasions since late 2021 (Silver 2022a and 2022b and this chapter), those doing the work of delivering adult basic education in Manitoba have taken the opportunity to respond to questions and to speak at length about their work. In the first study, thirty adult educators responded at length; in the second the number of respondents was thirty-six; in this study twenty-seven adult educators responded to the survey. What we were told in the latest survey is completely consistent with the findings in the two earlier studies. Austerity has been severe and of long duration in adult basic education in Manitoba. It has caused great damage. For educators, it has resulted in reductions in staffing levels, increased workloads and longer hours, high levels of stress and job dissatisfaction, reductions in the number of classes offered, class sizes much larger than what is best for adult learners, an inability to hire substitute teachers and therefore being forced to cancel classes when teachers are sick or at workshops, and the persistence of a large unmet demand for adult basic education.

All of this produces a significant opportunity cost. If there were increased investment in adult education, many more Manitobans would be able to improve their level of formal education. Many would then be able to pull themselves out of poverty, with benefits not only for themselves and their families but also for society as a whole; for example, in terms of reduced pressure on our healthcare system and improved levels of K–12 education. Replacing austerity with investment in adult basic education would contribute to the very important process of reconciliation. Families would be strengthened. Labour supply shortages would be reduced. Adult basic education produces multiple benefits. Austerity in adult education is short-sighted and disadvantageous to all in Manitoba.

Notes

1   For details on data sources used for provincial expenditures, employee staffing numbers, and full-time equivalent (FTE) positions in this chapter, see Preface.

References

Brownell, Marni. 2013. "Children in Care and Child Maltreatment in Manitoba: What Does Research from the Manitoba Centre for Health Policy Teach Us, and Where Do We Go from Here? Paper Presented for Phase III, Phoenix Sinclair Inquiry." Exhibit 139, Commission of Inquiry into the Circumstances surrounding the Death of Phoenix Sinclair. https://phoenixsinclairinquiry.ca/exhibits/exhibit139.pdf.

Brownell, Marni, Mariette Chartier, Rob Santos, Okechukwu Ekuma, Wendy Au, Joykrishna Sarkar, Leonard MacWilliam, Elaine Burland, Ina Kuseva, and Wendy Guenette. 2012. *How Are Manitoba's Children Doing?* Winnipeg: Manitoba Centre for Health Policy.

Brownell, Marni, Noralou Roos, Leonard MacWilliam, Leanne Leclair, Okechukwu Ekuma, and Randy Fransoo. 2010. "Academic and Social Outcomes for High-Risk Youths in Manitoba." *Canadian Journal of Education* 33, no. (4): 804–36.

Brownell, Marni, Randy Fransoo, and Patricia Martens. 2015. "Social Determinants of Health and the Distribution of Health Outcomes in Manitoba." In *The Social Determinants of Health in Manitoba,* 2nd ed., edited by Lynne Fernandez, Shauna MacKinnon, and Jim Silver. Winnipeg: Canadian Centre for Policy Alternatives–Manitoba.

Fernandez, Lynne, Shauna MacKinnon, and Jim Silver, eds. 2015. *The Social Determinants of Health in Manitoba.* 2nd ed., edited by Lynne Fernandez, Shauna MacKinnon, and Jim Silver. Winnipeg: Canadian Centre for Policy Alternatives–Manitoba.

Macdonald, David, and Daniel Wilson. 2016. *Shameful Neglect: Indigenous Child Poverty in Canada.* Ottawa: Canadian Centre for Policy Alternatives.

Silver, Jim, ed. 2013. *Moving Forward, Giving Back: Transformative Aboriginal Adult Education.* Halifax and Winnipeg: Fernwood Publishing.

———. 2022a. *Unearth this Buried Treasure: Adult Education in Manitoba.* Winnipeg: Canadian Centre for Policy Alternatives–Manitoba.

———. 2022b. *Building the Best Adult Education System in Canada: A Roadmap and Action Plan for Manitoba.* Winnipeg: Canadian Centre for Policy Alternatives–Manitoba.

Silver, Jim, Darlene Klyne, and Freeman Simard. 2016. "The Tools You Need to Discover Who You Are: Aboriginal Learners in Adult Learning Centres." In Jim Silver, *Solving Poverty: Innovative Strategies from Winnipeg's Inner City.* Halifax and Winnipeg: Fernwood Publishing.

SPCW (Social Planning Council of Winnipeg). 2020. *Manitoba Poverty Central: Manitoba Report Card Update—December 2020.* Winnipeg: Social Planning Council of Winnipeg.

———. 2021. *Manitoba: Missed Opportunities. Manitoba Child and Family Poverty.* Winnipeg: Social Planning Council of Winnipeg.

———. 2023. *Poverty, the Pandemic and the Province: Manitoba Child and Family Poverty, February 2023.* Winnipeg: Social Planning Council of Winnipeg.

TRC (Truth and Reconciliation Commission of Canada). 2015. *Canada's Residential Schools: The History*, Part 1, *Origins to 1939. The Final Report of the Truth and Reconciliation Commission of Canada.* Truth and Reconciliation Commission of Canada and McGill-Queen's University Press.

Chapter 5

WAVERING WELCOME: AUSTERITY IN THE IMMIGRATION SECTOR

Sarah Zell

"We desperately need the help," reflected a Manitoba Shared Health representative, referring to urgent labour shortages in healthcare. She was part of a provincially coordinated recruitment drive for nurses in the Philippines in February 2023, aimed at attracting and fast-tracking nurses through the immigration system to work in Manitoba (Thompson 2023). Her words echo those of employers in many other sectors—including hospitality, meat processing, manufacturing, and trucking—who were finding it difficult to fill vacancies and saw immigration as a way to address shortages. The recruitment was paradigmatic, in many respects, of the province's approach to immigration over the previous two decades. Manitoba is relatively unique in Canada in its use of immigration for "province-building" (Paquet 2019), as a way of addressing population and rural decline and economic development. After briefly contextualizing the role of immigration at the provincial level in Manitoba, this chapter examines recent changes in provincial funding and presents survey responses reflecting impacts on those administering and delivering immigration, settlement, and integration services. While Manitoba was an early advocate for provincial-level immigration control and is known for its warm newcomer welcome, cuts to the civil service workforce and provincial spending on immigration have reduced the province's capacity to support its pathbreaking immigration and settlement programs in recent years.

Immigration as an Economic Development Tool

Immigration is distinct from other provincial policy areas as it largely falls under federal jurisdiction. However, the province has a role in immigration; currently it "coordinates with other levels of government and local stakeholders to administer economic immigration programs focused on the skills and talent needs of Manitoba's employers," works "to promote the province as a destination of choice for international talent," and "administers funding to programs that support successful settlement outcomes among newcomers" (Manitoba 2022b, 43). Manitoba has an innovative immigration policy legacy, as the first province or territory to seek delegated authority from the federal government.

Prior to the 1990s, Manitoba's immigration-related policies were distributed across several departments, responsible for labour, education, citizenship, and families. In the 1990s, labour and immigration were centralized in one department, and the number of employees assigned to immigration increased (Paquet 2019). Despite austerity-minded limits on public spending and privatizations, Manitoba's Progressive Conservative (PC) government at the time invested heavily in immigration, developing an active recruitment strategy (Carter et al. 2008). Facing pressure from industry and rural communities, immigration was viewed not only as a social and humanitarian issue but as a tool for economic development and a "silver bullet" to address demographic and economic decline (243).[1]

The province negotiated for more power over immigration to ensure it would receive its "fair share" of newcomers, and in 1998, the Manitoba Provincial Nominee Program (PNP) was established. The program granted Manitoba greater control to determine immigration targets and criteria. Within the primary immigration pathways in Canada—economic, family, and humanitarian—the PNP is an economic program that emphasizes the selection of "skilled" workers for occupations in demand.[2] Significantly, it also allows temporary migrant workers and international students already working or taking post-secondary education in Manitoba to apply for permanent residency through a two-step process: migrants enter the country with temporary status and then apply to the PNP to immigrate.

Since the PNP's inception, immigration to Manitoba has surged. Fewer than 3,000 permanent residents arrived in 1998, but by 2011, 15,963 arrived, 77 percent through the PNP (Manitoba 2013). Manitoba also signed an addendum to its federal immigration agreement in 1999 and gained (until 2013) responsibility for delivering supports to newcomers.[3] The province funded settlement services, organizational capacity, and employment and language training services, investing its own resources on top of federal funding transfers. Manitoba's PNP and localized service delivery model were seen as successful in attracting immigrants and contributing to retention levels as high as 80 percent (Carter et al. 2012). In 2013, the federal Conservative government recentralized settlement services; however, the province continues to fund some settlement supports, including for temporary residents, and its focus on immigration as a tool for labour force growth and economic development has endured.

Recent Policy and Resource Changes

Department Priorities and Activities

Since 2016, there have been shifts in the provincial immigration sector. In 2016, immigration was moved to the new Department of Education and Training, signalling, at least in name, a more explicit link with advanced education.[4] In 2017, the department's mandate shifted to promoting Manitoba as a destination for not only skilled workers but also international students. Immigration was part of the International Education Strategy, dedicated to "promoting the internationalization of Manitoba campuses," seeing international students as potential immigrants and a means of enhancing Manitoba's "competitiveness for global talent" (Manitoba 2018, 69). Such measures were consistent with neoliberal immigration policies across Canada and globally, with subnational jurisdictions competing to "capture" workers as resources.

The PNP remained a mainstay of the department but underwent "renewal." In 2017, the department promised to eliminate the PNP application backlog and accelerate processing to six months or less for skilled workers (Manitoba 2017). It established a new PNP stream for international students completing programs at Manitoba post-secondary institutions. The following year Manitoba received the highest proportion of student applicants in the PNP's history. Part of the MPNP-Business stream was replaced by the Business Investor Stream, requiring candidates to successfully establish and run a business prior to becoming permanent residents (Manitoba 2019a). The province also introduced a $500 PNP application fee, announcing the revenue generated would fund settlement supports (Manitoba 2018).

In 2019/20, the immigration portfolio was restructured and moved under Economic Development and Training. In January 2021, it was moved to Advanced Education, Skills and Immigration, and in early 2023 it was moved yet again, to the newly formed Department of Labour and Immigration. In February 2022, the department created an Immigration Advisory Council, tasked with reviewing the entire continuum of provincial immigration programs, including the PNP, as well as surveying stakeholders and providing a roadmap for "program improvements" (Manitoba 2023). Its February 2023 report lists seventy recommendations organized around three primary areas: improving recruitment, streamlining the PNP to align with evolving labour needs, and enhancing settlement services to "encourage labour market attachment" and retention. It explicitly frames immigration as a tool "to advance Manitoba's economic prosperity" (9). The report signals renewed provincial attention to immigration but concludes by recognizing that "many of the recommendations . . . may require additional investment in Manitoba's recruitment, immigration and settlement systems and services" (30). It remains to be seen which actions the government will take in response—and what resources will be allocated to fulfill them.

Funding to the Sector

The provincial government funds activities to promote Manitoba and recruit immigrants, and it administers the PNP. The province also administers funding to support newcomer settlement and integration. Settlement service providers are primarily nonprofits but also include other organizations (e.g., educational institutions) that are seen as close to the communities they serve and best positioned to address their specific needs.[5] They receive funding from Immigration, Refugees and Citizenship Canada (IRCC) to deliver programming to newcomers (at no cost to them). These include employment-related services, English and French language training, orientation, and other supports.[6] Funding is allocated by province based on the number of immigrant landings, with additional consideration given to the number of refugees, to account for their unique settlement needs (they tend to require more and distinct supports compared to economic and family class immigrants). Generally, federal government funding supports only newcomers with permanent resident status. This means that most temporary residents and naturalized citizens are not eligible for IRCC-funded services (see Praznik and Shields 2018). These temporary residents include migrant workers (e.g., through various temporary foreign worker programs), international students, and asylum seekers (or refugee claimants). Provincial government funding is intended to complement federal funding, targeting the needs of temporary residents and unmet needs of other newcomers.

As immigration to Manitoba increased with the PNP, so did federal funding transfers. By 2012/13, the transfer to Manitoba had grown to more than $36 million, and dedicated provincial settlement staff had increased from four full-time equivalents (FTEs) in 1999 to around twenty-five (Clement et al. 2013). However, in 2012/13, the federal Conservative government recentralized settlement service delivery and restructured PNPs nationally, placing an annual cap on the programs. Since then, there has been a general trend of decreased provincial funding to immigration, as shown in in Figure 5.1. Manitoba's expenditure on immigration in 2013/14, excluding federal funding, was $11.04 million (adjusted for inflation).[7] Spending decreased over the following years, dropping to $7.28 million in 2019/20 (a 34 percent decrease since 2013/14). Spending increased again

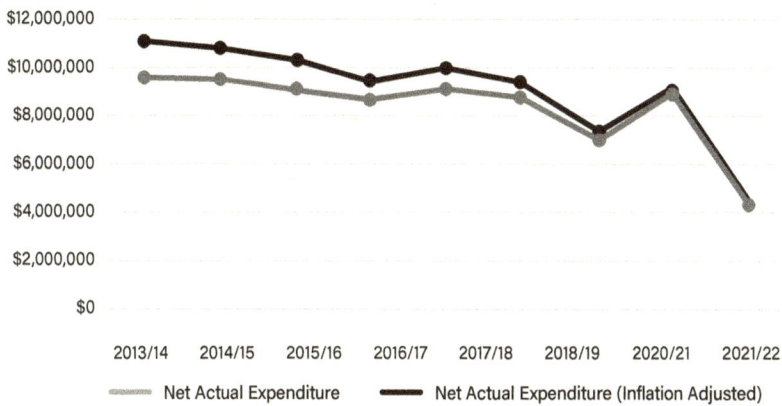

Figure 5.1. Manitoba provincial expenditures on immigration, 2013–2022.

in 2020/21, and then fell substantially to $4.21 million in 2021/22. It is important to note that new immigrant arrivals had also severely dropped in 2020/21, due to border closures, travel restrictions, and federal processing delays related to the COVID-19 pandemic.

Between 2013 and 2022, the number of new immigrants (permanent residents) in Manitoba remained relatively steady, with an average of around 15,000 each year over the twelve-year period. In 2020/21 that dropped to 10,197, due to the pandemic, but rebounded to 21,340 in 2021/22 with the reopening of the border and application processing (Statistics Canada 2022). In 2022, Manitoba received a record 21,645 permanent residents, the majority through the PNP (IRCC 2022). Analyzing expenditures in the sector compared to the number of new immigrants in the province, it is clear provincial funding per immigrant has decreased over the past decade (Table 5.1). Comparing actual expenditures with authorized budget allocations for immigration, the provincial government typically underspends in this area, by an average of around 3 percent of the authorized amount per year. Furthermore, these figures are for permanent residents, and do not include migrants arriving with temporary status. According to preliminary data from IRCC, in 2022 there were around 26,000 temporary residents in Manitoba; taking this into account, the provincial funding per migrant was even lower than indicated in Table 5.1.

Cuts to funding signal a reduction in the state's commitment to settlement supports. They align with broader neoliberal policy directions that increasingly limit family class and refugee intake in favour of economic class immigrants, presumed to settle more "successfully" and require fewer supports. Manitoba does have a long tradition of welcoming refugees. As part of federal initiatives, it settled refugees from Syria in 2015/16 and Afghanistan in 2021/22. It has also received more Ukrainians per capita than any other province since the early 2022 invasion of Ukraine (IRCC 2022). The federal government funds services for refugees.[8] The province provides supports for refugee claimants, though in cases of large humanitarian arrivals it may receive additional federal funding. The province funded a Refugee Response Community Coordinator at the Manitoba Association of Newcomer Serving Organizations (MANSO) to assist with Syrian refugee resettlement, and with increases in asylum seekers crossing from the United States into Manitoba in 2016/17, additional funding was

Table 5.1. Manitoba actual annual provincial expenditures on immigration (excluding federal transfers), 2013–2022 (adjusted for inflation in 2021 dollars).

YEAR	2013/14	2014/15	2015/16	2016/17	2017/18	2018/19	2019/20	2020/21	2021/22
Net expenditure (in millions)	$11.042	$10.743	$10.243	$9.475	$9.883	$9.300	$7.275	$9.024	$4.214
Net expenditure per new immigrant	$713	$726	$588	$604	$698	$584	$492	$858	$197

provided to cover housing-related and other costs (Hoyce 2017; Manitoba 2018). Manitoba also provided special funding to assist Ukrainian nationals arriving in Canada as temporary residents. However, these are often short-term, reactive funding injections. Cuts over subsequent years left some organizations attempting to deliver the same services with fewer resources. Stakeholders in the sector echo what is firmly established in the literature: while short-term supports may meet immediate needs and build capacity, immigrant settlement and integration are processes that take considerably longer than a year or two.

As it cut funding, the province also instituted cost-recovery measures to increase revenue; for example, by introducing PNP application fees. In 2019, it shifted settlement fund distribution, reinvesting the PNP application fee revenue into seventeen organizations across the province (Manitoba 2019b). These changes were criticized by many in the sector; for example, the fee was referred to as a "head tax" that creates an additional barrier to many applicants (Da Silva 2022). The move also, in effect, downloads some degree of funding for services to the very newcomers who would benefit from them.[9] In early 2022, the province responded to advocates by waiving the $500 fee for applicants from Ukraine and prioritizing those applications with a special PNP draw for Ukrainians (Manitoba 2022b). However, as one survey respondent reflected, "While many supports have been extended to Ukrainian newcomers, and a lot of provincial funding is associated with that, this is essentially a race-based policy. The Province is not extending the same supports to all temporary residents, and funding overall for settlement is reduced."

Funding to the sector has also been restructured. Over recent decades, there has been a shift at both federal and provincial levels away from core funding to organizations toward shorter-term, project-based funding (Lowe et al. 2017). This has created instability and competition across the sector. In 2022 and 2023, Manitoba's call for funding proposals came with new eligibility restrictions (e.g., for direct services only), and some organizations consequently lost substantial funding. Such cuts threaten the long-term vitality of affected agencies, the sector as a whole, and the well-being of the communities they serve.

Cuts to provincial funding especially affect humanitarian arrivals and newcomers with temporary status. Though Manitoba's immigration levels have remained relatively steady (apart from the brief pandemic-related drop), survey respondents noted that provincial funding reductions meant they had to provide fewer services to certain groups. For example, one organization was no longer able to support people with temporary status. This is especially concerning in the context of Manitoba's emphasis on the PNP and two-step immigration. Temporary residents, already marginalized by their status, generally do not qualify for federally funded settlement services, and must rely on provincial supports.[10] If they are unable to access services on arrival, it may be more difficult for them to settle and integrate well when they transition to permanent residency (and, eventually, citizenship). One survey respondent noted, "The impact of there being less funding and supports for non-permanent residents is that they experience greater challenges in their resettlement in Manitoba, since they are not eligible for as many services and supports."

In light of its cost cutting, several survey respondents and critics have questioned the province's commitment to its stated initiatives. For example, in the 2017 budget, the tuition fee rebate for graduating students who remained in Manitoba was phased out, and in 2018 the province made international students ineligible for provincial healthcare (saving $3.1 million). One civil servant noted it seemed "like a 'bait and switch' . . . a loss of protection for international students being promised benefits they did not receive." That same year, the province celebrated the thousands of jobs and $400 million that international students contribute to Manitoba's economy, as it was actively encouraging them to apply to immigrate (Denton 2021). As the international student healthcare example shows, impacts of austerity must be considered holistically. There has been decreased provincial funding to immigration since 2016, but immigration is interrelated with other provincial sectors—healthcare, education, housing, etc.—and measures that impact those areas also directly affect newcomer settlement and integration.

Impacts on Public Service Workers and Service Delivery

Shifts in policy and cuts to funding in recent years have impacted those working in the sector and the level and quality of services. Compared to other sectors, the number of people working on immigration in the provincial civil service is small, and there were few survey responses ($n = 5$). Respondents included public servants in the sector and professionals working in nonprofits receiving at least some provincial funding. This chapter also draws on responses from other areas, such as education, with overlapping mandates.

All respondents indicated that austerity measures implemented since 2016 have "greatly impacted" their organization's work. According to respondents, provincial government units have been restructured, moved, or eliminated. In several cases, provincial funding cuts led to the loss of positions. In one nonprofit, the province stopped funding a position, which meant the organization had to reallocate federal funding to the position and reduce service delivery to a particular client group. A few respondents noted the closure of an entire unit, resulting in reclassification of positions and significant portions of the division being moved to other jobs. Between 2016 and 2021, twenty FTE positions were eliminated, representing a 27 percent reduction in the immigration civil service workforce. Cuts were sometimes recommended with "no consultation with the [relevant unit] to even understand its work." One civil servant noted, "Once the government realized that there were actually jobs not getting done and jobs that were essential and no one was in charge, they placed those jobs on the side of the desk of already overworked people. They lost all their corporate knowledge of how [the sector] functioned, what the issues are, and what policies are needed to support and grow the sector." Respondents indicated this led to a loss of department strategy, a diminished "Manitoba 'brand,'" reduced coordination with federal partners, and increased precarity and insecurity.

Staffing shortages were mentioned in all responses, and workers experienced resource shortages and increased workload, including the assignment of more or longer shifts than desired. According to respondents, staffing cuts did not correspond with a reduction in work; rather, "it was passed around to other people, and some of the work just doesn't get done or gets done slower." This occurred while there was underspending of the authorized budget for these services. One respondent noted that since 2016, one-third of the positions in the unit they had supervised had become vacant and were not filled.[11] All respondents indicated that recent changes in the sector had negatively impacted working conditions, morale and employee mental health, and job satisfaction, and several were considering looking for employment elsewhere. One civil servant summarized their unit's experience as follows: "The government austerity since 2016 has been a disaster for [the sector] in the province of Manitoba. It will take years to rebuild the coordination and collaborative nature of the sector."

Furthermore, according to respondents, agreed-upon funding sometimes came with restrictive eligibility criteria, increased reporting requirements, and/or delays in its distribution.[12] Funding-related uncertainty or delays impacted organizations' capacity to plan for both programming and staffing. This caused, according to one nonprofit director, "constant stress," especially "for employees on precarious employment with delayed contracts." A few respondents suggested that rather than providing project-based funding, the province should provide multiyear core funding to key agencies. This would "greatly reduce administration costs and create greater access to programs for all." It would also mean less staff turnover and lower training costs.[13]

Overall, respondents indicated that austerity measures negatively affected service quality, particularly for lower-income users. Settlement services are a critical transition support to recently arrived newcomers and can have cascading effects over the longer term, impacting immigrants' economic and social integration outcomes. As one settlement organization employee reflected, "While there may be very short-term cost reductions to the province, critical social services are being eroded, with high stress and staff burnout in the community sector, more pressure on emergency services, and an increasingly divided society benefiting few, and further excluding marginalized groups like Indigenous, newcomer, and low-income Manitobans." Another respondent, reflecting on the cuts to international student healthcare, noted that while they might be more difficult to quantify, impacts of providing healthcare regardless of immigration status "would be far reaching," with fewer "health issues later on if access to Manitoba Health was provided to all newcomers." Austerity has negatively impacted those working in the immigration sector, and measures ostensibly intended to reduce costs in the short term may have detrimental longer-term costs.

Conclusion
Emerging from the COVID-19 pandemic, immigration received renewed attention from the province. In 2023, Manitoba estimated it would need about 15,500 new workers per year until at least 2025 to meet demands (Manitoba 2023). With interprovincial net out-migration and

population decline, immigration is seen as a key tool for ensuring that "we have people with the right skills at the right time, to quickly rebound from the pandemic and support economic resilience and growth" (Manitoba 2022c, 35). In 2023, the federal government announced record immigration levels, raising the annual intake target to 500,000 (Manitoba 2023), but it changed course in 2024 with a series of policy changes aimed at scaling back immigration. In October 2024, the annual target was reduced to 395,000, and the number of skilled immigrants allowed by Manitoba through the PNP was cut in half (Sanders 2025). The federal government also implemented measures to decrease the number of non-permanent residents in the country, including restrictions on the Temporary Foreign Worker Program and a cap on international students. Even as intake numbers were reduced, it is important to note that more than 40 percent of new permanent residents were to be drawn from temporary residents already living in Canada (Government of Canada 2024).

The province has a primary role in attracting immigrants and providing them settlement supports, and provincial funding for immigration is crucial, especially with recent cuts at the federal level. It fills important gaps in federally funded service provision. The PNP and other two-step immigration pathways continue to be drivers of immigration in Manitoba, and funding cuts especially affect those newcomers. Manitoba continues to negotiate with the federal government to increase its cap of provincial nominees and is making efforts to support those with temporary residence hoping to immigrate permanently (Manitoba 2025). As it strives to attract more immigrants to fill labour needs—at times through reactive, ad hoc measures such as the nursing recruitment mentioned at the start of this chapter—it must support the administration of those initiatives and provide supports so newcomers feel welcome. The state's material commitment to settlement sends an official message of welcome and inclusion. To fulfill its mandate on immigration and build thriving communities, Manitoba cannot waver; it needs strong public and service sectors to welcome and support immigrants once they arrive.

Notes

1   This aligns with broader neoliberal shifts in immigration policy that focus on the immediate, narrow economic benefits of immigration and view immigrants less as citizens with families and more as workers.

2   The PNP has had a diversity of other streams, some of which aimed to leverage existing family connections and social networks in Manitoba for family reunification and to rebuild smaller centres. Its focus on addressing labour market needs, though, contributes to larger trends toward employer-driven immigration (Labman and Zell 2021).

3   The agreement included an annual federal transfer to fund administrative and settlement services as well as the relocation of federal employees to Manitoba.

4   As a smaller, cross-sector policy area provincially, it is not surprising that the portfolio moves and "immigration" is occasionally dropped from the departmental name (Sanders 2016); however, the move perhaps signalled a more explicit link tying immigration to training/upgrading and an interest in encouraging international student immigration.

5   Compared with more laissez-faire settlement approaches elsewhere, Canada is seen as an international leader for its model of government-funded newcomer-serving organizations.

6   Services can be provided to newcomers directly or indirectly (i.e., indirectly supporting settlement by coordinating delivery or conducting research that informs services).

7   For details on data sources used for provincial expenditures, employee staffing numbers, and full-time equivalent (FTE) positions in this chapter, see Preface.

8   Government-assisted refugees are supported by the federal government, while privately sponsored refugees are expected to receive supports from their Canadian sponsors—effectively offloading settlement support to private citizens (Labman and Zell 2021).

9   Analysts have noted that this kind of "responsibilization," premised on an underlying presumption that migrants should be successful on their own, has contributed to the devaluation and underfunding of the entire settlement sector (Lowe et al. 2017).

10 The federal government made an exception for Canada–Ukraine Authorization for Emergency Travel visa holders, changing contribution agreements to reflect that this one group of temporary residents would be eligible for IRCC-funded settlement services from 1 April 2022 to 31 March 2025.

11 In 2021/22, across the Advanced Education, Skills and Training department, there was a vacancy rate of 18 percent (Manitoba 2022a).

12 One respondent noted that delays and increased reporting requirements were "constantly blamed on the Treasury." Rigid and increased reporting requirements stretch already thin organizational capacity and resources, and often have the effect of shifting accountability to the funder and away from the newcomer communities being served (Lowe et al. 2017).

13   This kind of project-based funding relationship with the government, and a lack of organizational autonomy, has also led to an "advocacy chill" in the sector, with umbrella groups such as MANSO increasingly monitored and service organizations less able to act as voices for the more marginalized community groups they serve.

References

Carter, Tom, Margot Morrish, and Benjamin Amoyaw. 2008. "Attracting Immigrants to Smaller Urban and Rural Communities: Lessons Learned from the Manitoba Provincial Nominee Program." *Journal of International Migration and Integration* 9: 161–83.

Carter, Tom, Sarah Zell, and Sarah Giesbrecht. 2012. *The Manitoba Provincial Nominee Program: An Evaluation of Manitoba's Principal Component of Immigration Policy.* Manitoba Immigration and Multiculturalism.

Clement, Gerald, Tom Carter, and Robert Vineberg. 2013. *Case Study: The Realigned System of Settlement Service Delivery in Manitoba 1999 to 2013.* Immigration Research West.

Da Silva, Danielle. 2022. "New Immigration Advisory Council Draws Praise but Also Calls for Quicker Fixes." *Winnipeg Free Press*, 15 February.

Denton, Peter. 2021. "Skills, Strategy, Bumf and Bargle." *Winnipeg Free Press*, 23 February.

Government of Canada. 2024. *Notice—Supplementary Information for the 2025–2027 Immigration Levels Plan.* https://www.canada.ca/en/immigration-refugees-citizenship/news/notices/supplementary-immigration-levels-2025-2027.html.

Government of Manitoba. 2013. *Manitoba Immigration Facts—2012 Statistical Report.* Manitoba Immigration and Multiculturalism. https://immigratemanitoba.com/wp-content/uploads/2017/11/manitoba_immigration_facts_report_2012.pdf.

———. 2017. *Annual Report 2016–17.* Education and Training.

———. 2018. *Annual Report 2017–18.* Education and Training.

———. 2019a. *Annual Report 2018–19.* Education and Training.

———. 2019b. "Province Announces $3 Million in New Funding to Strengthen Newcomer Support Services." News Release, 12 April. https://news.gov.mb.ca/news/index.html?item=45205.

———. 2022a. "2022 Committee of Supply—Briefing Binder Table." Advanced Education, Skills and Immigration, 23 September.

———. 2022b. *Annual Report 2021–22.* Advanced Education, Skills and Immigration.

———. 2022c. "Budget 2022—Supplement to the Estimates of Expenditure." Advanced Education, Skills and Immigration.

———. 2023. *Report of the Immigration Advisory Council.* Manitoba Immigration, February. https://immigratemanitoba.com/wp-content/uploads/2023/02/immigration-council-report_en.pdf.

———. 2025. "Manitoba Government Announces More Workers Will Be Able to Stay in Manitoba: Work Permit Extension Will Help Workers, Grow Manitoba's Economy: Marcelino." News Release, 15 April. https://news.gov.mb.ca/news/index.html?archive=&item=68439.

Hoye, Bryce. 2017. "Manitoba Boosts Funds for Asylum Seekers, Calls on Feds to Step Up." CBC Manitoba, 23 February. https://www.cbc.ca/news/canada/manitoba/manitoba-refugees-border-1.3995642.

IRCC. 2022. "Permanent Residents—Monthly IRCC Updates." Government of Canada, 31 December.

Labman, Shauna, and Sarah Zell. 2021. "The Shift Towards Increased Citizen-Driven Migration in Canada." In *Research Handbook on the Law and Politics of Migration*, edited by Catherine Dauvergne, 110–24. Cheltenham: Edward Elgar Press.

Lowe, Sophia, Ted Richmond, and John Shields. 2017. "Settling on Austerity: ISAs, Immigrant Communities and Neoliberal Restructuring." *Alternate Routes: A Journal of Critical Social Research* 28: 14–46.

Paquet, Mireille. 2019. *Province Building and the Federalization of Immigration in Canada*. Toronto: University of Toronto Press.

Praznik, Jessica, and John Shields. 2018. *An Anatomy of Settlement Services in Canada*. Building Migrant Resilience in Cities/Immigration et résilience en milieu urbain (BMRC-IMRU).

Sanders, Carol. 2016. "Immigration Disappears from Cabinet Titles." *Winnipeg Free Press*, 4 May.

———. 2025. "Manitoba Fights for More Skilled Workers after Ottawa Cut Program." *Winnipeg Free Press*, 20 January. https://www.winnipegfreepress.com/breakingnews/2025/01/20/provincial-nominee-program-allocation-cut-in-half.

Statistics Canada. 2022. "Estimates of the Components of Demographic Growth, Annual." Table 17-10-0008-01.

———. 2023. "Consumer Price Index, Annual Average, Not Seasonally Adjusted." Table 18-10-0005-01.

Thompson, Sam. 2023. "'A Humbling Experience': Manitoba Nursing Recruitment Trip is Underway in Philippines." Global News, 21 February. https://globalnews.ca/news/9500236/manitoba-recruiting-nurses-philippines/.

Chapter 6

CRITICAL CONDITION: HEALTHCARE IN MANITOBA

Katherine Burley, Robert Chernomas, and Ian Hudson

Both the financing and provision of healthcare in Manitoba are somewhat unique compared to other services provided by the provincial government. Because healthcare is universal in Canada, it is financed jointly by the federal and the provincial governments. Healthcare in all provinces is governed by the Canada Health Act, a piece of federal legislation that establishes conditions under which the provinces and territories may receive funding for healthcare services. These include public administration of care, comprehensiveness, universality, portability, and accessibility. The share that is covered by the federal government has declined over time, from approximately 35 percent in the 1960s, to around 22 percent in 2022 (Canadian Medical Association 2022). Since it was elected in 2016, however, Manitoba's Progressive Conservative (PC) Party prioritized its austerity agenda, often to the detriment of quality healthcare. This chapter will analyze the party's healthcare spending, the austere tools it utilized, and what healthcare workers say regarding the outcomes austerity produced.

Healthcare Spending by the Numbers

Figure 6.1 shows changes to the province's expenditures on healthcare between 2011 and 2015, and between 2015 and 2019. In nominal terms, Manitoba's healthcare expenditures increased 16.3 percent under New Democratic Party (NDP) leadership and 8.5 percent under PC leadership.

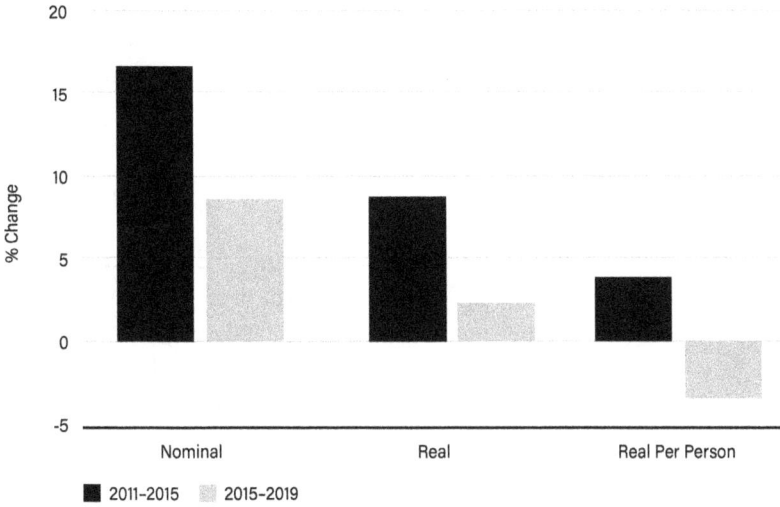

Figure 6.1. Percent change in Manitoba healthcare expenditure, 2011–2019.

Sources: CIHI 2021a, Table D.4.7.1; CIHI 2021b; Statistics Canada 2022a.

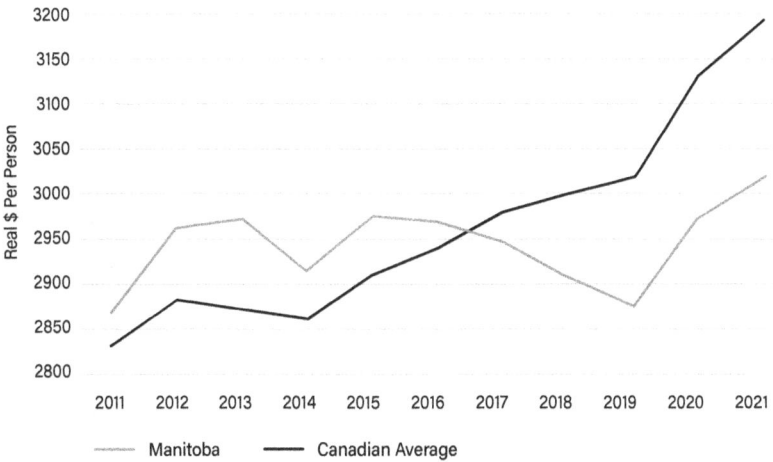

Figure 6.2. Annual real per capita provincial healthcare spending, 2011–2021.

Sources: CIHI 2021a, 2021b; Statistics Canada 2022a.

However, in order to calculate the real value of provincial expenditures, the effect of inflation must be considered. We accounted for inflation using the total healthcare implicit price index for Manitoba with 1997 as a base year. An accurate accounting of provincial spending also needs to account for the growing population. On a real per capita basis, expenditures rose from $2,869.90 in 2011 to $2,977.98 in 2015, but actually fell to $2,874.04 by 2019.

Turning to interprovincial comparisons, Figure 6.2 shows the annual real per-person total spent by Manitoba and the average spent by other Canadian provinces on healthcare from 2011 and 2021. While Manitoba was consistently in the top four provinces for provincial spending on healthcare during the NDP's reign, in the five successive years, it was consistently one of the lowest-spending provinces. Manitoba's per capita healthcare spending *did* increase during the COVID-19 years, as the PC government—like all governments—had to respond to extraordinary circumstances. Although Manitoba exceeded the Canadian average for COVID-19 specific funding in both 2020 and 2021, it performed well below the Canadian average in total healthcare spending.[1] This demonstrates that the entire increase in per-person healthcare spending was devoted to COVID-19 response funding, rather than to improving the system as a whole.

The PCs' Austere Tools

Healthcare providers in Manitoba had to contend with austerity in many forms during the PC administration. In April 2017, the PCs introduced their vision for overhauling the province's healthcare system, entitled Manitoba's Health System Transformation, a multiyear project intended to bolster healthcare coordination and reduce costs, which involved cuts, closures, and massive restructuring. Figure 6.3 presents a timeline of the various measures undertaken as part of the transformation strategy (Manitoba Health Coalition 2022). Their measures were far-reaching and included policy levers that affect both patients and providers. Therefore, while COVID-19 amplified Manitoba's crisis, the damage from the transformation strategy had already been building in the years prior. Regarding cuts, in addition to the mandated wage freeze on public sector workers discussed in the introduction, the PCs cancelled $1 billion worth of new health infrastructure projects in February 2017, less than a year after being elected, including a new CancerCare Manitoba facility, a personal care home in Lac du Bonnet, and several new clinics. They further cut all the regional health authorities' budgets for the 2017/18 fiscal year in March 2017, followed by additional cuts to staffing across the health authorities. The PCs also cut acute care by $14 million in their 2021 budget.

As to closures, then Minister of Health Kelvin Goertzen announced in April 2017 that the emergency rooms would close at Concordia, Victoria, and Seven Oaks Hospitals, and that the urgent care centre would close at Misericordia Hospital. This left only four emergency departments—including the Children's Emergency Department at the Health Sciences Centre (HSC)—equipped to treat patients in potentially life-threatening situations in the city of Winnipeg. Further, following the onset of the COVID-19 pandemic, many emergency rooms in rural and Northern Manitoba experienced closures, eighteen of which remained closed into the summer of 2022, and an additional thirty-four were on reduced hours (Hirschfield 2022).

Concerning restructuring, the province announced in 2017 that it would restructure and reorganize front-line care in the Winnipeg Regional Health Authority (WRHA), specifically at the HSC and Grace Hospital (CUPE 2017). To this end, position deletion letters were sent to 500 WRHA nurses beginning in August 2017, indicating that either the location of their work or the type of work they were doing—or both—were changing. If none of the available alternative positions were acceptable, nurses had the option to be laid off. As of May 2022, Grace Hospital had a 28 percent vacancy rate for nurses, while HSC had a rate of 18 percent for the same positions (Harewood 2022). A further 700 position deletion letters were sent to hospital support staff beginning in September 2017, including healthcare aides and housekeeping staff (CBC News 2017). Some workers lost their jobs entirely, while others had the option to be moved to a new one. Further, in September 2018, the WRHA announced it would consolidate its mental health services and its surgery services to three hospitals each, making care less accessible to patients when they need it.

The province also mandated a reduction in the number of bargaining units in healthcare in 2017. This process included a representation vote in 2019, forcing unions to compete against each other for the right to represent healthcare workers in the new structure (Hatherly 2019). This process required that unions dedicate considerable time and effort to electioneering rather than representing their workers.

Finally, the PCs contracted out services. In November 2019, the private company Dynacare closed twenty-six of its fifty-four diagnostic labs in Winnipeg, making patients travel further to access their services. The province also privatized its Lifeflight Air Ambulance program in September 2020 and extended the use of private stretcher service into rural Manitoba. The private provider Cerebra was contracted to provide home sleep studies, which cost considerably more than the public sleep clinic and raised red flags because it was both conducting diagnostic tests and selling the therapies—a recipe for overprescription (Roberts 2023). Further, Manitoba's nurses have reported a surge in contract or agency nurses being brought in to fill gaps left by previously full-time permanent positions, to which many of our respondents attested. In 2022/23, the province spent a total of $60 million on agency nurses, up 47 percent from the previous year (Da Silva 2023).

In the aftermath of the COVID-19 crisis, and with the state of Manitoba's healthcare the subject of considerable criticism, the province opened its purse strings in an attempt to recruit and retain workers. The 2022 Health Human Resource Action Plan promised to spend $200 million to add 2,000 workers. Although most health organizations cautiously welcomed the plan as a step in the right direction, the director of the Manitoba Health Coalition, Thomas Linner, criticized it for lacking metrics that could be used for tracking its success or failure. For example, how will the public be able to judge whether 2,000 people are hired? What kinds of workers will be hired? What is the timeframe for the hiring (Manitoba Health Coalition 2023)?

Healthcare System Outputs

It is clear that healthcare was included in the PCs' austerity agenda. However, if the restructuring of the system delivered increases in efficiency, health outputs might improve despite the decreased expenditure.

One way to assess the quality of the healthcare system is by looking at how easy and accessible it is to obtain care in times of need, often indicated by wait times (the median number of days for a patient to undergo the procedure after determining that it is required). Figure 6.4 shows the annual

CUTS AND CHANGES TO HEALTHCARE IN MANITOBA
2016-2022

September 2016
Health Minister Kelvin Goertzen announces Manitoba is considering adding private MRIs.
November 2016
$650,000 in funding used by the Manitoba Metis Federation (MMF) to employ five health staffers cut.

February 2018
Special Drug Program (SDP) merges with Pharmacare, meaning former SDP recipients have to pay a deductible for their medications.
July 2018
WRHA requests personal care homes cut their yearly budget by 0.25% for a second year in a row.
September 2018
WHRA to consolidate mental health to HSC, Victoria, and St. Boniface Hospitals and surgery to HSC, St. Boniface, Grace, and Concordia Hospitals by the end of 2018.
October 2018
1,200 previously-announced personal care home beds delayed from 2024 to 2025.
November 2018
• Upcoming staffing and recreation cuts announced for Deer Lodge Centre.
• Flin Flon Hospital suspends obstetrical delivery services temporarily.
• Province requests proposals for new private addictions facility.

January 2020
WRHA activates overcapacity flu plan, asking staff to work more shifts and postponing some elective surgeries.
March 2020
• With Manitoba's first COVID-19 cases, elective surgeries are delayed and prescriptions limited to 30-day supply.
• Province gives Morneau Shepell, a private company, $4.5 million to provide online mental health therapy.
April 2020
• Flin Flon closes only operating room.
• Province relies on Dynacare private labs to expand COVID-19 testing.
August 2020
Province awards contracts to two private and three public facilities to help resolve surgical backlog.
September 2020
• CancerCare consolidates care facilities from six to four.
• 50 health management positions cut across the province.
• Private STARS assumes air ambulance services from Lifeflight.
November 2020
• Red Cross called in to assist with COVID-19 outbreaks at Parkview Place and Maples personal care homes.
• Manitoba asks for volunteers at testing sites and healthcare facilities, rather than hiring workers.

January 2022
Government reorganizes its health portfolio into the care of three ministers - Minister of Health, Minister of Seniors and Long-Term Care, and Minister of Mental Health and Community Wellness.
April 2022
Province awards social impact bond to Shoppers Drug Mart to help curb smoking.
June 2022
18 rural and Northern ERs expected not to reopen in the summer after a year being closed, and 34 to be open only part-time.

February 2017
$1 billion of new health infrastructure projects cancelled.
March 2017
• All RHAs have their budgets cut for 2017-18.
• Public healthcare cut for international students.
April 2017
• Emergency and urgent care facilities to close at Concordia, Victoria, Seven Oaks, and Misericordia Hospitals.
• $4.2 million program to bring more doctors to rural Manitoba cancelled.
June 2017
• 197 healthcare jobs cut across the RHAs.
• Coverage reduced for blood glucose test strips for diabetes.
• 23 rural EMS stations to close.
July 2017
• WRHA cuts 24 positions, including 17 nurses at HSC.
• All but one QuickCare Clinic in Winnipeg will close.
August 2017
Position deletion letters sent to 500 WRHA nurses.
September 2017
111 healthcare aide positions cut at HSC as part of restructuring.
October 2017
40 nurses laid off at Victoria Hospital and 15 to be laid off at Deer Lodge Centre.
November 2017
$1 million funding cut for Winnipeg personal care homes.

April 2019
NDP FIPPA request reveals the province is relying increasingly on hiring nurses from private agencies to fill gaps since 2017.
May 2019
Berens River First Nation loses its four dialysis machines.
June 2019
• Concordia ER closes and becomes urgent care facility.
• US-based Access Health Imaging offering tests for fees in rural communities.
• Manitoba privatizes Lifeflight Air Ambulance program.
• Seven Oaks Hospital cuts full-time healthcare aide positions and increases nursing shifts to 12 hours.
July 2019
Seven Oaks ER closes and becomes urgent care facility.
November 2019
Dynacare, a private medical company, closes 26 of its 54 diagnostic labs in Winnipeg.

April 2021
Provincial budget cuts acute care by $13 million.
May 2021
• 18 COVID-19 patients airlifted out of Manitoba to Ontario.
• Viral sequencing of COVID-19 variants outsourced to private Dynacare labs.
November 2021
Vacant nursing positions in Winnipeg surpass 1,300.
December 2021
Province establishes Surgical and Diagnostic Recovery Task Force to resolve the 152,000-case backlog, focusing on negotiating contracts with providers and sending patients out of province if necessary.

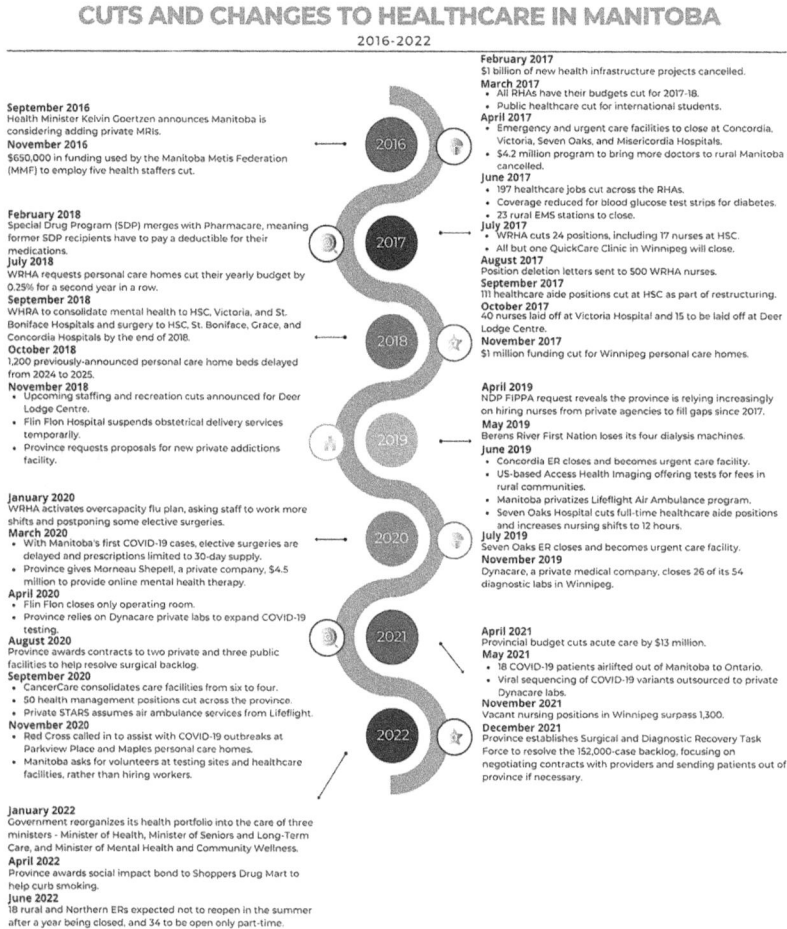

Figure 6.3. Timeline of cuts and changes to healthcare under the Progressive Conservatives in Manitoba, 2016–2022.

Source: Manitoba Health Coalition 2022.

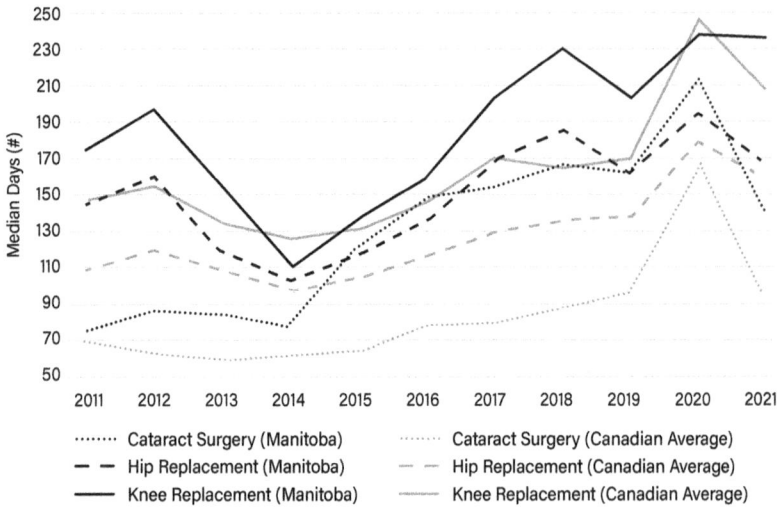

Figure 6.4. Annual provincial median wait times for elective surgeries, 2011–2021.

Note: Wait times are expressed as the median number of days for a patient to undergo the procedure after determining that it is required. Source: CIHI 2021c.

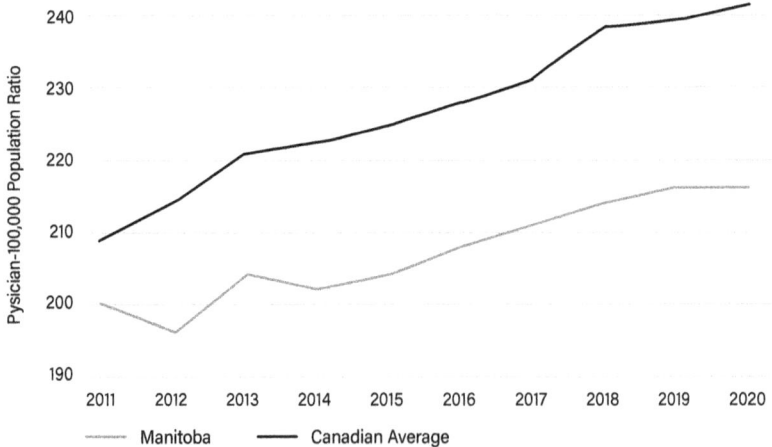

Figure 6.5. Annual provincial physician-to-100,000 population ratio, 2011–2020.

Source: CIHI 2021d.

median wait times for various surgeries in Manitoba and the average across all Canadian provinces from 2011 to 2021.

While Manitoba's wait times were longer than the Canadian average during the NDP's time in office, the gap widened under PC leadership. For instance, in 2015, Manitobans had to wait on average 56.9 days longer than patients in other provinces for cataract surgery. By 2019, that gap had widened to 64.7 days. During the first two years of the COVID-19 pandemic, wait times increased across the country, but Manitoba's wait times for cataract surgery and hip replacement surgery continued to outpace the Canadian average.

While Manitoba has had a consistently lower physician-to-population ratio over the past decade, the gap between Manitoba and other Canadian provinces widened after the PCs took office (Figure 6.5). In 2015—the last full year during which the NDP was in power—Manitoba had 204 physicians per 100,000 population, 20.4 fewer than the average of other Canadian provinces. By 2020, that gap had widened to 25.3.

We also looked at indicators related to those who work within the system. After all, it only makes sense that healthcare workers who are fairly compensated, feel supported by their peers and superiors, and are happy with their work environment are better equipped to provide quality care. From 2015 to 2022, the Canadian average nominal hourly wage for health-care and social assistance workers increased from $22.07 to $25.04. The case in Manitoba, however, was less straightforward. From 2015—the last full year during which the NDP was in government—until 2017, average hourly wages increased (Figure. 6.6). This increase, however, is attributable to contracts that were negotiated with the previous NDP government, which stretched into the beginning of the PC era. Many contracts negotiated between healthcare workers and various public health bodies expired in 2017 or 2018 (MAHCP 2022) and were only settled and ratified in the summer of 2023.

In 2017, the provincial government introduced legislation to mandate a two-year wage freeze on public sector workers' wages, followed by minuscule increases in the two successive years (Lambert 2022). Hourly wages for health and social assistance workers steadily declined in the years following, dropping below the Canadian average. A wage freeze alone cannot account for a decline in nominal wages. However, it is likely that

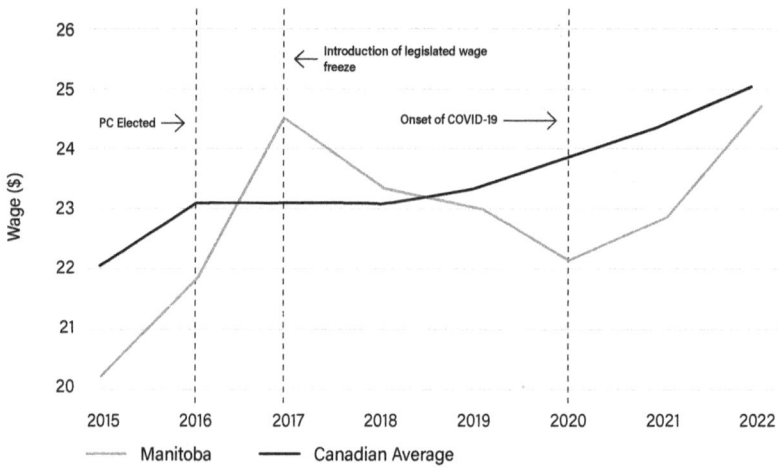

Figure 6.6. Annual provincial wage for health and social assistance workers, 2015–2022.

Source: Statistics Canada 2022b.

the freeze coincided with older, more experienced, higher-paid workers leaving the profession, and being replaced by less experienced, lower-wage workers. Between 2020 and 2022, wages offered to Manitoba's healthcare and social assistance workers finally began to rebound, likely due in part to the end of the legislated wage freeze, the negotiation of at least some new contracts with public sector unions, and wage top-ups for front-line workers in the context of the COVID-19 pandemic, made possible almost entirely by federal emergency funding (CBC News 2020; Dacey 2020). Still, though, Manitoban wages lagged behind the Canadian average.

Low wages and long hours are at least partly responsible for the very high vacancy rates in health professions in Manitoba. To take just a few examples, in 2023, nursing vacancy rates in the Interlake/Eastern Health Region were 36 percent, and in the Southern Health Region, 27 percent. The Southern Health Region rate had doubled from 2019 (Greenslade 2023). In January 2023, the vacancy rate for rural paramedics stood at 30 percent, more than three times higher than the 8 percent vacancy rate in 2020 (Baxter 2023). Manitoba's civil service workers in the Department of Health, who are responsible for administering healthcare in the province, had a staggering vacancy rate of 42 percent in 2022, the first year that the government reported vacancy rates by department (Government of Manitoba 2022, 62–67). High vacancy rates create a vicious spiral in which the remaining workers are forced to work longer hours and more overtime, making them more likely to seek employment in other professions, further increasing the vacancy rates and putting even more pressure on the remaining workers.

Survey Results: Perspectives from Manitoba's Healthcare Workers

In response to our survey, 471 public sector healthcare workers took the time to share their thoughts and opinions; 84 percent identified themselves as front-line workers and 75 percent identified as women. This section presents their responses on three main themes: privatization and contracting out; conditions of employment; and impact on service delivery.

Privatization and Contracting Out

Twenty-nine percent of respondents said more work in their area had been privatized since 2016. Overwhelmingly, the most frequently cited example of contracting out was the increased use of agency workers, particularly nurses, to perform jobs that were previously done by full-time, public sector staff. One supportive housing worker noted, "As we don't have enough staff, they have called an agency for workers at a way higher pay than [the regular staff] have ever been paid." Another worker expressed concerns with this model, as "the regular employee staff know the patients and the facility way better than a contracted provider can most of the time because of familiarity of the situational basis of the job and the facility's procedures." Therefore, contracting out jobs to private agencies not only makes public sector healthcare workers feel less valued, but also jeopardizes the consistency of patient care, a concern that was nicely summarized in a statement by Doctors Manitoba: "Our main concern with any new third-party contract is the potential for it to create duplication, fragmentation, or inefficiencies in the delivery of care for patients" (Piché 2023).

Conditions of Employment

We also asked healthcare workers if their conditions of employment— including their hours and workload—had been affected (Figure 6.7); 83

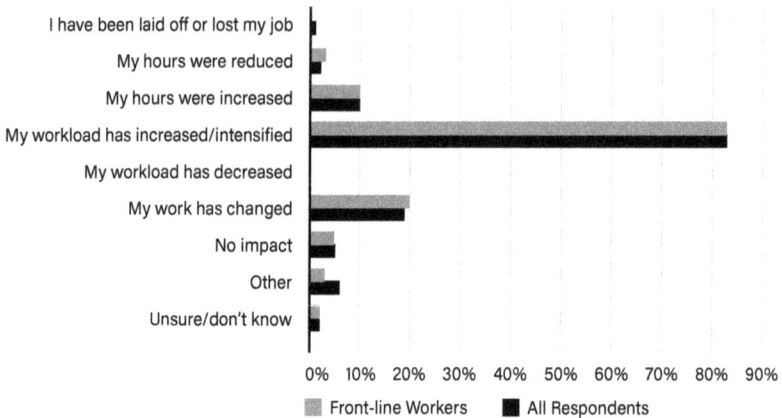

Figure 6.7. Survey responses: Impact of austerity on employment in healthcare.

percent said that their workload had increased. An Allied Health worker noted that "we are so short staffed in every area ... that we are all experiencing very heavy caseloads and performing many tasks outside our roles in trying to assist each other and make sure clients are safe." Recurring survey responses pointed to being short-staffed, being forced to work overtime on a regular basis, and being forced to take on more tasks than in the past.

Survey results on how health workers felt about their jobs were even more starkly negative. Between 85 and 90 percent of survey respondents working in the healthcare sector said that austerity measures worsened their working conditions, job satisfaction, mental health, and overall employee recruitment and retention (Table 6.1). Many respondents noted unfilled job vacancies, low wages, inconsistent or skipped breaks, and exhausting workloads. One long-term care worker said, "Previous to 2018, maybe 2019, this was a good place to work. It has now become a toxic mess. Everyone is working short and barely make enough to pay for the gas to come to work." Another worker expressed that emergency medical services workers in Winnipeg "regularly do not get breaks during 12-hour shift[s] . . . and regularly have zero ambulances to respond to emergency calls."

Table 6.1. Survey responses: Effect of austerity on conditions of employment.

	IMPROVED/ POSITIVE/MORE SATISFIED (%)	NO EFFECT (%)	WORSENED/ WORSE/LESS SATISFIED (%)	UNSURE/DON'T KNOW/OTHER (%)	NO AUSTERITY MEASURES IN MY AREA (%)
Effect on working conditions and job satisfaction	0	4	89	4	3
Effect on employee mental health	0	3	90	4	3
Effect on employee recruitment and retention	0	4	87	6	3

Numerous respondents talked about staff morale deteriorating in recent years, along with increased stress, exhaustion, burnout, and feelings of being undervalued in their workplace. One Allied Health worker noted that "employees are incredibly stressed and undervalued. Everyone is stretched so thinly and there is a very high rate of sick time being used. Many that would have worked longer are considering retirement." A WRHA social worker further said that "team morale in healthcare is low. Workers are burnt out. Many coworkers . . . often discuss how to get out of working in healthcare. The caseloads and job demands have increased and have put so much more pressure on staff . . . [who] don't have the time to provide quality care and honestly, there will likely be critical incidents that occur because of these pressures. The mental health of coworkers has noticeably declined." Darlene Jackson, president of the Manitoba Nurses Union, was reported saying that nurses, especially, were "experiencing unsustainable workloads and mandated overtime, which, combined with relatively lacklustre salaries and benefits, [had] them seeking employment in other provinces" (Harewood 2022).

These kinds of added stressors have made many healthcare workers leave or consider leaving their jobs. A large number of respondents said that they had left their job, considered leaving, retired earlier than they otherwise would have, or were actively looking for other positions or careers. A senior policy analyst reported that they "were on medical leave and a reduced work week, as well as anxiety medication, while the transformation occurred. [Their] mental health was impacted significantly. . . . [They] left [their] job of over 12 years with the Manitoba Government." Another health analyst said that austerity "led to the exodus of staff with significant experience and expertise, leading to overwork of remaining staff as well as reduced efficiency . . . [and] a significant loss of staff with not only experience and expertise, but passion and creativity, because they have burned out." Finally, in no uncertain terms, one paramedic poignantly expressed that they "can't wait to quit this hellhole." A report by Deloitte reveals similar results, saying that two-thirds of healthcare staff are experiencing burnout, and half are seriously considering looking for a new job (CBC News 2023).

Table 6.2. Survey responses: Effect of austerity on service delivery.

	IMPROVED/ POSITIVE (%)	NO CHANGE (%)	REDUCTION/ WORSENED (%)	UNSURE/ DON'T KNOW (%)	NO AUSTERITY MEASURES IN MY AREA (%)
Effect on service quality for the stakeholders/users of the service	0	7	75	13	4
Effect on service quality for lower-income service users	1	15	56	24	3
Effect on public safety	3	10	70	14	2

Impact on Service Delivery

Healthcare workers who responded to the survey overwhelmingly said that austerity policies led to a reduction in service quality, both for patients generally and for low-income patients, and expenditure restraints worsened public safety (Table 6.2). One worker said that "the lack of funding to support expanding our clinic and staff meant we had to make severe restrictions on our clinic's referral criteria. Patients who used to get care through our clinic no longer met the very stringent referral criteria."

We also asked healthcare workers about the specific ways in which their ability to deliver care had been impacted (Figure 6.8). More than 70 percent of respondents said that they were asked to provide the same or more care, but with fewer resources. Barely any survey respondents expressed that patient care had been improved as a result of the PCs' austerity agenda. The overwhelming majority of healthcare workers felt that austerity measures had a negative effect, and less than 5 percent felt that they had positive effect on the delivery of health services.

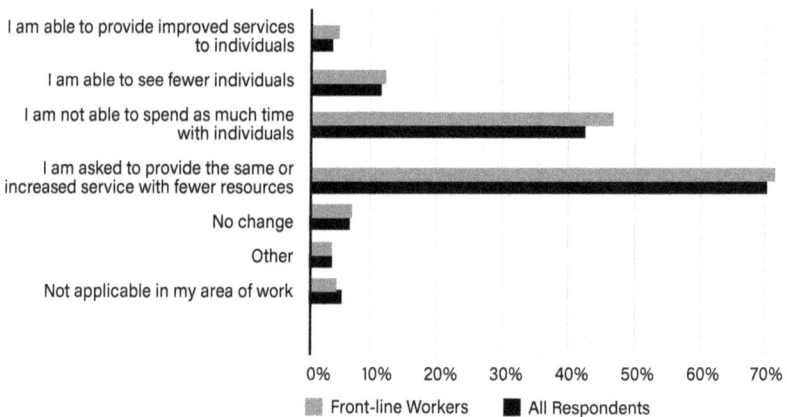

Figure 6.8. Survey responses: Impact of austerity on patient care.

Table 6.3. Survey responses: Will austerity save the public sector money?

	YES	YES, BUT TRANSFER COSTS TO OTHER AREAS	NO	NO AUSTERITY MEASURES IN MY AREA	UNSURE/ DON'T KNOW	OTHER
In the immediate or short term (within 1–2 years)	3% (13)	15% (69)	53% (243)	5% (25)	16% (74)	8% (35)
In the long term	3% (16)	8% (38)	70% (321)	5% (22)	12% (54)	2% (8)

Table 6.4. Survey responses: Evolution of provincial austerity.

	AUSTERITY IN MY AREA HAS BEEN RELAXED (%)	THE INTENSITY OF AUSTERITY HAS REMAINED ABOUT THE SAME (%)	AUSTERITY HAS BECOME MORE INTENSE (%)	UNSURE/DON'T KNOW (%)	OTHER (%)
The NDP government versus the PC government	2	11	65	20	2
Before versus after the start of the COVID-19 pandemic (March 2020)	7	27	50	14	3

It is clear that the healthcare respondents felt that austerity had a negative effect both on their work environment and on the quality of care they were able to provide. However, the justification given for austerity is often that it is necessary to control government spending. We therefore also asked respondents if they felt that the PCs' austerity measures had saved the public sector money in the short and long term (Table 6.3).

In their comments, a number of survey respondents discussed a shift in the approach to healthcare from proactivity to reactivity, meaning that patients were not seen until they were in, or close to, crisis, at which point they required more intense, more expensive care. Many also articulated what they saw as the consequences of constantly working short-staffed. They noted that instead of keeping or hiring regular staff, facilities often had to pay overtime to the staff that they do have, or bring in workers from private agencies, both of which end up being more expensive than maintaining a consistent, reasonably paid workforce. One crisis clinician noted that they "work a lot of overtime. In the long term, it doesn't make sense because they are paying the limited staff 1.5 times or 2 times regular pay for overtime, instead of just creating more fulltime positions."

Finally, we wanted to know how healthcare workers thought provincial austerity had evolved in Manitoba since the PCs took office. Budgetary frugality was not an approach held exclusively by the current government. While measures like program mergers, wage freezes, and staffing and resource reductions began under the NDP, we asked survey respondents if these types of measures had intensified under PC leadership (Table 6.4). The vast majority of respondents said that austerity had indeed become more intense since 2016, and even more so since the beginning of the COVID-19 pandemic, which is consistent with the data on real provincial spending on healthcare.

What we garnered from the healthcare workers who responded was that although the austere approach to healthcare is not necessarily exclusive to the PC party, it certainly intensified after it was elected. The vast majority of respondents not only acknowledged the presence of austerity in the healthcare sector, but also felt that it had a negative effect on their workplace and their ability to provide the best possible quality of care to patients. It is apparent that many workers felt frustrated, burnt out, and undervalued. This is unfair both to the workers themselves, as well as to the members of the public they are expected to treat, with the same level of care as they always have, but with less support.

Conclusion

The word "crisis" has been increasingly applied to healthcare in Canada, and the data in this chapter suggests that Manitoba fared worse than the national average by almost every measure. The survey results suggest that workers in the healthcare industry found their jobs increasingly stressful and unrewarding, and patient care increasingly compromised. These were not inherent, inevitable problems with a public healthcare system, but the result of deliberate political decisions.

Notes

1   All references to a "Canadian average" contained within this chapter refer to the average of the Canadian provinces.

References

Baxter, Dave. 2023. "Paramedic Job Vacancies in Rural Manitoba Have Tripled in the Last Two Years, M A H C P Says." *Winnipeg Sun*, 25 May. https://winnipegsun.com/news/provincial/paramedic-job-vacancies-in-rural-manitoba-have-tripled-in-last-two-years-mahcp-says.

Canadian Medical Association. 2022. "Healthcare Funding in Canada." 18 October. https://www.cma.ca/news/health-care-funding-canada.

C B C News. 2017. "More Than 100 Health-Care Aide Positions Will Be Cut as Part of W R H A Changes, Union Says." C B C Manitoba, 12 September. https://www.cbc.ca/news/canada/manitoba/support-staff-deletion-notices-1.4285988.

———. 2020. "Ottawa, Provinces and Territories Reach $4B Deal to Boost Essential Workers' Pay." C B C Manitoba, 7 May. https://www.cbc.ca/news/politics/essential-worker-pay-boost-1.5559332.

———. 2023. "Over Half of Manitoba Health-Care Workers Have Considered Quitting: Report." C B C Manitoba, 24 April. https://www.cbc.ca/news/canada/manitoba/health-care-workers-burnout-report-manitoba-1.6821278.

C I H I (Canadian Institute for Health Information). 2021a. "Provincial Government Health Expenditure by Use of Funds in Millions of Current Dollars, 1975 to 2021 (Table D.4)." Data set. National Health Expenditure Database. https://www.cihi.ca/en/national-health-expenditure-trends#data-tables.

———. 2021b. "Total Health Care Implicit Price Index, by Province/Territory and Canada, 1975 to 2021 (Appendix B.3)." Data set. National Health Expenditure Database. https://www.cihi.ca/en/national-health-expenditure-trends#data-tables.

———. 2021c. "Wait Times for Priority Procedures in Canada, 2008 to 2021." Data set. https://www.cihi.ca/en/explore-wait-times-for-priority-procedures-across-canada#additional-resources.

———. 2021d. "Supply, Distribution and Migration of Physicians in Canada, 2020, Historical Data." Data set. https://secure.cihi.ca/estore/productSeries.htm?pc=PCC34.

CUPE (Canadian Union of Public Employees). 2017. "WRHA Restructuring Will Result in Significant Cuts to Front-Line Care." 13 September. https://cupe.ca/wrha-restructuring-will-result-significant-cuts-front-line-care.

Da Silva, Danielle. 2023. "Private Nursing Costs Manitoba $60M." *Winnipeg Free Press*, 6 July. https://www.winnipegfreepress.com/breakingnews/2023/07/06/private-nursing-costs-manitoba-60m.

Dacey, Elisha. 2020. "Long List of Front-Line Workers to Receive Top-Up Cheques in Manitoba." Global News, 2 June. https://globalnews.ca/news/7015650/pallister-to-announce-details-of-120-m-wage-top-up-for-manitobas-essential-workers/.

Government of Manitoba. 2022. "2022/2023 Committee of Supply—Manitoba Health." 31 August. https://gov.mb.ca/asset_library/en/proactive/briefings/2022/health-cos-binder-2022-redacted.pdf.

Greenslade, Brittany. 2023. "Manitoba Nurses Quitting amidst Mandated Overtime, High Vacancy Rates, No Home-Life Balance." CBC Manitoba. 15 February. https://www.cbc.ca/news/canada/manitoba/manitoba-nurses-overtime-vacancy-rates-1.6747768.

Harewood, Keesha. 2022. "Manitoba Nurses Union Sounds Alarm over Nursing Position Shortage." Global News, 27 May. https://globalnews.ca/news/8875632/manitoba-nurses-union-nursing-position-shortage/.

Hatherly, Dana. 2019. "CUPE Wins Largest Share in Voting among Manitoba Health-Care Workers." CBC Manitoba, 22 August. https://www.cbc.ca/news/canada/manitoba/manitoba-health-care-workers-union-vote-1.5256771.

Hirschfield, Kevin. 2022. "ER Closures Expected as Doctors Concerned over Rural and Northern Manitoba Health Care." Global News, 22 June. https://globalnews.ca/news/8946949/er-closures-expected-as-doctors-concerned-over-rural-and-northern-manitoba-health-care/.

Lambert, Steve. 2022. "Unions Lose Bid to Appeal Manitoba's Wage-Freeze Law to Supreme Court." CBC Manitoba, 27 October. https://www.cbc.ca/news/canada/manitoba/manitoba-wage-freeze-law-appeal-supreme-court-1.6631468.

Manitoba Health Coalition. 2022. "MB Health Care Cuts & Changes." https://www.mbhealthcoalition.ca/timeline.

———. 2023. "Manitoba Health Coalition Statement in Response to Nursing Initiatives." 17 February. https://www.mbhealthcoalition.ca/manitoba_health_coalition_statement_in_response_to_nursing_initiatives.

Piché, Gabrielle. 2023. "At-Home Sleep Tests to Tackle Backlog." *Winnipeg Free Press*, 23 January. https://www.winnipegfreepress.com/breakingnews/2023/01/23/at-home-sleep-tests-to-tackle-backlog.

Roberts, Dan. 2023. "Why Is the Province Picking Private Care?" *Winnipeg Free Press*, 11 July. https://www.winnipegfreepress.com/opinion/analysis/2023/07/11/why-is-the-province-picking-private-care.

Statistics Canada. 2022a. "Annual Population Estimates on July 1st, by Age and Sex (Table 17-10-0005-01)." Data set. 28 September. https://www150.statcan.gc.ca/t1/tbl1/en/tv.action?pid=1710000501.

———. 2022b. "Job Vacancies, Payroll Employees, Job Vacancy Rate, and Average Offered Hourly Wage by Industry Sub-sector, Quarterly, Unadjusted for Seasonality (Table 14-10-0326-02)." Data set. 20 September. https://www150.statcan.gc.ca/t1/tbl1/en/tv.action?pid=1410032601.

Chapter 7

ENVIRONMENT AND NATURAL RESOURCES

Mark Hudson

Manitobans, like much of the rest of the world, are increasingly concerned with the state of the planet—including our own little corner of it. Global concerns like biodiversity decline and climate change are intertwined with local concerns about the water, air, and soil upon which we all depend. This chapter rolls together two existing government departments that are charged with overseeing the relationship between Manitobans and their natural environment. In 2022, the two relevant departments were Environment, Climate and Parks (ECP)[1] and Natural Resources and Northern Development (NRND). The people and offices responsible for environmental protection and approvals, resource management, parks, and climate have been subjected to disruptive, time-gobbling departmental and regional restructuring every couple of years since 2016. We have tracked these expenditures by function,[2] to provide assessments of whether and how austerity has affected the public sector's capacity to do everything from safeguarding our water, to remediating abandoned mine sites, to reducing our greenhouse gas emissions, to sustainably developing our forestry resources. This chapter also explores the experience of Manitoba-based environmental nongovernmental organizations (ENGOs), which play a crucial role in environmental monitoring, policy development, and public education in the province. Many of these have been impacted by provincial austerity since 2016. The major elements of resource development and environmental protection delivered by our public service are in Table 7.1. While we have opted to group these under a broad "environment" heading, these functions can sometimes be at odds

Table 7.1. Environment and resources: Departments, units, and allocations.

DEPARTMENT	UNIT	MAJOR ALLOCATIONS
Environment, Climate, and Parks	Parks and Trails	Parks
	Finances and Shared Services	Legislation, policy, coordination
	Environmental Stewardship	Compliance and enforcement; approvals, remediation
	Climate and Green Plan Implementation	Climate and green plan implementation; energy policy
	Water Stewardship	Water science and watershed management; drainage and water rights licensing; Office of Drinking Water; water stewardship initiatives
Natural Resources and Northern Development	Stewardship and Resource Development	Geological survey; mining, oil, and gas; forestry and peatlands; lands and planning; business development
	Resource Management and Protection	Fish and wildlife; Conservation Officer Program
	Manitoba Wildfire Services	Wildfire services; wildfire suppression

with one another. We roll them together because the public sector is a key player in environmental transformation, both in terms of environmental regulation, protection, or preservation, or in terms of resource extraction.

While programs and schemes to monetize, marketize, and privatize environmental sustainability proliferated globally starting in the 1980s, we rely heavily on the public sector to act in the public interest by regulating the impacts of industry, extraction, and agriculture on our lands, water, and air. Government is charged with attempting to facilitate the sustainable use of natural resources in the province, which requires monitoring, assessing, and providing parameters for resource development. We are also increasingly aware of the crucial role that government will have to play in the transition away from fossil-dependent industry, transportation, energy, and infrastructure. Governments around the world, including our own, have fallen short on all of these objectives for decades, and are failing now as climate targets are passed by almost as fast as they can be declared. Comparing across provinces on two major environmental indicators—conserved terrestrial area and greenhouse gas emissions—Manitoba's performance is middling. Manitoba is dead centre of the pack with 11 percent of its territory reported as "protected." That compares with a high of 19.6 percent in British Columbia to a low of 4.8 percent in Prince Edward Island (Government of Canada 2022). Manitoba currently has a single staff person working on protected areas. We perform considerably worse on greenhouse gas emissions, especially in terms of the trendline. Among the provinces, only Manitoba and Alberta increased their overall greenhouse gas emissions between 2005 and 2021 (Government of Canada 2023).

The current situation calls for an investment in our public capacities to monitor and regulate environmental impacts, reduce our greenhouse gas emissions, support conservation measures, and to provide Manitobans with access to nature-based recreation and education through parks. So, what has been happening?

Staffing

The most alarming data on this front are the staffing trends. We have lost almost a third (27.1 percent) of staff for the environment, conservation, and resource functions since fiscal year 2015/16. In 2018/19, staffing authorizations were slashed by 20 percent. Tracking staffing numbers year-over-year for specific functions is extremely difficult due to the very high rate of departmental restructuring and reorganization. However, looking at individual budget lines, some trends appear to emerge. The largest single segment of the ECP department's staffing is in Parks, and it accounts for the lion's share of the staff losses. From 249 full-time equivalent (FTE) positions in 2015/16, the Parks staff was reduced to a skeleton crew of 82.5 in 2018/19. Increases since then have raised the complement, but only to 127 in 2021/22.[3] Manitobans who camp, hike, and paddle in Manitoba's parks will not be surprised by these numbers, and it occurs in the midst of large increases in the use of parks. It remains to be seen how much of this was a product of travel limits and uncertainties during the pandemic, but in 2021, the first day of campground booking saw 11,000 reservations by 11 a.m., compared to 6,150 booked on the entire first day of booking the previous year (CBC 2021). The number of park users (not just campers) tripled during the pandemic, putting a huge strain on the limited campground staff to keep facilities clean and safe. Seasonal staff like campground attendants are getting harder and harder to recruit—especially for more remote areas—because of the high demands on staff and very low wages.

While Parks has the largest staff footprint in ECP, the crucial work of smaller parts of government has also been compromised due to staffing declines—and these may be of more serious concern to Manitobans. In 2020, the auditor general of Manitoba (AGM) produced a report on the provincial drinking water licensing and monitoring system. The Drinking Water Safety Act specifies that any water supplier must be licensed by the Office of Drinking Water, to be sure that suppliers are testing water and maintaining water quality standards. Among a long list of disturbing inadequacies, the AGM showed a huge rise in the number of licensed water systems in the province, from 662 in 2013/14 to 1,104 in 2018/19—a 53 percent increase. Meanwhile, total staffing had actually declined from thirteen to twelve over the period. Given the enormous increase in the number of systems to be licensed, caseloads per officer doubled. The AGM further found that a significant number of licensed water systems were operating without a certified operator, that there were high levels of noncompliance with standards in water systems operated by Indigenous and Northern Affairs, that public complaints were not tracked or documented, that enforcement actions were rare, and that the inspection process was insufficient and follow-up was spotty (AGM 2020).

Other staffing reductions in the context of increased requirements have taken place in Climate and Green Plan implementation, from a high of twenty-six FTEs in 2020/21 to twenty-three in 2021/22;[4] Environmental Programs and Remediation, down from twenty-three FTEs in 2017/18[5] to fifteen in 2021/22; and Environmental Approvals, down by two FTEs from 2015/16.

While it is not always easy to accurately pinpoint where there are reductions and where there are reallocations, persistent vacancies and staffing shortages show up not only in our aggregate numbers but throughout our survey responses, and sometimes even in the media. For example, the Conservation Officer Service (COS), now administered under NRND but previously under Sustainable Development, is now suffering an inability to recruit due to low wages. Twenty percent of the 102 positions remaining after reductions were vacant as of 2023, prompting a belated increase in the starting wage and reducing the qualifications for entry into the service. The Manitoba Government and General Employees' Union (MGEU) reported burnout for remaining officers (Da Silva 2023). This assessment is affirmed in the comments from our survey respondents, not just in the COS but across the departments.

Spending

A casual glance at inflation-adjusted expenditures for the functions currently undertaken by the two departments shows an increase from $195.1 million in 2015/16 to $230.3 million in 2021/22—an 18 percent increase. On a per capita basis, that took spending from $151 to $165 per Manitoban: a 9.6 percent increase. So why isn't this reflected in staffing levels, which, as we have seen, have fallen off a pretty big cliff?

Large, sporadic expenditure spikes dominate the pattern for ECP—particularly in 2018/19 ($115.6 million) and 2020/21 ($96 million). Many of these are accounted for by one-time investments in endowments and other funds, as the province has moved from directly funding environmental and conservation measures to doing so through the capitalization of trusts and endowments administered by private or arm's length organizations. The spikes also result from pass-throughs from other levels of government. This is not to say that some of those expenses are not worthwhile. For example, in the Climate and Green Plan Implementation office, there have been two significant increases in allocations. In 2018/19, the whopping increase from $1 million to $53 million is due to an allocation to the Growing Outcomes in Watersheds (GROW) funds. GROW funds provide payments to agricultural landowners for conservation, carbon sequestration, or watershed enhancement land modifications and management, following the logic that farmlands can provide ecological goods and services such as enhanced water quality and resilience to flooding. These programs need to be watched carefully, and a full assessment is beyond what can be done here. Sometimes, these programs can act as subsidies to municipalities and farmers with little by way of additional ecological benefit (Brears 2022; Dempsey and Robertson 2012). Another big, one-time increase in the budget came through a one-time allocation to Parks in 2020/21 to capitalize the Provincial Parks Endowment Funds. These funds supported just over $1 million in parks infrastructure and service improvements in 2022.

The increase in 2021/22 from $5.6 million to $11 million is due to a pass-through of federal dollars under the Low Carbon Economy Fund through Efficiency Manitoba and has (according to the public accounts) "no impact on Manitoba's bottom line."

A final spike is the very large increase in the allocation for Environmental Remediation and Programs, from $1 million in 2019/20 to $36 million in 2021/22. This results from the transfer of responsibility for orphaned and abandoned mine sites from Mining to ECP in 2020/21 and a large increase in the liability for those sites in 2021/22. These are sites where the original private developer either cannot be found or is unable or unwilling to carry out proper closure and remediation. In other words, this is a public subsidy to past private mine operators, in which the risks to environmental and human health have been socialized.

Spending on the functions and services currently falling under the department of NRND shows a small, inflation-adjusted drop from $105 million in 2015/16 to just over $103 million in 2021/22. This, however, masks a single-year increase in spending in 2019/20, which saw expenditure more than double from $93 million to $215 million before dropping again in the following year to $105 million (inflation adjusted). Almost half of the increase ($49 million) arose from contributions to the Fish and Wildlife Enhancement fund, the Oak Hammock Marsh Interpretive Centre, and the Fort Whyte Endowment; buybacks of Lake Manitoba Fisheries Licences; and the creation of a Conservation Trust endowment administered by the Manitoba Habitat Heritage Corporation. Another $7.5 million paid for improvements to the International Peace Gardens. A further $50 million is accounted for by the establishment of the Wetlands GROW Trust in 2019/20.

Privatization and Contracting Out

One-third of survey respondents said that work in their area had been privatized or contracted out. Activities mentioned ranged from garbage collection, e-licensing for park permits and forestry licences, infrastructure construction, air monitoring stations, seedling production, field surveys, Dutch elm disease removal, water sample lab analysis, and snow removal. The highest profile item within this outsourcing wave was the contract with Dallas-based Aspira to issue campground permits and hunting and angling licences. In addition to costing users an additional service fee, the service cost the province in the ballpark of half a million dollars per year, all flowing south of the border (CBC 2022). Also getting some attention was the closure of Pineland Nursery, which provided seedlings for reforestation (CBC 2018). We now purchase those trees from Saskatchewan and Alberta. The province's less visible forms of privatization and contracting out may be even more troubling. For example, one environmental officer reported that environmental audits once conducted by the province were now being self-conducted by industry. A front-line worker (not in Parks) commented that "privatization of services without consulting those directly involved caused more work for us in the end, because the private entity is delivering a substandard product and our clients are unsatisfied and complaining, which means we still have to satisfy them despite the private company being involved." In addition, the province's wildland fire aerial suppression services were contracted out in 2018 for a ten-year period to Babcock, a UK-based multinational defence, aerospace, and nuclear engineering services corporation. Former workers at Manitoba Government Air Services spoke at length in our survey about the excellence and efficiency of the formerly public air service, and the serious pains and frustrations during the transition to a privatized, for-profit service. Acknowledging that things have stabilized since what respondents described as a problem-riddled transition, one worker said, "As a taxpayer, the dissolution of the air service was unwarranted and from the beginning a more expensive avenue to take the public down." Meanwhile, at the level of decision making and planning, one respondent claimed that "internal decisions on sensitive topics are being farmed out to consultants. Previous levels of knowledge and capacity are greatly diminished."

Workers' Experiences of Austerity

The workers in this study fight wildland fires, build and maintain park infrastructure, monitor our water quality, patrol our parks, do environmental science, develop and implement conservation programs, manage the development of provincial natural resources, inspect and enforce regulations on waste disposal, develop and deliver public environmental programming and education, and do a host of other publicly valuable work.

Eighty-six percent of respondents reported that their work had been greatly or moderately impacted by austerity measures. The most common impact reported (54 percent) was an increase or intensification of workload—reflective of the decline in staffing, high rate of vacancy, and high turnover in some positions—and a corresponding decline in the province's capacity to protect our health and environment, maintain parks, and attempt to engage in sustainable resource development. This is true for both public sector workers and for those working in the nonprofit sector.

Nonprofits

Environmental nonprofits do extremely important work such as waste reduction, habitat conservation, or tree planting through public education, youth programs, environmental advocacy, and the development and analysis of environmental policy. Up until 2018, the province provided stable funding for some of these groups, which ENGOs used to leverage additional funds from foundations and granting agencies. The funding landscape for ENGOs has changed significantly since then, with less money coming directly from government, and more coming out of third-party-managed trust funds, often housed with the Winnipeg Foundation (where the workers are not unionized). For example, the Manitoba

Table 7.2. Survey respondents' occupations and areas of employment.

EMPLOYER		RESPONDENTS (83)
Nonprofit environmental nongovernmental organization (ENGO)		11
Province of Manitoba		
Environment, Climate and Parks	40	72
Natural Resources and Northern Development	32	

OCCUPATION	RESPONDENTS (83)
Front-line worker	39
Supervisor/manager	27
Senior manager	3
Other	14

Habitat Heritage Corporation, a Crown corporation, was privatized in 2021 and is now a nonprofit that administers the Conservation Trust Fund. The program to fund mitigation of lead in drinking water in schools and childcare centres is administered through an industry body, the Manitoba Environmental Industries Association. There are important implications here for democratic oversight and responsibility. As the deputy minister of finance stated in 2022, the goal of arranging funding through the Winnipeg Foundation to the tune of $388 million in funds (roughly generating, at 5 percent interest, $19 million annually) was "depoliticizing the decisions" (The Legislative Assembly of Manitoba 2022).

Significant sums of public money are now allocated by staff and appointed members of nonprofit boards, rather than by elected representatives and the public servants directly accountable to them.

The loss of core funding from the province created a huge problem of insecurity and instability among ENGOs. Of particular concern is that ENGO staff, rather than delivering their programs and getting stuck in on projects, are spending more and more of their time "cobbling together multiple smaller grants . . . preparing proposals, and reporting on successful applications." In addition, a major challenge for ENGOs is convincing any funder to be "first to the table." Provincial funding once played that role, allowing organizations to attract more private funding. New limitations on provincial funding provide additional obstacles, such as a focus on new projects (when ongoing projects, in order to be successful, still require funding). The increased workload required to simply maintain funding, along with the limits on the kinds of work that could be undertaken, has forced people out of the field: "Ultimately, I quit my job . . . and left the workforce completely, in large part as a result of austerity measures. The amount of labour that I was required to put in to simply maintain my position by seeking grants was unsustainable, and the strain on everybody in my NGO was palpable."

Public Sector Workers

Within the public sector proper, the survey responses tell a tale of failing infrastructure, reduced capacity to do crucial environmental monitoring and enforcement, outsourcing to private firms and consultants, and bruising, unsustainable workloads for remaining staff. One Parks worker painted a picture that would be familiar to most users: "We have stopped with building maintenance almost entirely. We stopped regular maintenance on most trails. New buildings and projects and equipment are planned but rarely happen and some are never finished. Others were never started. The quality of the finished projects is low grade. Sometimes with horrendous mistakes."

Eighty-one percent of participants responded that the austerity measures implemented in their area of work and related changes led to a reduction in the quality of service to stakeholders or users of the service. There were exceptions, though, where the stakeholder was a polluting industry. One of the two responses stating that quality of service to stakeholders had improved contextualized this claim by explaining that because business sees environmental regulation as burdensome red tape, less oversight and monitoring is welcome news to regulated industries. Site inspections and monitoring ranged between 135 and 165 annually from 2016/17 through 2019/20, falling to just 24 in 2020/21 and rising only slightly to 46 in 2021/22.

Staffing reductions, vacancies, and position eliminations left remaining workers with unmanageable workloads. The provincial wage freeze from 2016 resulted in increased staff turnover and high position vacancy rates, upping the workload burden. Respondents gave specific instances of positions being eliminated or remaining vacant over long periods, while the overall workload for remaining staff increased. One worker reported that, torn between short staffing and a duty to provide direct service to the public, they were regularly working sixty-hour weeks. A front-line equipment operator working for ECP reported that since 2019, they had been doing the job of "at least 2 other people who have left." Similarly, 58 percent of our respondents reported that they are asked to provide the same or increased service with fewer resources. Austerity-driven wages and work conditions also mean it is hard to recruit people with the right skills and training for jobs, putting additional strains on staff and managers, and hamstringing public capacities for environmental protection.

These effects of austerity are highly visible in workers' assessments of their workplaces, which paint a bleak picture of working conditions and morale. "More employees [are] going on stress leave, leaving fewer workers with increased workload, adversely affecting mental health of [those] remaining," stated one respondent. "Everyone is drowning and trying to grab for something to hold onto." Staff shortages, high position vacancy rates, increased numbers of tasks assigned to workers, and other resource shortages are reported to be widespread, as shown in Figure 7.1. With more casual and contract staff, as opposed to long-term, permanent staff, workers expressed a sense of isolation, and felt unsupported, unequipped, and constantly called on to take on more. As one worker put it, "Since the implementation of austerity there has been a noticeable reduction (possibly elimination) of camaraderie and support within the work environment. I have been isolated and unsupported, making my day-to-day tasks incredibly challenging to complete. This has been incredibly demoralizing."

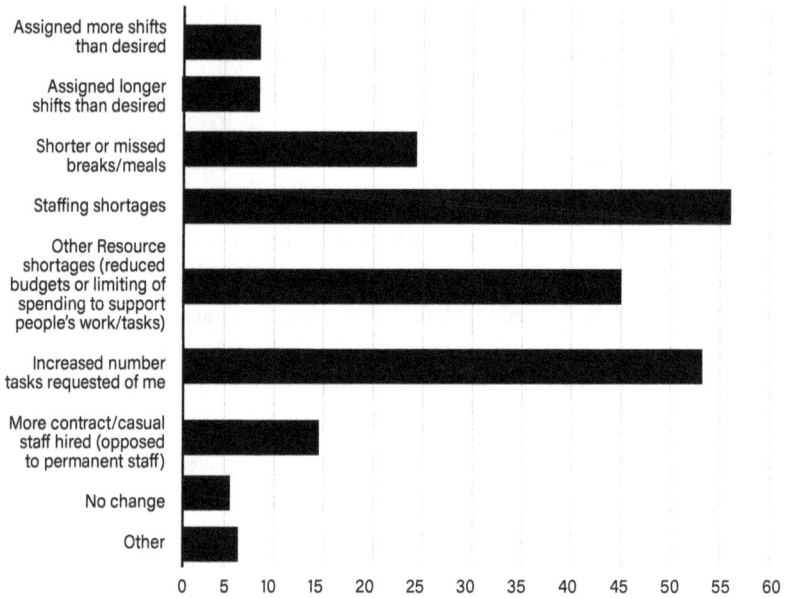

Figure 7.1. Percentage of respondents reporting changes to work scheduling.

Reduced Service, Safety, and Job Satisfaction Pay for Fictitious Savings

The consequences of austerity, in the eyes of public sector workers, are a toxic cocktail of worsened jobs, deteriorating public safety and service, declining environmental protection, and at best dubious savings. Sixty-two percent of our respondents perceive that expenditure cuts and restraints have, in their areas, worsened public safety. In addition to the negative effects mentioned above on the monitoring of pollution and drinking water, respondents cited limited resources to respond to bear encounters or night-hunting incidents, and inadequate or nonexistent oversight of contracted work as safety issues. Ninety-one percent reported worse working conditions and job satisfaction, likely also linked to the 90 percent who reported worsened worker recruitment and retention.

Meanwhile, 56 percent believe that the austerity measures, even in the immediate or short term, were either costing their own unit more money, or transferring costs to other units. That figure grows to 66 percent when considered over the long term. "Everything the [Progressive Conservatives] have done in the parks has increased costs now, and in the future," said one employee, citing new, exorbitant fees for GPS vehicle monitoring and garbage collection paid to private firms. Cuts to nonprofits also mean that other parts of the public service have increased costs. For example, whereas stable program funding for one ENGO meant that they could provide free or very low-cost programming in schools, now they have to charge schools or participants higher fees to cover costs. Overall, a full 78 percent of respondents believe the public is now getting less value for its money.

There is a consistent perception that workers—especially front-liners—have not been consulted or heard in the effort to trim budgets. A top-down approach has left workers frustrated, unable to contribute to finding efficiencies, and sometimes hamstrung in their work as a result of poorly conceived spending and cuts. Just under one-quarter of respondents strongly or somewhat agreed that they had been given meaningful opportunities to contribute ideas to save money in their area. Forty-two percent strongly or somewhat disagreed. When asked if their experience, expertise, and opinions were reflected in the actual expenditure reductions, only 5 percent somewhat agreed, and nobody strongly agreed. Thirteen percent of respondents agreed somewhat or strongly that the austerity measures reflected the experience, expertise, and opinions of front-line workers. Several workers elaborated on their frustrations with the lack of consultation, the lack of understanding on the part of senior management of the actual work being done, or missed opportunities for painless or less painful expenditure reductions. ENGO respondents reported that the sudden cut to their core funding was not signalled in advance; they were not warned or consulted, and it left them scrambling. One public servant replied that "no one asked any front-line workers for ideas to reduce spending or asked what areas might be less painful to lose vacant positions. Didn't have to agree, but no one asked."

Conclusion

In comments about who bears the costs of austerity, while many respondents spoke about themselves, their fellow workers, and the Manitoba public, others referenced the often invisible costs to Manitoba's natural environment. This reflects that many of these workers entered into and remain in public service not only for a paycheque but due to a respect and deep concern for our environment. The sense of mission for workers who interact directly with people, landscapes, and ecosystems is central to their morale and job quality. When austerity undermines their ability to protect and enhance the environment, and to provide an enriching experience to the public, they feel it deeply. "Forest sustainability will suffer," said one respondent. "Manitoba wildlife is paying the price," reported another. Others noted that the future costs of climate change to both humans and nonhumans, as we penny-pinch on environmental and climate-related programming and education, will dwarf any current savings. Budget savings, reported one worker, "come at a huge cost to Manitoba's natural resources." The quality of our water was another concern: "Lake Winnipeg, our beaches, and our wells are at risk," said one respondent. "Our lakes and rivers suffer," said another.

The urgency with which every jurisdiction and level of government must act to address ecological crises is widely recognized. Normally staid and conservative government, industry, and intergovernmental bodies are calling for deep, rapid investment in decarbonization, and to halt the collapse of biodiversity. This requires investment in monitoring, environmental regulation and enforcement, expansion of protected areas, conservation measures for habitat, flood mitigation, and carbon sequestration, and an all-of-government approach to greenhouse gas reductions. The austerity measures put in place since 2016 have, in the eyes of the public service workers trying to do the necessary work, critically undercut our capacity to provide Manitobans access to sustainably stewarded resources for recreation and development, to live up to our climate obligations and prepare for the effects of climate change, and to safeguard our soil, air, and waters.

Notes

1. In January 2023, Environment, Climate and Parks became Environment and Climate; Parks was reshuffled into Natural Resources and Northern Development.

2. For details on data sources used for provincial expenditures, employee staffing numbers, and full-time equivalent (FTE) positions in this chapter, see Preface.

3. Figures are from the Parks and Protected Spaces appropriation for all years except 2021/22; 2021/22 is from the Parks and Trails appropriation.

4. Staffing for climate change and air quality was also inadequate in 2015/16, at twelve FTEs. In 2018/19 the government passed its Manitoba Climate and Green Plan, under pressure from the federal government's Greenhouse Gas Pollution Pricing Act, adopted in 2018.

5. The relevant comparator budget line for 2017/18 is Sustainable and Green Initiatives.

References

Auditor General of Manitoba (AGM). 2020. "Provincial Oversight of Drinking Water Safety." September. Winnipeg: Office of the Auditor General of Manitoba. https://www.oag.mb.ca/_files/ugd/b32b68_92a19c1b7a3040569d6d64fa131efc49.pdf.

Brears, Robert C. 2022. "Payments for Ecosystem Services Financing Nature-Based Solutions." In Robert C. Brears, *Financing Nature-Based Solutions*. Palgrave Studies in Impact Finance. Cham, Switzerland: Palgrave Macmillan Cham. https://doi.org/10.1007/978-3-030-93325-8_7.

Da Silva, Danielle. 2023. "20 Percent Job Vacancy at Conservation Officer Service Prompts Wage Increase." *Winnipeg Free Press*, 14 March. https://www.winnipegfreepress.com/breakingnews/2023/03/14/20-job-vacancy-at-conservation-officer-service-prompts-wage-boost.

Dempsey, Jessica, and Morgan Robertson. 2012. "Ecosystem Services: Tensions, Impurities, and Points of Engagement within Neoliberalism." *Progress in Human Geography* 36 (6): 578–779.

Froese, Ian. 2022. "Manitoba Has Paid $1M in E-licensing Fees to U.S. Company Contracted to Sell Park Passes Online." CBC Manitoba, 21 April. https://www.cbc.ca/news/canada/manitoba/manitoba-park-fees-online-service-1.6426963.

Geary, Aidan. 2018. "Manitoba Closing, Selling Provincially Run Tree Nursery." CBC Manitoba, 3 May. https://www.cbc.ca/news/canada/manitoba/manitoba-pineland-forest-nursery-closes-1.4647742.

Government of Canada. 2022. "Canadian Protected and Conserved Areas Database." https://www.canada.ca/en/environment-climate-change/services/national-wildlife-areas/protected-conserved-areas-database.html.

———. 2023. "Greenhouse Gas Emissions." https://www.canada.ca/en/environment-climate-change/services/environmental-indicators/greenhouse-gas-emissions.html.

Hoye, Bryce. 2021. "Manitoba Campsite Reservations Surge on Opening Day amid Glitches, Hours-Long Waits." CBC Manitoba, 5 April. https://www.cbc.ca/news/canada/manitoba/manitoba-parks-campground-reservations-opening-day-1.5975797.

The Legislative Assembly of Manitoba. 2022. *Standing Committee on Public Accounts*, 31 May. https://www.gov.mb.ca/legislature/hansard/42nd_4th/pa_05/pa_05.html.

Chapter 8

SUPPORTING AND PROMOTING SAFE AND JUST COMMUNITIES?

Elizabeth Comack and Amelia Curran

Manitoba Justice's mission is "to support and promote safe and just communities for all Manitobans." The values of the department include: promoting a respectful work environment and recognizing people's commitment, performance, and achievements; valuing personal integrity, leadership, responsibility, participation, and teamwork; and encouraging outstanding client and community service, initiative, and innovation (Manitoba Justice 2021, 2). To achieve its mission, Justice's operating expenditure in 2020/21 was $695.7 million (82). Despite its large and increasing budget, austerity measures have been felt in Manitoba Justice. When asked whether their work has been impacted by the government's austerity measures aimed at reducing expenditures and balancing the budget, 95 percent (172 of 182) of Justice respondents surveyed answered in the affirmative.

What austerity measures have been implemented in Justice, and how have those measures impacted front-line workers and those they serve? Given the size of the department, we focus on three areas—Prosecution Service, Community Corrections, and Custody Corrections—with a view to understanding the measures undertaken by the Progressive Conservative (PC) government during its tenure and their import for supporting and promoting "safe and just communities for all Manitobans."

The KPMG Fiscal Performance Review

When the PC government came to power in April 2016, one issue it inherited was the province's high incarceration rates. In October 2015, 2,448 adults were being held in custody, representing 123 percent of the official capacity of the province's seven detention facilities. Two-thirds of those incarcerated were being held on remand—they had not been found guilty of an offence and were awaiting their day in court. Also concerning, 70 percent were Indigenous, even though Indigenous peoples represented only 15 percent of the total Manitoba population. Incarceration is expensive. In 2015, $233 million had been allocated for correctional services, an increase of 124 percent from 2005 (Marcoux and Barghout 2015).

Intent on reducing government spending, the PCs commissioned KPMG to produce a fiscal performance review. Released in September 2016, the report focused on identifying "cost improvement opportunities." "Justice System Reform" was identified as one area for cutting costs (KPMG 2016, 5–6). Several actions were recommended:

- Develop options for alternative justice programs for more minor offences and early triage of cases to remove minor/administrative cases out of the formal system.
- Consider ways (e.g., Lean process review) to encourage and facilitate a more holistic "sector" discussion and problem-solving to aid reform and ease cost pressure; the judiciary, police and legal aid contribute to pressures and should be part of the solutions.
- Consider changes to policy and procedures to reduce the number of people and length of stay in remand custody.
- Set targets for charge categories—monitor, assess, and adjust.
- Review provincial policing agreements and opportunities to enhance efficiencies and value for money (KPMG 2016, 185).

In the ensuing years, the PCs wholeheartedly embraced the KPMG review, as Manitoba Justice began implementing reforms to "bend the cost curve" (KPMG 2016, 72).

Manitoba Prosecution Service

"Burnout is happening. There will be a crisis in the courts very soon if nothing is done."

Prosecution Service is responsible for prosecuting criminal and provincial offences and conducting inquests. Crown attorneys prosecute cases under provincial statutes, the Criminal Code, and the Youth Criminal Justice Act. They also provide advice to police on charges, investigations, and procedures (Manitoba Justice 2021, 26–27).

Several initiatives were undertaken in Prosecution Service to create a "leaner" criminal justice process. One strategy had been initiated by the New Democratic Party (NDP) government. Started in 2015, the Intensive Case Assessment Process (ICAP) involves an initial assessment of cases as soon as charges are laid, identifying less serious matters that can be resolved more quickly and freeing up resources for more serious criminal matters. In 2017/18, ICAP was expanded in an effort to increase the number of cases referred to diversion programs (Manitoba Justice 2018a, 16). The KPMG report pointed to the volume of minor cases adjudicated by the courts. To address that issue, the Pre-Plea Triage Program was introduced in 2016 to reduce the number of traffic ticket matters scheduled for dispute hearings (Manitoba Justice 2021, 53). Also, in keeping with KPMGs recommendation to conduct a "Lean process review," a methodology designed to streamline processes and minimize costs, the Integrated Case Management Project (ICMP) was implemented in 2018/19 to reduce reliance on paper by providing online access to court records (Manitoba Justice 2019a, 43).

Another issue was the high percentage of people being remanded into custody. This issue had been raised in the 2014 auditor general's report on the management of adult offenders (OAGM 2014), but high remand numbers persisted. In 2016/17, 68 percent of the custody population was there on remand, one of the highest percentages among the provinces (Malakieh 2018). KPMG recommended developing strategies to reduce the number of people and length of stay in remand custody. Several moves were taken. In 2018, the Weekend Court Pilot Project in Winnipeg aimed to reduce the number of people held in remand over the weekend (Manitoba Justice 2019a, 43). In 2020, it was extended to Thompson, and an Evening Bail Program and Overnight Bail Program were implemented (Manitoba Justice 2020, 17).

Cost savings were also realized by keeping Prosecution Service staffing at minimal levels. According to Manitoba Justice annual reports, vacancies and underfilled positions saved $2.4 million, $2.5 million, and $2.8 million in Prosecution Service staffing costs in 2016/17, 2017/18, and 2018/19, respectively (Manitoba Justice 2017, 18; 2018a, 18; 2019a, 21). Nevertheless, those savings came at the expense of quality services. One worker commented, "Austerity has impacted us to such a significant extent that we are barely meeting our professional obligations as lawyers and are failing victims, families, and witnesses on a daily basis because we do not have the resources to provide adequate services."

Survey respondents said the vacancies occurred because of low salaries paid to Crown attorneys. One commented, "We are losing experienced Crowns to the private sector and other jurisdictions, where they are appropriately compensated. . . . As a result, this is negatively impacting the wellness, workload, and mental health of the remaining complement of Crown Attorneys. Morale at the Crown's Office is at an all-time low." Several respondents deemed the Crown's office to be "in crisis."

Community Corrections

"Increasing funding for access to basic needs like housing for clients would significantly impact recidivism rates and increase public safety overall."

Community Corrections provides services for individuals involved with the criminal justice system. In addition to preparing court reports, Probation Services supervises adult and youth offenders in the community (Manitoba Justice 2020, 35). The division also funds community agencies to carry out its programs.

Shifts were evident in the division once the PCs came to power. In 2017, the Elizabeth Fry Society (EFS) and John Howard Society (JHS) budgets were cut by 20 percent. EFS funding was cut by $50,000, while the JHS residential Bail Supervision and Support Program was eliminated, saving $166,000 (Malone 2017). The government also cancelled funding for Restorative Resolutions, a program that had received national attention for its success in reducing recidivism. Declining referrals and an intention to reallocate staff and resources were cited as reasons (Annable 2017).

In December 2017, the Responsible Reintegration Initiative (RRI) was announced. RRI involves releasing eligible offenders into the community to serve the remainder of their sentence. Probation officers were to meet regularly with clients, connecting them with housing, education, and jobs, and taking on additional responsibilities such as completing Employment and Income Assistance (EIA) intakes (CBC News 2017a).

Cost savings in Community Corrections were realized in a number of ways. In 2017/18, over $2 million was saved due to "vacant and under filled positions." Another $277,000 was left unspent due to "operational efficiencies and expenditure management," while $355,000 was reduced for programs and external agencies (Manitoba Justice 2018, 37). The cuts continued in 2018/19, with $4.5 million in savings due to vacant or under-filled positions, $445,000 due to "operational efficiencies and expenditure management," and $738,000 savings in community programs (Manitoba Justice 2019, 35). Similar patterns are found in the ensuing three years.

As one worker noted, "Reducing Probation Officers (or not filling vacant positions) reduces public safety and puts additional strain on police, healthcare, EIA, etc." Another remarked, "The cuts to community resources, social services, and healthcare have severely impacted the population I work with. There are less resources for individuals to access, and additional barriers placed on access to resources that are available."

Restorative Justice

"Imagine if we could help people instead of warehousing them."

Restorative justice (RJ) was a key plank in the PCs' 2018 Criminal Justice System Modernization Strategy. The strategy was founded on four objectives:

- Reduce crime, improve community safety, and reduce the number of individuals coming into conflict with the law and the criminal justice system.
- Deal with each case in a manner appropriate to the seriousness of the offence and circumstances of the offender.

- More effectively use RJ options to improve public safety, reduce delays in the court system, and ultimately reduce reliance on incarceration, especially in the case of Indigenous offenders.
- Reintegrate offenders from custody to the community with essential supports to prevent further offences and future contact with the criminal justice system (Manitoba Justice 2018b, 2).

RJ has become popular in criminal justice circles as an alternative to traditional practices. In contrast to incarceration, RJ advocates argue that a more effective response to crime involves making offenders aware of the harm they have caused and providing the supports necessary to repair that harm. RJ also involves community-based justice, as community members (including victims) collectively decide on appropriate measures (Johnstone 2002).

RJ has potential to transform how we respond to social harms. As it gained in popularity, however, RJ has become a "catch-all" phrase used to refer to a wide variety of practices for settling a legal matter (Randall 2013). Given its adaptability, RJ is easily diluted. This adaptability "can lend to its application within a very conservative politics" by "holding offenders accountable for crimes that are perceived to be solely the result of their individual choice," thereby "individualizing criminal activity and victimization with little regard for the structural conditions that make crime possible" (Woolford and Nelund 2019, 195).

In introducing the Modernization Strategy, then justice minister Heather Stefanson quoted from the 2017 Speech from the Throne: "Our government is committed to being tough on crime but also tough on what causes crime" (Manitoba Justice 2018b, 1). Yet "no promise was made to add the anti-poverty and decolonizing work that would be necessary for a transformative restorative justice to address the roots of crime and not just its symptoms" (Woolford and Nelund 2019, 198).

One appeal of RJ is the potential to reduce government spending, a factor acknowledged in the Modernization Strategy (Manitoba Justice 2018b, 5). Without addressing structural conditions, however, RJ "supplements and supports the dominant [criminal justice system], playing no more than a marginal role within this system by offering a more cost-effective approach for dealing with the small stuff" (Woolford and Nelund 2019, 197). As one front-line worker commented, "The current government wants to let offenders out of custody as it is cheaper to supervise them as opposed to pay for them to stay in jail. But they don't have the necessary resources in place to support them, EIA, housing, addictions, etc."

RJ was advanced by the previous NDP government in its Restorative Justice Act of 2014. A key component of the act was the establishment of a Restorative Justice Advisory Council (RJAC) comprised of community members with recognized expertise in delivering community-based programs and services. The council was charged with advising Manitoba Justice on designing, implementing, and monitoring RJ programs. In 2017, as part of their cost cutting, the PCs eliminated the RJAC (CBC News 2017b), thereby undermining community input on RJ in the province. Instead, the government focused on its Restorative Justice Branch (RJB) and Restorative Justice Centres (RJCs). RJB funds and oversees agreements with RJ service providers, while RJCs are intended to increase the number of referrals. Nevertheless, RJ referrals remained stable—4,937 in 2018/19 and 4,811 in 2021/22 (Manitoba Justice 2023a).

Custody Corrections

"Corrections is sorely under-funded. We do not help inmates, we simply house them."

Custody Corrections manages adult offenders sentenced to less than two years and remanded adults. It also manages youth held in custody. The branch represents the largest expenditure area in Justice. The lion's share of spending involves labour costs. In 2018/19, 31 percent of Justice funding ($203.9 million of $660.1 million) went to salaries and benefits in Custody Corrections (Manitoba Justice 2019a, 74–75).

KPMG noted that Justice was one of two departments that had incurred significant overtime costs (KPMG 2016, 74). A 2019 departmental briefing indicated that efforts were being made to reduce that expense: "In 2018/19, the Department reduced overall overtime costs by $3M in comparison to the previous year" (Manitoba Justice 2019b, 19), which included a $723,000 reduction in Custody Corrections for salaries and benefits (Manitoba Justice 2019a, 74).

While there may be lower overtime costs overall, there are also fewer staff. Staff shortages have resulted in what one employee described as an "overtime crisis": "The overtime crisis and safety issues has increased the number of employees quitting, going on disability, or accessing workers' comp. It also created an overtime crisis from the number of staff quitting or requiring time off to get healthy." Corrections staff repeatedly said under-staffing results in long-term costs. One respondent explained, "Every staff in jail that misses a shift due to mental health is replaced at double the cost through overtime plus the cost of their sick time so in total triple the cost. Ensuring a good work environment through proper funding and staffing will save money in the long term."

The PCs also cut costs by freezing wages. These cuts affected the well-being and safety of staff: "Staff are leaving at an alarming rate and going to other higher paying federal jobs, resulting in a dangerous work environment." Respondents maintained that investing in staff actually saves costs: "Offer competitive wages to encourage recruitment, more staff means less overtime. Provide high quality mental health supports to reduce burn out. Less staff burned out means more staffing, which in turn means less overtime. It also lowers the Province's central training costs as retaining staff means less new hires are needed."

Other moves bent the cost curve in Corrections. In 2018, ManCor Prison Industries, which provided training opportunities for inmates, was cancelled. Cancelling the programs was expected to save $920,000 a year and free up eleven staff positions for redeployment within Corrections (Annable 2018). Front-line workers saw benefits to these programs; they "would teach offenders life skills, but we also made the inmate clothing at the jail." That work "has now been contracted out to the private sector, resulting in higher costs and supply issues." The government said it was focusing instead on the RRI. However, one worker commented, "We released a lot of inmates deemed to be lower risk to reoffend with a program called 'RRI.' This directly in my opinion has resulted in worsening of public safety. These individuals received no corrective programming and were simply released because of the higher institutional counts and lack of staff to do the work."

To cut more costs, the PCs announced the closure of the Dauphin Correctional Centre (DCC) in January 2020. Correctional workers were to be transferred to other institutions. Justice Minister Cullen had indicated that the sixty-seven inmates at the DCC would be accommodated at other jails. However, every correctional centre in the province except one was over capacity (Unger 2020). According to one worker, "With the closure of DCC we now have increased needs in other facilities and increases in inmates and inmate needs."

Despite efforts to reduce incarceration numbers, average daily adult custody and remand counts remained stable. In 2014/15, 2,387 adults were in custody (65 percent on remand); in 2019/20, there were 2,158 (72 percent on remand) (Manitoba Justice 2023b and 2023c). Custody counts began to fall, however, with the COVID-19 pandemic. Adult inmates near the end of their sentences were released, as were youth in open custody. Direct lockups and other noncriminal detentions were suspended. The courts prioritized bail hearings to reduce the custody numbers (Skelly 2020). By 2021/22, the custody count was reduced to 1,649 (72 percent on remand) (Manitoba Justice 2023b and 2023c).

While custody counts were down, workloads in Manitoba's correctional facilities were not, especially for nurses. As one worker said, "Workload has doubled due to COVID," creating added stress for an already short-staffed workforce.

In July 2022 the government closed the Agassiz Youth Centre, saying that youth custody numbers were dropping. With the closure, 109 Justice staff would be redeployed and youth transferred to the Manitoba Youth Centre (CBC News 2022). The announcement caught workers by surprise. As one worker commented, "Staff was confronted with the fact of closure and left to scramble in what they would have to do next. Quit or relocate or driving large distances to other centres in order not to lose their jobs."

Overall staffing complements in Manitoba Justice decreased during the PC government's tenure. In 2016/17 there were 4,310 Justice employees; this fell by 15 percent to 3,664 by 2020/21 (Manitoba Civil Service Commission 2017, 49; 2021, 47). Custody Corrections saw significant reductions. On 28 February 2021, 27 percent (432) of the authorized 1600 full-time equivalent positions in Custody Corrections were vacant (Sanders 2022).

Unfilled positions were a prominent concern for respondents. One worker noted, "Reduced staffing leads to overworked and overtired staff that are unable to proactively stop the violence that occurs in our jails. This leads to increased healthcare costs. And staff being exposed to brutal violence leads to mental health issues that cost thousands in lost productivity." Another stated, "The PC government has set back Manitoba Corrections by decades. Staff suffering from PTSD at increased levels, inmate lawsuits are up. We lose staff who may never be able to work again and are now reliant on the social system for support."

One worker commented on the precarious nature of their employment: "All staff hired as correctional officers are part-time however expected to work as many hours as are available, which has typically been full-time or more." Another remarked that "part-timers are continuously on eggshells. They don't belong to a team, must work all units on always different hours of the day and night. . . . There are staff with young families who are overly stressed about their job."

Austerity measures create a cycle difficult to break. Increased workloads and precarious work make retention and recruitment increasingly difficult. As one worker commented, "We became less attractive to work for—and we work short every day."

Investing in Public Safety

"Please read. I don't do surveys as a rule, so to do this says things need to change."

Over half (55 percent) of Justice respondents believed that austerity measures had led to a reduction in service quality for low-income service users, calling into question the ability of Manitoba Justice to deliver "outstanding client and community service." In turn, these measures impeded the safety and justice mission of Manitoba Justice. The absence of required supports negatively impacts community safety. A probation officer commented, "Clients who have reduced access to social services in the community have been at an increasing risk of relapse into substance use, reoffending, and reincarceration. Unhoused clients are breaching conditions or reoffending and being released immediately with no housing options or inadequate or unsafe housing options. This is resulting in more trips to the ER as well as more arrests (increasing police budgets and Court costs)."

As well, despite Manitoba Justice's values of promoting a respectful work environment and valuing workers' participation and teamwork, austerity measures have impacted the well-being and safety of workers, leading one correctional officer to say, "Many staff report that they feel like their safety concerns are not important."

Since the criminal justice system can be a source of trauma and insecurity in the lives of vulnerable Manitobans, ensuring safe and just communities is inseparable from addressing social and economic exclusion (CCPA–MB 2020). Respondents repeatedly spoke of "justice" within this wider framework of community support. As one worker put it, "The public service ought to be focused on the needs of the community (i.e., addictions, mental health, public safety, accessible housing, education, health, environmental protection, etc.) and how to best achieve those based on community input, data, and structured continuous improvement methodologies. Austerity for austerity's sake is costly to Manitobans." Another worker agreed, adding, "We need to actually do the work of reconciliation and understand that Indigenous Manitobans have a legacy of trauma and systemic oppression that has created over representation in justice, child welfare, and poor health determinants."

The strain on both workers and those they serve can be reduced by broadening our understanding of justice and providing civil service jobs within well-funded, proactive justice strategies. One correctional officer's plea—"We *need* more recognition for the very difficult job we do, we *need* mental help support, and we *need* to have time to recharge from all the horror we see inside the jails"—asks us to envision renewed public spending on justice that does not rely on incarceration.

Safe and just communities are not achieved through austerity. Indeed, 75 percent of Justice workers noted that expenditure cuts and restraints have worsened public safety. Public safety requires government investment, resources, and support. Reliance on the carceral system is reduced only when community supports are robustly available through healthcare, housing, and social services. Rather than quick fixes that have little social and financial value over time, the focus should be on the long-term cost savings that come with crime reduction. To the extent that cost cutting negatively impacts the government's ability to address the social inequalities at the root of crime, then what we save in short-term gains costs us in public safety—the main thing Manitoba Justice should be focused on.

References

Annable, Kristin. 2017. "Pallister Government to Eliminate 'Ground-Breaking' Restorative Justice Program." CBC Manitoba, 30 May. https://www.cbc.ca/news/canada/manitoba/restorative-resolutions-elimated-manitoba-1.4136961.

———. 2018. "Manitoba Government Ends Employment Training Program for Provincial Inmates." CBC Manitoba, 1 May. https://www.cbc.ca/news/canada/manitoba/jail-mancor-closes-employment-1.4642073.

CBC News. 2017a. "Low-Risk Inmates Released Early through Manitoba's New Probation Model." CBC Manitoba, 19 December. https://www.cbc.ca/news/canada/manitoba/new-probation-model-manitoba-1.4457138.

———. 2017b. "Manitoba Axes, Shrinks 25 Government-Appointed Boards." CBC Manitoba, 4 December. https://www.cbc.ca/news/canada/manitoba/manitoba-government-boards-cut-1.4432693.

———. 2022. "Agassiz Youth Centre in Portage la Prairie Closing due to Falling Incarceration Numbers." CBC Manitoba, 24 March. https://www.cbc.ca/news/canada/manitoba/agassiz-youth-centre-closing-1.6396167.

CCPA–MB (Canadian Centre for Policy Alternatives–Manitoba). 2020. *Change Starts Here: Manitoba Alternative Provincial Budget 2020.* Winnipeg: Canadian Centre for Policy Alternatives–Manitoba. https://www.policyalternatives.ca/wp-content/uploads/attachments/Alt%20Provincial%20Budget%202020-7.pdf.

Government of Manitoba. 2017. *Annual Report 2016–2017.* https://www.gov.mb.ca/justice/publications/annualreports/pubs/annualreport1617.pdf.

———. 2018a. *Annual Report 2017–2018.* https://www.gov.mb.ca/justice/publications/annualreports/pubs/annualreport1718.pdf.

———. 2018b. "Criminal Justice Modernization Strategy." https://www.gov.mb.ca/justice/pubs/criminaljusticereform.pdf.

———. 2019a. *Annual Report 2018–2019.* https://www.gov.mb.ca/justice/publications/annualreports/pubs/annualreport1819.pdf.

———. 2019b. "Departmental Briefing Election 2019."

———. 2020. *Annual Report 2019–2020.* https://www.gov.mb.ca/justice/publications/annualreports/pubs/annualreport1920.pdf.

———. 2021. *Annual Report 2020–2021.* Manitoba Justice. https://www.gov.mb.ca/justice/publications/annualreports/pubs/annualreport2021.pdf

———. 2023a. "Restorative Justice and Other Diversions." https://www.gov.mb.ca/justice/cjsm/diversion.html.

———. 2023b. "Custody Population." https://www.gov.mb.ca/justice/cjsm/custody-pop.html.

———. 2023c. "Remand Percentage." https://www.gov.mb.ca/justice/cjsm/remand.html.

Johnstone, Gerry. 2002. *Restorative Justice: Ideas, Values, Debates.* Cullompton, UK: Willan Publishing.

KPMG. 2016. *Manitoba Fiscal Performance Review, Phase 1 Report.* 30 September. https://www.gov.mb.ca/asset_library/en/proactive/fpr-phase-1.pdf.

Malakieh, Jamil. 2018. *Adult and Youth Correctional Statistics in Canada, 2016/2017.* Ottawa: Statistics Canada. https://www150.statcan.gc.ca/n1/en/pub/85-002-x/2018001/article/54972-eng.pdf?st=tIqJHSCm.

Malone, Kelly. 2017. "'It's Really Hard for Us to Swallow': Manitoba Prisoner Advocates Get 20% Funding Cut." CBC Manitoba, 16 June. https://www.cbc.ca/news/canada/manitoba/elizabeth-fry-john-howard-funding-cut-manitoba-1.4164949.

Manitoba Civil Service Commission. 2017. *Annual Report 2016–2017.* Government of Manitoba. https://www.gov.mb.ca/csc/publications/annrpt/pdf/2016-17_annualrpt_en-fr.pdf.

———. 2021. *Annual Report 2020–2021.* Government of Manitoba. https://www.manitoba.ca/csc/publications/annrpt/pdf/2020-21_annualrpt_en-fr.pdf.

Marcoux, Jacques, and Caroline Barghout. 2015. "Manitoba Jails Bursting at the Seams Even Though Crime Rates Continue to Fall." CBC Manitoba, 29 October. https://www.cbc.ca/news/canada/manitoba/manitoba-jails-busting-crime-rate-falling-1.3293068.

OAGM (Office of the Auditor General–Manitoba). 2014. *Managing the Province's Adult Offenders.* March. https://www.oag.mb.ca/_files/ugd/b32b68_7d769ebd1e-be435cbf72be0e8b8a1958.pdf.

Randall, Melanie. 2013. "Restorative Justice and Gendered Violence? From Vaguely Hostile Skeptic to Cautious Convert: Why Feminists Should Critically Engage with Restorative Approaches to Law." *Dalhousie Law Journal* 36 (2): 461–99.

Restorative Justice Act. SM 2014 c. 26. https://canlii.ca/t/54rsb.

Sanders, Carol. 2022. "Fix Justice Staffing Problem at Home First: MGEU." *Winnipeg Free Press*, 13 September. https://www.winnipegfreepress.com/breakingnews/2022/09/13/fix-justice-staffing-problem-at-home-first-mgeu.

Skelly, Greg. 2020. "Memorandum: Manitoba Corrections Notice to Judiciary." 15 April.

Unger, Danton. 2020. "Fact Check: Nearly All of Manitoba's Correctional Facilities Are Over Capacity." CTV News, 27 January. https://www.ctvnews.ca/winnipeg/article/fact-check-nearly-all-of-manitobas-correctional-facilities-are-over-capacity/.

Woolford, Andrew, and Amanda Nelund. 2019. *The Politics of Restorative Justice: A Critical Introduction.* 2nd ed. Halifax and Winnipeg: Fernwood Publishing.

Chapter 9

LOOKING FOR "A WAGONLOAD OF LUCK" ON "THIS CAPITALIST EARTH": WORKERS' PERSPECTIVES ON INCOME ASSISTANCE AND DISABILITY SUPPORT

James P. Mulvale

Introduction

The Government of Manitoba's Department of Families delivers an income support program called Employment and Income Assistance (EIA). This program broadly resembles similar programs in the other provinces and territories across Canada, and collectively these programs are often referred to generically as "social assistance" or (colloquially) "welfare." The EIA program has three categories: general assistance, EIA for single parents, and EIA for persons with disabilities.[1] The Department of

Families also administers other support programs including: drug, dental, and optical services to EIA recipients (and children in care); other income supplements for low-income renters, seniors, and expectant mothers; and programs specifically for persons with severe and prolonged disabilities, including a new income support program separate from EIA, residential care facilities, day services, transportation, respite, crisis intervention, and investigation of abuse and neglect.

EIA is a "last resort" income support measure for those who fail to qualify for other more generous and less stigmatized programs such as Employment Insurance, public pensions for the elderly, or Workers' Compensation. EIA is means-tested, has elaborate rules and regulations to determine eligibility, and pays benefit levels that are well below the poverty line. When measured against Canada's official poverty line (based on the Market Basket Measurement of essential goods in Winnipeg), EIA benefits only reach 42 percent of this threshold for single people considered employable, 58 percent for single people with a disability, 76 percent for a single parent with one child, and 70 percent for a couple with two children (Maytree 2021).

On the positive side, in 2014 the New Democratic Party (NDP) government in Manitoba launched a new housing benefit called Rent Assist. This benefit replaced the old shelter allowance component of EIA and the previous Rent Aid program, which were both very inadequate. Rent Assist provides a housing subsidy for low-income people renting in the private market based on the gap between their income and 75 percent of median market rent (Brandon and Hajer 2019). Rent Assist is available to those who do not receive EIA as well as those who do. The program has been a significant improvement in financial aid to low-income Manitobans, although there were worries about reduced eligibility and benefit levels in the wake of the election of the Progressive Conservative (PC) government in 2016 (Cooper et al. 2020).

The discussion which follows is based on data from a survey conducted in late 2022 of provincial public servants and staff of community organizations contracted to deliver provincial programs. Of the total of 2,078 survey respondents across all government programs, seventy-seven persons were working in delivering EIA, other income-tested benefits, and support to persons with disabilities. Seventy-nine percent of this sample worked directly for the Manitoba government in the Department of Families, while the remainder worked in nonprofit agencies with government funding to deliver benefits and support. Of people working directly for the government, 69 percent worked with persons with disabilities. A substantial majority (71 percent) of the EIA respondents identified as front-line workers. The survey respondents were geographically dispersed (43 percent in Winnipeg, 57 percent in other parts of Manitoba). They were mostly female (82 percent), had considerable job experience (an average of sixteen years), and were highly educated (with 83 percent holding a post-secondary diploma or degree).

Effects of Government Austerity on EIA Delivery

Provincial government austerity measures related to EIA and disability support can be measured in a variety of ways. Regarding staff available to deliver programs, there has been a decline in the number of positions since the PCs took power in 2016. During this period the number of full-time equivalent (FTE) positions for EIA and disability support delivery has decreased from 1,522 to 1,306, a decline of 14 percent. These figures are for positions *available*, not actual staff filling these positions. The vacancy rate across the entire Department of Families was 19 percent in 2022. Agencies providing support for persons with a disability have also faced massive vacancy rates due to low wages set by the province (MacLean 2022). Both cutting the number of positions *and* allowing a generally high staff vacancy rate (almost one in five) are having significant deleterious effects on program delivery and quality of service in EIA and programs supporting persons with disabilities, including on many occasions service users not even being able to reach or even identify their EIA worker.[2]

Another way to measure austerity is to look at government spending. Government spending on EIA and disability support declined in inflation-adjusted dollars from $530 million in 2018/19 to $445 million in 2021/22. Under the NDP government before 2016, annual per capita expenditure on EIA and disability support (based on the total population of Manitoba and adjusted for inflation) grew from $817 per person in 2010/11 to $924 in 2016/17. In the first full fiscal year after the PCs took power (2017/18), this figure actually increased to $941 per capita, likely as a result of bureaucratic lag as the new government required time to assert its control over programs and expenditures. Per capita expenditures[3] started declining the following year, and by 2021/22 the PC government had reduced expenditure on EIA to $855 per Manitoban, a decline of 9 percent from its peak in 2017/18.

The rigour of austerity is evident in survey responses. Over two-thirds of respondents (69 percent) reported that austerity was harsher under the PC government compared to the previous NDP government. A strong majority (83 percent) indicated that austerity measures had led to "a reduction in the quality of service for stakeholders/users of the service." As to effects of austerity measures on staff, 70 percent of respondents reported an increased and intensified workload, and 92 percent reported "worse working conditions and job satisfaction." Deterioration in employee mental health was reported by 95 percent. Examples of this mental health toll provided by Department of Families staff included:

- "I see my community living casework team struggle every single day. They deal with the most vulnerable people in the downtown Winnipeg area. When we hear about murders and fires and that there's an adult involved in those, it's often one of our clients. The mental health effect on those caseworkers is unreal."
- "People don't want to come to work; they cry at their desk; they're overwhelmed with their case load; they're overwhelmed with clients who are in addiction treatment, clients on the street, and these are all folks who have developmental disabilities or intellectual disabilities of some sort. They need more ... casework staff."

A majority of respondents (63 percent) felt that austerity would lead to "worsened public safety." One EIA case counsellor commented that there was an "inability to complete tasks that help participants become independent from EIA, [which] leads me to believe that crime statistics would show an increase. ... EIA issues very little [benefit money] compared with meaningful employment."

One of the supposed merits of austerity is that it will lead to "lean government" and greater efficiency of the public service. The respondents to this survey emphatically disagree with this argument. Most of the respondents (57 percent) were of the view that "austerity measures would increase costs in both my area of work and for the public sector as a whole." Almost nine out of ten (87 percent) saw austerity measures as leading to "less value for money" in public services. The survey respondents cited particular aspects of poorer outcomes in program delivery (that would likely lead to *lower* efficiency): 15 percent indicated that they were not able to see as many individuals as they used to; 31 percent stated that they were not able to spend as much time with individuals as previously; and 45 percent were "asked to provide the same or increased service with fewer resources." Only 3 percent of respondents indicated "no change" in service quality in the wake of austerity measures, and no one saw opportunities for improved services.

One respondent suggested that austerity may in fact *decrease* efficiency. Having to do "more with less" may lead to quick or sloppy decision making, which in turn may trigger reversals of some decisions by EIA workers that are appealed. Other comments bearing on service quality, efficiency, and accountability included:

- "[There is] nothing to encourage quality workers applying or staying, so service has gone down, as employees exemplify the organization's lack of care to those we serve."
- "Severe lack of staff, mandating and redirecting staff around has left staff overworked and exhausted."—Employee with a nonprofit organization (NPO) that provides services to people with disabilities
- "There is no accountability [of] agencies that are not overseen by a civil servant."—Community service worker, Community Living disABILITY Services (CLDS)

Part of "efficiency" in the public service is preparing documents in ways that streamline work but also generate necessary information. One respondent described the impossibility of adequately documenting their work under conditions of austerity: "Due to limited ability to complete all tasks, my work is being reviewed more.... Even if I ... worked 5 days a week plus volunteered overtime without responding to my phone or emails and missing every meeting, [my reporting] still wouldn't be completed to standards."

On the flip side of this question—the proposition that budget *increases* would create opportunities for "higher quality services [provided] in a cost-effective way"—64 percent of respondents agreed with this proposition (compared to 8 percent who disagreed and 28 percent who were unsure or didn't know). Many different improvements were envisioned by respondents if austerity were to be reversed, and adequate resources were to be provided. Some of these ideas were:

- More preventative or early intervention measures;
- Facilitating social engagement for people with disabilities;
- Stronger client engagement and referral links with organizations serving persons with disabilities;
- Using certain community-based facilities on a twenty-four-hour basis;
- More availability of ASL interpretation for those with hearing loss or impairment;
- Better safety planning and provisions for vulnerable clients;
- More support for service users facing multiple barriers;
- Better continuity of services for families (related to decreased staff turnover); and
- Behavioural and psychological services.

A very strong theme in these responses was that more funding for staff in EIA and disability support could lead to lower caseloads; this in turn could enable better quality and more comprehensive support for service users.

Respondents expressed concerns about how austerity measures have been implemented; 78 percent of respondents reported that "management or other senior government officials" failed to adequately explain or justify them. Seven in ten respondents either somewhat disagreed (10 percent) or strongly disagreed (60 percent) with the proposition that "the work-related experience, expertise and opinions of front-line workers in my area of work were reflected in the austerity measures implemented." One EIA case counsellor gave an example of such lack of consultation: "Numerous times myself and my colleagues gave feedback to management about the unmanageable amount of work due to high case load numbers, but our input was ignored, and case load numbers continue to increase."

The devaluation of the work of public servants under regimes of austerity can be expressed in very concrete and mundane ways, including in the quality of the physical work environment. One Department of Families respondent cited this example: "[We] didn't have a lunchroom, not even a sink to wash our cups in. Our toaster was taken away as the sockets were overloaded. We had a crappy microwave, a dodgy kettle and a [coffee machine] spread out in various places."

On the question of privatization, respondents were asked for their views on whether or not "the private sector would perform your unit/ organization's tasks in a more efficient manner." Seventy-two percent replied no, while only 8 percent said yes, and 20 percent were unsure or didn't know. The concerns of the "no" respondents included less commitment to the welfare of service users if EIA and disability services were delivered in the private sector:

- "Compassion is required, not a pure business approach." —Support worker
- "The private sector needs to make money, to make money you need to close files. That would not be done in a caring and effective manner if done by a private organization worried about their bottom line."—EIA case counsellor
- "Disability advocacy is not a for-profit job."—Employee with an NPO that serves people with disabilities

Respondents were also concerned that if responsibility for service was placed outside government,[4] then service quality would decline and there would be less accountability.

- "[The] private sector would squeeze more clients into the workloads of individual workers as their goal is to maximize profit, not service. There is no way on this capitalist earth that the private sector would seek to provide better outcomes for the clients."—Family Services employee
- "I believe my team is skilled and educated to support this population and [that the] private sector may not have that experience and/or accountability for participant safety/risk." —Social worker, Disability Services
- "The responsibilities that are being outsourced such as case management are often falling to individuals with less education and experience, resulting in a deterioration of the quality of services to the individuals [whom] my program supports." —Community service worker, CLDS

- "We provide interdisciplinary services in one area. With funding cuts to our comprehensive service, [this] often ends up creating a series of compartmentalized and disconnected services that clients spend more time in to achieve service."
—Employee with an NPO providing clinical services and specialized care to individuals with developmental disabilities

Respondents were also concerned about maintaining a stable and suitably qualified workforce in the years ahead in the context of austerity. Eighty-seven percent of respondents indicated that austerity had "worsened employee recruitment and retention." Seventy-two percent indicated that they would consider changing to another job. One Department of Families employee gave the example of their own workplace: "In the team of five [that] I was in, four of us are/were looking for new jobs."

The austerity agenda was in full swing when the COVID-19 pandemic arrived in early 2020. Sixty percent of survey respondents indicated that "provincial austerity in my area of work has become more intense" since then. One NPO respondent working with persons with developmental disabilities stated that "COVID measures 'put the nail in the coffin' and permanently changed the type, the amount, and the way we offer services to clients."

A resource coordinator in the Department of Families described the effects of the pandemic on staff: "Most of us had been with government for years, by the time COVID hit, and we felt micromanaged, we were disrespected, we were not given proper equipment to do our jobs, and the expectations were even higher of our positions. Many of us have children or elderly parents to look after [and] some of us had both, and yet family accommodations were denied over and over."

To summarize, the data above indicate the dramatic gulf in perceptions of austerity between the staff delivering EIA and disability support and Manitoba's former PC government. The government had a strong neoconservative ideology that made judgments on the relative "deservingness" of those receiving provincial income benefits (Mulvale 2020), as well as a strong neoliberal orientation on the need to cut government expenditures, taxes, and regulations in the hope that an unfettered business sector will create prosperity (Hajer and Fernandez 2021). This ideologically driven austerity has had very significant negative impacts on public servants supporting low-income and disabled Manitobans. Both staff and service users have been paying a huge price for government apathy and even antipathy toward poor and marginalized Manitobans.

Rethinking the EIA Model

The survey included a question soliciting respondents' views—as people who actually deliver EIA and disability support—about the program model. Respondents could indicate the view that EIA was "well adapted to the needs of clients," that it required "minor adjustment and improvements," or that it required "a fundamental overhaul." Over half (52 percent) of the respondents saw the EIA model as requiring a "fundamental overhaul." When the "unsure/don't know" responses are taken out the calculation, two-thirds (30 of 44, or 68 percent) of respondents saw the need for fundamental change in the way EIA is structured and delivered.

Many respondents made observations on EIA that amount to a broad indictment of the way in which the program currently operates:

- "They've now centralized EIA delivery for our participants on our program, which means they no longer have an EIA case counsellor assigned to their file and now only have a generalized telephone number or email that they can contact. The clients are now experiencing longer wait times, unable to speak to someone specific and it has now become impersonal . . . we can no longer work collaboratively on a specific file together and the wait [time] for a simple answer which we [used to] get in a matter of hours now takes 1–2 days if not longer and the answers are not always consistent due to it not being the same worker you deal with every time." —Department of Families employee
- "The ability of EIA staff to 'help' participants [has] been taken away. EIA workers are systematically handcuffed from providing any meaningful service to participants. The EIA worker used to be able to refer to employment programs, [but] this is no longer the case."—Community service worker, CLDS
- "Staff can't provide in-depth case management to a caseload of 150 all with significant barriers to employment and/or

education. Individuals are blamed for *systemic failures.*"—Case manager/counsellor (emphasis in original).

Respondents characterized the current EIA model of income support in the context of austerity as "very punitive," with "clients [who] are starving having to wait extended periods for small cheques." Comments of the oppressive and dysfunctional aspects of EIA included:

- "The 'heavy hand' of government 'cutting off the cheque' [is used] as a threat."—Senior policy analyst, Department of Families
- "The microscopic involvement in people's lives is too colonial."—Policy analyst, Department of Families
- "There are not enough collateral resources available to people (mental health, housing, proper medical attention) [and] clients are often treated horribly. Some of us staff actually care and want to help our clients but management is more focused on statistics and just getting people off the program."
  —EIA worker, Department of Families case counsellor

EIA was also portrayed as a dead end for those in the program:

- "EIA provides no real way for those receiving assistance to exit the program without a wagonload of luck. Workers are unavailable for communication, benefits do not provide enough money to search for work effectively, there is no support for learning to become self-employed or starting a business, and funds are frankly insufficient to cover the cost of living most of the time."—Manitoba Family Services employee

Thus, it is clear that the majority of survey respondents had a strong desire to move beyond the current austerity-driven dysfunctional mess of EIA delivery. Several respondents offered constructive ideas for positive change. One theme that came up regularly was the desirability of recovering and strengthening EIA's role in proactive case management to facilitate opportunities and supports for service users. Another theme was respondents' wish to be able to interact with service users in more individualized and unhurried ways that would constitute positive helping relationships. Being good case managers and building positive and professional helping relationships is especially important in work with service users who face multiple structural, community, and individual barriers in their lives, as is the case with many EIA recipients.

Social assistance caseworkers in Ontario have articulated similar ideas about improving cash benefits and personal and programmatic supports for clients. As part of an extended discussion about work and income security held in Toronto in 2019, social assistance workers expressed their preference for the more comprehensive, generous, and unconditional model of basic income over the current means-tested social assistance model that is in place across the country (OBIN 2020). Like their Manitoba counterparts, these Ontario workers identified poor working conditions in delivering social assistance in its current form (OBIN 2020, 19). "Anxiety levels are also very high for workers in the ODSP [Ontario Disability Support Program][5] offices because there are too many cases, too much ongoing restructuring, and too many people not doing the jobs for which they were trained and educated. Many staff positions required clerical and administrative skills, not social work skills."

The Ontario workers also stated that "for [social assistance] caseworkers, basic income represents an opportunity to become a true support for people instead of a punitive gatekeeper" (OBIN 2020, 18).

Many social assistance workers in both Manitoba and Ontario want to move beyond being gatekeepers and "welfare cops" enforcing eligibility and behavioural requirements for people receiving benefits. While some changes have been made in Manitoba, including the recent introduction of a distinct benefit program for those with prolonged and severe disabilities (Government of Manitoba n.d.), punitive approaches continue for others. Workers are eager to work with clients in positive ways to improve their life circumstances. For such positive change to occur, governments must abandon austerity and embrace new ways of thinking about income security in a world facing many different forms of precarity in the economy, public health, and the natural environment.

Conclusion

Social assistance and disability support caseworkers can be thought of as "street level bureaucrats" (Lipsky 2010) who deliver a state program that is governed by policies and rules, but that also has built into it a degree of worker discretion in delivering benefits to those who need them. One can hope that workers give service users the benefit of the doubt when they assess client needs and make decisions about eligibility for support. It is clear from the comments in this survey that public employees delivering EIA and disability supports do indeed have the best interests of those whom they serve at heart.

EIA in Manitoba, like other social assistance programs across Canada, carries a lot of neoconservative and neoliberal ideological baggage. Many politicians, senior bureaucrats, and members of the public believe that social assistance should dichotomize the poor into categories of deserving and undeserving. They believe that the preeminent (or perhaps only) goal of temporary income support should be labour market activation. They believe that the "less eligibility" principle (that keeps social assistance rates below the lowest wage levels) can spur those receiving benefits to seek paid employment regardless of their health status, family circumstances, or other challenges in life.

In such a context, EIA caseworkers have very little room to manoeuvre as street-level bureaucrats (or even as empathetic fellow human beings) trying to do the best they can for the people whom they serve. Austerity measures make an inadequate and stigmatizing social assistance system worse. The inability of government employees or contractors to provide legislatively mandated programs leaves people abandoned and forces them to rely on emergency and meagre support from voluntary organizations. Austerity means that the mental and emotional toll on workers is high, and service users are often very poorly treated.

But EIA caseworkers also can speak with authority about the needs and aspirations of their fellow Manitobans whom they assist. Public servants on the front line have potential roles to play in challenging and overthrowing austerity in the program area of income security and support for persons with disabilities. Working in concert with allies such as union leaders, community activists, and advocates for better models of income security and practical support, EIA workers can help to construct systems in Manitoba that ensure an adequate income, strong social support, human dignity, and social inclusion.

Notes

1   The Department of Families' 2021/22 annual report indicates that 61,948 individuals received some form of EIA in that fiscal year. Of these, 22 percent were on general assistance, 37 percent were single parents, and 41 percent were persons with disabilities. There was a small number of special cases (under 1 percent, $n = 424$) in which children, aged persons, and residents of crisis facilities received EIA.

2   Based on feedback from leaders of organizations advocating for persons with disabilities.

3   For details on data sources used for provincial expenditures, employee staffing numbers, and full-time equivalent (FTE) positions in this chapter, see Preface.

4   It appears that some survey respondents interpreted "privatization" to mean downloading services to nonprofit community agencies.

5   The Ontario Disability Support Program pays somewhat higher benefits than Ontario Works, the social assistance program for persons who are assessed as nondisabled.

References

Brandon, Josh, and Jesse Hajer. 2019. *Making Space for Change: The Story of Manitoba's Rent Assist Benefit.* Winnipeg: Canadian Centre for Policy Alternatives–Manitoba. https://www.policyalternatives.ca/news-research/making-space-for-change/.

Cooper, Sarah, Jesse Hajer, and Sheyna Plaut. 2020. *Fast Facts: Now, More Than Ever, We Need Rent Assist Helping Manitobans.* Winnipeg: Canadian Centre for Policy Alternatives–Manitoba. https://policyalternatives.ca/publications/commentary/fast-facts-now-more-ever-we-need-rent-assist-helping-manitobans.

Government of Manitoba. n.d. "Manitoba Supports for Persons with Disabilities." https://www.gov.mb.ca/fs/manitobasupports/news-and-media/index.html.

Hajer, Jesse, and Lynne Fernandez. 2021. *COVID-19, Austerity and an Alternative Social and Economic Policy Path for Manitoba.* Winnipeg: Canadian Centre for Policy Alternatives–Manitoba. https://policyalternatives.ca/publications/reports/COVID-19-austerity-and-alternative-social-and-economic-policy-path-manitoba.

Lipsky, Michael. 2020. "Dilemmas of the Individual in Public Services." In *Street-Level Bureaucracy: Dilemmas of the Individual in Public Services.* 2nd ed., edited by Michael Lipsky. New York: Russell Sage Foundation.

MacLean, Cameron. 2022. "Low Pay Leads to 'Revolving Door' of Adult Support Workers in Manitoba, Mom Says." CBC Manitoba, 11 July. https://www.cbc.ca/news/canada/manitoba/adults-intellectual-disabilities-staffing-shortages-1.6515156.

Maytree. 2021. *Welfare in Canada.* https://maytree.com/welfare-in-canada/.

Mulvale, James P. 2020. "Income Security in a Time of Pandemic: Neo-Liberalism Meets the Coronavirus in Manitoba." In *COVID-19 in Manitoba: Public Policy and the Pandemic,* edited by Andrea Rounce and Karine Levasseur, 163–72. Winnipeg: University of Manitoba Press. https://uofmpress.ca/files/9780887559501_web.pdf.

OBIN (Ontario Basic Income Network). 2020. *Rethinking Work and Income Security in the 21st Century: The Case for Basic Income and Work.* Basic Income Working Session, June. https://basicincomecoalition.ca/wp-content/uploads/2022/08/Case-for-Basic-Income-for-Work.pdf.

Chapter 10

AUSTERITY AND CHILD WELFARE

Shauna MacKinnon

In this chapter we focus on the experiences of members of the Manitoba Government and General Employees' Union (MGEU) and Canadian Union of Public Employees (CUPE) who were employed in the Manitoba child welfare system. We learned from respondents that, although austerity was creating very real and direct challenges in child welfare, there was something more deeply troubling happening because of a decades-long neoliberal approach within the broader context of colonial policies and practices, including residential schools, and the resultant trauma. Many of the children and families involved in the Child and Family Services (CFS) system are dealing with multiple traumas including, as one respondent commented, "serious mental health issues, more dangerous drug use, violence and a general lack of regard for self and others." The impact of deep poverty, racism, and intergenerational trauma is apparent, and the system continues to fail children and families. Workers who responded to the survey (see the preface for details) told us that the challenges for children and families caught up in the child welfare system are becoming much worse. Issues are far more complex because of deep poverty, systemic racism, and a growing sense of hopelessness and despair.

Seventy-two workers responded to surveys sent to MGEU and CUPE workers employed by child welfare agencies. The majority of workers (fifty-seven) indicated employment with the General CFS Authority. The remaining fifteen respondents reported working for an Indigenous child welfare authority or child welfare agency. Although the General Authority represents a relatively small percentage of the total number of workers in Manitoba's child welfare system, their perspective provides a window into the impact of provincial austerity measures on their working conditions and on the families that they support.

Despite the growing and pressing need, the resources allocated to the problem were dwindling, according to provincial expenditure data. Spending did increase in 2017/18 by approximately $45 million, but has trended downwards since then and was below 2015/16 levels by 2019/20.[1] In inflation-adjusted terms, spending on child welfare decreased 7.5 percent over that period. By 2021/22, spending was 11 percent below 2015/16 levels in inflation-adjusted terms.[2]

Background and Context

In Canada, child welfare services are provincially and territorially funded and legislated, except for federally funded services to First Nations peoples living on reserves. In accordance with individual agreements negotiated between First Nations communities, provincial and territorial governments, and the federal government, an increasing number of First Nations are delivering child and family services under provincial and territorial legislation. In addition, several community-based organizations provide prevention supports to children and families.

The child welfare system in Canada has long been criticized as an oppressive system that focuses far too much on apprehension over prevention. Furthermore, it has been highly criticized as systemically racist and a continuation of the colonial system that gave us residential schools (TRC 2015). Indigenous children continue to be overrepresented in the child welfare system across Canada. Indigenous children account for 53.8 percent of all children in foster care in Canada, according to Statistics Canada's 2021 census. This has gone up slightly from the 2016 census, in which 52.2 percent of children in care under the age of fourteen were Indigenous. At the time, only about 8 percent of children in Canada were Indigenous. In Manitoba, 91 percent of children in care are Indigenous, yet Indigenous children only account for 27 percent of the child population. Scathing analyses of child welfare in Canada and Manitoba are highlighted in many reports, including national reports by the Royal Commission on Aboriginal Peoples (1996), the Truth and Reconciliation Commission of Canada, and the National Inquiry into Missing and Murdered Indigenous Women and

Girls, as well as Manitoba reports by the Review Committee on Indian and Métis Adoptions and Placements (Kimelman 1984), the Aboriginal Justice Inquiry (AJI) (Hamilton and Sinclair 1991), and the Inquiry into the death of Phoenix Sinclair (Hughes 2014).

In Manitoba, the most significant effort to overhaul the system began in 1994 with the Framework Agreement Initiative[3] signed by the Government of Canada and Manitoba First Nations. In January 2007, the Assembly of Manitoba Chiefs voted to dissolve the agreement, citing concerns about negotiations with the federal Conservative government which took office in 2006. The recommendations outlined in the 1991 AJI report were shelved by Manitoba's Conservative government when elected in 1992. Although some progress toward devolution was made through the Aboriginal Justice Inquiry–Child Welfare Initiative (AJI–CWI) (Manitoba, MMF, AMC, MKO) launched by the New Democratic Party (NDP) in 2000, it falls far short of the desired self-governance. A 2018 report from the Legislative Review Committee, *Transforming Child Welfare Legislation in Manitoba: Opportunities to Improve Outcomes for Children and Youth* (Government of Manitoba 2018) emphasizes the need to fully implement the devolution of child welfare services in Manitoba.

Devolution in Manitoba

Services for children and families in Manitoba are delivered through a complex system involving multiple agencies operating under provincial legislation. The Child and Family Services Division of the Department of Families oversees family supports and protection services to children, delivered under the mandate of The Child and Family Services Act (CFSA), The Adoption Act, and the Child and Family Services Authorities Act (CFSAA). In accordance with the devolution process that commenced in 2000 and in response to the recommendations outlined by the AJI, the CFSAA created four authorities: the First Nations of Northern Manitoba CFS Authority (Northern Authority), responsible for administering and providing support to seven First Nations CFS agencies; the Southern First Nations Network of Care (Southern Network), responsible for administering and providing support to ten First Nations CFS agencies; the Métis CFS Authority, responsible for administering and providing support for two Métis CFS agencies; and the General CFS Authority, responsible for administering and providing support to eight non-Indigenous CFS agencies/regional offices. The four authorities oversee services, disperse funds, and ensure that culturally appropriate services are delivered by their respective agencies consistent with relevant legislation.

Some Indigenous youth are served by non-Indigenous agencies through the General Authority, especially when placed in emergency care, including temporary shelters and group homes. In Winnipeg, where the majority of survey respondents work, families enter the system through the All Nations Coordinated Response Network (ANCR) and are initially placed in the care of Winnipeg Child and Family Services emergency shelters. So, while Indigenous children and families are typically supported through Indigenous authorities and agencies, many Indigenous children and families, particularly in Winnipeg, are at least temporarily in the care of a non-Indigenous agency.

Changes in Child Welfare since 2016

There have been significant changes to the CFS system since 2016, mainly affecting services and support for Indigenous children and families. On the positive side, An Act Respecting First Nations, Inuit and Métis Children, Youth and Families became law in 2019 and came into effect in 2020. It affirms the rights and jurisdiction of Indigenous peoples in relation to child and family services and sets out nationally applicable principles including the best interests of the child, cultural continuity, and substantive equality. This federal law includes national standards with which provincial legislation must align.

In 2020, the courts ruled against the Manitoba Government for its practice of ordering CFS agencies to hand over the money they received from the federal Children's Special Allowance (CSA). The federal CSA is meant to ensure children in care receive the same federal funding that other children receive through the Canada Child Benefit and Child Disability Benefit. The CSA clawback occurred from 2006 to 2019. It was determined by the courts to be unconstitutional and discriminatory against Indigenous and disabled children (Petz 2022). It is estimated that the province misappropriated over $334 million in benefits—including $251 million from Indigenous CFS agencies in 2024.

After piloting the model in 2019 with nine agencies, the Manitoba government announced a fundamental shift in its approach to funding CFS, moving to the single-envelope funding (SEF) model in 2019 as opposed to allocating funding per child in care. The government argued that this would allow agencies greater flexibility and discretion over the design and delivery of services. The efficacy of this approach is contingent upon the amount of funding in the envelope. Notably, SEF does not provide for exceptional circumstance that may lead to unforeseen costs, such as complex medical needs for a child or travel expenses for family members. Under this system, each of the four Authorities receive a block of funding based on the previous year's data on children in care. The premise is that this gives Authorities greater flexibility on how funds are allocated, which in theory opens up opportunities for preventative measures and eliminates financial incentives to bring children into care. Although greater discretion over the use of funds is welcomed, there are grave concerns with the amount in the "envelope" and the potential for it to erode over time. Critics of block funding have reason to be concerned and warned of the dangers of block funding, describing it as being used as "the fall guy for fiscal restraint" (Torjman and Battle 1995, 1). We have since seen the erosion of transfers to the province through block funds for social assistance, post-secondary education, and healthcare (Moscovitch and Thomas 2015).

The move to a block fund in child welfare was particularly concerning given the Manitoba government's implementation of austerity measures that included cuts in spending, wage freezes, privatization, and vacancy management. The implementation of block funding coincided with a rapid decline in Child Protection branch spending since 2017/18. A number of workers surveyed reported cuts in their departments and being told by their supervisors that SEF was the cause.

Funding Responsibility for Child Welfare

Funding for mandated child welfare in Manitoba is provided through both federal and provincial governments (Table 10.1). Federal or provincial funding is determined at the time a child enters care. A child who has, or is eligible for, treaty status, and whose parents are normally living on-reserve at the time the child enters care, is deemed a federal funding responsibility. All other children are deemed a provincial responsibility.

Table 10.1. Federal and provincial funding for children in care.

AUTHORITY	2021-03-31			2022-03-31		
	TOTAL CHILDREN	PROV. FUNDING (%)	FEDERAL FUNDING (%)	TOTAL CHILDREN IN CARE	PROV. FUNDING (%)	FEDERAL FUNDING %
First Nations of Northern Manitoba CFS Authority	2,935	61	39	2,920	62	38
Southern First Nations Network of Care	4,765	73	27	4,257	73	27
Métis CFS Authority	1,131	100		1,093	100	
General CFS Authority	1,019	100		926	100	
Totals	9,850			9,196		

Source: Government of Manitoba 2022, 102.

Funding is provided to the four CFS Authorities, which then allocate funds to their member agencies. The province of Manitoba funds the operations of each Authority. First Nation CFS agencies operating under the Southern and Northern First Nations CFS Authorities are financed 60 percent by the province and 40 percent by the federal government. This percentage split was based on the approximate division of children in care off- and on-reserve, as First Nation CFS agencies are responsible for both. Two agencies—Animikii Ozoson Child and Family Services and the Child and Family All Nations Coordinated Response Network (ANCR)—are funded 100 percent by the province, as are the Métis and the General CFS Authorities.

The Federal Government's Role

It is important to note that federal government funding is specifically for children in care on-reserve, and there has been a significant discrepancy in the amount received. In 2007, this discrepancy led to a complaint to the Canadian Human Rights Tribunal and the ruling in 2016 that the funding of child welfare services on-reserve is discriminatory. In September 2019 the federal government was ordered to compensate First Nations children who were placed in the on-reserve child welfare system. In 2023, a settlement agreement was reached and approved by the federal court. The first claims period for compensation began in March 2025. In 2021, the federal government passed the United Nations Declaration on the Rights of Indigenous Peoples Act, noting that the legislation "provides a roadmap for the Government of Canada and Indigenous peoples to work together to implement the Declaration based on lasting reconciliation, healing, and cooperative relations" (Government of Canada 2023). Importantly, these federal laws and agreements with Indigenous people will have implications for child welfare policy in Manitoba.

Provincial Funding

Funding for children in care off-reserve is provided by the Department of Families through two main programs: Child Protection, and Strategic Initiatives and Program Support (SIPS). SIPS is an important initiative as it funds nonmandated services that support children and families. The provincial Child and Youth Services Division works in close collaboration

Table 10.2. Manitoba funding allocations to child welfare service providers.

| SERVICE PROVIDER | FUNDING 2021/22 ($000S)[a] | | |
	SINGLE-ENVELOPE FUNDING	GROUP CARE[b]	TOTAL
First Nations of Northern Manitoba CFS Authority	83,239	5,471	88,710
Southern First Nations Network of Care	167,767	13,021	180,788
General CFS Authority[c]	66,535	12,068	78,603
Métis CFS Authority	52,882	7,492	60,374
Directorate programs	5,294	4,387	9,681
Authority subtotal	**375,717**	**42,439**	
Treatment centres/group care grants[d]	24,452		
Other agencies/programs[e]	11,177		
Emergency Placement Resources Program[f]	24,452		
Total	**498,490**		

Source: Government of Manitoba 2022, 109.

a The table reflects the distribution of provincial child and family services funding in Manitoba since the implementation of the single-envelope funding (SEF) model in 2019/20. CFS agencies were funded by their mandating authority from within the applicable SEF allocations above.
b Group care funding was provided by the department directly to service providers in 2021/22 which provided care for children in the care of a CFS agency.
c Winnipeg CFS and Rural and Northern CFS do not receive funding from their mandated authority. However, their direct program expenditures have been included in the above allocation.
d Grant funding for providers not associated with group care funding.

e Funding to community-based agencies to provide operating funding and program-specific funding.
f The Emergency Placement Resources Program, including emergency foster homes managed by third-party service providers and provincially licensed emergency shelters, was also funded by the Department.

with the CFS Authorities and their member agencies to compile service statistics for the Manitoba Families annual report. The Department of Families 2021/22 annual report shows funding allocations (Table 10.2) during that time.

The table reflects the distribution of provincial child and family services funding in Manitoba since the implementation of the single-envelope funding (SEF) model in 2019/20. CFS agencies were funded by their mandating authority from within the applicable SEF allocations above.

As stated earlier and as illustrated in Table 10.1, 91 percent of children in care are Indigenous. Most are in the care of Indigenous-led agencies associated with the Northern Authority, the Southern Authority, or the Métis Authority. Very few of these agencies are unionized workplaces represented by either MGEU or CUPE, and therefore the number of survey respondents working for Indigenous agencies was limited. Fifty-five of the sixty-nine respondents to our survey indicated they were civil servants employed by the Manitoba government. Only nine respondents indicated employment with an "Indigenous authority or child welfare agency." Given the much higher number of workers employed with Indigenous agencies compared with non-Indigenous, it is possible that the perspectives reflected in this survey were not necessarily representative of child welfare workers across the province and in particular those working for Indigenous agencies.

Austerity and Neoliberalism

Austerity measures during the period of study aligned with the decades-old neoliberal approach, continuing to exacerbate inequality and erode public investment with devastating implications for vulnerable children and families as well as those employed to serve them. However, the child welfare system served as a mechanism to oppress minorities long before the ascendancy of neoliberal capitalism. Although improvements have arguably been made in Manitoba in recent decades, they have been relatively minimal and have transpired only because of resistance—as in the case of the AJI–CWI. Nonetheless, the root causes that lead children and families to become entangled in the child welfare system in the first place remain unresolved.

Workers face the overwhelming challenge of working within a system that is perpetually underfunded and focused more on fixing people rather than the systems that oppress them. As described below, workers surveyed raised several concerns.

A survey respondent from Winnipeg Child and Family Services commented on the erosion of support for children and families:

> If we had more financial support the children in care would have better resources and housing options. Children who are permanent wards would have better support and opportunities to be successful adults. The current rates to support kids are the same as 10 years ago. We can't do the basics like feeding and clothing them appropriately at today's cost. We have lost funding for sports and activities that children should be able to participate in. We have lost good homes because the foster care model is based on a charity model and people are not paid to do the job of caring for traumatized children. Educational opportunities for older youth should be expanded so they can be successful adults.

This individual went on to describe the broader impact of neoliberal policies that neglect to provide youth in care with necessary supports: "Adults in jail, homelessness and suffering in poverty largely are products of the child welfare system. The more we can provide teaching and support [in] the early years [the more] we will save over the lifetime. The more we invest in mental health, education and recreation the better outcomes will be for children and the next generation."

Austerity, Neoliberalism, and Job Cuts

All but four respondents said that that they had been affected by staff shortages and increases in workload. Twenty-three respondents spoke about an increased use of contract and casual staff, and about the growing use of third-party private for-profit service providers such as Complete Care and Drake Medox. They noted high turnover due to poor wages, burnout, and insufficient training. One long-time family support worker

Table 10.3. Full-time equivalent positions and vacancies across Child and Family Services General Authority, 2019/20 to 2021/22.

FISCAL YEAR	2019/20		2020/21		2021/22	
AUTHORITY	TOTAL FTES	VACANT ON 31 MARCH	TOTAL FTES	VACANT ON 31 MARCH	TOTAL FTES	VACANT ON 31 MARCH
General Authority	21	3	21	7.6	21	5
Winnipeg CFS	237.6	35.7	234.7	29.3	234.7	40
Rural and Northern CFS (formed in 2020/21)			113.5	25	113.5	17
Jewish CFS	4.6	0	4.6	0	4.6	0
CFS Central Manitoba	55	1.5	56	2.75	59.45	11.38
CFS Western Manitoba	88.83	2	88.13	4	86.27	4
Total	407.03	42.2	517.93	68.65	519.52	77.38

noted an increase in violence and workers' reluctance to report it in fear of retribution.

Workers felt that government attempts at cost savings were doing more harm than good for children and families as well as workers. Sixty-seven respondents felt that austerity measures were having a negative impact on workers' mental health. Sixty-five said that austerity made it more difficult to recruit and retain workers. Fifty-two respondents said the impact of austerity measures led them to think about looking for another job. One respondent noted the lack of consistency that comes with high staff turn-over is detrimental to outcomes: "When workers remain with a client for a long period of time they are more likely to have an impact."

Concerns about recruitment and retention were supported by government statistics obtained through a freedom of information request. Table 10.3 shows FTEs and vacancies across the General Authority and its agencies from 2019 to 2022. There was a total of 77.38 vacant positions in 2021/22, and more than half of these vacancies were direct service workers. A total of 26 of the 40 vacant positions at Winnipeg CFS were SP4 Social Service Worker positions.

Survey respondents were asked to compare expenditure restraint under the NDP government prior to 2016 versus that of the Progressive Conservative (PC) government after 2016. Forty-nine individuals said it became more intense, nine respondents said it was about the same, and the remainder were uncertain except for one person who said things had improved. Forty-eight respondents said austerity became more intense after the COVID-19 pandemic. When asked about the state of austerity measures under the leadership of Brian Pallister versus Heather Stefanson, forty-two respondents said it remained the same while twenty-one said it became more intense.

A support worker with Family Services summed up the situation under the PC government this way:

> Over the last several years we have been working without a contract. The needs of our youth in Manitoba have changed dramatically over the last decade. The government has put out a very basic description of our job description which could not be further from the truth. We deal with severe mental health issues on a regular basis. We are dealing with gang violence,

weapons, drug use on a regular basis and we are often assaulted. Moreover, the emotional impact on the children in care and trying to provide them with adequate counselling while they are with us is not within the educational means of all the employees. We are the front line for these children, and I think they should hire people with more education and experience working with our indigenous youth. Putting our youth on a better path early will save money in the long run. We all worked very hard long hours and should not have to pick up 36 hours of overtime every 2 weeks just to survive. Many of us have a degree or diploma and deserve more than $20 an hour.

Another respondent, a long-time emergency placement services worker, said this: "When I first started working for CFS it was a better organization. The children have a lot more issues now and there is so much more mental illness . . . so many kids are violent and want to hurt staff. We get very little support from management, and it is so frustrating. Our biweekly shelter budget has not increased in 24 years, yet groceries have skyrocketed. Also, our pay is way too low. We should be civil servants [like] our coordinators, then maybe we would get the pay and respect we deserve."

Conclusion

Manitoba's child welfare system has long been fundamentally flawed, and its problems historically exacerbated in the context of increasing poverty, inequality, and racism and the lack of political will to take the bold steps needed to transform it. Child and family service workers and advocates have long pointed to systemic injustices in child welfare and governments' failure to do what is necessary to keep children out of the system. Those working in child welfare offer an important perspective from the front lines. They need to be better supported through increased staffing and wages and better working conditions. However, there has been a long list of studies telling us that keeping children and families out of the child welfare system should be a priority and this cannot happen without significant government investment in the health and well-being of vulnerable children and families to ensure they have all the opportunities available to others. As described throughout this chapter, the PC government moved in the opposite direction. Despite an initial increase in funding for child welfare in 2017/18, funding declined by 2022 to 11 percent below 2015/16 levels when adjusted for inflation. While a move to block funding led to more discretion for agencies on how to spend the money, this model did not result in increased funding to child welfare agencies, while services delivered by the province through Winnipeg CFS and Rural and Northern CFS continued to see cuts.

The workers that responded to our survey told us that, at the time, the government continued to fail by implementing government-wide austerity measures that pushed families more deeply into poverty, further complicating the lives of those struggling to make ends meet. Until governments overhaul the foundations of the child welfare system as well as other oppressive systems that serve to perpetuate poverty and exclusion, the problems articulated by these workers during the study will not be resolved.

Notes

1   Expenditure based on Community Service Delivery Division of Winnipeg Child and Family Services and Rural and Northern Child and Family Services (when reported separately) and the Child and Youth Services Division's Strategic Initiatives and Program Support and Child Protection branches.

2   This estimate nets out the reduction due to Family Conciliation Services being transferred from the Child Protection branch to the Justice Department. Based on Justice annual report adjustments of five-year expenditure data, between 2019/20 and 2020/21, this transfer accounted for a decrease of approximately $2.5 million. Government of Manitoba annual reports available at https://www.gov.mb.ca/fs/about/annual_reports.html.

3   Information about the Framework Agreement Initiative is available at https://waapihk.com/2023/05/05/the-framework-agreement-initiative/.

References

Census 2021. "Portrait of Youth in Canada: Indigenous Peoples." https://www150.statcan.gc.ca/n1/pub/11-627-m/11-627-m2021085-eng.htm.

Government of Canada. 2019. An Act Respecting First Nations, Inuit and Métis Children, Youth and Families. SC 2019, c. 24. Justice Laws Website. https://laws.justice.gc.ca/eng/acts/F-11.73/index.html.

Government of Manitoba. 2018. *Transforming Child Welfare Legislation in Manitoba: Opportunities to Improve Outcomes for Children and Youth*. Report of the Legislative Review Committee. Manitoba. https://www.gov.mb.ca/fs/child_welfare_reform/pubs/final_report.pdf.

———. 2022. *Manitoba Families Annual Report 2021–22*. whttps://www.gov.mb.ca/fs/about/pubs/fsar_2021-2022.pdf.

———. 2023. "Implementing the United Nations Declaration on the Rights of Indigenous People Act." Department of Justice. https://www.justice.gc.ca/eng/declaration/index.html.

———. n.d. The Child and Family Services Act. SM 1985-86, c. 8. https://web2.gov.mb.ca/laws/statutes/ccsm/_pdf.php?cap=c80.

———. n.d. The Child and Family Services Authorities Act (CFSAA). SM 2002, c. 35. https://web2.gov.mb.ca/bills/37-3/b035e.php.

Hamilton, Alvin C., and Murray Sinclair. 1991. "Report of the Aboriginal Justice Inquiry." Accessed 8 June 2023. http://www.ajic.mb.ca/reports/final_ch01.html.

Hughes, Edward N. 2014. "Inquiry into the Circumstances Surrounding the Death of Phoenix Sinclair." Accessed 8 June 2023. http://www.phoenixsinclairinquiry.ca/.

Hurley, Mary C., and Jill Wherrett. 1999. *The Report of the Royal Commission on Aboriginal Peoples*. PRB 99-24E. Parliamentary Research Branch. October. https://publications.gc.ca/Collection-R/LoPBdP/EB/prb9924-e.htm.

Kimelman, Edwin C. 1984. *No Quiet Place: Review Committee on Indian and Metis Adoptions and Placements Final Report to the Honourable Muriel Smith, Minister of Community Services*. Manitoba Community Services. https://fncaringsociety.com/publications/no-quiet-place.

Moscovitch, Allan, and Ginette Thomas. 2015. *A New Social Care Act for Canada*. Canadian Association of Social Workers (CASW). https://www.casw-acts.ca/files/a_new_social_care_act_for_canada.pdf.

National Inquiry into Missing and Murdered Indigenous Women and Girls. n.d. *Reclaiming Power and Place: The Final Report of the National Inquiry into Missing and Murdered Indigenous Women and Girls*. https://www.mmiwg-ffada.ca/final-report/.

Petz, Sarah. 2022. "Judge Sides with Indigenous CFS Agencies, Rules Manitoba Government Misused Benefits Meant for Kids in Care." CBC Manitoba, 19 May. https://www.cbc.ca/news/canada/manitoba/childrens-special-allowance-fund-judge-decision-1.6459229.

Province of Manitoba, The Manitoba Métis Federation, The Assembly of Manitoba Chiefs, and The Manitoba Keewatinook Ininew Okimowin. 2007. "Aboriginal Justice Inquiry—Child Welfare Initiative." Accessed 8 June 2023. http://www.mb.ca/.

Report of the Royal Commission on Aboriginal Peoples. 1996. Accessed 1 June 2023. https://www.bac-lac.gc.ca/eng/discover/aboriginal-heritage/royal-commission-ab-original-peoples/Pages/final-report.aspx.

Torjman, Sherri, and Ken Battle. 1995. *The Dangers of Block Funding*. Caledon Institute of Social Policy. https://maytree.com/wp-content/uploads/479ENG.pdf.

TRC (Truth and Reconciliation Commission of Canada). n.d. "Truth and Reconciliation Commission of Canada." https://nctr.ca/about/history-of-the-trc/truth-and-reconciliation-commission-of-canada/.

Chapter 11

HOMES FOR DOLLARS: AUSTERITY AND THE MANITOBA HOUSING AND RENEWAL CORPORATION

Sarah Cooper

Introduction

Access to good quality, affordable housing has long been a pressing issue in Manitoba. In 2016, 11.4 percent of all Manitoba households (including 25.8 percent of renter households) reported that their housing cost more than 30 percent of household income, was too small for the household, and/or required major renovations; and that the household could not find suitable or adequate housing for less than 30 percent of household income in the same area. In 2021, this figure had dropped to 10.1 percent of all Manitoba households, including 22.0 percent of renter households (Statistics Canada 2022).[1] Before 1993, the federal government funded public, nonprofit, and cooperative housing programs to provide housing that was affordable to low- and moderate-income households; since then, provincial governments have held primary responsibility for low-cost housing provision (Suttor 2016).

In Manitoba, housing policy and programming is led by the Manitoba Housing and Renewal Corporation (MHRC). Despite its role as a Crown

177

corporation, the Department of Families has been gradually absorbing MHRC, and in 2021/22, all MHRC employees and the operating budget were transferred to the Department (Manitoba Families 2022). MHRC is responsible for the provision of public housing, as well as overseeing government-subsidized housing provided by nonprofit and cooperative housing organizations. It is also mandated to influence the housing market to benefit Manitoba households and to "enhance the affordability of, and accessibility to, adequate housing for Manitobans, particularly those of low and moderate income or those with specialized needs" (The Housing and Renewal Corporation Act 2022). Revenues to MHRC come primarily from sales of provincial land, rents paid by tenants, and contributions from provincial and other governments. MHRC spends money on a variety of rent subsidies and programs, including for housing operations, repairs, and new construction (Manitoba Families 2022).

As a proxy for provincial operating support for housing, Figure 11.1 presents the provincial operating grant to MHRC minus the corporation's surplus.[2] From 2010/11 to 2014/15, provincial operating support to MHRC was relatively stable, ranging from a high of $89 million in 2010/11 to a low of $70.8 million in 2014/15 in inflation-adjusted (2021) dollars; it then jumped to $104.4 million in 2015/16 and $120.7 million in 2017/18 before peaking at $144.1 million in 2020/21 during the COVID-19 pandemic (Hajer 2023). Once pandemic spending had slowed, MHRC's funding from the province reduced slightly to $129.9 million in 2021/22 (Hajer 2023). Capital asset values show a different pattern over this period. As part of the New Democratic Party (NDP) initiative to increase and reinvest in public housing stock, the book value of MHRC's tangible capital assets increased from $288 million in 2011/12 to $826 million in 2017/18, but then dropped to $753 million by 2021/22 (Manitoba Housing and Community Development 2013; Manitoba Families 2017, 2018, 2022). Staffing numbers also show declines under the Progressive Conservative (PC) government. Until 2021/22, staffing numbers were not publicly reported by MHRC, but data obtained through correspondence with the Manitoba Government and General Employees' Union (MGEU) show that between 2016 and 2021, the number of members MGEU represented fell from 372 to 240.

These figures tell a confusing story: On the one hand, operating funding for housing increased substantially after 2016 under the newly

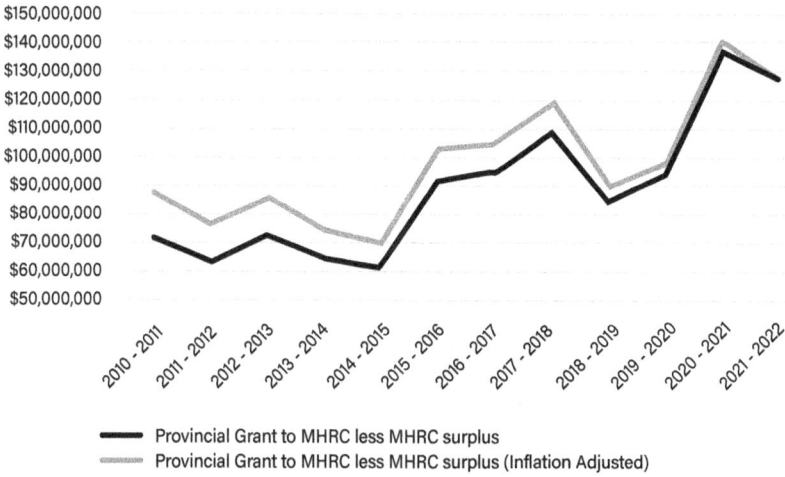

Figure 11.1. Provincial funding to MHRC less the MHRC surplus, 2011–2022.

elected PC government, in part as a response to the COVID-19 pandemic in 2020. On the other hand, the value of MHRC's capital assets fell by $73 million by 2021/22, and staffing numbers, based on the number of MGEU members, show a dramatic decline of 36 percent. This raises the question of where the new funding for MHRC is going. Although operating support from the province has been increasing, *how* housing needs are being addressed is shifting toward the market, with funding increasingly being used to support privately owned and nonprofit-owned housing rather than publicly owned and operated housing.

A Shift Away from Public Provision of Low-Cost Housing

Over the past ten years, low-cost housing policy in Manitoba has undergone substantial changes. These changes, which include greater reliance on Rent Assist, the transfer or sale of public housing units to private and nonprofit housing providers, and the National Housing Strategy, reflect a shift away from government provision of low-cost, nonmarket housing toward a focus on housing provision through the private market.

Although technically an income supplement managed by the Employment and Income Assistance (EIA) program in the Department of Families and therefore not part of the MHRC budget, Rent Assist is intended to subsidize renters' housing costs in private or nonprofit housing. Rent Assist is a universal program available to any household with an income below a given cut-off, including both households that are working and those receiving social assistance. The original program, announced in 2014 and fully implemented in 2015, covered the difference between 25 percent of household income and 75 percent of Winnipeg's median market rent (MMR). In the earlier years of the PC government, reductions to eligibility and the freezing of benefits for single people resulted in fewer households receiving less support (Froese 2019), but in 2021 the maximum non-EIA Rent Assist benefit was increased to 80 percent of MMR, increasing benefit levels. Although Rent Assist is an expensive program for the province, costing over $138 million in 2018/19, it has resulted in substantial improvements in housing and income stability for recipients (Cooper, Hajer, and Plaut 2020; Government of Manitoba 2021). As a universal program, it represents a substantial investment in housing support, but also a dramatic shift away from brick-and-mortar provision of social housing toward subsidies to the private market.

Paralleling the growth of Rent Assist is a shift away from provincially owned and managed housing. In 2017, the province released a fiscal performance review report by KPMG that examined the current state of social housing policy in Manitoba (KPMG 2017). The report recommended transferring public housing assets to private and nonprofit housing organizations in order to reduce spending, and indeed, from 2016 to 2022, the number of units owned by Manitoba Housing dropped from 18,200 to 16,400 (a decrease of 9.9 percent), and the number of units directly managed by Manitoba Housing dropped from 14,200 to 11,700 (a decrease of 17.6 percent) (Manitoba Housing and Community Development 2016; Manitoba Families 2022). While the management of most public housing units was transferred to nonprofit housing organizations, many units were sold to private developers, including the well-publicized sale of 373 units at 185 Smith Street (Grabish 2018, 2019). At the same time, the number of new units being built dropped, and maintenance budgets were reduced, leading to an overall reduction in investment in public and nonprofit social housing.

The third change is the implementation of the 2017 National Housing Strategy (NHS) through the 2018 NHS Bilateral Agreement. The Agreement lays out cost-matched funding from the federal government for a variety of housing programs, including for new housing construction, renovation of existing housing, and housing supplements for populations at greater risk of housing insecurity (Government of Manitoba 2020, 2019). The National Housing Council (2022) has critiqued the NHS for failing to produce housing that will move low-income households out of core housing need. It also argues that, even if the NHS meets its targets for developing new and maintaining existing community housing units, there will be almost 100,000 fewer units of low-cost community housing than were available in 2015. Although data for Manitoba is not yet available, these criticisms suggest that the province should not rely on the NHS to address the urgent need for low-cost housing in Manitoba and should instead develop its own low-rent housing.

Additional Factors

At the same time as these major changes in policy were taking place, three additional factors have shaped Manitoba's low-cost housing system. The first is the COVID-19 pandemic. Beginning in March 2020, a series of shelter-at-home and other health orders closed many public-facing businesses. The result was, for many households, a financial crisis: how to pay for rent, food, and other essentials without income? The province of Manitoba responded by temporarily freezing rents, postponing non-urgent eviction hearings, and providing new funding to support physical distancing measures in shelters for those experiencing homelessness. The province also provided one-time cash transfers to support vulnerable households, and the Government of Canada provided the Canada Emergency Response Benefit, an income support for workers who had lost income as a result of the pandemic (Cooper and Hajer 2020). Although the public policy response to the pandemic has abated, provincial housing policy has not addressed the systemic issues that shape core housing need, nor has it taken advantage of the opportunity to address housing as a public health requirement. Instead, low-cost housing has returned to business-as-usual.

The second factor is the expiry of federal and provincial funding agreements with nonprofit and cooperative housing providers that were put in place decades ago to subsidize social housing. These agreements enabled housing providers to offer low rents, but as they expire, housing providers must find ways to continue to offer low-cost housing without ongoing funding. This often requires increasing rents and changing tenant mixes, reducing the number of deeply subsidized units (Cooper 2015). In extreme cases, the end of agreements may result in the sale of buildings to private for-profit landlords, as has happened with Lions Place in downtown Winnipeg (Bernhardt 2023). The province announced a plan to address these expiring agreements through a new block funding model in May 2023, but the full plan has not yet been approved by government, and the initial funding committed ($1.4 million) is a small fraction of the estimated need.

Third, rents continue to increase, especially at the lower end of the market as part of an ongoing commodification of housing. In 2020 the rent increase guideline was 2.4 percent, but was frozen from April to October 2020; in 2021 it was 1.6 percent (Residential Tenancies Branch, n.d.; Hoye 2020). The guideline was set at 0 percent for 2022 and 2023, but despite these low guidelines, average rents have jumped. Rents increased by 11.7 percent in 2020; by 10.3 percent in 2021; and by 9 percent in the first six months of 2022 (Da Silva 2022). This is due to above-guideline increases (which are allowed when a landlord can demonstrate that they are making capital improvements to the property) and to newer and high-rent units not being subject to rent controls. The consequences are fewer low-cost units available in the private market and, as incomes rise much more slowly than rents, a gradual pricing out of lower-income households from the rental market.

Workers' Perspectives

In light of the pressures in Manitoba's housing market, particularly at the low end of the market, staff at the province and at nonprofit organizations funded through provincial programs were surveyed. Twenty-seven responses to the survey were received from individuals whose work relates to housing. These included eighteen respondents from the province of Manitoba (including staff in the Department of Families and Manitoba Housing) and nine respondents who work in housing-related positions at nonprofit organizations. Respondents work in all regions of Manitoba, with fifteen focusing on Winnipeg, seven focusing on all of Manitoba, and the remaining five focusing on rural and northern regions. For the most part, this section focuses on feedback from the provincial workers, but also includes feedback from the other, nongovernment employees where relevant.

Presence of Austerity over Time

Austerity has played a clear role in decision making about provincial housing policy and programming for the past several years. Eighty-three percent of provincial respondents said that their work was greatly impacted by the Government of Manitoba's austerity measures aimed at reducing expenditures and balancing the budget, with the remainder saying their work was moderately impacted. Respondents identified austerity measures such as reductions in spending, changing priorities, and a transfer of responsibility away from the government to the private or nonprofit housing sector. They also mentioned increasing workloads because of changing expectations and shortages caused by positions left vacant for months. Half of the respondents said that program work in their area had been reduced, including entire programs being eliminated and tasks being scaled back; one stated, "Program development decreased, development of affordable housing decreased, improvements to the supply of current affordable housing decreased." In addition to these cutbacks, 44 percent identified privatization and contracting out in their area, with one-third specifically mentioning the sale or transfer of public housing buildings to community-based organizations, and multiple respondents noting that maintenance and repair work is increasingly contracted out. As one Manitoba Housing property manager noted, "Maintenance staff is about half of what it once was due to retirements/career changes and nobody [has been] hired to replace them."

Austerity is not, however, a static process. Priorities for housing policy have shifted over the past several years. Rent Assist, as well as disinvestment in and the sale and devolution of provincially owned and managed housing, demonstrate the new policy focus on market solutions. One Manitoba Housing project officer noted that "there used to be significant [provincial] capital for the development of affordable housing under the NDP. Now most funding comes from the federal government." Another commented that while funding has increased overall, there are no plans to hire more staff. Seventy-two percent of respondents said austerity has intensified over time. During the pandemic, when spending on housing increased, 39 percent said austerity had become more intense, while the same proportion (39 percent) said it had remained the same. Since Premier Stefanson took office in November 2021, 67 percent said that the level of austerity has remained about the same, and 17 percent said the level of austerity had intensified.

Impact of Austerity on Service Quality and Value for Money

The result of these measures has been, according to 83 percent of provincial respondents, a reduction in the quality of service. More specifically, 78 percent indicated that they were being asked to provide the same or an increased level of service with fewer resources, and 39 percent said they were not able to spend as much time with individuals. The vast majority of provincial respondents (94 percent) felt that the austerity measures implemented in their area led to a reduction in service quality for low-income service users.

A majority of nonprofit respondents (56 percent) also identified a reduction in service quality, especially due to inadequate funding and support from the province. This is likely a result in part of the increased workloads and higher vacancy rates in essential positions, which make it more difficult for nonprofit respondents to connect with provincial staff. One property asset advisor noted that when funds are not provided for regular maintenance of housing properties, there is "lost value for all stakeholders." Likewise, a nonprofit property manager noted that there were fewer "government staff available to respond to issues as they arise," resulting in a "significantly slower response rate to necessary problem solving." A third nonprofit respondent, an executive director, stated that the "lack of prevention equals more houselessness, more desperation, more crime, more violence." These comments suggest a short-sightedness implicit in the province's austerity agenda, one with potential long-term implications for low-cost housing provision as nonprofit housing providers reconsider how much support they are getting from the province.

Of course, these austerity measures might be justified if they result in increased efficiency and savings over the long term. However, only a small minority of provincial respondents (11 percent) felt that the austerity measures implemented in the housing area would save money for the public sector as a whole, and only 17 percent expected that the austerity measures would create long-term savings. Only one said that the measures would result in better value for money for Manitobans. In contrast, 83 percent of provincial government respondents anticipated that the austerity measures would result in less value for money for Manitobans.

When asked about the implications of austerity measures, 33 percent suggested that costs were simply being transferred to other parts of the public sector, 61 percent expected increases in costs over the long term, and 44 percent anticipated that the result will be an increase in costs for both Manitoba Housing and the broader public sector. One respondent noted the importance of proactive action, saying that in the long run, "higher needs and less support/resources equals a greater need to reinstate previous support and develop additional resources." Likewise, among nongovernment respondents, 78 percent said the austerity measures would result in the same or less value for money for Manitobans. Two commented on the importance of investment in the maintenance of housing assets; as one property manager said, "If you don't properly manage and maintain property its value can decrease rapidly to the point where the real estate could actually be lost, and not-for-profit real estate is very valuable." Public and nonprofit housing represents a substantial decades-long public investment. Homelessness, housing need, and the loss of property value and housing units can be prevented with subsidies to maintain housing quality, but this approach requires forward thinking and funding.

Austerity and Working Conditions at the Province

Austerity measures have also resulted in increased workloads and longer timeframes for filling job vacancies, as well as stress and challenges for provincial employees: 89 percent said that the austerity measures implemented in their area led to worse working conditions and job satisfaction, and 94 percent said that austerity measures had worsened employee mental health. One described poor morale and high levels of stress, saying, "Feeling like your hard work is not recognized and being told someone else could do it better for less doesn't make you want to give it your best and if there's a chance you lose your job, not great for morale." As a result,

67 percent were less satisfied with their jobs, and none reported a positive impact. While it is certain that the COVID-19 pandemic contributed to stress for workers both within and outside the government, it seems clear that the work environment, including the pressure to do more with less resources, plays a substantial role in worsening working conditions.

Addressing Austerity

Improving the current working conditions and addressing the impacts of austerity measures on programming and service quality, including access to housing, for low-income households will not be simple. Some respondents suggested that the private sector has more resources and would be more focused on front-line service provision than the province. This may be in part because provincial spending is increasingly directed toward private services (e.g., contracting out of maintenance, or providing rent supplements rather than direct provision of public housing).

Other respondents—67 percent of provincial respondents and 33 percent of nonprofit respondents—said that they did not think the private sector would perform their unit or organization's tasks in a more efficient manner. They highlighted the lack of public accountability and the lack of incentive in the private sector to provide social housing, with comments including:

> "I don't believe that the private sector is equipped to address the issues that we deal with, they don't have the same mandate and political influence to work with the tenants and will not address the increase in homelessness as there may be an increase to evictions."

> "The private sector is not driven by the same values that we [in the nonprofit sector] are. Both the level of service and quality of service would be reduced."

These comments suggest that there is a need for nonmarket strategies to deal with social priorities that cannot be addressed through a profit-oriented private sector. However, nonmarket strategies will require funding. Most provincial respondents (72 percent) indicated that if their budget was increased, their area of work would have opportunities to provide greater value for money for Manitobans, while the remainder were unsure.

Increases in budgets could be used to fully staff units and provide "better service and less burn out for staff." Twenty-eight percent mentioned the importance of maintaining both public and nonprofit housing portfolios to improve tenant outcomes, with comments including:

> "[With additional funding,] we could maintain our current housing portfolios to offer more affordable housing, we could address some of the capital projects to increase security and maintain housing units. We could hire more trained, educated staff to support our current tenants and perhaps have funding to build new affordable housing units."

> "Housing and support services would lead to less eviction [and] more occupancy."

Some provincial respondents (17 percent) discussed the need for more staff, including front-line workers, with "smaller workloads for tenant services to help support our tenants in a more meaningful way." Two suggested a reduction in the number of managers to reduce micro-management and redundancy, and one mentioned the need for more mentorship and training "from seasoned employee[s] to newer employees." These suggestions reflect a deep concern among provincial staff for adequate investment in public and nonprofit low-cost housing, sufficient staff levels to carry out programming and policy making, and a long-term focus on prevention of housing need.

Conclusion

Although spending on housing continues to increase in Manitoba, there is a slow but steady policy focus on the provision of housing through the market. While Rent Assist provides substantial benefits to tenants, it essentially acts as a transfer to landlords, with no long-term investment in nonmarket low-cost housing. The transfer of ownership and management of public housing units to private landlords and nonprofit housing providers points to the privatization of a public resource. Finding low-cost housing is complicated by above-guideline rent increases that push average rents ever upwards; expiring subsidies for long-term, low-cost, nonmarket housing; provincial disinvestment from housing provision; and insufficient low-cost housing provision through the National Housing Strategy.

Provincial and nonprofit survey respondents emphasized the negative implications of the province's austerity measures, including a reduction in service quality, potential loss of housing assets, and poor working conditions. They also mentioned the transfer of public housing to nonprofit and private housing providers and the contracting out of maintenance and other services. This may explain why the province has increased funding to MRHC in the last few years despite the lack of investment in new housing: to compensate for more expensive private delivery, a finding clearly identified by workers in the transportation and infrastructure department (see Chapter 16 in this volume).

Public service workers in housing also noted that the public and nonprofit sectors are needed to provide low-cost, nonmarket housing. The end result of a provincial shift in housing policy toward the market and austerity is a gradual destabilization of access to housing, especially for the households with the lowest incomes and highest needs. Without strong, long-term investment in public and nonprofit housing, the resulting forecast for low-income households is grim.

Notes

1   The drop in percentage of households in core housing need from 2016 to 2021 is likely partly attributable to the federal and provincial governments' short-term COVID-19 pandemic benefits, especially the Canada Emergency Response Benefit (CERB) payments.

2   We subtract the surplus from the provincial grant, as surpluses go toward paying down government debt as opposed to supporting housing operations. MHRC generally ran annual surpluses under the PC government, averaging $16.2 million from 2016/17 to 2021/22, compared to under the NDP going back to 2010/11, where MHRC on average posted deficits averaging $3.6 million.

References

Bernhardt, Darren. 2023. "Rally at Lions Place Urges Halt to 'Shameful' Sale of Downtown Winnipeg Seniors' Complex." CBC Manitoba, 19 January. https://www.cbc.ca/news/canada/manitoba/lions-place-rally-housing-winnipeg-1.6719192.

Cooper, Sarah. 2015. "A Terrific Loss: The Expiring Social Housing Operating Agreements in Manitoba." In *Poor Housing: A Silent Crisis*, edited by Josh Brandon and Jim Silver, 143–56. Winnipeg: Fernwood Publishing.

Cooper, Sarah, and Jesse Hajer. 2020. "The COVID-19 Policy Response for Renters and Persons Experiencing Homelessness in Manitoba." In *COVID-19 in Manitoba: Public Policy Responses to the First Wave*, edited by Andrea Rounce and Karine Lavasseur, 173–80. Winnipeg: University of Manitoba Press.

Cooper, Sarah, Jesse Hajer, and Shayna Plaut. 2020. "Assisting Renters: Manitoba's Rent Assist in the Context of Canada's National Housing Strategy." Winnipeg: Canadian Centre for Policy Alternatives–Manitoba and Manitoba Non-profit Housing Association. https://www.policyalternatives.ca/wp-content/uploads/attachments/Assisting%20Renters.pdf.

Da Silva, Danielle. 2022. "'They Can't Afford Food . . . They Can't Afford Rent.'" *Winnipeg Free Press*, 11 November. https://www.winnipegfreepress.com/breakingnews/2022/11/11/they-cant-afford-food-they-cant-afford-rent.

Froese, Ian. 2019. "No Households Cut Off from Rent Assist This Year, but Anti-poverty Group Warns Single Adults Being Left Behind." CBC Manitoba, 3 June. https://www.cbc.ca/news/canada/manitoba/manitoba-rent-assist-benefits-frozen-1.5158402.

Government of Manitoba. 2019. "Governments of Canada and Manitoba Sign 10-Year Housing Agreement." News Release, 11 June. https://news.gov.mb.ca/news/index.html?item=45386.

———. 2020. "Governments to Invest More Than $17.5 Million to Connect Vulnerable Manitobans with Safe, Stable Housing." News Release, 17 December. https://news.gov.mb.ca/news/?item=50076.

———. 2021. "Province Investing More Than $4 Million in Manitoba Housing Properties to Improve Tenant and Community Safety." News Release, 15 January. https://news.gov.mb.ca/news/?archive=&item=50241.

Grabish, Austin. 2018. "Manitoba Housing Sells Downtown Highrise That's Been Vacant for 3 Years." CBC Manitoba, 17 May. https://www.cbc.ca/news/canada/manitoba/manitoba-housing-sells-downtown-highrise-that-s-been-vacant-for-3-years-1.4668401.

———. 2019. "Province Has Sold Off 94 Manitoba Housing Properties since 2016, Documents Show." CBC Manitoba, 2 November. https://www.cbc.ca/news/canada/manitoba/manitoba-housing-properties-sold-off-1.5381628.

Hajer, Jesse. 2023. "Austerity in Manitoba." Manitoba Research Alliance. 29 August. https://mra-mb.ca/austerity-in-manitoba/.

Hoye, Bryce. 2020. "Retiree's Fight against 30% Rent Hike Points to 'Broken Rent-Control System': Manitoba NDP." CBC Manitoba, 1 December. https://www.cbc.ca/news/canada/manitoba/manitoba-rent-hydro-increase-pandemic-covid19-1.5823733.

KPMG. 2017. "Manitoba Fiscal Performance Review. Phase 2 Report Business Case: Rationalization from Reorganization." https://www.gov.mb.ca/asset_library/en/proactive/fpr-phase-2-2.pdf.

Manitoba Families. 2017. *Manitoba Families Annual Report 2016–2017*. Province of Manitoba.

———. 2018. *Manitoba Families Annual Report 2017–2018*. Province of Manitoba.

———. 2022. *Manitoba Families Annual Report 2021–2022*. Province of Manitoba.

Manitoba Housing and Community Development. 2013. *Manitoba Housing and Community Development Annual Report 2012–2013*. Province of Manitoba.

———. 2016. *Manitoba Housing and Community Development Annual Report 2015–2016*. Province of Manitoba.

National Housing Council. 2022. "Analysis of Affordable Housing Supply Created by Unilateral National Housing Strategy Programs." https://assets.cmhc-schl.gc.ca/sites/place-to-call-home/pdfs/analysis-affordable-housing-supply-created-unilateral-nhs-programs-en.pdf.

Residential Tenancies Branch. n.d. "Rent Increase Guidelines." Province of Manitoba.

Statistics Canada. 2022. "To Buy or to Rent: The Housing Market Continues to Be Reshaped by Several Factors as Canadians Search for an Affordable Place to Call Home." *The Daily*. Ottawa. https://www150.statcan.gc.ca/n1/daily-quotidien/220921/dq220921b-eng.htm.

Suttor, Greg. 2016. *Still Renovating: A History of Canadian Social Housing Policy*. Montreal: McGill-Queen's University Press.

The Housing and Renewal Corporation Act. 2022. CCSM c. H160. https://canlii.ca/t/55ck6.

Chapter 12

AUSTERITY VERSUS MANITOBA WOMEN

Mara Fridell

Women, Social Reproduction, and Support Security

As they continue to be excluded from the wealth required to thrive in our world, how are women workers and women in poverty doing in Manitoba after seven years of austerity? In this chapter we look beyond any agency, set of agencies, or functional specialization. While this chapter does provide analysis from agencies traditionally tasked with addressing "women's issues" in the province, we enlarge our frame to include both empirical data from workers across Manitoba's public sector and comparativist social science. We seek a valid grasp of the broader encompassing dynamics of austerity, particularly on women in our province—both as public sector workers and as the people who pick up the slack from diminished public services, performing the feminized work of social reproduction in homes and communities.

We have to start by recognizing social reproduction work. Social reproduction denotes the intelligent, skilled labour we pour into keeping life—workers, children, elders, families, communities, and ecosystems— surviving and thriving. It is *feminized* work, and by that we mean that our economy and polity methodically fail to recognize its essential social and economic contributions. Social reproduction work includes healthcare and therapy; day care; elder care; art; environmental research and advocacy; educating, retraining, and organizing working people and communities; city and regional planning in support of democratic development; healthy housing, food, transportation, sports, and movement for all; restorative justice, reconciliation, and practising healthy, balanced self-esteem and boundaries for collaborative connection; the democratization of policy, law, institutions, and budgets; newcomer integration; and moderating infrastructure barriers for people with disabilities. Social reproduction work is human and environmental capacity-building work; it is support security—as opposed to suppression security, which takes the form of surveillance, policing, and incarceration, but also chemical restraints on many forms of life.

Conventionally, we discount the support security work reproducing healthy life, and we confusedly account for that work as a cost to the economy (Fridell and Turnbull 2014). Private property rights and militarism are our societal anchors, automatically disposing us to suppression security (Enloe 2013; Gilmore 2022; Gilmore and Murakawa 2024; Hanieh 2025; Kumanyika 2020). Unevenly enforcing decapacitation and disconnection becomes our default priority, crowding out support security. Without organized egalitarian intervention, our suppression-security bias snowballs into stunted human development and so stunted regional and economic development; into rampant inhumanity as well as the crises of our biosphere, hydrosphere, atmosphere, and lithosphere.[1]

To help motivate the recognition and restoration of support security for broader thriving, we will here review what is at stake, using survey, interview, economic outcomes, and comparative data to clarify the impacts of the accumulated burden of austerity on women's work and security in Manitoba.

Feminized Carework Discounted

Over the past half century, women around the world have stood in the bull's eye of austerity, as governments serve to disorganize, degrade, stymie, and strip down the support security foundation[2] laid by the extension of political rights, civil rights, and the social rights undergirding the welfare state (Bakker 2007; Dabrowski 2021; Enloe 2013; Hormel 2016; Lonergan 2015; Sutton 2010). Austerity funnels women—often deprived of the pay required to live in our society—into performing most of the triage work required to keep the workforce, consumers, and citizens alive if not thriving (Federici 2004; Fraser 2022; Matthei 2022; Simpson 2017).

Austerity policies were accelerated in this century after the 2008 global economic crisis. Citing the work of Diane Elson (1991) and other feminist economists, the UK-based Gender and Development Network has documented and summarized austerity policy and its impact on women: "Policy responses to the global economic crisis increasingly included drastic public spending cuts—or austerity measures—with an overwhelmingly disproportionate effect on women and girls." Canadian researchers from Isabella Bakker (Bakker and Gill 2003; Bakker 2007) to Canadian Centre for Policy Alternatives Senior Researcher Katherine Scott (2023, 2024) have documented how women's work, and especially poorly valued women's care work, is discounted across austerity crisitunities, including most recently the COVID-19 pandemic.

Deploying the political techniques of "balancing" budgets, under-spending announced budgets, regressively cutting taxes, neglecting infrastructure, privatizing and offloading services, and replacing taxpay-ers' skilled, paid decent work with junk jobs,[3] austerity in Manitoba has targeted social reproduction institutions including healthcare, Family Justice services, long-term care, in-home care, childcare, and education. Austerity has amplified and extended crises in women's carework, house-holds, and communities. Hospitals and families, for example, are juggling a variety of health problems deferred in and arising from successive years of lockdowns instituted to manage the engineered undersupply of care-workers and healthcare resources. Austerity's radical discounting of human development and care requirements had stripped workers and families of protective cushioning at the same time that it increased the risk of emergen-cies, resulting in rampant health damages to youth inflicted by the extended suspension of developmental connection; health damages to working-years adults by pandemic labour misallocation, social isolation, and burnout; and deferred healthcare.

If you have had a loved one with a progressive disability like demen-tia, you may have preferred to protect them from extra-debilitating stress with aging-in-place supports. Health and aging expert Laura Funk cites Marier's 2021 finding that Manitoba has one of the more robust home care programs left in Canada. Yet, threatening "home care transforma-tion," austerity politicians appeared to have Manitoba's publicly delivered home care program in their gunsights, and the home care program has a fundamental vulnerability: As in other provinces, its mandate is merely to supplement family care. Thus, the province will delegate to relatives the primary responsibility for care of its clients; the Winnipeg Regional Health Authority's (WRHA) direct-managed care program is marketed as a subsidy to private agency service; and if short-staffed, the WRHA contracts out services to the private sector. Following the crisis-chain playbook (Klein 2007), austerity strategists have insufficiently funded a public service in demand; underfunding generates gruelling crises in service provision, repelling workers and resulting in a consequent crisis of workforce recruitment and retention; these public sector service crises then serve as the plausible emergency which austerity managers use to justify clientelism, gifting private clients the public budgets of dissolved public services. Dependent on vulnerable workers with little support cushioning, privatized home care services strip down care quality, and so continue the austerity trend of transferring social reproduction work onto unpaid family caregivers. These are usually women, spread thin across too many off-loaded obligations, from regressively taxed, undervalued jobs to regressively taxed, underpaid, and unpaid household and community carework.

The survey of workers conducted for this study demonstrates that austerity governance amplifies crises upon families, as well as upon the Child and Family Services (CFS) Justice system supporting families. "Financial stressors are the main stressors on families," a typical respondent reported, adding that subjected to austerity, "financial stress is high and has grown over the past generation." By imposing additional crises that propel family dissolution, "austerity translates into higher CFS demand." As the lack of childcare supports and rising inflation combine, there is more need for mediation and child support payments. Moms are the main beneficiaries of public support, public employees report; and "since the pandemic, fathers have not been able to make their support payments." In a vicious spiral, families' diminished survival capacities put more pressure on thinned public supports.

Austere dismissal of the demanding, skilled work of fostering human connection has resulted in disarray across Justice institutions. "Justice is in turmoil," one respondent noted, continuing, "Because of government cutbacks, Child and Family Services (CFS) is constantly understaffed, especially up North." Employees reported that Family Resolution Services consolidated eight branches in 2020 and cut half of the Child Support staff, diminishing capacity even as concussive public emergencies mounted, childcare support languished, and price gouging and the cost of living billowed. Among other agencies, "Family Resolution Services and Victim Services has staffing gaps because of the difficulty of the work." Because employees were under the rule of austerity, there is no succession planning; and, lacking sufficient paid stress days, childcare, and even office space, the expanding and increasingly demanding workload is breaking employment. "Retention is collapsing," a CFS interview respondent reported, affirming our survey consensus, where 86 percent of women and 84 percent of men workers reported worsened employee recruitment and retention. One respondent put it simply: under austerity conditions, "staff just can't do it."

Support Security Displaced

Although women's work as social reproducers in families, communities, and public service is besieged across the board by austerity, within the Commonwealth tradition, governing women is largely constrained to managing social neglect's outcomes via domestic violence policy, as well as to marginal public expenditure on supporting women as representatives of—and triage workers in—families and communities maintained in poverty, crisis, and trauma. Accounting for inflation, actual funding to the two women's budget lines, the Manitoba Status of Women Secretariat and Family Violence Prevention, fell by $1.3 million between 2016 and 2023. Their budgets reduced in previous planning, provincial spending on these women's supports dropped notably in the pandemic crisis years of 2020/21, despite increasing need.

Manitobans suffer severe family and sexual violence, and it has gotten worse with the rise of global inequality. Over the past decade, demand for Family Violence Prevention services, for example, has increased by half, with 18,000 calls to their crisis hotline in 2021. In addition to the crisis line, Manitoba maintains ten women's shelters and four protective residences for abused women and their children, nine women's resource centres, and additional programming, including counselling, support groups, and training. Because much social reproduction work must be conducted within shelter, the dismantling of social housing and a dearth of state capacity to alleviate homelessness continue to undermine our women's resource centres in their work of supporting households in poverty communities.[4] Still, this study's respondents reported that with MLA support, substantial federally matched provincial money has been committed to ameliorate the problem of gender violence, particularly as a sharp increase in domestic violence (one of the "shadow pandemics" inflicting women) was unleashed in homes during the "perfect violence storm" of the isolating, stressful, and trauma-triggering pandemic lockdowns (Statistics Canada 2022).

Data collection was prohibited by public health guidelines, a respondent said, "but shelters were full, and we had some insight, delivering food hampers to 150 neighbourhood families two times a month." Researchers have noted that victims of the "shadow pandemics" and other dysfunctions of forced isolation suffer ongoing knock-off damage, from trauma to addictions, to induced autism-like symptoms in children, to Type II diabetes, to child marriage, to severe developmental disruption and diseases of malnourishment and chronic stress, for some examples (Flor et al. 2022; Phung et al. 2023). "Trauma and healing supports are needed, but they're not coming," a study respondent warned, citing as well mental health impacts on poverty sector careworkers.

Austerity governance maintains Manitoba's poverty-service agencies without coordination capacity, a study respondent observed. A lack of coordinating infrastructure incentivizes an institutional culture of "lateral violence," with irrational competition spinning out into decapacitated service providers. Manitoba advocates for women in poverty are struggling to overcome their structural decapacitation by convening to develop collaborative capacity, political literacy, communicative capacity, vision, and confidence. "I'm hopeful," a respondent ventured; but government backing is needed to moderate inequality and austerity's damages.

There is a constructive model that flashed across Winnipeg during the COVID-19 pandemic. A study respondent recommended an emergency cultural shift similar to the temporary but stunningly effective one instituted to coordinate ten agencies, including the Winnipeg Foundation, federal, provincial, and municipal agencies, and the United Way. Pan-organization coordination pooled resources and talent for more effective housing support, drop-in support, food security, and outreach. With a pivot toward support security, poverty-servicing public and nonprofit agencies were no longer on probation. Funders dropped their restrictions. Social work professionals were trusted to implement their expertise and improve their work together. Detailed accountability burdens were significantly eased. But extending this lesson from the state of emergency into an effective anti-poverty campaign flies into austerity headwinds. With the COVID-19 pandemic fading, the sector is back to scrappy play. "Now, though I am an experienced, proven professional and leader running a three million dollar 'business' every day, we're back to spending our time counting bus tickets," a respondent rued. Our capacity to support the women working and caring for families and communities is hamstrung by, as a respondent named it, "accounting culture"—a component of austerity's sexist, anti-worker bias proscribing a cost-benefit analysis of the displacement of support security by suppression security, including the accounting surveillance imposed upon resource-deprived communities.

Manitoba's Women on Austerity

Feminized work is heavily discounted (see Evans-Boudreau et al. 2023). Feeding over time into wealth-inequality crises, the gender pay gap in Manitoba is an objective measure of our self-defeating *misperception* of feminized support security work as inessential—desultory, disposable, a waste of resources.

Women are allowed a better chance in unionized public sector work than in the private sector. The draw of women toward union-protected public sector employment is reflected in the composition of public unions like the Manitoba Government and General Employees' Union (MGEU), with a nearly two-thirds female membership; and representatively, two-thirds of respondents in the survey are women. Seventeen percent of the civil workforce was slashed leading up to the pandemic, when the Progressive Conservative (PC) government cuts disproportionately removed women's health and women healthcare workers, nurses, post-partum care and lactation consultants, and gynecology and menopause healthcare workers, as well as public physiotherapists, emergency room staff, and low-wage, racialized healthcare workers (Sampert 2017). Observing in 2017 that it is Manitoba's women in the provincial austerity program's firing line, journalist Shannon Sampert reported with unease, "Because women are most often tasked with providing care in the private or domestic sphere, when the public sphere no longer provides services, it's expected those services will then be picked up by the private sector," which means particularly *women* "are expected to pick up the slack." The failure to perceive women's existing workload creates and exacerbates crises and emergencies.

The survey data informing this Women's chapter was contributed by twenty-five Manitobans mostly supervising or otherwise employed in nonprofit or contract social work with women, along with a few provincial supervisors and employees working primarily on behalf of women. The austerity game plan prescribed reducing family and community services, which exacerbated burnout among service providers. All respondents reported that their work was at least moderately impacted by austerity governance, and most reported their work was greatly impacted. Over three-quarters of these respondents reported that their workload has increased and intensified in distressing ways that wear workers down. A respondent explained, "The people we work with can't afford the basic necessities of life. EIA [Employment and Income Assistance] rates haven't kept up with inflation, and everything is more expensive, so more people are relying on non-profits like ours for access to basic needs like food, diapers, housing, washrooms, phones. And we have fewer resources to provide, so we are stretched thinner and not able to do the work in the caring way people need." Another reported that the PC government imposed "massive" budget cuts, causing "reduction in services available to community, as well as additional burnout for staff." Another conveyed distress at the sprawling toll on human lives in Manitoba. "When you cut social supports, the problems and root causes don't disappear," front-line workers reminded us. "We are seeing increasing need and more acute abuses experienced by populations we serve." A respondent reported that the official end of government COVID-19 supports resulted in budget cuts at odds with ongoing pandemic and pandemic policy tolls and the needs of women, their families, and their communities in poverty. "We were struggling before COVID-19. COVID-19 placed our services in the forefront and exposed how serious the conditions are in our sector: Dangerous work, low pay, under-trained staff."

Managing services provided under the provincial Status of Women portfolio, many respondents feel keenly the difficulty of recruiting and retaining social service workers in such critical, low-paid, punishing work conditions. As inflation mushrooms, wages have to be sufficient to channel women into these hard, discounted jobs. Under the province's crumbling, caving surface, social service workers supporting women are plagued by "burnout, because staff are fighting against colonial, oppressive, racist, capitalist, conservative systems that are killing people." Like women workers across Manitoba, they reported that chronic stress has impacted their physical and mental health and enjoyment of work. These results echo and amplify the experience of women workers responding throughout the study survey, who found themselves burdened by increased work responsibilities and resource shortages as budgets and staff were cut and work was contracted out and privatized.

Working conditions suffer under austerity governance. Eighty-eight percent of women workers reported worse working conditions and plummeting work satisfaction, 83 percent reported a decline in job satisfaction, and no women reported improved job satisfaction in austerity Manitoba. The majority (90 percent) reported worsened employee mental health as a result of austerity; 40 percent of women workers surveyed reported that worker safety had declined. A lot of workers (including 67 percent of women workers) wanted out of Manitoba in austerity.

Austerity left half of respondents stripped of resources, more perilously serving the same or increased numbers of clients. Three-quarters of women workers responding to the survey observed service declines as a result of austerity. Over half of women workers advised that with the imposition of austerity, service to Manitobans in poverty declined; and they confirmed that as austerity undercuts support security, public safety has declined. Recognizing austerity's capacity to induce a public sector crisis, 65 percent of women workers nonetheless expected that the private sector would deliver inferior performance in their work area.

Manitoba's women workers view conservative politics as contributing to their declining and even repulsive working conditions. Sixty-four percent of Manitoba's women workers believed that austerity worsened since 2016 under PC governance, and women workers (7 percent) were even less likely than men (13 percent) to report any improvement when the PC Party's Heather Stefanson replaced Brian Pallister as premier.

Austerity governance has burdened Manitobans with inappropriate, counterproductive, and costly reforms. Across the survey, workers of Manitoba overwhelmingly agreed that they were left out in the cold when austerity was imposed; they were not consulted, and they did not benefit from reasoned explanation. Only 8 percent of women workers saw their informed reform recommendations adopted; and according to 67 percent of women workers, front-line workers' expertise is missing from austerity interventions. Sixty-four percent of women workers told us that they can offer Manitobans better value for money strategies than austerity. Manitoba's women workers hold a very dim view of austerity as a politi-cal-economic strategy: 41 percent advised that in the short term, austerity measures increase costs, and an additional 18 percent reported that the cost reductions in their departments are merely transferred as cost increases to other departments. Their longer-term read on austerity governance is worse. Seventy percent predicted that austerity in their line of work will either hurt Manitobans economically or shuffle costs around from their department to others. "Less value for money" is far and away most women workers' view of austerity.[5] Manitobans' overwhelming experience of austerity has been workload intensification, resource depletion, diminished public services, declining work conditions, and torpedoed health.

Austerity Culture Preys on Manitoba Women

Austerity governance does not just cut funding to the collective goods and services we need to survive and thrive; it also fosters a crippling culture of contempt. Underfunding essential social reproduction work and maintaining communities in crises is justified by the everyday disrespect dumped upon feminized social reproduction work and workers. While promoting another PC party bill (Bill 35) attacking Manitoba's teachers, austerity politicians cynically leveraged sexual assault and social media's infamous capacity to inflict mental health damage into a media shaming campaign targeting public educators broadly, initiating the institution of an online public stockade where under-supported teachers' every slip in judgment is judged and paraded before the public as if it were continuous with sexual predation and church-run residential school genocide.

Today's online social-credit shaming spectacle targeting teachers is designed by austerity politicians to reinforce a conceit: that in the dirty trenches of economic and social crises, feminized careworkers are always on probation as the root social problem to sanctimoniously attack. We do not treat public school educators as reprobates because that is the way to protect children. We treat public school teachers as a class of reprobates because we are being misled again to misrecognize authoritarian, patriarchal inegalitarianism as caring, just as we were misled through the residential school era. It's a *Handmaid's Tale* on repeat: The compulsion to deploy shame to manipulate the feminized, public social reproduction workers among us is a childish reflex in a province so entirely *dependent* upon those workers' contributions, from their care-worn, skilled labour to their taxes. It is time to activate our adult relational capacities instead.

Conclusion: Democratize Economic Institutions, See and Support Social Reproduction Work

Women's vital contributions remain subject to multiple forms of exclusion; they are made invisible, denied and discounted, policed, and expropriated. People learn to withhold credit and cooperation from most women, and in an inequality society, this is exacerbated in crises. Failing to support social reproduction work sufficiently, our institutions maintain and manage our lives in a perpetual series of crises.[6] Like other bargains, discounted social reproduction allows decision makers to flatter themselves savvy market masters, but it undermines our foundations and welfare, and our human right to development. The cost of failing to recognize and reward the breadth of women's innovative work supporting life, and the public goods and services that begin to make this collective work in the context of a complex economy and society, is intergenerational stunting and trauma, and regional underdevelopment (Therborn 2013). The cost of valorized public goods and services is a reduction in yacht sizes (Chernomas, Hudson, and Hudson 2019). In Manitoba, with its vast ghost Lake Agassiz, that is a cost that should be not just bearable but a priority.

Because we observe that historically, political parties have only shifted off austerity under organized egalitarian pressure, and because the most crippling error of the austerity restoration is the erroneous belief that democracy is a done deal and only requires refinement at the margins, we know there are two fundamental requirements for abating the surging flow of austerity crises: first, we need to recharge the *egaliberte*[7] ideas that can divide elites and create space for developing democratic policies and institutions; second, we need to restore working-class organizing capacity.

Sociologist-organizers Jane McAlevey and Ruth Rittenhouse Morris are among the researchers who have helped diverse workers and their communities worldwide rebuild that capacity. More likely to be excluded from the benefits of elite collaboration, and saddled with unrecognized, underpaid but required reproductive work in crisis, women and people of colour have always played critical roles in the crucial historical moments of rethinking and reorganizing toward *egaliberte*. Reforging democratic infrastructure is the foundation for the support security that will allow us to collaborate in work that is truly innovative and productive *because it reflects the breadth of human thriving.*

Notes

1   Because Black Rock's Morris Pearl believes "the rich have begun to monopolize resources and opportunity in a way that jeopardizes social stability and economic growth," the former managing director of the world's largest asset management firm is part of a reviving interest in progressive taxation (Smith 2023). Historically, elite splintering has opened opportunities for organized egalitarian interventions.

2   The support security foundation is realized in the public assets, resources, quality credit, and cooperation bravely envisioned, organized, and introduced by previous organizing and struggle (McAlevey 2016; Piketty 2020).

3   See Gøsta Esping-Andersen (1990, 207), for a comparative analysis of junk jobs policy.

4   "Women and their households need safe, stable, and deeply affordable housing now," women's centre leaders advise. "BC public investment in rent-geared social housing provides the effective model for housing Canadians."

5   Our study found that a very small sample of thirty-one survey respondents identifying as trans, nonbinary, or other gender stood out from the predominant trend for their comparative comfort with austerity, in stark contrast to the reported experience of over 1,900 surveyed workers self-identifying as women and men. However, everyone tended to agree that austerity created repugnant working conditions.

6   The model for suppression security at the expense of support security can be seen starkly in the 2024–2025 Trump policies (Tait 2025).

7   *Egaliberte* denotes freedom based on equality, in contrast to the more elitist, postwar liberal and conservative, economistic versions of freedom.

References

Bakker, Isabella. 2007. "Social Reproduction and the Constitution of a Gendered Political Economy." *New Political Economy* 12 (4): 541–56.

Bakker, Isabella, and Stephen Gill. 2003. *Power, Production, and Social Reproduction: Human In/Security in the Global Political Economy*. London: Palgrave Macmillan.

Chernomas, Robert, Ian Hudson, and Michael Hudson. 2019. "A Political Economy for Yacht Owners." In *Neoliberal Lives: Work, Politics, Nature, and Health in the Contemporary United States*, 1–23. Manchester: Manchester University Press.

Dabrowski, Vicki. 2021. *Austerity, Women and the Role of the State: Lived Experiences of the Crisis*. Bristol: Bristol University Press.

Elson, Diane. 1991. "Structural Adjustment: Its Effect on Women." In *Changing Perceptions: Writings on Gender and Development*, edited by Tina Wallace and Candida March, 39–53. Oxford: Oxfam.

Enloe, Cynthia H. 2013. *Seriously! Investigating Crashes and Crises as if Women Mattered*. 1st ed. Berkeley: University of California Press.

Esping-Andersen, Gøsta. 1990. *The Three Worlds of Welfare Capitalism*. Princeton: Princeton University Press.

Evans-Boudreau, Anna, Oyindamola Alaka, Lorna A. Turnbull, Jesse Hajer, Natalie Dandenault, and Kristine Barr. 2023. *Tired of Waiting: Rectifying Manitoba's Pay Gap*. Winnipeg: Centre for Policy Alternatives, 23 April. https://www.policyalternatives.ca/wp-content/uploads/attachments/Pay%20Equity%20full%20report.pdf.

Federici, Silvia. 2004. *Caliban and the Witch: Women, the Body and Primitive Accumulation*. Brooklyn: Autonomedia.

Flor, Luisa S., Joseph Friedman, Cory N. Spencer, John Cagneya, Alejandra Arrieta, Molly E Herbert, Caroline Stein et al. 2022. "Quantifying the Effects of the COVID-19 Pandemic on Gender Equality on Health, Social, and Economic Indicators: A Comprehensive Review of Data from March, 2020, to September, 2021." *The Lancet*, 2 March. https://www.thelancet.com/article/S0140-6736(22)00008-3/fulltext.

Fraser, Nancy. 2022. *Cannibal Capitalism*. New York: Verso.

Fridell, Mara, and Lorna Turnbull. 2014. "Resilient Feminism: Social Movement Strategy in a Conservative Regnum." In *Counting on Marilyn Waring: New Advances in Feminist Economics*, edited by Margunn Bjørnholt and Ailsa McKay, 247–62. Bradford: Demeter Press.

Gender and Development Network. 2018. "The Impact of Austerity on Women." Submission to the United Nations Independent Expert on Foreign Debt and Human Rights. https://www.ohchr.org/sites/default/files/Documents/Issues/Development/IEDebt/WomenAusterity/GenderDevelopmentNetwork.pdf.

Gilmore, Ruth Wilson. 2022. *Abolition Geography*. New York: Verso.

Gilmore, Ruth Wilson, and Naomi Murakawa, eds. 2024. *Change Everything: Racial Capitalism and the Case for Abolition*. Chicago: Haymarket Books.

Hanieh, Adam. 2025. *Crude Capitalism: Oil, Corporate Power, and the Making of the World Market*. New York: Verso.

Hormel, Leontina M. 2016. "Marx the Feminist?" *Monthly Review* 67 (8): 57–61.

Klein, Naomi. 2007. *The Shock Doctrine: The Rise of Disaster Capitalism*. Toronto: Penguin Random House Canada.

Kumanyika, Chenjerai. 2020. "Ruthie Wilson Gilmore Makes the Case for Abolition." *The Intercept*, June 10. https://theintercept.com/2020/06/10/ruth-wilson-gilmore-makes-the-case-for-abolition/.

Lonergan, Gwyneth. 2015. "Migrant Women and Social Reproduction under Austerity." *Feminist Review* 109 (1): 124–45. https://doi.org/10.1057/fr.2014.43.

McAlevey, Jane F. 2016. *No Shortcuts: Organizing for Power in the New Gilded Age*. Oxford: Oxford University Press.

Marier, Patrik. 2021. *The Four Lenses of Population Aging: Planning for the Future in Canada's Provinces*. Toronto: University of Toronto Press.

Mattei, Clara E. 2022. *The Capital Order: How Economists Invented Austerity and Paved the Way to Fascism*. Chicago: University of Chicago Press.

Mineo, Liz. 2022. "Shadow Pandemic of Domestic Violence." *Harvard Gazette*, June. https://news.harvard.edu/gazette/story/2022/06/shadow-pandemic-of-domestic-violence/.

Olsen, Gregg M. 2021. *Poverty and Austerity amid Prosperity: A Comparative Introduction*. Toronto: University of Toronto Press.

Organizing for Power (O4P). "Rosa Luxemburg Stiftung." https://www.rosalux.de/en/o4p.

Phung, Ryan, Jessy Burns, Ana Hanlon-Dearman, Mara Fridell, Stefanie Narvey, and M. Florencia Ricci. 2023. "Association between Autism Spectrum Disorder and Parental Immigration among a Cohort of Preschool Children in Manitoba." Canada Paediatric Society annual meeting.

Piketty, Thomas. 2020. *Capital and Ideology*. Cambridge: Belknap Press.

Sampert, Shannon. 2017. "Women Feel Budget Cuts the Most." *Winnipeg Free Press*, 7 December.

Scott, Katherine. 2023. "Canada's Gender Pandemic Response: Did It Measure Up?" Winnipeg: Canadian Centre for Policy Alternatives, 8 March. https://policyalternatives.ca/publications/reports/canadas-gender-pandemic-response-did-it-measure.

———. 2024. "Work in Progress." 8 May. Winnipeg: Centre for Policy Alternatives. https://policyalternatives.ca/publications/reports/work-progress.

Simpson, Leanne Betasamosake. 2017. *As We Have Always Done: Indigenous Freedom through Radical Resistance*. Minneapolis: University of Minnesota Press.

Smith, Talmon Joseph. 2023. "The Greatest Wealth Transfer in History Is Here, with Familiar (Rich) Winners." *New York Times*, 14 May. https://www.nytimes.com/2023/05/14/business/economy/wealth-generations.html.

Statistics Canada. 2022. "Many Shelters for Victims of Abuse See Increases in Crisis Calls and Demand for External Supports in the First Year of the COVID-19 Pandemic." *The Daily*, 12 April. https://www150.statcan.gc.ca/n1/daily-quotidien/220412/dq220412b-eng.htm.

Sutton, Barbara. 2010. *Bodies in Crisis: Culture, Violence and Women's Resistance in Neoliberal Argentina*. New Jersey: Rutgers University Press.

Tait, Robert. 2025. "Trump Proposes Cutting $163bn in Non-defense Funds and Boosting Military." *The Guardian*, 2 May. https://www.theguardian.com/us-news/2025/may/03/trump-budget-cuts-health-education-military.

Therborn, Göran. 2013. *The Killing Fields of Inequality*. Cambridge: Polity.

Varoufakis, Yanis. 2023. *Technofeudalism: What Killed Capitalism*. New York: Melville House.

Chapter 13

SLASHING ROSES: AUSTERITY, SPORTS, AND THE ARTS IN MANITOBA

Brenda Austin-Smith

*The arts are the roses that make our lives worth living . . . people always say,
"but what about the potholes?" And I always say well, yes, we need to fix the
potholes so we can drive to the theatres—we need both. It's not either/or.*
—*Gail Asper (Kavanagh 2017)*

Manitoba has a reputation as a province that punches above its weight
in creative, cultural, and recreational activities. Marquee organizations
such as the Royal Winnipeg Ballet, the Winnipeg Symphony Orchestra,
the Winnipeg Jets, and the Winnipeg Blue Bombers draw crowds,
attract donors, sell season tickets, and make the province's capital city
an important one for those who enjoy sports and the creative arts.
Other seasonal events such as Festival du Voyageur, the Winnipeg Folk
Festival, the New Music Festival in Winnipeg, the Harvest Festival and
Exhibition in Winkler, and the Morden Corn and Apple Festival receive
critical provincial support. Various museums across the province do
as well, including the Royal Aviation Museum of Western Canada, Le
Musée de Saint-Boniface, the New Iceland Heritage Museum in Gimli,
the Mennonite Museum in Steinbach, the Canadian Fossil Discovery
Centre in Morden, and several others. Many other community-focused

organizations receive provincial funding through grants received via the Manitoba Arts Council. So do individual artists, artist groups, and arts and amateur sports organizations. Government funding for sports ranges from tax breaks and gambling revenue for professional sports clubs ($16.6 million in 2019 from the city and province) to targeted support through programs such as the Arts, Culture and Sport in Community Fund (Kives 2019). Whether the events and activities are profit or nonprofit, held in a community pitch, concert hall, or artist-run gallery, provincial support is a critical part of the arts and sports environment in the province.

Planning for Austerity

When the new Progressive Conservative (PC) government launched a head-to-toe "return on investment" analysis of cultural projects in 2017, it was the centrality of provincial funding to this sector that made this announcement potentially ominous. While the previous New Democratic Party (NDP) government had intended something similar, the election of 2016 forestalled that action, leaving a new government to conduct the first review of policy and funding since 1990. The framing of the test in those terms—the first strategy review of sports and culture priorities in over thirty years—was a built-in rationale for whatever the result revealed. The political utility of the gap in analysis was not lost on the new leadership. Minister Rochelle Squires observed in a CBC article at the time that the "previous administration" had not increased funding for the sector, and that the PCs had inherited "a major cultural deficit" (Kavanagh 2017). But Squires did not commit to more funding, even after admitting Manitoba had slipped to "the middle of the pack" in terms of its funding for the area.

The 2019 policy document *Our Way Forward: Manitoba's Culture Policy and Action Plan* emerged from that 2017 exercise. Its contents reflect the business priorities of the PC government in recasting the realm of creativity, recreation, and culture as one defined by investment, management, growth, and marketization. For example, the first guiding principle of the blueprint for action is "contribution to the economy," with "creativity" and "diversity and access to culture" next in the list. "Indigenous culture" is the fourth priority listed. *Our Way Forward* is characterized by language reminiscent of literature on the "culture industry," a term with roots in the anti-capitalist theorizing of the Frankfurt School (2020) that has long since been repurposed to justify the existence of the arts primarily as they contribute to capital. The concept of the culture industry, as Ieva Moore writes, implies "a foundation of competitiveness," and recasts creativity as an asset subject to economic policy (2014, 739). The definition of cultural activities as deserving of government funding if they serve economic ends emerges in reference to the "consumers" of culture, to "cultural entrepreneurs," to culture as an economic driver, and to a vision of ever-deepening business partnership, increased volunteering, private philanthropic support, and continuing growth as sector goals. The vision expressed in *Our Way Forward* echoes neoliberal economic policies in Australia and the UK, in which notions of the creative economy, the creative nation, art-centric business, and knowledge economies took hold after 1994 (Moore 2014, 739). It is, as Moore observes of similar documents and positions in the UK post-1997, cultural policy as economic policy, with sports, tourism, parks, and other cognate areas included under the category of "the creative industries" (2014, 740).

Our Way Forward commits to supporting export readiness for cultural products; making cultural programs for labour force development responsive to industry needs; and ensuring "alignment with Manitoba's strategic priorities" in reviewing. Other priorities articulated in the plan include reducing the complexity of the grant application process and supporting the "modernization" of the Manitoba Arts Council's assessment process. The plan's introduction also forecasts shifts in the Department of Sport, Culture and Heritage itself, ventriloquizing the government's intentions by attributing them to everyday Manitobans who, it seems, saw "an opportunity for a strengthened partnership between the culture sectors and Travel Manitoba" (2019, 7).

In a cultural environment conditioned by austerity, funding for sports, culture, and the arts is shaped by assessments of return on investment over considerations like artistic merit or community needs. Existing social inequalities are not reduced but rather reinforced when funding attitudes are guided by the determination to reduce public spending—and perhaps especially, public spending on activities and events whose outcomes are not as tangible and objectively quantifiable as those provided by a new bridge or wider roads. While the 2019 policy document touts the economic activity associated with culture (it directly employs over 20,000 Manitobans and accounts for 2.7 percent of the province's gross domestic product) the immeasurable effects of recreation and the arts on those who participate in these activities do not merit discussion. Heritage is cast in preservationist terms rather than as something always in the making. High-profile organizations that operate on a subscription basis with similarly high-value donor contributions are likely to benefit from provincial supports, including tax breaks, in ways very different from amateur community-based recreational and arts organizations that do not offer subscriptions or programs that appeal to high-income earners in a direct way. Non-marquee organizations that serve rural and inner-city users and communities rely more on public monies because the user base does not have the disposable income necessary to pay directly for the recreational and cultural experiences available to other communities with more disposable income and more access to successful funding paths.

Austerity in Action

The policy document adopted by the PCs in 2019 provided a roadmap for austerity budgeting in the Sport, Culture and Heritage Department, one the provincial government has followed with only a few short-term deviations. Tracking the area expenditures and changes to full-time equivalent positions (FTEs) in the Ministry between 2016 and 2022 reveals significant decreases to funding and staffing that reduce overall support for recreational and cultural efforts province-wide. The execution of that vision turns up, for example, in a 2017 announcement of cuts to Sport Manitoba, with that government agency directed to apply the decrease to salaries and operations rather than grants (Annable and Lee 2017).

Data from the Government of Manitoba Estimates of Expenditure[1] show a decline in funding to the Ministry between 2015/16 and 2021/22 of 13 percent when adjusted for inflation (Hajer 2023). Despite some one-time specific expenditures, the base trend of spending in this period is downward. These one-time expenditures appear in the annual reports (Hajer 2023). For example, in 2018/19 the film and video production tax credit increased by $22 million, while sports grants assistance increased by $4.5 million for support of the 2023 World Police and Fire Games. There was also a one-time $17 million contribution to the Heritage Resources Fund and the Military Memorial Preservation Fund. Similarly, there was a $47.5 million increase in sports grants noted in the annual report as related to Investors Group Field for a capital reserve fund and construction deficiencies and for an international curling centre of excellence—again, all one-off spends. That same year also saw a temporary infusion of funds to support increased grants to organizations participating in the celebration of Manitoba's 150th anniversary, while the film and video production tax credit increased by another $12 million. In 2020/21, the budget of the Ministry enjoyed a briefly positive blip in the form of $33 million as nonrecurring costs associated with the architectural renovation projects (the Dome Building) and the establishment of the Bay Building Heritage Preservation fund. Expenditures in this sector peaked briefly in the run-up to the banner anniversary of the province, held there for a year, and then fell sharply to a level *below* that of 2015/16—the year Rochelle Squires pointed to as indicative of the NDP's "cultural deficit."

It is also critical to realize that this department was tasked with managing more files over this six-year period than it had been in 2016. For example, costs that attend the department's new responsibility for the Francophone Secretariat have been included, as have the costs of moving Tourism back into the department in 2021/22. Despite this net increase in portfolios, then, total inflation-adjusted expenditures for Sport, Culture and Heritage (including Francophone Affairs) decreased from $106.3 million in 2015/16 to $92.5 million in 2021/22. The one-off spends in 2018/19 and 2019/20 were rapidly offset by decreases in funding across the department. The comparison is stark: total expenditure on sports, recreation, arts, culture, and heritage per Manitoban was $66 in 2021/22, down from $82 in 2015/16.

Plummeting Funds, Disappearing People

Austerity means more than direct funding cuts, of course. It takes the form of privatizing services that used to be publicly funded, contracting out jobs that government workers already do, and reducing the number of staff available to do the work of public service. Replacing full-time workers with part-time ones is also a method of cost cutting, albeit one that is harder to track. You cannot tell if the person standing at the desk of a provincial park office, or the person who designed a display at a museum you visited on the weekend, has benefits and a pension plan. Nevertheless, cross-referencing records of F T E s in the department between 2016/17 and 2021/22 with other information shows F T E s in the department dropped from 204 to 154 over this period (Hajer 2023). Though it is impossible to tell how many of these F T E positions were filled versus left vacant, Public Service Commission reports tell us the real number of employees in each government department. In 2017 there were 210 employees in this department, while in 2022 there were 95. Even accounting for the 54 F T E positions hived off when Communication Services Manitoba left the department, and the 24 F T E positions that moved out of the department with Translation Services in 2017/18, that leaves 126 F T E positions staffed by only 95 bodies and a reported vacancy rate of 26 percent (Hajer 2023). A combination of direct funding cuts, vacancy management (e.g., not filling positions), and part-time appointments consistent with austerity measures has dramatically reduced staffing levels in a department that the government claimed was central to building "our cultural capacity" and that would support "a dynamic environment where artists, cultural entrepreneurs and the cultural industries can flourish" (Government of Manitoba 2019, 1).

Working in Austerity

Numbers go only so far in conveying the effects of austerity as a philosophy and a management practice. What brings data to life are the experiences of public workers in this department over this period. The sections that follow offer readers an understanding of how these austerity measures have affected the working days of those charged with delivering excellent services to the Manitoba residents who deserve them.

Thirty-five employees in Sports, Culture and Heritage responded to the survey described elsewhere in this volume, and many provided additional remarks on the survey and in interviews. They answered questions about the nature of their jobs under the Manitoba P C government and shared their analyses of what the government's decisions have meant for families, communities, and the general public who contribute to, engage in, and enjoy sports and culture in this province. The workers surveyed held positions at several levels of the department and on the community side of services. Their observations fill in gaps that might otherwise have been created had only one stratum of employees responded. Some respondents were comfortable identifying themselves as front-line workers, coordinators, managers, analysts, and administrators. Others preferred not to be identified as working in a particular position. Most said that their responsibilities involve services provided to the entire province rather than to a specific region. Both rural and urban communities were thus affected by changes to their work.

Working Conditions under Austerity

"Added duties to cover for the laid-off positions means that people are feeling overworked, underpaid, and will burn out."

Seventy-nine percent of the employee respondents reported that their work was greatly or moderately affected by the government's austerity moves; only 15 percent felt no impact at work. The effect was most dramatic both for those laid off and for the 50 percent who reported an increased or intensified workload. Duties from laid-off workers have been transferred to others, even as areas are not permitted to replace people, leaving positions vacant. One person reported that their unit had been cut from over twenty people to fewer than ten, with a 57 percent increase in workload. The result, reported one worker, was having to put in regular overtime to complete duties associated with the job. Funding cuts for organizations that deliver public services with provincial funding means employees must spend more of their time fundraising than before. Cost cutting and frozen budgets have affected everything from supplies to salaries. "I haven't received a raise in three years," said one person, while another described paper and equipment shortages affecting their ability to print or photocopy.

One person described having been handed senior management responsibilities with no departmental support or financial compensation. A detailed description of working in austerity conditions came from someone who said, "I consider my workload to be unsustainable. We are currently short-staffed (three unfilled positions and one person is leaving soon). There are no plans to fill two of those positions and the position of the person who is leaving will take months to fill. Everyone's workload has increased as a result. I feel like I can't keep up." A respondent remarked that staff cuts reduced their unit to such an extent that it became "non-functional" until more people were slowly added over the following four years. These observations not only confirm the reality of austerity but also show how poorly planned the measures were, reducing some areas to absurdly low levels of capacity.

"The government asked for input from staff but had no intention of listening or acting on any suggestions."

The haphazard effect of austerity measures is itself a result of failures to consult and respect the expertise of public sector staff. Not one of the respondents felt that their experience, expertise, and opinions were reflected in the reduction plans implemented in their area. Some reported that there were no formal or public consultations on the changes and no discussions with staff about the rounds of job losses experienced over the last five years. One employee sounded incredulous that anyone from the government could have consulted Arts and Culture staff and still proceeded with cuts; "otherwise the government should have provided more, not less, funding to our sector." Another had this to share: "The strain on resources in our area, and the lack of interest in public service expertise, resulted in decision-making without foundation in understanding the challenges, needs or problems, or any in-depth policy analysis of potential solutions, risks and impacts." As one person put it, "My area of work could save policy analysts time, save the government money by providing specialized services and extend services across Manitoba."

Service to the Public under Austerity

When asked if work was scaled back or eliminated in response to austerity measures, 41 percent of respondents answered yes. Many explained in comments that their unit could not deliver as much programming because of cuts, the scale of certain performances had been reduced, or they could not do as much research for the position because they need to pick up the critical work of others who had left and not been replaced. Austerity has also affected the support some units can offer to others: "We can host fewer workshops and training events. Additionally, other organizational community roles such as research, resource sharing, networking, and communications have been significantly reduced." One person mentioned the dissolution of the Manitoba Community Service Council, which provided funding for nonprofit, volunteer, recreation, and social service organizations to secure equipment and computers. This person mentioned a government promise to distribute that funding to municipalities, but said there is no evidence that actually happened. Still other respondents shared that they can do only 50–70 percent of essential curatorial work because of an increased workload from staff losses. Despite claims in the government's 2017 plan document, respondents commented that elimination of staff working in heritage areas meant that "dramatically less" planning, conservation, and actual work is possible, including the provision of support for the discovery of unmarked or hitherto unknown burial sites of Indigenous people of public significance that the department would be responsible for managing. So drastic is the reduction in staff that in some areas, respondents said, "fulfilling our legal mandate is now impossible."

"I am burnt out, trying to do as much with less."

Forty-five percent of respondents reported being asked to provide the same or increased service with fewer resources than before. Twenty-eight percent either were not able to see the same number of individuals as before or could not spend as much time with them as before. "Not all responsibilities can be filled and [there is] a much greater delay to stakeholders," said one employee. The outlier was one fortunate respondent who reported being "pleasantly surprised" that there were no cuts to base funding in their area. One commentator added, "Any reduction in services or safety are immaterial to this government. They don't respect public servants and their work, and similarly have no interest [in] whether their policies hurt or help middle- or low-income Manitobans." Connecting the department to indirect and long-term health concerns, one respondent observed that "greater funding for the arts can positively impact mental health and in some ways, for youth, is a crime prevention tool." Another worker added this comment: "Sport in my opinion is long-term healthcare. Funding cuts affect programming which will affect *health* in the *short* & long term" (emphasis in original). One employee speculated that services are likely reduced for low-income Manitobans because admission costs have increased, creating a financial barrier to access.

Financial Responsibility under Austerity

"They ended up increasing costs in both my area of work and for the public sector as a whole."

Fifty percent of respondents thought that the savings from austerity in the short term did not save the public any money, with 18 percent clarifying that savings in one area often resulted in costs to other branches and other levels of government. For some nongovernment organizations, austerity measures took the focus away from the provision of services and redirected it to searching for other funding sources. One person commented that the austerity measures were hard to justify "when we need to print materials to preserve them for future generations." Some shared that immediate savings went to a cut to the education levy, the tax paid by employers with a permanent establishment in Manitoba, and that in the end, rebuilding capacity would cost Manitobans much more in the future. No employees reported that the implemented measures in their area resulted in better value from tax dollars spent on public services. Instead, 68 percent thought austerity would result in poorer services. Respondents commented that cuts to sports and recreation "will negatively impact health, social & community services in the long term." Respondents also made the point that austerity affects the maintenance of properties, artifacts, and other holdings, as well as the staff who best know how to "keep up appearances" and work with outdated databases and inadequate storage for various collections. Respondents returned again and again to the deterioration of working conditions and the consequent effects on the services Manitobans deserve, all of which detracts from the savings goals that justified the austerity moves in the first place: "The enormous strain on staff from heavy workloads, staff shortages and time pressures has created a vicious circle of staff turnover, brain drain, high rates of sick/ stress leave and increased strain on staff who remain. Limited training and mentoring resources are expended on staff who then leave after only working months. Term employment positions are a poor investment of public resources for similar reasons."

Seventy-one percent of respondents reported either no change or intensified austerity in the wake of the election that replaced Brian Pallister with Heather Stefanson. In some instances, there had been cuts for years before 2016 under the NDP. Cuts to one area over the last thirty years have resulted in an effective 30–35 percent funding reduction, something current austerity has only made worse. When asked if there was a role for the private sector in the provision of their area's services, 77 percent said no. Respondents noted that their department provides services for those without many resources, and that privatizing would put profit over serving community needs. Others pointed out that the arts and culture sector "is about so much more than making money" which would make privatization "disastrous!" All who commented stressed the contradictions between private mandates and public ones. Arts, culture, and amateur sports do not generate profit; neither do museums that concentrate on science and culture. "Any efficiencies," said one person, "would be at the expense of services."

"If the government listened to the professional, experienced, skilled and educated members of the public service, Manitobans would be amazed at the resulting superior services."

The knowledge and dedication of public service workers in the Ministry is an under-tapped resource, according to the 88 percent of respondents who shared ideas for increased value for money for Manitobans with an increase to their budgets. Cultural institutions "have decades of experience" working with tight budgets. Respondents saw many ways to seize partnering opportunities, share resources, manage data, make community training more effective, and increase access to lower-income families with more funding and more staff. Respondents also had lots of suggestions for improving the efficiency of their departments even if funding did not improve. Among these were synchronizing grant opportunities; sharing staff among volunteer arts organizations in rural areas; forming consultation committees in the sector to develop ideas and plans; keeping funding under the Community Services Branch for arts organizations; and adopting automated processes to cut down on wasteful manual practices.

Conclusion

"Austerity has damaged the fabric of our province."

In closing remarks, respondents from the Ministry of Sport, Culture and Heritage surveyed the damage done to their units from years of austerity, some predating the current government, but nevertheless amplified by the PCs. "This government has completely disregarded any evidence of the resulting damage to public services and showed no empathy for its employees and the majority of Manitobans," said one. Another identified a pattern in arts funding cuts "spreading the funding from the have nots to the haves." Fears that further cuts "could kill off arts organizations," especially in rural areas, and that staff could not fulfill their current mandates for service ran throughout these final comments. "This erosion of public service capacity has been demoralizing and damaging," said one. "The only thing keeping the lights on . . . is the unwavering devotion to our profession and belief that what we do is important to Manitobans."

Notes

1   Expenditure data comes from the Government of Manitoba's Annual Reports on the Estimates of Expenditure and Supplementary Information (2019/20 to 2021/22) and Volume 3: Supplementary Schedules and Other Statutory Reporting Requirements (2010/11 to 2018/19). These documents are published as part of the government's annual public accounts reporting process and can be found in Manitoba's Provincial Annual Report and Public Accounts Archive: https://www. gov.mb.ca/government/finances/financial-reports-archive.html. For compilation and synthesis of this data see Jesse Hajer, "Austerity in Manitoba" (Hajer 2023).

References

Annable, Kristin, and Donna Lee. 2017. "2017 Manitoba Budget: Arts, Sports Programs to See Big Cuts." CBC Manitoba, 11 April. https://www.cbc.ca/news/canada/manitoba/manitoba-budget-arts-culture-programs-1.4064794.

Government of Manitoba. 2019. *Our Way Forward: Manitoba's Culture Policy and Action Plan*. March. https://www.gov.mb.ca/asset_library/en/culture/culture-policy-action-plan.pdf.

Hajer, Jesse. 2023. "Austerity in Manitoba." Manitoba Research Alliance. 29 August. https://mra-mb.ca/austerity-in-manitoba/.

Horkheimer, Max, and Theodor W. Adorno. 2020. *Dialectic of Enlightenment*, edited by Edmund Jephcott and Gunzelin Schmid Noeri. Redwood: Stanford University Press.

Kavanagh, Sean. 2017. "PC Government Will Establish 'Return on Investment' Test of Social and Cultural Products." CBC Manitoba, 3 January. https://www.cbc.ca/news/canada/manitoba/arts-culture-squires-pc-government-infrastructure-1.3917263.

Kives, Bartley. 2019. "City and Province to Provide Winnipeg Pro Sports With $16.6M This Year." CBC Manitoba, 6 March. https://www.cbc.ca/news/canada/manitoba/winnipeg-manitoba-pro-sports-subsidies-1.5041908.

Moore, Ieva. 2014. "Cultural and Creative Industries Concept—A Historical Perspective." *Procedia: Social and Behavioral Sciences* 110: 738–46.

Chapter 14

AUSTERITY IN THE DEPARTMENT OF ECONOMIC DEVELOPMENT, INVESTMENT AND TRADE, AND IN THE DEPARTMENT OF AGRICULTURE

Fletcher Baragar

This chapter examines the effect of the austerity policies implemented by the Manitoba provincial government on work and workers in the province's Department of Agriculture and Department of Economic Development, Investment and Trade (EDIT). The relevant years extend from 2016 through to 2022, which are the years of Progressive Conservative (PC) Party rule. The first section provides an overview of the responsibilities and goals of the EDIT and Agriculture departments, and of the organizational restructuring incurred by those departments during this period. The next section examines the effects of the austerity agenda through the expenditure budgets and the employment levels in each of the departments.[1] That is followed by a closer and more detailed account of the effect of the austerity measures on the work and work experience of the employees in those departments. A brief conclusion closes the chapter.

Overview of the Departments

In its *Annual Report 2021–2022*, EDIT stated that the department is "responsible for driving economic growth for Manitoba through investment, trade and a skilled and diverse workforce" (Province of Manitoba 2022c, 8). The stated mission of the Department of Agriculture is to "foster the sustainable growth of Manitoba producers and agri-processors through innovative, reliable support services" (Province of Manitoba 2022b, 18). Both departments are directly concerned with aiding and sustaining economic growth, but whereas the focus of Agriculture is directed toward a key provincial industry and its linkages to other industrial sectors, the remit of EDIT involves elements of the larger, province-wide framework shaping economic development and growth. Practical concerns of direct producers resonate strongly within Agriculture. Especially pronounced in recent decades has been the growth and influence of agribusiness, a development that has been well-received by the PC government. By contrast, the larger, macro-oriented concerns of EDIT have favoured a more top-down approach, which lends itself to the articulation and implementation of policies and programs that emerge as manifestations of abstract principles and a prevailing ideology, rather than from the imperatives of pragmatic problem solving.

Whether measured in terms of the annual budgetary allocation, or in terms of employment, neither Agriculture nor EDIT ranks among the larger of the provincial departments. Expenditures for 2021/22 for Agriculture and for EDIT were $645 million and $282 million, respectively (Province of Manitoba 2022a, 48–49). As of 31 March 2022, Agriculture employed 324 workers and EDIT employed 292 (Province of Manitoba 2022d, 47). Core staffing levels in 2021/22, expressed in terms of full-time equivalent positions (FTEs),[2] were 392 for Agriculture and 369 for EDIT.

The composition and attendant responsibilities of government departments evolve over time. Reconfiguration has been very evident in EDIT over the 2016 to 2022 period. Under the previous New Democratic Party

(NDP) administration, the department operated as the Department of Jobs and the Economy. In 2016, under the auspices of the new PC government, the department was reconstituted as the Department of Growth, Enterprise and Trade. A new mission statement articulated the orientation of the new administration: "The Department . . . is committed to increasing prosperity for Manitobans by partnering with entrepreneurs and community leaders to develop and implement initiatives that will strengthen Manitoba's economy and create jobs" (Province of Manitoba 2017b, 4). Entrepreneurs and community (read: business) leaders were conceptualized as the key agents, and they were to take on active roles not only as directors and managers of private sector business but also in an advisory capacity with respect to the formulation and implementation of provincial economic policy. A significant development here was the formation of the Premier's Enterprise Team, described as "an independent advisory panel of entrepreneurs that will provide advice and recommendation for job creation and economic development across Manitoba" (Province of Manitoba 2016). The panel replaced the Premier's Economic Advisory Council which, under the NDP, had representation from both business and labour.

Further restructuring occurred in October 2019, and then again in 2021, culminating in the establishment of the new Department of Economic Development, Investment and Trade on 18 January 2022. As a result of these restructurings and their attendant mission reorientations, numerous departmental units and divisions, such as resource development, labour, advanced education, immigration, and apprenticeship and training (which at one time or another had comprised parts of the department under its previous iterations) were no longer constituent elements of EDIT.

In addition to the musical chairs of department restructuring, the 2016 change of government brought a different perspective on the definition of economic development. The previous NDP administration's approach to economic development tilted toward acceptance of the principles of Community Economic Development (CED), which stresses the interconnection between economic, social, and environmental outcomes with an emphasis on community ownership and control of the economy. Economic development under the PCs was designed to meet the needs of employers and garner the support of business under the assumption that pro-business policies would create broad prosperity. This change in priorities resulted in resource reductions in areas that promoted CED. For example, under the NDP the province employed analysts to assist with the formation and development of cooperatives, but those responsibilities were eliminated under the PCs. The NDP funded a Social Enterprise Strategy to promote businesses with explicitly social goals, such as providing training and employment for the unemployed. The PCs did not renew the Social Enterprise Strategy after 2018.

Under the PCs, heightened attention was given to "partnerships," where partnership between business, industry, and government was seen as fundamental to creating an environment conducive to "economic success." The strategic role of these partnerships was articulated in the government's Economic Growth Action Plan, which was launched in December 2018. As stated in the news release of 6 December 2018, the Action Plan was envisaged as constituting a new and "modern approach to supporting economic development in the province." Furthermore, the government indicated that a "first critical step" would be to establish "new governance structures . . . to ensure decision-making and co-ordination functions are in place to enable a whole-of-government approach in implementing the action plan." Phase 1 of the Action Plan included, along with the establishment of an Economic Growth Committee of Cabinet, a new Manitoba Economic Development Office "to lead economic development initiatives and projects with business, industry and stakeholders" (Province of Manitoba 2018b). The Economic Development Office became part of the department after the 2019 restructuring. With the 2021 restructuring, institutional support was in place to advance the view of partnerships associated with the Action Plan. As noted in the department's *Annual Report 2020–2021*, the objective of its Industry Programs and Partnership division was to support the "whole-of-government approach to implementation of the Manitoba Growth Action Plan in collaboration with business, industry, partner organizations and other levels of government" (Province of Manitoba 2021b, 17).

Internal reorganization also occurred in Agriculture during the 2016 to 2022 period. In 2015, the department existed as the Department of Agriculture, Food and Rural Development. In 2016/17, the new PC government transferred the Rural Development unit to the newly reconstituted Department of Growth, Enterprise and Trade (Province of Manitoba 2017b, 43), and what was formerly Agriculture, Food and

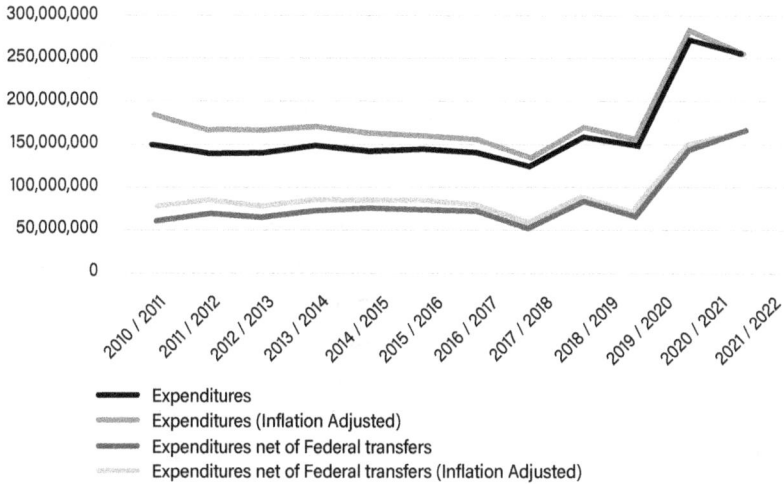

Figure 14.1. Department of Economic Development, Investment and Trade expenditures, 2010/11 to 2021/22.

Sources: Government of Manitoba 2016a, 2016b, 2017a, 2017b, 2018a, 2018b, 2021a, 2021b, 2021c, 2022a, 2022b, 2022c, 2022d; Statistics Canada 2023.

Rural Development then simply became Manitoba Agriculture. A further and more substantial organizational change came in 2019/20 with the addition of the Resource Development and Water Stewardship units. This expanded department was, however, short-lived: by 2021/22, both of the recently added units had been moved out, this time to Natural Resources and Northern Development. Restructuring was also precipitated with an initiative by the department to consolidate rural service offices and shift more services to online portals rather than via in-person interactions. The government news release stated that the initiative would "leverage existing synergies with Manitoba Agricultural Services Corporation" (Province of Manitoba 2021c). However, this endeavour to bring together and "modernize" the provision of selected rural services involved the closure of twenty-one department offices in rural Manitoba and the elimination of in-person service in an additional nine rural communities (MGEU 2021).

The Onset of Austerity

Figure 14.1 presents expenditure data, adjusted according to the methodology outlined in the volume preface, for EDIT. The data cover twelve years (2010/11 to 2021/22), the first six of which coincided with the NDP administration, and the latter six with the PC. The first series are the actual expenditure figures, but the second series adjusts for inflation by converting those nominal expenditure values into 2021 dollars. Changes in the level of expenditures in the inflation-adjusted figures thus reflect changes in the real value (i.e., actual amount of goods and services that can be purchased) of the sums presented.

As indicated by Figure 14.1, real expenditures in EDIT were on a mild but discernable downward trajectory prior to the arrival of the PCs in 2016. Initially, the new administration continued the trend, and in their second year (2017/18) the spending squeeze was especially pronounced. The trend was noticeably reversed in 2018/19, and it is significant that 2019 was also an election year. Real expenditures tightened again the following year, but the department budget was redrawn in the face of the COVID-19 pandemic crisis. Expenditures, driven primarily by COVID-19-related financial and grant assistance programs to businesses,[3] soared in 2020/21, and even with an easing of the crisis in 2022, the 2021/22 level of real expenditures in EDIT was still 58 percent higher than it had been in 2015/16 when the PCs took office.

Note that a significant portion of EDIT's budget is financed through transfers from the federal government that are targeted to particular programs, and particularly toward programs pertaining to labour market training. These transfers vary considerably on a year-to-year basis, but they are substantial, ranging from 25 percent to, on occasion, more than 50 percent of the department budget. Netting out these transfers yields a clearer measure of the provincially driven expenditures and thus the extent to which an austerity agenda manifests itself in terms of the department's appropriations. When viewed through these more discriminating lenses, the downward trend in real departmental expenditures under the NDP government disappears as the expenditure squeeze really only comes with the new PC government. Even with the spending boost from 2017/18, real expenditures in 2019/20, net of the federal transfers, were only 86 percent of the 2015/16 level.

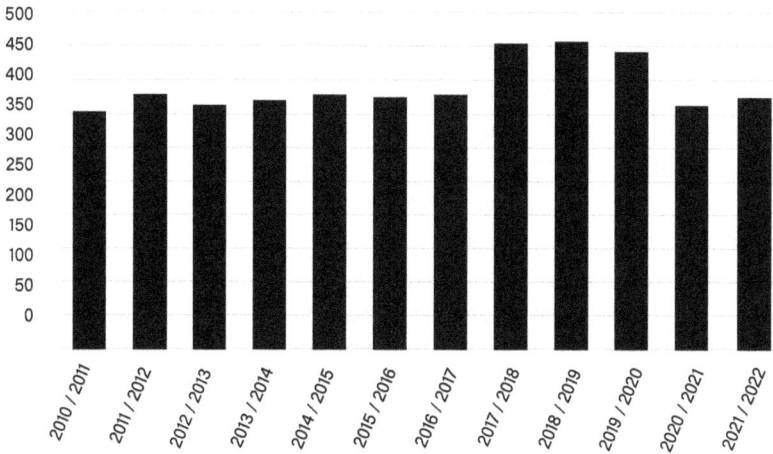

Figure 14.2. Department of Economic Development, Investment and Trade full-time equivalent positions, 2010/11 to 2021/22.

Sources: Government of Manitoba 2016a, 2016b, 2017a, 2017b, 2018a, 2018b, 2021a, 2021b, 2021c, 2022a, 2022b, 2022c, 2022d.

In terms of EDIT staffing positions, as measured by FTEs, the level has, apart from the 2017 to 2020 interval, remained relatively steady (Figure 14.2). The elevated level of the three 2017 to 2020 fiscal years can be attributed to the temporary transfer of the Skills and Employment Partnerships to Advanced Education, with the likely result that former EDIT staff and work activity was integrated with other workers, thereby swelling the FTE figures for this (temporarily) relocated subunit. Once these responsibilities were shifted back under the auspices of EDIT, FTE levels reverted to the norm (Jesse Hajer, email message to author, 23 February 2023). FTEs, however, are not necessarily filled, and the presence of a number of job openings and a lack of urgency in seeking to fill those openings can be another means by which an austerity program affects the workplace. Calculations of actual employee numbers in EDIT and its equivalent suggest a drop in employment from 345 employees in 2015/16 to 292 employees in 2021/22, which amounts to a substantive drop of 15 percent (Province of Manitoba 2022d; Jesse Hajer, email message to author, 23 February 2023).

Expenditures in the Department of Agriculture are presented in Figure 14.3. The data shows that after the 2011 flood-induced surge of departmental expenditures for fiscal 2011/12, there is a mild downward trend in the aggregate expenditures spanning both the NDP and PC years. However, a substantial portion of these expenditures—ranging from 68 percent to over 80 percent, depending on the year—are comprised of funding for risk management, credit, and income support programs, some of which are financed, to varying degrees, by federal institutions. No employees lodged in Agriculture, nor any Agriculture FTEs, are consequently attributed to the risk management, credit, and income support programs, notwithstanding the enormous share that these programs command of the department's budget. Furthermore, the levels of expenditures for these programs are to some degree sensitive to external factors such as weather or broader economic conditions that can dramatically affect producer incomes. Removing this category of expenditures from the totals for Agriculture allows for a more refined depiction of the larger discretionary fiscal stance of the government. With this removal, the residual department expenditures are plotted in the bottom two series of Figure 14.3.

As illustrated in Figure 14.3, the level of the remaining expenditures in Agriculture experienced a real increase in the first two fiscal years of the PC government, rising from $38.8 million (in 2021 dollars) in 2015/16 to $52.8 million in 2017/18. The ensuing four years, however, saw progressively smaller appropriations. For 2021/22, the expenditures (in 2021 dollars) had decreased to $45.6 million, down 14 percent from its 2017/18 level. Staffing in the department, as measured by FTEs, had held steady around 393 from 2013/14 through to the end of fiscal 2017/18. Since then, however, in tandem with the post-2017/18 drop in real expenditures (excluding the risk management, credit, and income support programs), FTEs dropped from 393.0 to 380.5, a decrease of 3.2 percent (Government of Manitoba 2017a, 2021a, 2022b). As noted above, some FTEs may not be filled, resulting in job vacancies of varying duration. Actual employment figures (adjusted) for the department show a slight increase over the 2016 to 2022 interval, rising from 319 to 324 employees, an increase for the period of 1.5 percent (Province of Manitoba 2022d).[4]

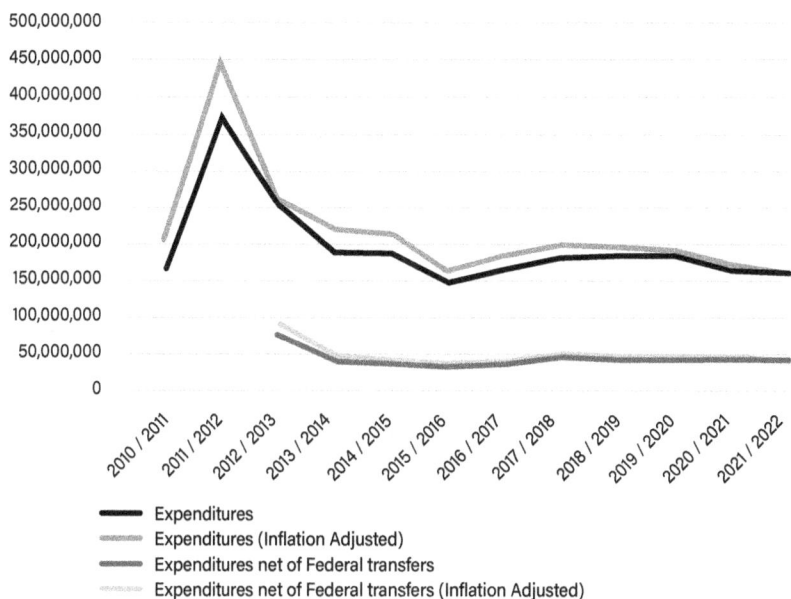

Figure 14.3. Department of Agriculture expenditures, 2010/11 to 2021/22.

Sources: Government of Manitoba 2018a, 2021a, 2022b; Statistics Canada 2023.

In reviewing the publicly available data on budgetary expenditures, jobs, and employment in EDIT and Agriculture, the contrasting incidence of the austerity-inspired agenda is evident. For EDIT, tightening of the budgetary screws was a feature of the early years of the new PC administration, and was especially pronounced in 2017/18, but Tory-style fiscal probity was cast aside as expenditures escalated with the arrival of the COVID-19 pandemic. Employment positions in terms of FTEs tended to hold constant over the period (save for the special circumstances of 2017 to 2020), but actual employee numbers declined. For Agriculture, the budgetary screws were loosened in the initial years of the new PC government, but fiscal tightening emerged after 2018 and remained in play, showing, at the aggregate level, no change in course consequent to the ubiquitous challenges of the COVID-19 pandemic. A slight decrease in Agriculture FTEs occurred over the 2016 to 2022 period, but, in sharp contrast to EDIT, employment levels held firm and ultimately registered a small increase.

Workers and the Labour Process

The implementation of austerity measures by the PC government adversely affected workers in EDIT and Agriculture. The public mantra of the new government was to get Manitoba back onto a "responsible fiscal path" while "protecting front-line services" (Friesen 2016). In practice, though, imposing fiscal restraint, bolstered by official rhetoric pledging to eliminate "wasteful government spending"—in a larger context of a province with a growing population and expanding economy beset with episodic challenges in the forms of bouts of extreme weather and a global pandemic—makes the protection of services problematic. Top-down directives from the Premier's office through to senior management initiated the organizational changes and the reporting and assessment criteria associated with the new agenda, but the burden of reconciling these objectives on a day-to-day basis fell largely upon the public sector employees in the two departments.

In the 2022 survey[5] of EDIT and Agriculture workers, 91 percent of the respondents indicated that their work had been affected by the government's austerity measures. A majority (60 percent) indicated that their own personal workloads had increased. A number of factors contributed to this outcome. For example, managers endeavouring to eliminate waste and find cost savings in their units led to pressure on existing employees to intensify their work activity and do more things as part of their job. The potential for budgetary savings by not filling open positions in a timely manner shifted the burden to remaining workers to find ways to fill the gaps. In other instances, positions were eliminated entirely, and remaining workers were left to cope with managing the load. Overall, 24 percent of respondents reported the existence of staff shortages in their unit. Another worker reported that in their unit, jobs were retained but hours were reduced across the board, and that, with the reduced hours, workers were nonetheless expected to deliver the same level of service. Ten percent of respondents stated that they had taken shorter work breaks or even had missed breaks altogether in order to attend to the volume of work that needed doing.

In a large, complex organization such as the provincial government, the quest to achieve cost savings and enhance value for money across the board lends itself, from a managerial perspective, to embracing measures that seek out and potentially exploit efficiency gains that could be realized through administrative reorganization. That was very much a part of the strategy adopted by the PC government. Large-scale organizational changes affecting the areas of responsibility and range of services offered by both EDIT and Agriculture have been touched on in previous sections in this chapter, but those changes had direct effects on workers and the work environment in both departments. The implementation of the austerity agenda, including the reorganization and restructuring, was very much a top-down, managerial-driven project, and it is significant that survey respondents in EDIT and Agriculture reported that they were not consulted regarding the nature and timing of the reorganizations or the form of their implementation. In the workplace, that implementation was disruptive and chaotic. Survey respondents reported that reorganizational changes resulted in frequent turnover of supervisors and managers, often resulting in lack of continuity and consistency regarding concrete workplace practices and allocations of responsibilities. The organizational changes also brought changes in unit priorities, job descriptions, and reporting practices, all of which increased costs incurred in learning and implementing new policies and procedures and raised levels of uncertainty and stress among the workers. Some individual workers reported that the reorganizations resulted in their being transferred to a different physical work location, resulting in extra costs at the personal level, such as increased commute times to and from work. Another worker opined that the maelstrom of reorganization worked to undermine union protection for workers and thus offered managers a "broad license" for "bullying and staff abuse." In many cases, the reorganizational changes were not so much one-offs but recurring. One respondent from EDIT remarked, "My branch has been 'reorganising' for a decade."

Overall, the impact on workers has been adverse. For 93 percent of the survey respondents, the government's austerity measures have worsened their working conditions and job satisfaction; 89 percent of the respondents believed that the measures have also impaired worker recruitment and retention; and 75 percent indicated that they themselves, as individuals, have been driven to consider job opportunities elsewhere.

Workers surveyed were also very skeptical about whether cost savings had actually been realized; the expected savings that purportedly were still to be realized; and the degree to which front-line services had been protected. With respect to costs, respondents pointed out that staff turn-over is costly, and that austerity has worked to raise turnover rates. Ongoing deterioration of working conditions further erodes job satisfaction, and higher work intensity carries increased likelihood of burnout among existing workers. Eliminated positions or unfilled vacancies can appear as short-term successes insofar as they lower current budgetary expenses, but budgetary costs associated with turnover and replacement are carried forward to future budgets, and the loss of the knowledge and skills of departing workers contributes to the erosion of the unit's stock of human capital and thus also of potential value-added over future years.

The ability of the department to deliver the services incidental to its mandate has also been impaired. When asked about the impact of the austerity measures on the quality of the services provided, 76 percent of the respondents indicated that service quality had declined (a further 13 percent reported that they were unsure or did not know if there was a change in the quality of service). Some 50 percent of respondents noted that they were being asked to provide the same or increased level of services for stakeholders and users but were given fewer resources by which to achieve that. For those directly interacting with the public or other stakeholders, 19 percent of respondents stated that they were simply not able to spend as much time with their clients as they could previously, and 18 percent revealed that they were forced to see fewer clients due to resource and time constraints. Only 15 percent of respondents said that the austerity measures would result in positive savings and better value for money in the short term. For the long term, only 7 percent envisaged positive outcomes here, whereas 46 percent anticipated negative results. Interestingly, 24 percent of the respondents indicated that some long-term positive gains would be realized in their "areas," but that some of the costs associated with achieving those gains would in fact be transferred elsewhere.

Conclusion

For the EDIT and Agriculture departments, evidence of the PC govern-ment's implementation of the austerity agenda after assuming office in 2016 can be extracted from annual aggregate data on the expenditures, employment levels, and FTE positions of those departments. This data, however, does not on its own suffice to critically assess the degree to which the government has met or approached its broad objectives of reducing waste, being fiscally responsible, and maintaining front-line services. Evidence from front-line workers themselves suggests that the putative fiscal improvements to the budgetary bottom line from changes in these departments may in part be merely a short-term phenomenon, and furthermore one that has imposed considerable human and economic cost on the public sector workers in those departments. Those workers also suggest that, notwithstanding their own efforts, the provision of the front-line services for which the two departments are responsible have been compromised. There is mounting evidence that Finance Minister Cameron Friesen was correct when, in the 2016 Budget Speech, he stated that "sweeping austerity measures will not work" (Friesen 2016).

Notes

1   For details on data sources used for provincial expenditures, employee staffing numbers, and full-time equivalent (FTE) positions in this chapter, see Preface.

2   Full-time equivalents (FTEs) are "a measure for the number of positions. Every full-time regular position represents one full-time equivalent position." Other, non-full-time positions "are measured in proportional equivalents" (Province of Manitoba 2022d, 59). So, for example, a subdepartment or subunit with a staffing allocation of 1.50 term FTEs could have this allocation filled by employing one full-time employee (52 weeks) and one half-time employee (26 weeks), or alternatively, three half-time employees (26 weeks each), or perhaps even with six part-time employees (13 weeks each).

3   Major COVID assistance programs included the wage subsidy program, and the Long Term Recovery Fund and training support for businesses and workers (see Province of Manitoba 2021c, 17–18, 34–35).

4   These employment figures do not include employees in the Rural Development unit, which was transferred from Agriculture to Growth, Enterprise and Trade (later EDIT) in 2016/17 (Jesse Hajer, email message to author, 23 February 2023).

5   Of forty-six respondents, thirty-one (67 percent) were in Agriculture, and fifteen (33 percent) were in EDIT.

References

Friesen, Cameron. 2016. *The 2016 Manitoba Budget Address*. Government of Manitoba, Department of Finance, 31 May. https://www.gov.mb.ca/finance/budget16/papers/speech16.pdf.

Government of Manitoba. 2016. "Premier Announces Appointments to the Premier's Enterprise Team." Media Bulletin, 8 December. https://news.gov.mb.ca/news/index.html?item=40112&posted=2016-12-08.

———. 2017a. *Annual Report 2016–17*. Department of Agriculture. https://www.gov.mb.ca/agriculture/reports-expenses/pubs/2016-2017-annual-report.pdf.

———. 2017b. *Annual Report 2016–2017*. Department of Growth, Enterprise and Trade. https://www.gov.mb.ca/jec/reports/pdfs/16_17_get_ar.pdf.

———. 2018a. *Annual Report 2017–18*. Department of Agriculture. https://www.gov.mb.ca/agriculture/reports-expenses/pubs/2017-2018-annual-report.pdf.

———. 2018b. "Manitoba Launches Economic Growth Action Plan." News Release, 6 December. https://news.gov.mb.ca/news/index.html?item=44819&posted=2018-12-06.

———. 2021a. *Annual Report 2020–21*. Department of Agriculture and Resource Development. https://www.gov.mb.ca/agriculture/reports-expenses/pubs/annual-report-2020-2021.pdf.

———. 2021b. *Annual Report 2020–2021*. Department of Economic Development and Jobs. https://www.gov.mb.ca/jec/reports/pdfs/20_21_edj_ar.pdf.

———. 2021c. "Province to Provide New Service Delivery Options for Rural Clients." News Release, 6 January. https://news.gov.mb.ca/news/index.html?item=50183&posted=2021-01-06.

———. 2022a. *Annual Report and Public Accounts 2022*. https://www.gov.mb.ca/asset_library/en/proactive/20222023/public-accounts-2022.pdf.

———. 2022b. *Annual Report 2021–2022*. Department of Agriculture. https://www.gov.mb.ca/agriculture/reports-expenses/pubs/agr-annual-report-21-22.pdf.

———. 2022c. *Annual Report 2021–2022*. Department of Economic Development, Investment and Trade. https://www.gov.mb.ca/jec/reports/pdfs/21_22_edit_ar.pdf.

———. 2022d. *Annual Report 2021–2022*. Public Service Commission. https://www.manitoba.ca/csc/publications/annrpt/2021-22-annualrpt_en-fr.pdf.

MGEU (Manitoba Government and General Employees' Union). 2021. "Manitoba Government Plans to Shutter Services for Farmers, Rural Businesses and Communities," *News and More*, 8 January. https://www.mgeu.ca/news-and-resources/the-latest/news/2048/article-2048.

Statistics Canada. 2023. "Table 18-10-0005-01 Consumer Price Index, Annual Average, Not Seasonally Adjusted." https://www.150.statcan.gc.can/t1/tbl1/en/tv.action?pid=1810000501.

Chapter 15

TARNISHING THE CROWN: THE IMPACT OF AUSTERITY ON MANITOBA'S PUBLIC CORPORATIONS

Lynne Fernandez and Niall Harney

Crown corporations such as Manitoba Hydro (MH), Manitoba Public Insurance (MPI), and Manitoba Liquor and Lotteries Corporation (MBLL) are financially self-contained, government business enterprises. They are publicly owned and tend to provide high-wage, unionized jobs while operating under public mandates and remitting profits to provincial treasuries for reinvestment into public services. In 2022, Manitoba Crown corporations (or "Crowns") contributed $1.81 billion to provincial coffers (Manitoba Government Budget 2023). Crowns have had to comply with austerity measures introduced since the Progressive Conservatives (PCs) took power in 2016. Austerity measures targeted unionized staff and management and reduced capital expenditures, while increasing opportunities for profit making in the private sector. Government communicated orders through mandate letters and directives/orders-in-council, as well as through communiques between the premier, ministers, and boards of directors and executives of Crown corporations. For example, in 2017 a sweeping mandate from the Minister of Crown Services ordered all Crowns to reduce front-line and managerial staff by 15 percent (Annable

2017). Austerity measures also hinged upon passage of various pieces of controversial legislation which increased political interference in Crown corporation operations while undermining oversight by the Public Utilities Board (PUB). The cumulative effect on all three Crowns was to shrink the managerial and front-line workforce, interfere with collective bargaining through the imposition of wage freezes, stymie operations at all three Crowns while increasing private sector engagement, and shrink government's role. Staff at all three Crowns reported safety issues and service reduction due to austerity.

Manitoba Hydro

MH is an integrated utility which generates, transmits, and sells electricity and natural gas throughout the province. It trades electricity in four wholesale markets in the U.S. and Canada and sells power to the U.S., Saskatchewan, and Ontario (Manitoba Hydro 2023). It contributed $497 million to provincial revenues in 2022/23 (Da Silva 2022a).

In February 2017, following the order to reduce its workforce by 15 percent, MH cut 900 positions, almost entirely through a voluntary departure program in which employees were offered a buyout to leave. Both the CEO and Board Chair said such deep cuts, combined with double-digit rate increases, were necessary to put the utility's finances in order (Glowacki 2017). This narrative underscored Hydro's refusal to negotiate a wage increase while a shrinking workforce dealt with inflation, disruptions from COVID-19 and adverse weather events (Hoye 2021). The utility received mandate letters (Minister of Crown Services 2019a) and directives/orders-in-council, including a directive to sell the utility's surplus fibre-optic capacity to an out-of-country corporation and to cooperate with the government-commissioned inquiry into two large capital projects built under the previous New Democratic Party (NDP) government: the Keeyask Generating Station and Bipole III transmission line (Directive to Manitoba Hydro Electric Board). Former Saskatchewan premier Brad Wall was appointed as inquiry commissioner and report author. Wall's criticisms combined technical problems that arose during construction with assumptions about future demand (Wall 2020, 11, 21) that willfully ignored the importance of new export contracts. His analysis became suspect when Hydro announced it had secured thirty-year contracts totalling $5 billion to sell power to Saskatchewan, something Wall would have known (Lett 2021). According to a Hydro source, "This was huge news for us. But we knew it was not consistent with the current government's attempts to make the previous government look bad over the construction of Keeyask and Bipole. You can only assume [the Saskatchewan power sale] was deliberately covered up because it didn't serve their political purposes" (Lett 2021).

Wall also understated or dismissed key background information on Bipole III (CMC Consultants 2007) and Keeyask, including approval of the level of debt taken on (Public Utility Board 2014, 164). He stated that a public-private partnership (P3) may have mitigated cost overruns (26). Critics note that P3s can drive prices higher and open a back door to privatization. P3 promoters claim risk is allocated away from government, but this claim has been sorely tested by real-world experiences (Loxley 2010, 18–39). The report recommended that MH cut costs, sell off non-core functions, and reduce debt (Wall 2020, 147). Some recommendations are now enshrined in the controversial Bill 36, The Manitoba Hydro Amendment and Public Utilities Board Act.

Concerns about Bill 36 included the increase of political interference, decrease in transparency, unwarranted concerns with MH debt levels, and loss of expert advice on rate increases and project development for MH and MPI (Da Silva 2022b; PUB Coalition 2022). According to Dale Friesen of the Manitoba Industrial Power Users Group, Bill 36 "politicizes energy rates, focuses too much discretionary power within government while constraining the authority of the regulator. It lacks an emphasis on independent, qualified review and transparency" (Province of Manitoba Hansard). As for debt reduction, Friesen stated that MH's debt load has not "prevented Manitoba Hydro from financing a large portion of its long-term debt at favourable rates on extended terms" (Province of Manitoba Hansard).

The bill states, "The retail supply of power by persons other than Manitoba Hydro is allowed in limited circumstances" (The Manitoba Hydro Amendment and Public Utilities Board Act, 3), potentially allowing the privatization of electric vehicle charging stations. The bill authorizes landlords, condominium corporations, and housing cooperatives to produce and sell power to tenants (2–3). These provisions are controlled by regulation under a subsection of the bill. It is not clear if customers will pay the same rates as MH customers, or what guarantees they will have in the case of outages. Roughly 32 percent of Manitobans live in multifamily housing units (Statistics Canada 2017), so these changes open the door to substantial privatization of the residential market. Finally, the bill stipulates that rates for a class of customer cannot vary "based on affordability or other socio-economic factors" (22), making it impossible to protect First Nation communities or low-income customers from rate increases.

Bill 36 passed in November 2022, definitively wrestling oversight away from the PUB. The government no longer has to adhere to the PUB's expert-informed rulings regarding project development, how to calculate the debt/capitalization ratio, or how to service the debt (PUB Coalition 2022). Government can now arbitrarily increase rates when it could more fairly use money it collects from various fees MH pays to government to avoid rate increases (Public Utility Board 2014, 227–28). It also opened inroads to privatization (Lambert 2022), indirectly justified reducing the workforce, and put MH's reliability record at risk.

Manitoba Liquor and Lotteries

MBLL is the monopoly wholesaler and distributor of liquor and cannabis in Manitoba. It runs sixty-three liquor stores and operates casinos and lotteries distribution. MBLL profits contribute to provincial general revenue in support of healthcare, education, and other social and community services (Manitoba Liquor and Lotteries 2023). Government interventions placed constraints on MBLL capital and staffing expenditures beginning in 2017. These constraints, in turn, stymied MBLL's operations, creating space within liquor and cannabis retail markets for the private sector while increasing demands on remaining staff. Abandonment of a $75-million consolidation plan for MBLL's five offices in a new headquarters on Kennedy Street was the first instance of capital spending constraint. This move marked a departure from the previous government's development strategy which would have revitalized Winnipeg's core (Lett 2016).

In 2017, Manitoba became one of two provinces to fully privatize cannabis retail. The growth, enterprise and trade minister stated that exclusively private retail "eliminates the need for public investment in storefronts" (Global News 2017). Fully privatized cannabis retail draws in the lowest share of government revenue relative to models in other provinces (Statistics Canada 2019). Further, intervention by the premier to prevent capital investment in Club Regent Casino resulted in the resignation of MBLL's board chair over concerns of ministerial overreach and excessive restraints on investment by Crown corporations (Kusch 2019a). Mandates to restrain capital and operational spending were renewed in 2019. The new mandate letter ordered MBLL to "increase the dividend paid to the Province through the development and implementation of operational efficiencies. This should be accomplished without increasing the corporation's capital investment, liquor or gaming footprint in the province" (Minister of Crown Services 2019b). Without latitude to invest in business expansion, increasing the provincial dividend (profits) would have to come from demanding higher sales from a workforce beleaguered by wage restraint legislation (see Chapter 3). The 2017 management staff reduction targets of 15 percent drew criticism as they did not align with any analysis of Crown corporation business structures (Annable 2017). An audit of management staff reductions conducted in 2018 showed over 20 percent of management positions at MBLL were eliminated (MNP LLP 2018). The 2019 mandate letter called for further staff reductions of 8 percent. Crown corporations that had already met their targets were directed to search for further opportunities to cut staff (CBC News 2019).

When compared to other western Canadian provinces, Manitoba's liquor retail model has typically maximized the diversion of profits to the provincial treasury while limiting the social harms of liquor access (Flanagan 2016). Despite this enviable situation, plans for more private sector liquor retail and distribution appeared in several bills, starting in November 2020. Bill 40 allowed for the sale of all liquor products at any location with a retail licence, diverging from the existing model which limits the sale of full MBLL product lines to MBLL liquor marts. Bill 40 and its successor Bill 42 did not receive royal assent. Liquor privatization was revived in early 2023 under Bills 9 and 30. Bill 9 is a near carbon copy of Bill 42, while Bill 30 adds to preceding legislation by allowing for liquor sales in grocery stores through a five-year pilot program. The privatization of liquor retail will leak profits to private retailers, as has happened in Alberta, where liquor retail was fully privatized in the 1990s (Flanagan 2016).

Manitoba Public Insurance

MPI is the sole provider of auto insurance, motor vehicle registration, and driver licensing in Manitoba. MPI products are compulsory for all drivers and administered on a nonprofit basis (Manitoba Public Insurance 2023).

MPI also received mandates to cut staff expenditures beginning in 2017. However, orders for MPI to *increase* direct payments to private insurance brokers put austerity's real goals in plain view. MPI eliminated 28 percent of management positions in 2017/18, the largest reduction of the three Crowns. A further 8 percent reduction followed in 2019 (CBC News 2019). In line with wage freeze legislation influencing bargaining with other public sector workers (Chapter 3), MPI management was directed to offer wage freezes for MPI staff in November 2020 (*Winnipeg Free Press* 2021). The government used COVID-19 related "budgetary unknowns" to justify wage freezes, while traffic reduction during lockdowns had reduced MPI costs, allowing the corporation to issue $500 million in rebates between May 2020 and February 2022 (CBC News 2022).

In 2019, during contract negotiations between MPI and the Insurance Brokers Association of Manitoba (IBAM), the government issued two directives to MPI management: first, to extend the existing contract with IBAM for two years at a commission rate higher than MPI's board would agree to; and second, to give control of future online renewals to insurance brokers (Kusch 2019b). Both directives contravened MPI's own analysis, which showed administration of online renewals exclusively through MPI would save millions of dollars for the corporation (in commission reductions) while maximizing MPI's return on investment for the online renewal system being developed. These directives were followed up by an order-in-council directing MPI to enter conciliation with IBAM, resulting in a five-year agreement which gave brokers a percentage of online renewals, increasing commissions by $23 million (*Winnipeg Free Press* 2021). The agreement between MPI and IBAM was signed in November 2020, the same month ministers directed MPI to freeze staff salaries.

In 2020, MPI launched an overhaul of its IT system under the title "Project Nova." Initial budget estimates for Project Nova were $100 million, but the budget has since ballooned to $290 million (CBC News 2023). Planning and management of Project Nova has relied heavily on private consultants rather than internal management and IT expertise, revealing a costly preference for contracting out at MPI.

Employee Survey Results

Of the 130 Crown corporation employees who responded to our survey, 32 percent work for MH, 26 percent for MBLL, and 42 percent for MPI. Respondents were attached to various parts of the province, with the majority being in Winnipeg (69 percent). When asked if their work had been affected by austerity measures, 46 percent stated their work has been greatly affected and a further 32 percent stated their work was moderately affected. Only 10 percent indicated their work was unaffected by provincial austerity measures. While 10 percent of respondents indicated their work was unaffected by austerity measures, these respondents did fill out the remainder of the survey and are therefore counted in subsequent questions.

Staff Cuts and Declining Morale

Eighty percent of respondents said that austerity measures have worsened job satisfaction, and 86 percent believed that austerity has worsened employee recruitment and retention. Since the PCs took power in 2016, MH, MBLL, and MPI have all cut staff in line with provincial mandates for 15 percent reductions in management positions and 8 percent reductions in overall staff. Respondents overwhelmingly commented that they were expected to "do more with less," with 76 percent stating their workload has intensified or increased since the onset of austerity measures, and a further 72 percent indicating that they were asked to provide the same or increased service with fewer resources. According to one electrician, "Workload has increased as there are no longer proper staffing levels for the hours it takes to complete all work, resulting in worker fatigue and burnout. Jobs are pushed to following years or ignored, and at times shortcuts are taken."

According to MH employees, the erosion of staff has led to succession problems: "A lack of hiring [at MH] has caused problems that are just beginning to be felt . . . we are almost out of qualified staff to fill necessary positions in a trade that takes two and a half years of schooling and two years of training before being qualified." As a result, stress levels are up, and morale has worsened. Comments included: "I no longer have any pride in the fact that I work for Manitoba Hydro. My stress levels have increased exponentially in the past three or four years. The company's failure to negotiate fairly or competently . . . has led to ridiculously low morale throughout the company"; and "I love my job and the people I work with, but the austerity measures have made everything more difficult to do; it has made people insecure about their future. I have seen coworkers have mental health crises; it all just adds unnecessary stress to everybody's lives."

Similar concerns were repeated by MBLL and MPI employees. One staff member at MBLL reported, "Almost every area I work with is completely under resourced for the growing business. When they first announced cuts, positions were left vacant leaving another employee to do two jobs. . . . Many good employees are leaving, and I haven't seen this [amount of] turnover in my fifteen years working at MBLL." Another employee at MPI outlined grave understaffing and turnover: "We are at critical staffing levels in several departments and all departments rely on each other. Taking zeros for our last contracts, no COVID-19 benefits, [no] cost of living . . . makes me apply for additional jobs or another job that would provide the proper resources and staffing for the level of work." The concerns expressed by these employees over chronic understaffing and diminished capacity spill over into service and safety issues.

Loss of Service and Safety

When asked how austerity impacted quality of service and safety, 76 percent said austerity reduced quality. Across Hydro, MBLL, and MPI, staff noted neglected maintenance, service delays, cut corners, and reduced customer service, leading to larger long-term costs. One MH lineman noted that "neglecting maintenance and maintaining low staff levels is courting disaster in the future once the infrastructure starts failing and we'll be at the mercy of contractors with too few trained staff." This observation was confirmed by another MH employee: "With the added cost in errors in documenting and poorer quality installations, the cost will be the same, if not higher in the long term." Service to MH customers could be improved with more staff: "We would be able to maintain an up-to-date infrastructure that would be more resilient to customers' needs and environmental impact."

Staff at MPI echoed observations that staff shortages were reducing service quality and increasing long-term costs: "Because of staffing shortages, customers and plaintiff councils are increasingly upset . . . vehicles are off the roads significantly longer which leads to higher rental costs . . . bigger storage bills and less customer service. The department I worked in prior would typically have two to four complaints a month . . . the complaints now are about fifteen to twenty [per month] and we have two less staff members."

MBLL employees identified the elimination of training time and high turnover diminishing customer service: "Training has always helped our liquor marts [deliver] stellar customer service. Many of those training opportunities are gone now and newer staff don't have the same ability to get that knowledge . . . senior staff have less time to devote to training." With staffing constraints, the corporations are turning more to a common austerity practice: contracting out.

Contracting Out

Our survey results confirmed that contracting out and privatization take different forms within and between Crown corporations, covering work including:

- janitorial, maintenance, and administrative support
- specific trades such as electrical, welding, painting, and mechanics
- outside vendors for shipping and transportation
- IT support
- management, and
- developers.

Contractors are recruited to the Crowns in different ways:

- They do the work of retired employees who are not replaced.
- They fill in for striking workers.
- They fill in when staff is overworked or to avoid paying overtime to staff.
- Job descriptions are carved up and contracted out to different companies.
- Parts of jobs on large-scale projects are being outsourced to private companies.

- Experienced employees take voluntary departure and then take jobs in the private companies that MH hires.

Staff at MH, MPI, and MBLL identified that institutional knowledge was being lost when employees left, and that contractors did not have the same breadth of experience or training as public sector employees. When asked if the private sector could perform their jobs more efficiently, 74 percent said no. MH exhibited the most pervasive use of contractors. It uses contract workers in many of the areas noted above, from meter reading and tree trimming to building stations and line construction. MH also contracts out the design and installation of infrastructure. Employees noted that MH hires out-of-province contractors, and MH technicians noted that using private contractors can increase costs: "The majority of the time we are training/working with contractors so they are supervised, which adds to the cost"; as well, "there are a lot of systems and procedures in place to provide a safe workplace for us and the public. Adding contractors would only further complicate things, possibly making it more dangerous and unreliable."

Employees at Crown corporations noted that the prevalent use of contractors and consultants, exemplified by but not limited to Project Nova, resulted in increasing costs and turnover. According to one IT worker, "The cost-saving measures taken have created a lot of inefficiencies.... Frequently hiring new consultants and [releasing] old ones instead of investing in current permanent employees creates a lot of overhead for training and slows down work output because of a lack of familiarity with technology." At MPI, employees noted a greater reliance on direct repair shops to do estimates, with diminished oversight from MPI estimators to ensure costs are reasonable.

MBLL staff reported the fewest instances of contracting out; however, contract janitorial services were noted. The passage of Bills 9 and 30 will significantly privatize liquor retailing in Manitoba.

Final Thoughts Offered by Respondents

We received some very insightful responses when we asked Crown corporation employees for their overall impressions of austerity. One employee shared: "MHs upper management put in place by the current government is running the company's infrastructure into the ground with their short-sighted planning. Most field departments are understaffed and take years of training." The employee pointed to the 2021 Texas power crisis, noting that while a similar grid failure "may not be an imminent problem [in Manitoba], it is one that will take years to address if it is not handled before it gets to that point and unlike Texas our weather will cause significantly worse problems than theirs." Finally, this employee's observations succinctly state what happens when austerity runs its course: "I am a conservative at heart and I fully agree with 'trimming the fat.' However, you do need a small amount of 'fat' to protect the core. Pallister cut the fat, and then went straight on to the bone. You cannot continue to undervalue the people providing the services necessary to keep this province running. What you will end up with is qualified and skilled people changing professions or retiring early because they are fed up. What you will be left with is staff that are ill-equipped to handle the stress/workload and simply quit."

References

Annable, Kristin. 2017. "Manitoba Government Orders Management Cuts to Health Authorities, Agencies." CBC Manitoba, 15 March. https://www.cbc.ca/news/canada/manitoba/health-region-staff-cuts-1.4025653.

CBC News. 2019. "Manitoba Crown Corporations Pushed to Cut Overall Staff by 8%." CBC Manitoba, 1 May. https://www.cbc.ca/news/canada/manitoba/maniotba-crown-corporations-cuts-1.5117800.

———. 2022. "MPI Dishes Out 3rd Rebate of the Pandemic, Averaging $328 per Customer." CBC Manitoba, 2 February. https://www.cbc.ca/news/canada/manitoba/manitoba-public-insurance-rebate-1.6335626.

CMC Consultants. 2007. "Bipole III Transmission Routing Study." September. http://manitobawildlands.org/pdfs/BipoleIIITrRoutStudy_2007.pdf.

Da Silva, Danielle. 2022a. "Friesen Weighs Down Current Hydro Profit Buzz." *Winnipeg Free Press*, 23 June. https://www.winnipegfreepress.com/breakingnews/2022/06/23/friesen-weighs-down-current-hydro-profit-buzz-with-talk-of-future-woes.

———. 2022b. "Industrial Electric Consumers Slam Provincial Hydro Bill." *Winnipeg Free Press*, 12 October. https://www.winnipegfreepress.com/breakingnews/2022/10/12/industrial-electricity-consumers-slam-provincial-hydro-bill.

———. 2023. "MPI Chief Info, Tech Officer Resigns." *Winnipeg Free Press*, 2 June. https://www.winnipegfreepress.com/breakingnews/2023/06/02/mpi-chief-info-tech-officer-resigns.

Editorial. 2021. "Freeze Demand at Odds with MPI Payouts." *Winnipeg Free Press*, 14 January. https://www.winnipegfreepress.com/local/2021/01/13/freeze-demand-at-odds-with-mpi-payouts.

Flanagan, Greg. 2016. "Balancing Convenience with Social Responsibility: Liquor Regulation in Manitoba." September. Winnipeg: Canadian Centre for Policy Alternatives–Manitoba. https://policyalternatives.ca/publications/reports/balancing-convenience-social-responsibility.

Glowacki, Laura. 2017. "Manitoba Hydro to Shrink Workforce by Roughly 900 Positions." CBC Manitoba, 3 February. https://www.cbc.ca/news/canada/manitoba/manitoba-hydro-reductions-1.3966055.

Government of Manitoba. "Budget 2023." https://www.gov.mb.ca/budget2023/summary-budget-and-financial-updates.html.

Hoye, Bryce. 2021. "Manitoba Hydro Workers Strike amid Allegations of Government Meddling in Contract Dispute." CBC Manitoba, 23 March. https://www.cbc.ca/news/canada/manitoba/manitoba-hydro-union-workers-reject-offer-1.5960353.

Kusch, Larry. 2019a. "Ousted MLL Chair Disputes Premier's Story, Says Province Overstepped." *Winnipeg Free Press*, 26 February. https://www.winnipegfreepress.com/breakingnews/2019/02/26/ousted-mll-chair-disputes-premiers-story-says-province-overstepped.

———. 2019b. "Tory Meddling Could Cost MPI Millions, Boost Autopac Rates." *Winnipeg Free Press*, 24 June. https://www.winnipegfreepress.com/breakingnews/2019/06/24/tory-meddling-could-cost-mpi-millions-boost-autopac-rates.

Lambert, Steve. 2022. "Manitoba Considers More Private-Sector Work with Crown-Owned Energy Utility." CTV News Winnipeg, 30 November. https://winnipeg.ctvnews.ca/manitoba-considers-more-private-sector-work-with-crown-owned-energy-utility-1.6175779.

Lett, Dan. 2016. "PCs Love Scandals So Much They Make Them Up." *Winnipeg Free Press*, 19 November. https://www.winnipegfreepress.com/local/2016/11/19/pcs-love-scandals-so-much-they-make-them-up.

———. 2021. "Hydro's $5-billion Deals with Saskatchewan 'Deliberately Covered Up.'" *Winnipeg Free Press*, 23 March. https://www.winnipegfreepress.com/breakingnews/2021/03/23/manitoba-hydros-5-billion-deals-with-saskatchewan-deliberately-covered-up.

Loxley, John, with Salim Loxley. 2010. *Public Service Private Profits: The Political Economy of Public-Private Partnerships in Canada*. Winnipeg: Fernwood Publishing.

Manitoba Hydro. "About Us." Accessed 2 March 2023. https://www.hydro.mb.ca/corporate/.

Manitoba Liquor and Lotteries. "About Us." Accessed 2 March 2023. https://www.mbll.ca/content/about-us.

Manitoba Public Insurance. "Who We Are." Accessed 2 March 2023. https://www.mpi.mb.ca/pages/who-we-are.aspx.

Martin, Riley, Lauren McNabb, and Amber McGluckin. 2017. "Pot to be Sold from Private Retail Locations in Manitoba, Supply Handled by Liquor and Lotteries." Global News, 8 November. https://globalnews.ca/news/3848058/manitoba-offers-first-glimpse-at-plan-for-cannabis-legalization-tuesday/.

Minister of Crown Services. 2019a. "Letter to Chair of Manitoba Hydro Electric Board." 24 April. https://www.gov.mb.ca/asset_library/en/executivecouncil/mandate/hydro_mandate_letter.pdf.

———. 2019b. "Letter to Chair of Manitoba Liquor and Lotteries Corporation." 24 April. https://www.gov.mb.ca/asset_library/en/executivecouncil/mandate/mbll_mandate_letter.pdf.

MNP LLP. 2018. "Audit of Management Staff Reductions for Select Crown Corporations." 9 November. https://www.manitoba.ca/asset_library/en/proactive/audit-of-management-staff-reductions-select-crown-corporations.pdf.

Province of Manitoba Hansard. 2022. "Legislative Assembly of Manitoba. The Standing Committee on Social and Economic Development." 11 October. https://www.manitoba.ca/legislature/hansard/42nd_4th/sed_08/sed_08.html.

PUB Coalition. 2022. "Preparing a Presentation on Bill 36, *The Manitoba Hydro Amendment and Public Utilities Board Amendment Act*. A Guide by the PUB Coalition." September. https://protectpub.ca/wp-content/uploads/2022/09/Speaking-to-Committee-Bill-36-.pdf.

Public Utility Board. 2014. *Report on the Needs For and Alternatives To (NFAT) Review of Manitoba Hydro's Preferred Development Plan*. http://www.pubmanitoba.ca/nfat/pdf/finalreport_pdp.pdf.

Sanders, Carol. 2021. "MPI Customers Owed Larger Rebate, Rate Cut: Customers Group." *Winnipeg Free Press*, 12 October. https://www.winnipegfreepress.com/breakingnews/2021/10/12/mpi-customers-owed-larger-rebate-rate-cut-consumers-group.

Statistics Canada. 2017. "Census in Brief: Dwellings in Canada." 3 May. https://www12.statcan.gc.ca/census-recensement/2016/as-sa/98-200-x/2016005/98-200-x2016005-eng.cfm.

———. 2019. "Analysis in Brief: The Retail Cannabis Market in Canada: A Portrait of the First Year." 11 December. https://www150.statcan.gc.ca/n1/pub/11-621-m/11-621-m2019005-eng.htm.

The Legislative Assembly of Manitoba 2016–2017. "Bill 20." https://web2.gov.mb.ca/bills/41-2/b020e.php.

The Manitoba Hydro Amendment and Public Utilities Board Act. SM 2009, c. 17. https://web2.gov.mb.ca/bills/42-4/pdf/b036.pdf.

Wall, Brad. 2020. "Economic Review of Bipole III and Keeyask." November. https://manitoba.ca/asset_library/en/proactive/2020_2021/ERBK-Report-Volume1.pdf.

Wharton, Jeff. "Respecting Manitoba's Response to the Economic Review of Manitoba Hydro- Keeyask and Bipole III Projects." Directive to Manitoba Hydro Electric Board. https://www.gov.mb.ca/asset_library/en/proactive/20212022/directive-mh-review-bipole-keeyask.pdf.

Chapter 16

SOMETHING NEEDS TO CHANGE: AUSTERITY IN MANITOBA TRANSPORTATION AND INFRASTRUCTURE

Holly Scotland and Jennifer Keith

In 2021, the Canadian Centre for Policy Alternatives (CCPA) published a report examining the impact of austerity measures on the Department of Infrastructure. Using the same data-gathering processes as those used in the present volume, the report laid the foundation for the findings further developed in this book. Drawing heavily on worker perspectives, the report warned that the government's "multi-year push for privatization aimed at reducing the size of government and the public service" would erode internal capacity and be challenging to reverse (Keith et al. 2021, 68). It identified three common austerity approaches utilized by government: "a reduction in workforce through attrition, assets being sold off or not replaced, and a lack of government investment in the resources that remained" (Keith et al. 2021, 38).

These austerity measures were articulated in a fiscal performance review initiated by the Progressive Conservative (PC) government in 2016/17. The review, conducted by KPMG (an audit, tax, and advisory firm), looked at government programs and spending and identified the Department of Infrastructure as one of four departments which would require "significant transformation" for the government to achieve its mandate to control spending, better provide value for money, and efficiently allocate resources without negatively impacting front-line services (KPMG 2017, 5). The report recommended the government consider "alternative delivery options," such as outsourcing maintenance services to the private sector, and options for private ownership of assets used to maintain public services (KPMG 2017, 80). It was proposed that the department could reduce the size of the civil service by taking advantage of natural attrition, eliminating programs and services, and shifting the government's focus to regulation and oversight of services rather than delivery (KPMG 2017, 142).

In 2018, PricewaterhouseCoopers (PwC) was awarded a contract to review the service delivery model for the department and to develop options and recommendations for a modern, flexible, and adaptable service delivery model (Manitoba 2018, 20). Changes to the department since the review included: transfer of Vehicle and Equipment Management Agency (VEMA) to the Finance Department and then to Central Services; privatization of all Manitoba Government Air Services; an increase in the number of provincial snow clearing, pavement marking, and seal coating contracts; and automation of the Motor Carrier Permitting Application System, which is responsible for ensuring that large oversized tractor trailer loads are routed safely throughout the province.

The CCPA report found that these widespread changes resulted in "a decline in service quality . . . worsening work conditions for workers and reduced accountability to the broader public" (Keith et al. 2021, 4). The report goes on to outline that privatization and contracting out of public services has not been shown to result in cost savings or value for money, despite claims by the government that this was their motivation (Keith et al. 2021, 69). In fact, in recent decades there is a clear trend in other jurisdictions of reversing privatization due to failure to deliver on cost savings and quality expectations along with concerns regarding transparency and accountability (see Keith et al. 2021, 62–64). The report concludes that the government's actions appeared to be "dictated by ideology as opposed to rigorous analysis" and that "Manitobans along with the public service were paying the price" (Keith et al. 2021, 70).

The report also detailed worker suggestions for improving efficiencies. This included investing in staffing to enable all necessary jobs to be

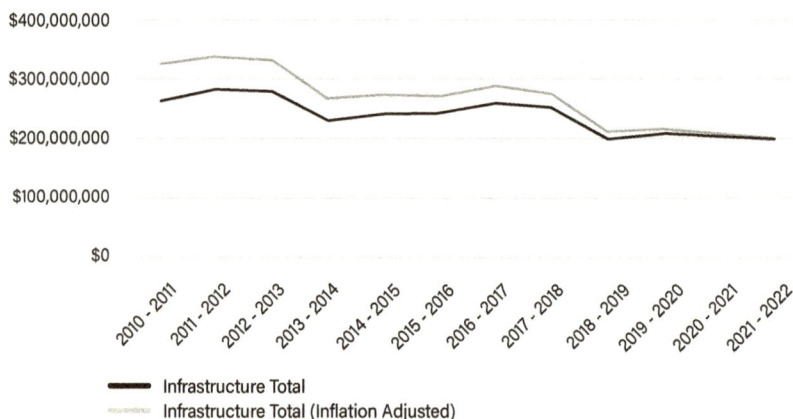

Figure 16.1. Total actual Department of Transportation and Infrastructure expenditures (inflation adjusted), 2010/11 to 2021/22 fiscal year.

done, restoring capacity for in-house delivery of services, bringing wages in line with the private sector to improve recruitment and retention of experienced workers, improving long-term strategic planning instead of constantly changing priorities, utilizing existing assets more strategically, and developing hybrid models for service provision. The current study, completed eighteen months after the original CCPA report, provides an opportunity to evaluate whether the government has continued its problematic course of privatization.

Overview of Manitoba Transportation and Infrastructure

Since the publication of the CCPA report, the department's name has changed to Manitoba Transportation and Infrastructure (MTI). The vision of the department is "to connect and protect Manitoba" with a mission "to ensure safe, reliable, and sustainable infrastructure and services for Manitoba and its communities" (Government of Manitoba 2022, 25). MTI is responsible for all public infrastructure (including highways, roads, bridges, airports, and marine services); flood control; motor carrier regulations, safety services, and emergency preparedness; emergency response; and disaster recovery (Government of Manitoba 2022, 13).

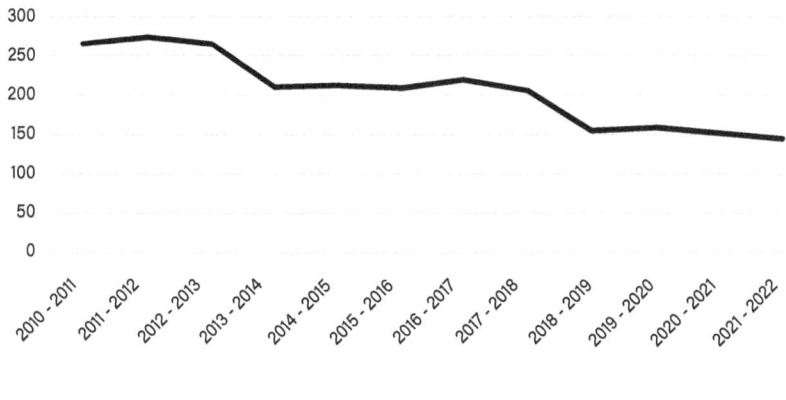

Figure 16.2. Annual provincial per capita infrastructure spending (inflation adjusted), 2010/11 to 2021/22.

Figure 16.1 depicts operating expenditure amounts, adjusted historically to match the current composition of the department.[1] Department expenditures made a steep decline in 2018/19 but have remained relatively stable since, with only a small decline over the past three years. Between 2016/17 and 2021/22, operating expenditures fell by 22 percent or $58 million, a 30 percent drop when adjusting for inflation.

Expenditures per capita have also declined (Figure 16.2). In 2011/12, per capita expenditures were at an all-time high of $275. This figure fell to $212 in 2013/14, then remained relatively stable until 2018/19, when it fell to $157; it then continued to decline and reached an all-time low of $145 in 2021/22.

Between 2016 and 2022 the number of FTE positions has fluctuated. In 2016/17 there were 1,937. This number rose to 2,057 in 2018/19 but fell over the next three years to 1,820 by 2021/22.

Despite only a 6 percent decrease in FTEs between 2016 and 2022, the actual number of employees has suffered a far more devastating fate. While government reporting makes it difficult to get an accurate vacancy rate year to year, between 2017 and 2022 the department lost 550 employees, as demonstrated in Table 16.1.

Furthermore, the vacancy rate in 2022 was an astonishing 36 percent, based on data published in Committee of Supply documents (Manitoba Transportation and Infrastructure 2022) (2022 Committee of Supply

Table 16.1. Year-over-year change in number of employees, Manitoba Transportation and Infrastructure Department (formerly Department of Infrastructure), 2017–2022.

YEAR	NUMBER OF EMPLOYEES	YEAR-OVER-YEAR CHANGE	
		NUMBER	%
2017	1709		
2018	1645	-64	-3.7
2019	1425	-220	-13.4
2020	1267	-158	-11.1
2021	1219	-48	-3.7
2022	1159	-60	-4.9
Total change compared to 2017		**-550**	**32.2**

Manitoba Transportation and Infrastructure as of 27 April 2022 Briefing Binder, 18). This means that despite the relative stability in FTEs, there were far fewer boots on the ground year to year.

Presence of Austerity Then and Now

The CCPA report by Keith et al. (2021) gathered survey data from 124 Department of Infrastructure and VEMA workers and conducted follow-up interviews with ten respondents. Respondents, who had an average of twelve years of experience, represented a cross-section of the department, including front-line workers (54 percent), supervisors/ managers (33 percent), and other employees. The data for the current study came from a similar cross-section of respondents. Of sixty-eight survey respondents, 56 percent identified as front-line workers, 29 percent as supervisors/managers, and 6 percent as senior management. The average number of years with the government of this survey group was higher than in the earlier study at seventeen years.

Comparing survey responses from 2021 to responses to the current survey suggests that austerity measures have continued and become more problematic. In 2021, respondents reported there was a decrease of 30–50 percent in the workforce at all levels, making it difficult for those who remained to maintain service quality, with significant risks to public safety (Keith et al. 2021, 38). Hiring freezes, which began in 2016, left many positions vacant for years. As staffing levels were reduced, operations could no longer be maintained, leading to closures and seemingly arbitrary redeployment of workers and assets. More recent data show that vacancy rates remain high at 36 percent in 2022,[2] and respondents report that a lack of staff in all divisions and at all levels continues to worsen. There are supervisors who are operating equipment because of lack of front-line staff, and front-line staff who have had to take on supervisor roles because of lack of management. This shortage of staff means that fewer commercial vehicles are being inspected, expensive equipment is not being maintained and is underutilized, and work formerly done in-house is being contracted out to keep up with demand. One respondent reported, "I have been required to cover for multiple positions as vacancies were not filled . . . in order to attempt to make up for this shortfall our department is now hiring engineering service providers to perform the functions our staff used to do."

Chronic staff shortages have led to one of two outcomes: work is contracted out or it does not get done. The reduction in staff and the resulting high vacancy rate has meant a loss of expertise and difficulty compensating for this loss. One worker reported, "We lost all legacy knowledge in our organization due to the [austerity] measures with no succession plan in place and it took months to fill positions with no one to train new recruits." The decrease in the number of employees (Table 16.1) supports the claim that the workforce has continually deteriorated, although at a decreasing rate.

In 2021, 54 percent of respondents reported that their work had already been impacted by austerity. Eighteen months later this number had risen to 94 percent. When asked how their work had been impacted, 55 percent said their workload had intensified or increased, 11 percent said hours had increased, 5 percent had been laid off or lost their job, and 19 percent said their work had otherwise changed. Furthermore, all but 3 percent reported some form of change to their work scheduling such as staff shortages, increased number of responsibilities, shorter/missed breaks, other resource shortages, or the presence of more contract or casual staff.

Contracting out and privatization of work has also increased. In the most recent survey 67 percent of MTI employees reported that some or all of their work had been privatized or contracted out to private companies. This was up from 52.5 percent in 2021. Areas contracted out include everything from routine maintenance work to highly skilled essential or quality assurance work. As one respondent put it, "Everything [is being contracted out] at an inflated cost for mostly subpar workmanship that has to be redone by my men for a lower wage. What a joke. You've succeeded in breaking the backs and spirits of many honest, hardworking men and women . . . all while the private sector gets fat."

Another respondent was concerned that the quality of work and materials used was deteriorating now that private contractors are overseeing their own work. The high standards that were once the hallmark of Manitoba Infrastructure can no longer be expected.

Consultation on Austerity Measures

Workers reported being demoralized over the lack of communication, along with poor pay and the threat of privatization. Even big changes such as eliminating two regions and redefining the boundaries of the remaining three regions was not communicated to workers. The result of this lack of transparency and accountability left workers feeling uncertain and insecure and has resulted in many leaving their position with the government.

Among those who responded to our survey, 84 percent disagreed or strongly disagreed that they had been meaningfully consulted on changes resulting from austerity measures. This number remained constant between the two surveys. However, there were some improvements in this area. In 2021, only 7 percent of respondents felt that their work-related experiences were reflected in ongoing changes, while in the current survey this number improved to 18 percent.

Impact of Austerity on Service Quality

In the current survey the number of respondents who felt austerity measures had led to a reduction in service quality for stakeholders grew to 87 percent from 71 percent in 2021. Additionally, over 60 percent of respondents reported being asked to provide the same or improved service with fewer resources or not being able to spend as much time with individual users. Forty percent felt that there had been a reduction in service quality for low-income users. Finally, none of the respondents in the current survey felt that there had been an improvement in service quality to stakeholders or that they were able to provide improved service to users because of implemented austerity measures. One respondent commented on their perception of the quality of work performed by the private sector, saying, "I find that they are not doing as much QA/QC [quality assurance/ quality control] as the civil servants have. There are more delays, quality of work has deteriorated, and costs have increased."

One stark example of this is the provision of Justice services in northern communities. As predicted by department employees, privatizing air transportation services has resulted in 50–70 percent of flights being cancelled, making lawyers, judges, and community members feel like "someone is playing a joke on them" (Sanders 2023).

Service Quality and Public Safety

In both the 2021 survey and the current survey, 54 percent of respondents felt public safety was being compromised due to austerity measures. However, between 2021 and the current survey, the percentage of respondents who believed that expenditure cuts and restraints had worsened public safety increased from 55 percent to 66 percent. One respondent commented that "transportation services have been severely reduced in the province and are now creating dangerous roads and highways for the public . . . funding must greatly increase to improve public safety on the roads."

The increasing concern for public safety is higher and more explicit in the responses for MTI than for many of the other departments. Workers identified their work as directly affecting public safety, and when their ability to do that work is compromised so is the safety of the Manitobans whom they serve. The most obvious area of potential impact to public safety is road maintenance. Respondents expressed concern with having to "fulfill the duties of 12 to 14 workers ... on the backs of 4 to 6 workers." Workers gave examples of their inability to keep roads safe, such as not replacing broken highway signs or repairing and replacing guardrails that protect motorists. Other areas of concern for public safety include air ambulance services and water bombing during forest fire season, services that have been contracted out, leaving "northern and rural communities ... with less capable airplanes, and a lower level of service." Respondents also point to commercial vehicle inspection, saying that a "lack of manpower means less inspection [for compliance] when the industry is growing ... [meaning] the public is not very safe."

Nowhere is the impact on the life of Manitobans more evident than in the provision of air ambulance services. Since the privatization of Manitoba Government Air Services, there have been reports of a lack of care during medical transports, and most tragically, the loss of a life. In May 2021, Krystal Mousseau died after her medical evacuation flight from Manitoba to Ottawa was unsuccessful. As predicted by doctors and pilots, privatized medical transport service providers did not have the experience or equipment to deal with Ms. Mousseau's condition (Lambert 2021).

Cost Saving and Sustainability

Respondents in the 2021 study believed that because private companies are motivated by profits, they are more likely to take shortcuts in equipment maintenance and service provision compared to the public sector, who respondents believed are concerned with delivering the highest quality service while maintaining efficiencies. Similar sentiments continued to be expressed by respondents in the current survey. One worker stated, "Privatization is a temporary savings . . . business[es] are out to make money, so they want to do the job ... the cheapest and fastest way possible, so they themselves turn a profit. The public sector has one goal. That is to do a good job and make life in our local areas safe and looking great."

Those who did believe that austerity represents a real cost saving to the public sector remained low across the two surveys: 6.5 percent of respondents to the 2021 survey felt there were short-term savings, and 3 percent in the current survey. As for long-term savings, only one respondent in the current survey thought there would be savings. It is important to note that among those who believed there were cost savings, some felt it was only achievable by putting public safety in jeopardy.

Many respondents pointed out that initial cost savings would eventually result in more money being spent. One worker noted, "Failure to repair things that need it will only be more costly in the future due to prolonged disrepair." Another employee commented, "We have [had to] send out our own staff to open up the roadways as contractors just couldn't achieve a consistently satisfactory open roadway. So, the government paid someone else to do the job and we had to go and do it anyway. Pay twice for the same job and that contractor pays his employees 5 to 10 dollars more than any one of my co-workers."

Workers also questioned the cost savings of selling off expensive government assets. One pilot explained, "Manitoba Government Air Services ran 22 aircraft with 80 employees for a cost recovery amount of $16 million per annum. We ran the cheapest government air service in Canada! . . . there was no case made for savings, and the drain of talented people in the years after affected the safe delivery of the service."

Another respondent also questioned the logic of selling off assets: "[Premier] Pallister and [then Minister of Infrastructure] Schuler sold equipment for pennies on the dollar. There should be an investigation into the price they received for the Amphibexes and other specialty equipment they sold."

Finally, numerous employees suggested that the loss of institutional knowledge and technical expertise created by leaving vacancies open for so long would result in greater costs in the long run.

Impact on Working Conditions

"What's happened in our department over the last six years has negatively affected public safety (lack of preventative maintenance, increased emergency response time), [and] the employees' physical and mental health (frustration and workload). The benefits of working for government are no longer there and recruiting new employees now that they are beginning to hire again has become difficult."

The above response to the recent survey is an indication that the impact of austerity on working conditions predicted in 2021 has been not only realized but exceeded two years later. Today, the main issues continue to be heavy workload, inadequate wages relative to industry standards, and low morale. An astounding 90 percent of workers said that austerity measures had led to worse working conditions and job satisfaction, 91 percent felt that austerity had negatively impacted employee mental health, and 90 percent said it had increased the difficulty in recruiting and retaining employees. Perhaps not surprisingly, not a single worker felt that working conditions, job satisfaction, mental health, or recruitment and retention had improved because of austerity measures. One worker said that they were unsure whether they could "keep up the physical demands and work-load if no new staff are hired." Regarding wages, another worker noted, "The municipalities around the city of Winnipeg pay their staff $8–12 dollars more per hour to start. That is a serious reason to look elsewhere." Even now that some areas within the department are beginning to hire, wages continue to be an issue for recruitment. One worker reported,

> We had the opportunity to hire this year, but we did not hire as many as needed . . . a lot of the ones that did get a job [offer] refused the job offer once they found out their starting wage and what they would top out at. The majority of the time we end up getting disgruntled employees for the wages we offer and it's sad because it wrecks a good working crew which should be a crew of six but is only a crew of two. . . . Our system is broken and disappointing. This goes right from the summer students to senior management.

A result of being underpaid and overworked is that workers consistently experience low morale. One respondent stated, "Morale in the workplace has been horrible. Myself and co-workers have seen a significant decline in mental health, even before the pandemic." Additionally, 60 percent of respondents to the current survey felt that worker safety had worsened due to privatization and contracting out, 62 percent of respondents reported looking for a job outside of government, and 12 percent of respondents stated they had already left. One employee wrote, "I don't like to discuss that I am a civil servant as I am unable to provide a safe and reliable service that all . . . Manitobans once relied on . . . it wasn't perfect 5 to 10 years ago, but it was not in any way this badly managed and operated."

Promising Policy Ideas

Besides filling vacancies and paying staff higher wages to encourage staff retention, other suggestions for improving efficiency and lowering costs included: training staff; enforcing construction specifications across the board between private and public contractors; placing subject matter experts who have the technical expertise to understand the impacts of their decisions at the level of deputy minister or assistant deputy minister; and lowering the rates VEMA charges for renting out equipment. Manitoba Government and General Employees' Union (MGEU) even offered to collaborate with the department to make significant improvements based on a report that provided numerous strategic recommendations; however, the department did not pursue the offer. Notably, 59 percent of respondents believed there were opportunities to provide a higher quality of services in a cost-effective way if budgets were increased in their area.

Of the 13 percent who said there were no opportunities to improve efficiency or reduce expenditure, the reason cited most often was that it was simply too late now that so many staff and physical assets had been lost. It was also pointed out that costs could have been saved if "they . . . contracted out some of the programs the air service was operating and kept the air ambulance and water bomber programs."

Conclusion

"Something needs to change. Five years ago, this was a good place to work. Not anymore."

Transportation and infrastructure play a key role in achieving and maintaining a high standard of living in the province. Well-designed infrastructure is a key driver of economic prosperity as it connects people and products, creates jobs, and improves productivity. Networked infrastructure such as transportation ensures Manitobans have access to essential services vital to their safety and security. Despite the critical nature of these assets and services, and their direct linkage to safety and prosperity, the current government continues to ambitiously implement austerity measures. The CCPA report (Keith et al. 2021) and those who participated in surveys and interviews at the time issued a warning: if the trajectory of the government toward aggressive austerity measures did not change, things would get worse. These warnings fell on deaf ears, and although the Conservative government might finally be recognizing the wisdom of their workforce, significant damage has been done, as predicted. Employees have left, government spending continues to dwindle, and staff are focused on damage control and triage rather than planning, growth, and programs and services. There is no doubt now: the public service and Manitobans are paying the price.

Notes

1   For details on data sources used for provincial expenditures, employee staffing numbers, and full-time equivalent (FTE) positions in this chapter, see Preface.

2   Authors' calculation based on Manitoba Transportation and Infrastructure (2022).

References

Keith, Jennifer, Jesse Hajer, and Michael Conway. 2021. *Hard Infrastructure, Hard Times: Worker Perspectives on Privatization and Contracting Out of Manitoba Infrastructure.* Winnipeg: Canadian Centre for Policy Alternatives–Manitoba. https://www.policyalternatives.ca/publications/reports/hard-infrastructure-hard-times.

KPMG. 2017. *Manitoba Fiscal Performance Review Phase 2 Report, Business Case: Rationalization from Reorganization.* https://www.gov.mb.ca/asset_library/en/proactive/fpr-phase-2-2.pdf.

Lambert, Steve. 2023. "Family of Manitoba Woman Who Died After Aborted Medical Flight Sues Province." Canadian Press, 9 March. https://www.ctvnews.ca/winnipeg/article/family-of-manitoba-woman-who-died-after-aborted-medical-flight-sues-province/.

Manitoba Transportation and Infrastructure. 2022. "2022 Committee of Supply Manitoba Transportation and Infrastructure as of April 27, 2022." https://gov.mb.ca/asset_library/en/proactive/briefings/2022/mti-cos-binder-2022-redacted.pdfhttps://gov.mb.ca/asset_library/en/proactive/briefings/2022/mti-cos-binder-2022-redacted.pdf.

MERX. 2018. "15Q09222018—Review of Manitoba Infrastructure's Services Delivery Model." 22 November. https://www.merx.com/mbgov/manitobafinance/solicitations/Review-of-Manitoba-Infrastructure-s-Services-Delivery-Model/0000137341.

Sanders, Carol. 2023. "Report Predicted Northern Court Crisis After Privatization." *Winnipeg Free Press,* 11 February. https://www.winnipegfreepress.com/breakingnews/2023/02/11/report-predicted-northern-court-crisis-after-privatization.

VEMA (Vehicle and Equipment Management Agency). "About." Accessed 28 April 2023. https://www.vema.gov.mb.ca/about/.

Chapter 17

AUSTERITY IN LABOUR AND CONSUMER PROGRAMS: FALSE ECONOMIES, REDUCED SERVICE, DEMORALIZED STAFF

Julie Guard

The Manitoba government's relentless pursuit of austerity has eviscerated programs upon which Manitobans rely as workers and consumers, undermining the safeguards and supports that have been won through decades of struggle. Budget cuts, staff reductions,[1] and privatization in the labour and employment and consumer protection divisions in the pursuit of fiscal austerity have undermined the public services that are paid for by all Manitobans, creating barriers to access, lowering benefits, and reducing the quality of the social and legal supports that sustain the quality of life and work for people in the province. Staff reductions, contracting out, and declining resources in labour programs have weakened Manitobans' assurance of safe workplaces where their rights will be protected. Consumer protections have been undermined, and programs designed to increase the transparency of public expenditures have been cut. Demoralized staff in these programs struggle to provide service as their numbers shrink, causing workloads to increase. Many have left their jobs or are biding their time until retirement.

This chapter evaluates the impact of the Progressive Conservative (PC) party's austerity measures on public services and staff in the Labour Division and the Consumer Protection Division. The province's 688,000 wage earners and their households depend on the services provided by the Labour Division, and as consumers, homeowners, or renters, we all rely on the work of the Consumer Protection Division. These government services support a stable economy and are intended to ensure that Manitobans can count on fair treatment as workers, consumers, and tenants, and can seek redress when things go wrong. Based on data generated for this project and on anonymous surveys conducted with workers in these divisions, this chapter explores the effects of austerity on the branches, boards, and offices of the Labour Division, including the Employment Standards branch, Workplace Safety and Health, the Workers Compensation Board, the Worker Advisor Office, and the Labour Board, as well as the Consumer Protection Division and its Residential Tenancies branch.

Austerity Budgeting and Anti-union Animus

Since being elected in 2016, Manitoba's PCs have imposed a neoliberal, austerity-driven agenda that deploys staff reductions, wage freezes, and anti-labour legislation to shrink the public sector and disempower its unions. Some of the worst effects are felt by the province's many low-waged workers—the very workers who need the services of labour programs and tenancy protection the most. Shortly after they took office, the government froze the minimum wage at $11, aligning themselves with the pro-business Chamber of Commerce (Ahmed 2022) as opposed to the more progressive Canadian Centre for Policy Alternatives, which advocated raising the minimum wage to a living wage (Apata, Hajer, and Harney 2022). Holding to that position, the government raised it by only 15 cents in 2018 and then by small increments until 2022. Only in the midst of the COVID-19 pandemic and after other provinces had raised theirs was it increased to $13.50, and not until April 2023 did they raise it to $14.15—still less than a living wage, but more in line with other provinces (Government of Canada 2022). As low-waged workers struggle to get by, cuts to public sector budgets have enabled the PCs to institute tax breaks that disproportionately benefit the wealthy while portraying themselves as the only fiscally responsible option. Government underspending has shrunk the size of the labour and consumer protection workforces and undermined the services those workers provide—services upon which Manitobans rely. Between 2015/16 and 2021/22, labour program budgets (adjusted for inflation) have been cut by 26.4 percent. Yet these are the provincial services that keep workers safe, offer help when they encounter problems at work, and support free and fair collective bargaining.

In tandem with cuts to labour programs, the government has engaged in what many have identified as an across-the-board assault on organized labour, with a particular animus toward public sector unions (Edmond 2021; Press Progress 2019). Soon after taking office, they increased barriers to union certification and proposed other changes that would have undermined workers' rights. Most egregiously, they mandated an across-the-board wage freeze on the public sector. Courts subsequently described the measure as "draconian," rendering "meaningful collective bargaining impossible" and violating unions' rights under the Charter of Rights and Freedoms (Cardozo 2020).

While public sector unions were organizing against the wage freeze, forced amalgamations, and attacks on collective bargaining, the government was slashing budgets. From 2016 to 2021, labour programs, including the Labour Board, Employment Standards, and Workplace Safety and Health (WSH), lost 17.6 percent of their budgets, equivalent to 26.4 percent in 2022 dollars or over $4.3 million, a real reduction of 31.7 percent per Manitoban. Public sector workers in these departments experienced those cuts most directly as a sharp decline in program staffing. Between 2016, when the PCs took power, and 2021, full-time equivalent (FTE) staff numbers in labour programs declined by 15.2 percent. Such drastic cuts increase workloads, undermine morale, and jeopardize staff's ability to deliver quality services. People working in these departments reported that "key departments... are extremely short-staffed." Staff report "having to do 1.25 to 1.5 jobs for most of the year but getting paid for one," and "experiencing a high degree of burnout." Working people have struggled for many decades to achieve the rights that protect the safety of working Manitobans, ensure they are treated fairly, and provide them with recourse when these rights and protections are violated. Staffing reductions and budget cuts have put those rights in jeopardy.

Most Manitobans who have a work-based complaint seek help from Employment Standards. This branch is the first and often the only point of contact for workers who have been denied pay, fired unfairly, or forced to work unpaid overtime, or encountered other problems with their employer. Employment Standards staff inform workers and employers about their rights and obligations and enforce compliance with the legislated minimums that underpin workers' most basic rights. They intervene to resolve workplace conflicts, including compliance with minimum wages, hours of work, and legal holidays, as well as terminations and resignations. Workers who are not protected by a union, but who believe their employer has violated the Code, have little recourse but to file a complaint. Yet staffing in this department has declined by 9.6 percent since the PCs took power. The issues that bring workers to this office are frequently urgent, but the branch is no longer providing unscheduled, drop-in service. Instead, workers who need help are advised to call for an appointment or get advice from the staff at its call centre (Government of Manitoba, Employment Standards n.d.).

Austerity versus Safe and Healthy Workplaces

In 2022, Manitoba's Labour, Consumer Protection and Government Services Minister Reg Helwer promised that "all Manitobans . . . have the right to a healthy workplace" (Government of Manitoba 2022). Jon Reyes replaced Helwer in January 2023 and, according to labour watchers, has initiated changes in the department. Yet barring significant improvements, that right may still be denied to the many thousands of Manitobans who are injured at work every year. During the Tories' term in office, Manitoba has had the highest rate of time-loss injuries of any province (Tucker and Keefe 2021). The Workers Compensation Board (WCB) accepted 24,003 workplace injury claims in 2021, an increase of 1,348 over 2020; many more were filed and rejected. More of those injuries (3,512) were defined as severe than in 2020 (3,051). Twenty of those injured workers whose cases were reported died in 2022, six more than in the previous year (Workers Compensation Board of Manitoba 2021, 27–28; Wilson 2022). Yet those numbers, although alarming, minimize the extent of the problem. Only 75 percent of Manitoba's workforce is covered by Workers Compensation, the lowest coverage rate of any province, meaning that workers in many sectors of the economy lack access to WCB support and benefits. Moreover, employers are incentivized to suppress claims because their premiums are calculated on the basis of injuries reported. A 2010 investigation by the Manitoba Federation of Labour found that claim suppression was endemic and that significant numbers of workplace injuries were not reported (Manitoba Federation of Labour 2010). A subsequent report commissioned by the WCB in 2013 found that as many as 57 percent of injured workers did not apply for WCB benefits (Prism Economics and Analysis 2013, 41). Workers' advocates point out that government has taken no action to improve these outcomes and contend that, if anything, the situation has worsened (Manitoba Federation of Labour 2022). Indeed, the government's failure to even mention claim suppression in its November 2022 review of the Workplace Safety and Health Act suggests that it does not perceive it to be a problem and that the review is unlikely to address it (Government of Manitoba 2022).

The WSH branch enforces the regulations that are in place to protect Manitobans at work. Yet the rising numbers of reported work-related injuries and deaths contradict Minister Helwer's assurances. Parts of the public sector, particularly healthcare, report higher than average workplace injuries (Workers Compensation Board 2021, 12; Safe Work Manitoba 2023). Workers' advocates claim that rather than putting the onus on employers to ensure that their workplaces are safe, injured workers are obliged to prove that their injury or illness was caused at work (Stefanation 2023). A 2013 study found that over 80 percent of claims were disallowed on that basis (Prism Economics and Analysis 2013, 66). In addition, the Act does not address most work-related diseases. But instead of strengthening workplace protections and oversight, the government has weakened the regulations, allowing the department to dismiss appeals they consider frivolous or vexatious without review. Following the same deregulatory agenda, the PCs have dismissed concerns raised by the Manitoba Federation of Labour by scrapping automatic adoption of occupational exposure limits on hazardous materials. Instead, they promise to review substances flagged as hazardous every three years, but without an obligation to adopt changes (Manitoba Federation of Labour 2022).

As workplace injuries and fatalities increased, the province cut WSH staff, reducing the number of employees who enforce the regulations intended to make workplaces safer. The department's random inspections aimed at reducing noncompliance with the regulations are a critical part of that work. The department reports that WSH staff conduct 5,000 workplace inspections annually in response to 8,500 phone calls and hundreds of emails. Similarly, officers issue approximately 7,500 improvement orders requiring employers to address violations in a timely manner and 400 stop-work orders in response to an immediate hazard (Government of Manitoba, Manitoba Workplace Safety and Health n.d.). Yet this work is hampered by a steady decline in staff. Between the time this government took office in 2016 to 2021/22, the branch has lost 20.7 percent of its budget in real terms, equal to 26.7 percent per Manitoban, and lost 9.9 percent of its staff.

Reduced Support for Injured Workers

The thousands of workers who are injured every year depend on the WCB, which provides crucial support to those workers, their employers, and the community by replacing workers' lost income during recovery and supporting their safe return to work. Returning injured workers to work has obvious social and economic benefits, and although many injuries are not reported or not accepted by the Board as legitimate workplace injuries, those whose claims are accepted report positive outcomes. According to the WCB's 2022 annual report, 83 percent of the injured workers to whom it has provided service report a satisfactory return to work; 72 percent had their claims paid within fourteen days; and 82 percent rated their experience with the WCB as positive.

WCB staff attributed those results to their own knowledge and skills, acquired over many years of service, and collective dedication to their jobs, but report that cuts to the services they offer and to staffing levels have jeopardized their ability to provide services to injured workers and undermined morale: "Morale and engagement are the worst I have ever experienced. We feel disrespected and undervalued." Many worry that austerity will be achieved by contracting out more jobs. "I have decades of experience that is not replaceable. This would be lost with contracting out and result in a significant reduction to client service," said one respondent. Claimed another, "We are trained and dedicated public servants. That commitment just does not exist with private sector workers."

WCB workers point out, moreover, that austerity measures "have zero [benefit] to taxpayers." Unlike other Labour programs, the WCB is funded solely by employer premiums and its own investments, rather than the province. Budget cuts do, however, benefit employers. The WCB's annual reports highlight the Board's success in providing "financial relief to eligible employers" (Workers Compensation Board of Manitoba 2021, 22). When its revenues exceed its funding target—that is, when it is able to deliver services at a cost lower than projected—the Board returns the surplus to employers or reduces their premiums, or both.

The Board's budget has increased every year but so has the annual surplus it returns to employers. In 2021, it returned $71 million, or 40 percent, of eligible employers' premiums. In 2020, it returned $36 million (Workers Compensation Board of Manitoba 2020, 9). Several of those surveyed blamed the cuts on the Board's practice of refunding employer premiums from its budget surplus. One worker reported that staff had to do "more work for less money. Yet, our employer returned over $100 million in rebates."

In addition to refunding employer premiums, from 2016 to 2020, it has consistently reduced them (Workers Compensation Board of Manitoba 2020, 9). The premiums paid by employers in Manitoba are the lowest in the country (Workers Compensation Board of Manitoba n.d.). In short, the WCB's actual operating and staffing costs appear to have declined even as its budget appears to have risen. The WCB does not report on its staffing levels, but its 2021 annual report notes that operating expenses were $8.4 million (7.3 percent) below budget, due in part to delays in hiring. Reduced or delayed hiring is consistent with the survey responses of WCB staff. Respondents reported that budget cuts and staffing deficits have increased their workloads and made work more difficult. According to one, injured workers are often unable to reach their WCB agent by phone: "On a weekly basis, I am receiving phone calls from workers who cannot get hold of [their agent] because we are so understaffed." Several reported that they are unable to provide timely, high-quality service because of staff shortages. "We only have time to do the bare minimum," reported one. "Caseloads are at an all-time high [but] injured workers and employers are not receiving the level of service they are used to [and] expect," said another.

Others reported that the years-long salary freeze has made pay uncompetitive and recruitment difficult. According to one respondent, "We can't attract staff or keep the ones we currently hire." Staff who retire or take stress leave are not replaced, creating "more work for less individuals," slowing delivery of services to injured workers, and eroding morale.

At the same time, benefit levels remain low. Although benefit levels are pegged at 90 percent of the workers' net earnings, research conducted for the WCB in 2013 found that actual benefit levels averaged between 54.4 percent and 43.3 percent of gross earnings (Prism Economics and Analysis 2013, 36). Benefit levels may have improved since then, but the formula for calculating workers' net earnings is unchanged. That formula deducts estimated income tax, payroll, and other deductions, including premiums for benefits for which injured workers who are off work may not even be eligible (Workers Compensation Board of Manitoba 2023). Workers' advocates contend that benefits have long been inadequate (Smith 2002) and have not increased in real terms since the 1980s. They argue that any surplus should be used to raise the benefits paid to injured workers rather than being returned to employers. Instead, austerity objectives are met by maintaining current benefit levels and reducing operating and staffing costs.

The Worker Advisor Office works closely with the WCB; its staff provide help to workers who make WCB claims. Although the number of injured workers seeking support from the WCB has increased, the branch has lost 22 percent of its budget, equivalent to 28 percent per Manitoban in real dollars since 2015/16, a loss that parallels its 11.1 percent loss of staff positions. The PC government created a new department, the Employer Advisor Office, to assist employers in interpreting WCB regulations. This includes helping employers to manage WCB claim costs and qualify for the Prevention Rebate Program, among other matters. However, aside from its website, little information is available about this office, including the rationale for its creation or any data related to its budget or staffing (Government of Manitoba, Employer Advisor Office n.d.).

Labour Peace and Third-Party Dispute Resolution

Manitoba's Labour Board facilitates collective bargaining, arbitrates workplace disputes, and enforces the rules for the 34.6 percent of Manitoba workers who are union members and their employers (Government of Canada 2023a). They all depend on the Board to maintain fair and reasonable labour relations and, in the process, stabilize the economy. Despite significant infringements on collective bargaining that left virtually the entire public sector hamstrung at the bargaining table, the Board has functioned well, helping unions and employers negotiate collective agreements and resolve disputes. Manitoba workers have been under exceptional pressure during recent years, many working without a contract, being forced to work mandated overtime, and experiencing stress and other workplace hazards, while under a provincially imposed wage freeze and other efforts to undermine collective bargaining in the public sector. Yet even in this hostile climate, the Board's record of supporting unions and employers to reach a negotiated agreement is the envy of other jurisdictions (Robinson 2022).

Despite its impressive record of assisting the parties to achieve equitable outcomes in labour relations, the Labour Board has suffered significant budget cuts. Since 2015/16, the Board has lost 41 percent of its funding in inflation-adjusted dollars (equal to 45 percent per person) and 38.3 percent of its staff complement. Some of this loss may be attributable to the elimination of the Conciliation and Mediation branch in 2019, which accounts for seven of the nine full-time equivalents (FTEs) lost to the Board. The branch provided third-party support for dispute resolution—a service essential to maintaining harmonious labour relations. It had an excellent reputation with employers and unions who trusted the advice of its mediation experts (Manitoba Federation of Labour 2019). But the government severed it from the Labour Division as a cost-cutting measure (Government of Manitoba 2018). Now, parties needing advice to resolve contentious issues in labour relations are directed to a list of mediators, for whom they pay out of pocket. Transferring these services to the private sector effectively privatizes the cost of an important public service.

Virtually every branch of the Labour Division has endured budget cuts, including those that do not provide direct services to the public, for which the loss of staff and budget cuts is more difficult to assess. Operating out of the public gaze but providing essential support to the Labour Division and other parts of the public sector, the Legislative Development office provides technical expertise and knowledge on legislation and regulatory requirements. Always a small branch, with only seven FTEs in 2015/16, its staff have shrunk to a posted four FTEs in 2021/22. Even that appears to understate the branch's actual losses. The dramatic decline in its expenditures, which dropped by 70 percent in real dollars, equivalent to 72 percent per Manitoban, suggests that most of those positions are no longer filled.

Consumer Protection and Residential Tenancies

Consumer Protection, which is also part of the portfolio of the labour minister, has seen similarly drastic cuts to staffing and budgets. The Consumer Protection Division administers the legislation that protects Manitobans as consumers. Its staff provide information about buying a house or condominium, debt management, scams and frauds, and identity theft, and enforce the rules for the retail market. It administers the Residential Tenancies Act, which is intended to create fairness in the rental market. Staff adjudicate disputes between tenants and landlords, resolving over 400 such cases every year (Government of Manitoba 2022). Enforcement of the Act is necessary to ensure that the legislation that protects the rights of tenants, landlords, and consumers is effective. Yet cuts to consumer protection programs totalled almost $2 million, equivalent to 14.7 percent in today's dollars, a loss of some 20.8 percent per Manitoban, from 2016 when the PC took office to 2021. During the same period, FTEs in consumer protection programs declined 8.5 percent.

One of the consequences of these cuts is reduced access to services, as staff struggle to manage ever-larger workloads. One survey respondent reported that their team had been reduced by 80 percent and that they were unable to keep up with the calls for service from the public. But rather than increasing staffing, some of the work was privatized, and the rest was off-loaded to another, also overburdened, branch. Another response to inadequate staffing was to offer more services online. The result was more convenient for some, but effectively off-loaded work from paid staff to clients.

Survey responses from people working in these offices were overwhelmingly critical of the effect of austerity in their areas. Just over 90 percent reported that austerity had created worse working conditions and less job satisfaction. Workers reported that they "don't feel valued." Over 60 percent reported that austerity led them to consider leaving their current job, and another 6.67 percent reported that they had already done so. Over 30 percent reported staffing shortages, in addition to 30.5 percent who reported that they had been assigned extra work and 13.48 percent who reported other resource shortages. Some observed that the work in their area had simply been shifted to another overburdened office or contracted out. Several described a staffing crisis, workers suffering from burnout, and a lack of respect. One commented, "We have already been stripped to the bone."

In addition to worsened recruitment and retention, over 85 percent reported that austerity was damaging employees' mental health. Over 80 percent reported that austerity undermined the quality of service they are able to provide. Almost none reported any cost savings in their area. Asked if the private sector would perform the work more efficiently, almost 70 percent did not believe the private sector could do a better job or be more efficient. One explained that "the work is specialized and takes years to learn and execute with proficiency." Another observed, "my job requires a lot of institutional knowledge" that would be lost if services were delivered by the private sector. They also cited lack of accountability, lack of commitment, and conflict between service provision and profit. Over 70 percent believed that austerity became more intense when the PCs took office. One commented, "I think we have been in austerity so long we can't think of new ways to serve the public."

Conclusion

The Manitoba government has preemptively promised "historic help" to Manitobans. Such hubris stands in sharp contrast to the evidence in this chapter. Rather than helping, the government's austerity measures have abrogated rights won by decades of struggle and undermined protections that workers and consumers need and that are paid for by our taxes. Austerity policies have left public sector workers demoralized and exhausted, unable to provide the care and support that vulnerable, abused, underpaid, and injured workers need and upon which consumers and tenants rely. The erosion of these crucial public services not only undermines our collective economic well-being; it presages a less secure society in which we can no longer rely on the state to protect our rights.

Notes

1 For details on data sources used for provincial expenditures, employee staffing numbers, and full-time equivalent (FTE) positions in this chapter, see Preface.

References

Ahmed, Jamil. 2022. *3 Factors Affecting Business: Manitoba's Inflation, Unemployment, and Minimum Wage Increase.* The Winnipeg Chamber of Commerce, 12 September. https://winnipeg-chamber.com/chamber-blog/3-factors-affecting-business-manitobas-inflation-unemployment-and-minimum-wage-increase/.

Apata, Michael, Jesse Hajer, and Niall Harney. 2022. *Manitoba Living Wage Update 2022.* Winnipeg: Canadian Centre for Policy Alternatives–Manitoba. https://policyalternatives.ca/sites/default/files/uploads/publications/Manitoba%20Office/2022/08/MB%20Living%20Wage%20Update%202022.pdf.

Cardozo, Rachel. 2022. "Manitoba Legislation Limiting Wage Increases for Public Sector Workers over Four-Year Period Violates Charter of Rights, Court Holds, Given Unjustified Interference with Collective Bargaining." CanLII Connects, 12 August. https://canliiconnects.org/en/summaries/71787.

Edmond, Lucas. 2021. "Brian Pallister's Long War on Unions Must Mark a New Era for Labour in Manitoba." *Canadian Dimension*, 13 January. https://canadiandimension.com/articles/view/brian-pallisters-long-war-on-workers-must-mark-a-new-era-for-labour-in-manitoba.

Government of Canada. 2022. "General Hourly Minimum Wage Rates in Canada since 1965." 12 September. https://minwage-salairemin.service.canada.ca/en/since1965.html.

———. 2023. "Work Stoppages by Sector and Year." 28 February. https://www.canada.ca/en/employment-social-development/services/collective-bargaining-data/work-stoppages/work-stoppages-year-sector.html.

Government of Manitoba. 2018. "Government Introduces Labour Relations Amendment Act." Press Release, 28 November. https://news.gov.mb.ca/news/index.html?item=46406.

———. 2022a. "Manitoba Government Launches Five-Year Review of Workplace Safety and Health Act, Associated Regulations." 30 August. https://news.gov.mb.ca/news/index.html?item=56178&posted=2022-08-30.

———. 2022b. *Manitoba Residential Tenancies Commission Annual Report 2021–2022.* https://www.gov.mb.ca/cp/residtc/pubs/2021%202022%20annual%20report.pdf.

———. 2022c. "Workplace Safety and Health Act Review." https://engagemb.ca/workplace-safety-and-health-act.

———. n.d. "Employment Standards." https://www.gov.mb.ca/labour/standards/index.html.

———. n.d. "Employer Advisor Office." https://www.gov.mb.ca/labour/eao/.

———. n.d. "Workplace Safety and Health." https://www.manitoba.ca/labour/safety/.

Manitoba Federation of Labour. 2010. "An Investigation into the Incidence of WCB Claims Suppression." June. https://mfl.ca/system/files/mfl-report-files/Claim%20 Supression%20Final.pdf.

———. 2019. "Manitoba Federation of Labour Statement on Pallister Government's Closure of the Manitoba Conciliation and Mediation Branch." 12 March. https:// mfl.ca/manitoba-federation-of-labour-statement-on-pallister-governments-clo- sure-of-the-manitoba-conciliation-and-mediation-branch/.

———. 2022a. "2022 MFL Health and Safety Report Card." June. https://mfl.ca/ node/2054.

———. 2022b. "2022 Review of the Manitoba Safety and Health Act." November. chrome-extension://efaidnbmnnnibpcajpcglclefindmkaj/https://mfl.ca/wp-con- tent/uploads/2022/12/MFL-2022-Submission-WSH-Act-Review.pdf.

Press Progress. 2019. "4 Times Brian Pallister Attacked Workers' Rights and Left Manitobans with Less Money in Their Pockets." 19 July. https://pressprogress. ca/4-times-brian-pallister-attacked-workers-rights-and-left-manitobans-with-less- money-in-their-pockets/.

Prism Economics and Analysis. 2013. *Claim Suppression in the Manitoba Workers Compensation System: Research Report.* https://www.wcb.mb.ca/sites/default/files/ Manitoba%20WCB%20Claim%20Suppression%20Report%20-%20Final-1.pdf.

Robinson, Colin. 2022. Labour Board Chair, class presentation in LABR 2300, 29 September, University of Manitoba.

Safe Work Manitoba. 2023. *Manitoba Workplace Illness and Injury Statistics Report.* https://www.safemanitoba.com/topics/Pages/Injury-and-illness-statistics.aspx.

Smith, Doug. 2002. "Turning the Tide: Renewing Workers Compensation in Manitoba." Winnipeg: Canadian Centre for Policy Alternatives–Manitoba. https://policyalternatives.ca/sites/default/files/uploads/publications/Manitoba_ Pubs/mb_workers_comp.pdf/.

Stefanation, Gratton. 2023. "Safe Workers of Tomorrow," guest lecture in LABR 2300, 31 May, University of Manitoba.

Tucker, Sean, and Anya Keefe. 2021. *2021 Report on Work Fatality and Injury Rates in Canada.* University of Regina, 21 October. https://www.researchgate.net/ publication/390980150_2021_Report_on_Work_Fatality_and_Injury_Rates_ in_Canada_Work_Fatality_and_Injury_Rates.

Wilson, Jim. 2022. "Manitoba Reports Increased Injury Rate in 2021." *Canadian Occupational Safety*, 22 July. https://www.thesafetymag.com/ca/news/general/ manitoba-reports-increased-injury-rate-in-2021/414326.

Workers Compensation Board of Manitoba. 2020. *Annual Report 2020.* https://www. wcb.mb.ca/annual-report-2020.

———. 2021. *Annual Report 2021.* https://www.wcb.mb.ca/flowpaper/wcbannualre- port2021/docs/13555-WCB-Annual-Report_Web.pdf?reload=1651611527061.

———. 2022. *Annual Report 2022.* https://www.wcb.mb.ca/2022-annual-report-re- veals-strong-finances-and-benefits-of-return-to-work-program.

———. n.d. "How Premiums Are Calculated." https://www.wcb.mb.ca/ how-premiums-are-calculated.

Chapter 18

"IT DID NOT MAKE SENSE": AUSTERITY IN INDIGENOUS RELATIONS AND RECONCILIATION IN MANITOBA

Jennifer Keith and Niigaan Sinclair

In April 2022, Manitoba's Auditor General Tyson Shtykalo tabled his Independent Audit Report titled *Manitoba's Implementation of The Path to Reconciliation Act*. While legally mandated under the Act to devise a plan to build Indigenous and non-Indigenous relationships in all sectors of Manitoba, the report pointed out that the Manitoba Progressive Conservative (PC) government—overseen by former premiers Brian Pallister from 2016 to 2021 and Heather Stefanson from 2021 to 2023— had "not developed a strategy for reconciliation" (Auditor General Manitoba 2022, 1).[1] As Shtykalo flatly states, "In this audit we wanted to determine whether the Government has been fulfilling its commitments under the [Path to Reconciliation] Act. . . . Unfortunately, it hasn't" (Auditor General Manitoba 2022, 1). This lack of strategy in the province means that "efforts towards reconciliation are hampered, ultimately lacking focus and vision" (Auditor General Manitoba 2022, 1). In other words: the Manitoba government received a big "F" on their report card on reconciliation.

When discussing reconciliation, it is crucial to acknowledge the historical relationship shaped by the legacy of colonization. This context underscores the significance of genuine engagement with Indigenous communities to rebuild trust and address systemic inequalities. According to Shtykalo, Manitoba's failure is due to a lack of communication with Indigenous communities and organizations, poor reporting and missed deadlines, and evidence that provincial representatives treat Indigenous leaders and civil servants with disrespect. As Shtykalo observed, "Government representatives would decide something, then meet with Indigenous peoples to tell them of the decision, and then publicly claim engagement has occurred" (Auditor General Manitoba 2022, 22). Citing other situations, Shtykalo remarked, "Government representatives would sometimes invite Indigenous peoples to a meeting but give them insufficient time to research and prepare" (Auditor General Manitoba 2022, 22), or, damningly, "the Government of Manitoba would only engage with Indigenous representatives when it needed something from them (for example, access to their land)" (Auditor General Manitoba 2022, 22).

This is an unfortunate statement for a province located on the traditional territory and ancestral lands of the Anishinaabeg, Anishininewuk, Dakota Oyate, Denesuline, and Nehethowuk Nations and the Inuit, and the homeland of the Red River Métis (The Legislative Assembly of Manitoba 2023). It is, however, evidence that Manitoba is ground zero for Canadian colonization. After violent negotiations with the Métis provisional government, Manitoba became the country's first province after confederation in 1870 with a land area of approximately 160 square kilometres (Assembly of Manitoba Chiefs n.d.). Canada then negotiated treaties and interpreted them in ways which removed Indigenous peoples from their lands to make room for non-Indigenous settlement, farming, mining, and forestry, and other purposes that benefited settlers and the Canadian government. Between 1871 and 1910, Canada entered into Treaties 1 to 6, Treaty 5 adhesion, and Treaty 10. These treaties covered the new boundaries that were drawn for the province of Manitoba in 1912, expanding the province to the place we see today.

Violence that dispossessed Indigenous peoples from their ancestral lands and way of life is not just a part of the past. Sadly, it continues to inform the relationship between Indigenous peoples and all Manitobans. Government policies continue to be unapologetically racist and assimilationist, resulting in human rights abuses like over-policing and over-incarceration of Indigenous people, rampant poverty among Indigenous communities, and the ongoing high numbers of murdered and missing Indigenous women, girls, and Two Spirit people. While changes began to occur in the 1960s and 1970s (largely due to Indigenous victories in politics and in the Supreme Court, and demands for recognition of Indigenous rights), Manitoba's history of colonialism continues to influence and impact the province in profound ways. Even when laws are passed to recognize Indigenous rights—such as in Section 35 of the Constitution Act of 1982—these remain largely undefined or, worse, defined by non-Indigenous institutions, leaving colonial violence in the province, for the most part, unaddressed and ongoing.

Today, there are sixty-three First Nations in Manitoba, represented by individual Chiefs and Councils and traditional forms of government (Assembly of Manitoba Chiefs n.d.). The Red River Métis are represented by the Manitoba Métis Federation (MMF) organized into seven regions and a number of community-level locals (Manitoba Métis Federation n.d.). Additionally, there are fifty Northern Affairs Communities, and a significant percentage of their populations identify as Indigenous. There are also large urban populations of Indigenous people. This means that the Indigenous population in Manitoba is as diverse as the nations they come from. There are, of course, countless cultural, historical, and social differences; for instance, seventeen northern First Nations are not accessible by an all-weather road, and 43.9 percent of the First Nations population live off-reserve (Government of Canada n.d.). In 2016, it was estimated that 223,310 people, accounting for approximately 18 percent of the total population of Manitoba, identified as First Nations, Inuit, or Métis (Statistics Canada 2017). This suggests that every single Manitoban, Indigenous or not, either works with, lives alongside, or is married to an Indigenous person.

From Municipal Affairs to Indigenous Reconciliation and Northern Relations

Prior to 1970, Indigenous communities in Manitoba were under the purview of the Department of Municipal Relations—a sign of how the province viewed treaty rights, Indigenous rights, and the role of First Nations and Métis communities. From the 1970s to 2016, Indigenous issues were separated from Municipal Relations and became the central focus of departments called Native Affairs, Northern Affairs, and Aboriginal and Northern Affairs. However, within government Indigenous issues were generally left to be spearheaded by Indigenous leaders like Elijah Harper, Eric Robinson, and Oscar Lathlin. In the April 2016 provincial election, the PC Party of Manitoba defeated the New Democratic Party (NDP) and collapsed Indigenous and Municipal Relations together again—one of the first indications that then premier Pallister and his government did not recognize their unique legal obligations or relationship with Indigenous peoples. This move was short-lived, however, and by the following year, municipal responsibilities were again separated from Indigenous issues when the Department of Indigenous and Northern Relations was formed. This title remained until 2019 when "Reconciliation" was added, making it the Department of Indigenous Reconciliation and Northern Relations—a change that remains to this day.

Although it is encouraging that reconciliation has taken a prominent place in the title of the department, it is surprising that it took until 2019 for that change to occur. Four years earlier, the Truth and Reconciliation Commission of Canada (TRC) published their final six-volume report, the culmination of over six years of studying and gathering testimony on the issues and impacts of residential schools. The report details the depth of the destructive impact the residential school system has had on Indigenous communities and how it relates to a long history of colonization that has deeply damaged the relationship between Indigenous peoples and non-Indigenous peoples—particularly in places like Manitoba. The report also provided direction with ninety-four Calls to Action.

Responding to the work of the TRC, the provincial NDP government passed the The Path to Reconciliation Act in 2016. This legislation set out the government's commitment to advancing reconciliation and compels the government to publish an annual report which details government-wide activities and progress toward reconciliation (Path to Reconciliation Act 2016). Inheriting this legislation, Manitoba's newly elected PC government had a legal obligation to address this work and take action to create a Manitoba with more peaceful relationships than the past.

In fact, moves like responding to the TRC and The Path to Reconciliation Act are a part of recent nation-wide changes between Indigenous communities and Canada. The past decade has been witness to national movements like Idle No More, #CancelCanadaDay, and various Indigenous-led environmental movements to protect Indigenous territories from resource development. The result of these resistance efforts has been increased societal and political attention to Indigenous issues, creating a degree of political pressure for politicians and leaders to address some of the issues faced by Indigenous peoples, communities, and families. In 2016, Canada reformed its approach to providing services for First Nations children, and Jordan's Principle, a child-first, needs-based principle used in public policy and administration, was implemented to support access to health and social services. That same year, a national inquiry into murdered and missing Indigenous women and girls was held; its final report was published in 2019. A big step occurred in 2021 when the federal government passed the United Nations Declaration on the Rights of Indigenous Peoples Act, which provides a road map for the Government of Canada and Indigenous peoples to work together to implement the UN declaration.

These moves and the work of Indigenous activists for over a century and a half have led to a more comprehensive understanding in Canada of what it means to renew and repair relationships with Indigenous peoples—what is often called reconciliation. Best articulated by the TRC, reconciliation represents commitment and investment in the ongoing work of "establishing and maintaining respectful relationships" which "involves repairing damaged trust by making apologies, providing individual and collective reparations and following through with concrete actions that demonstrate real societal change" (The Truth and Reconciliation Commission of Canada 2015, 16). Provinces, in particular, have the unique opportunity to lead this work by moving away from policies that maintain contemporary colonial control toward a diplomatic relationship that recognizes Indigenous sovereignty.

Manitoba's Department of Indigenous Reconciliation is on the front lines of this important work on behalf of Manitobans. In the 2022/23 annual report for the department, the minister is tasked with "the advancement of reconciliation and strengthening of Indigenous relations in Manitoba, fulfillment of Manitoba's constitutional responsibilities to Indigenous communities, and supporting the provision of municipal programs and services to Northern Affairs Communities" (Government of Manitoba 2022, 12). The department fulfills the ministers responsibilities by: providing policy direction related to Indigenous communities and communities in Northern Manitoba; developing initiatives to advance reconciliation; ensuring constitutional obligations to Indigenous communities are met; establishing and implementing Crown consultation policies; implementing agreements with Indigenous communities; supporting growth, independence, and autonomy of northern communities, as well as their infrastructure, services, and programming; and promoting good governance for northern communities (Government of Manitoba 2022, 13).

Much of this work is in on-the-ground activities and initiatives that can profoundly impact the day-to-day lives of Indigenous peoples in Manitoba. In 2021/22 the department reported that they "created new initiatives to address the many challenges Indigenous people and northern communities faced in light of the COVID-19 virus" (Government of Manitoba 2022, 3). This included monitoring outbreaks, ensuring essential services were maintained, and arranging vaccination clinics. The department also led "provincial responsibilities in the negotiation and implementation of Treaty Land Entitlements and other agreements in Manitoba" and the response to recommendations of the *Provincial Oversight of Drinking Water Safety Report* (Government of Manitoba 2022, 3). With regards to reconciliation, the province supports the identification, investigation, protection, and commemoration of unmarked burial sites on the grounds of former Indian Residential Schools, and leads the response to the Calls to Justice to address violence against Indigenous women and girls (Government of Manitoba 2022, 3). While Indigenous peoples will always have a unique relationship with the Crown, this list of initiatives demonstrates that the province plays a critical role in advancing work that leads to real change in Indigenous communities and for Indigenous peoples.

Austerity Measures

Department annual reports[2] supplemented with survey data reveal that despite the important role this department has in advancing reconciliation and fulfilling the Crown's obligation to Indigenous peoples, it was not spared the aggressive austerity measures brought forward by the PC government. Annual reports demonstrate that department budgets and staff were cut in the first five years after the PC government took office— impacting ongoing, important work and the relationships Indigenous communities relied on.

Survey respondents provide context and insight into these cuts. A total of seven respondents identified that they worked in the area of Indigenous Reconciliation and Northern Relations. Of these seven respondents, the majority (five) were Manitoba public sector workers, while two worked with a nonprofit organization. They were a small, but accomplished group with an average of sixteen years of experience. All but one respondent reported that their work had been negatively impacted by the government's austerity measures aimed at reducing expenditures and balancing the budget.

In 2010/11 the total actual expenditures, adjusted for inflation, for activities related to Indigenous Reconciliation and Northern Relations was almost $47 million. This number gradually fell year after year until it reached an all-time low of $28.5 million in 2018/19. In 2019, the total expenditures rose to almost $54 million, but the department's expenditures were $24.5 million over budget (Government of Manitoba 2020, 31). Of these unbudgeted expenses $999,000 was related to a "contingent liability" and $25.7 million to the "payment of a remaining loan due to the conversion of the Loan Act Program to Capital Grants . . . plus principal and interest requirements for the Department's Loan Act Program" (Government of Manitoba 2020, 12). Unplanned infrastructure and capital expenditures included investments in roads, water and wastewater systems, waste disposal sites—such as a new regional facility in the Dauphin Parkland area and a temporary water treatment system to replace one destroyed by fire. By the following year, spending returned to levels more typical of this government at just over $29 million.

Full-time equivalent (FTE) positions in the department suffered a similar fate. By the end of the NDP mandate in 2015/16, the department had ninety-one FTEs (Government of Manitoba 2016, 42). The following year the number of positions fell to eighty-two (Government of Manitoba 2021, 33). Over the next four years the FTEs fluctuated until resting at eighty-one FTEs in 2020/21 (Government of Manitoba 2021, 33).

FTEs are only part of the story. As seen in other areas, this government has used attrition to shrink the public service. Although vacancy rates for the department were only published for 2022, a year where the department saw a shockingly high rate of 22 percent, employee counts in previous years reveal many positions were left vacant. From 2017 to 2022, the number of persons employed by the department fell from eighty-four to sixty-five. Workers responding to the survey reported that it was difficult to fill vacant positions because the pay was less than that offered by competitors such as Manitoba Hydro and the Government of Canada, and it was known that the chronic understaffing resulted in poor working conditions.

High vacancy rates in the department resulted in additional and intensified workloads for existing staff. Not only were employment positions left vacant, but consultant contracts were also allowed to expire without renewal, resulting in department staff assuming this work on top of their existing responsibilities. As a result, the majority of respondents reported deteriorating job satisfaction and declining mental health. It became increasingly difficult to recruit and retain qualified workers, further compounding the problem. One department staff shared their frustration: "I am a helper, my co-workers are helpers and when we were all benched and could not assist the communities in the capacity we were accustomed to, it affected everyone. Personally, it was hard not being able to fully carry out my duties and still be expected to report on the quarterly requirements. . . . Because of the cuts I felt that I was unable to complete all my job duties however the expectation was to do so and it did not make sense."

The majority of respondents reported that the austerity measures resulted in a reduction in the quality of services and public safety. The quality of programming was impacted as "fewer staff equals fewer projects," and staff reported not having the capacity to work on all existing initiatives and projects. This resulted in emerging issues having to be shelved as there was no capacity to respond to them due to excessive workloads.

Respondents also reported the frustrations of having no ability to visit communities, and no funding to invest in critical community programming. One respondent from the department noted that "when the cuts came, front-line staff were benched and only under extreme reasons, were staff able to travel."

Despite these attempts at saving money, 80 percent of the respondents felt that the cuts either transferred costs to other areas of the public service or ended up increasing costs in the public sector as a whole. One worker explained, "The cuts affected the services and supports to forty-eight communities. Administration, Public Works, Fire and Community Safety programs and community infrastructure were all affected by the cuts, and now to play catch-up and bring things back to a level they were at before the cuts will cost more in the long run."

Despite these drastic steps to reduce expenses, the majority of workers reported that neither management nor other senior officials gave any explanation or reasoning for the austerity measures or consulted with staff on cost-cutting opportunities. One staff reported that "front-line staff were not aware or involved, they were left to figure things out for themselves."

All but two respondents, who were unsure, felt that if there were more resources for their work, the value for money for Manitoba taxpayers would increase. They reported that if front-line staff were given adequate funding and freedom to travel to communities, they would be better able to support communities and "help them to become more self-reliant and mindful of their operating budgets."

One staff member felt that if vacancy rates were significantly reduced and competitive salaries offered, it would encourage retention of qualified staff "and add value for money through the reduction in on boarding and training new hires" that had become the norm in recent years. Furthermore, staff reported that efficiencies would improve "if there was greater investment in front-line workers, and if those workers were provided with the tools and operating budget to ensure that services, they were hired to provide, were in fact being provided."

Spending and staffing levels recovered somewhat in 2021/22. That year, actual expenditures for the department were $38.2 million. FTEs also increased by nine for a total of ninety, though the number of employees fell by four to a total of sixty-five. Increased expenditures were the result of funding for Urban Indigenous Vaccination Clinics and the Indian Residential and Day School Burial Sites Action Plan (Government of Manitoba 2022, 35).

Expenditure and FTE data (although not employee counts) are consistent with survey respondent reports that the department had "become more generous" since the change in leadership. Unfortunately, employees are fed up with working conditions and reported that recent changes were useless as no one wants to work for the government anymore. One respondent commented that increased spending and staffing should not be surprising, but that they were skeptical it would result in positive changes for communities. Frustration with the situation was evident: "With an election looming in 2023 it would only make sense that the current Government is increasing spending . . . IRNR [Indigenous Reconciliation and Northern Relations], as a whole, has seen staffing increases. However, in saying that, the focus of Government seems to be on policy and not field work." Instead of policy work, respondents felt that in order to make a difference in the work they did and for the communities they served, they needed adequate time and resources and, most importantly, the ability to visit the people and communities they serve.

Conclusion

Manitoba and Manitobans benefit in countless ways from the treaties and historical relationships with Indigenous nations. As a society, Canada is only recently coming to an understanding of how Canada's colonization efforts have harmed and continue to harm Indigenous peoples. If reconciliation is to come into being in Canada and Manitoba, this involves deep commitment, consistency, and a willingness to create a country different from the one we inherited. To do this important work the government must adequately fund and staff the Department of Indigenous Reconciliation and Northern Affairs.

We both participated in some of the discussions that took place during the drafting of The Path to Reconciliation Act. At the time, everyone involved hoped that this step would help Manitoba to find its way off an old colonial road where Canadian prosperity came at the expense of Indigenous peoples while Indigenous communities were mistreated, underfunded, and left behind. The new road would prioritize the creation of respectful relationships that honoured Indigenous peoples and required the provincial government to create and execute a plan of action on reconciliation for the betterment of all Manitobans. Much thought and deliberation went into the principles of respect, engagement, understanding, and action that were to inform and guide government activities. We were both present when the bill went to its third reading and was ultimately unanimously passed into law. At the time, it seemed like a progressive change, and we both hoped it would be implemented in the spirit and intent with which it was drafted.

Unfortunately, Manitoba's former PC government veered off the road that they were set on. While some may appreciate a government's use of austerity measures to rein in spending and balance budgets to promote financial stability, funding levels for Indigenous initiatives have always been far lower than for programs and services serving the general public. Over time, the already inadequate expenditures for Indigenous Reconciliation and Northern Relations were further reduced, resulting in government employees feeling overwhelmed with expanding responsibilities and reduced resources alongside policies that have taken precedent over community-based action and relationships. This was not reconciliation, but instead a continuation of the ongoing crisis created by the historic underfunding of Indigenous initiatives and communities.

There was little in the approach by Manitoba's PC government that suggested this trajectory was changing—an opinion we shared with Manitoba's Auditor General in 2022. As Manitobans who believe in the need for reconciliation, we know that the old path of colonization, violence, and acrimony between Indigenous and non-Indigenous peoples is fraught. Decorating this road with a rhetoric of reconciliation while operating under austerity, underfunding, and report cards of failure does not serve the needs of this province needs and has resulted in far greater costs than it would take to adequately resource and support a project of building relationships and rectifying the past. In a province where nearly one fifth of its citizens are Indigenous, the Manitoba government must take the lead and address the harms of the past through planning, delivery, and action.

Notes

1   This chapter was written in Summer 2023 before the election of the New Democratic Party government of Wab Kinew. Timelines and information have been updated wherever possible.

2   For details on data sources used for provincial expenditures, employee staffing numbers, and full-time equivalent (FTE) positions in this chapter, see Preface.

References

Assembly of Manitoba Chiefs. n.d. "About AMC." Accessed 20 February 2023. https://manitobachiefs.com/about/about-amc/.

Auditor General Manitoba. 2022. "Manitoba's Implementation of *The Path to Reconciliation Act*." April. https://www.oag.mb.ca/audit-reports/manitoba's-implementation-of-the-path-to-reconciliation-act-2022.

Government of Canada. n.d. "First Nations in Manitoba." Accessed 21 February 2023. https://www.sac-isc.gc.ca/eng/1100100020400/1616072911150.

Government of Manitoba. 2016. *Aboriginal and Northern Affairs Annual Report 2015–2016*. https://www.gov.mb.ca/inr/resources/pubs/ana-annual-report-2015-2016.pdf.

———. 2020. *Manitoba Indigenous and Northern Relations Annual Report 2019–2020*. https://www.gov.mb.ca/inr/resources/pubs/inr-annual-report-2019-2020.pdf.

———. 2021. *Department of Indigenous and Northern Relations Annual Report 2020–2021*. https://manitoba.ca/inr/resources/pubs/inr-annual-report-2020-2021.pdf.

———. 2022. *Manitoba Indigenous Reconciliation and Northern Relations Annual Report 2021–2022*. https://www.gov.mb.ca/inr/resources/pubs/inr-annual-report-2021-2022.pdf.

Manitoba Métis Federation. n.d. "Government Structure." Accessed 8 May 2025. https://www.mmf.mb.ca/government-structure#:~:text=Locals:,you%20belong%20to%20a%20Local.

The Legislative Assembly of Manitoba. 2023. "Land Acknowledgement." Accessed 21 February 2023. https://www.gov.mb.ca/legislature/about/land_acknowledgement.html.

The Path to Reconciliation Act. 2016. Bill 18. SM 2016, c. 5. 5th session, 40th Legislature. https://web2.gov.mb.ca/bills/40-5/b018e.php.

Statistics Canada. 2017. *Focus on Geography Series, 2016 Census*. Statistics Canada Catalogue no. 98-404-X2016001. Ottawa, Ontario. Data products, 2016 Census.

Truth and Reconciliation Commission of Canada. 2015. *Honouring the Truth, Reconciling for the Future: Summary of the Final Report of the Truth and Reconciliation Commission of Canada*. Truth and Reconciliation Commission of Canada. https://nctr.ca/publications-and-reports/reports/.

Chapter 19

THE IMPACT OF AUSTERITY ON MUNICIPALITIES

Orly Linovski

Introduction

Canadian municipalities are often referred to as "creatures of the province." Municipal powers are created by provincial legislation, with limited options to raise revenue. Despite this, municipalities are responsible for a wide variety of social, community, sanitation, safety, and transportation services. In Manitoba, as across Canada, the majority of revenue for municipalities comes from three sources: transfers from other levels of government, property taxes, and user fees. Two of these sources— property taxes and user fees—are largely seen as regressive (with a larger impact on lower-income households) and unable to keep pace with the demand for municipal services (Thompson et al. 2014; Kitchen, Slack, and Hachard 2019).[1]

Despite revenue sources remaining largely unchanged, municipalities are facing demands to address issues that go well beyond their traditional responsibilities, such as addressing climate change, critical housing affordability, immigrant settlement, and ongoing public health crises (Kitchen, Slack, and Hachard 2019, 2). The share of infrastructure that municipalities are responsible for has doubled in the last seventy years, with increasing maintenance and replacement costs (Thompson et al. 2014, 18). While the COVID-19 pandemic exacerbated many of the issues faced by municipalities—and underscored their role in providing front-line services—the unsustainable fiscal futures faced by municipalities across the country are ongoing (Federation of Canadian Municipalities 2020). In Manitoba, these issues are exacerbated by a provincial freeze on unconditional funding to municipalities that has been in place since 2016 (Lambert 2023), and key changes such as the elimination of transit cost-sharing agreements.[2]

In addition to direct financial support to municipalities, the province provides municipal advisory services, land use and community planning support, and support for regional service delivery and critical infrastructure. These services for municipalities are key in ensuring the protection of the public interest and in maintaining long-term social, environmental, and fiscal sustainability. The provision of these types of professional services has experienced significant changes, with the widespread outsourcing of government services (Blymke 1995; Saint-Martin 1998, 2000). As part of the "new public management" ideology, private sector consultants were perceived to be more efficient and less politically oriented, and to offer more "value for money" than in-house government staff (Blymke 1995; Christensen and Laegreid 2001). For example, from 1981 to 2001, there was a 647 percent increase in Canadian government spending on policy consultants, accompanied by "a disproportionate reduction in the number of operational and administrative support employees" (Perl and White 2002, 53–55). Despite this, outsourcing policy and professional services is not necessarily less expensive than directing resources to building in-house capacity, particularly when the full costs of outsourcing—such as transaction costs and the costs of supervising and managing external consultants—are accounted for (Perl and White 2002). Critically, a lack of public sector capacity to manage consultants can result in a lack of oversight and concerns about the protection of the public interest (Linovski 2018, 2021).

In this context of constrained municipal resources and government outsourcing, austerity measures at the provincial level can have wide-ranging and significant impacts on municipalities and the services they provide. This chapter examines how changes to funding levels, departmental priorities, and the contracting out of services impact the municipal sector, including employees, residents, and the public interest more broadly.

Municipal Context and Funding in Manitoba

Across Canada, the proportion of the population living in urban areas has been increasing (Statistics Canada 2022), and Manitoba has seen similar trends. Between 2011 and 2021, the populations of the majority of the largest municipalities have increased, in some cases more than 25 percent (Table 19.1). Critically, since 2011, more than 75 percent of the new population increase in Manitoba has occurred in the eight largest cities.

In addition to population changes, municipalities are addressing increasingly complex issues, such as climate change, homelessness, housing affordability, public health, immigration, refugee settlement, and aging infrastructure (Thompson et al. 2014; Federation of Canadian Municipalities 2020). Despite this, funding to the Department of Municipal Relations has remained largely static over time, both to support provincial department activities and to provide direct financial assistance to municipalities (Figure 19.1).[3] While there was a jump in financial assistance from 2020 to 2021, partially as a result of federal flow-through COVID-19 pandemic support, funding has decreased or largely stagnated over the long term. For example, after adjusting for inflation and changes in branch composition, support for Community Planning, Permitting, and Development decreased by more than $6.6 million, or 14 percent, between 2012/13 and 2021/22 (Government of Manitoba 2022). Direct financial support for municipalities has also largely not kept pace. Support for municipalities in 2022 was only 6 percent higher than in 2013, despite double-digit population growth in most large municipalities and pressing challenges facing municipalities. When adjusting for inflation, total financial assistance to municipalities per Manitoban fell from $280 to $244 between 2015/16 and 2019/20. In 2021/22, funding was still 11 percent below 2015/16 levels.

While budget data shows stagnation in funding for municipalities and municipal services, as a cautionary note, one survey respondent raised concern about how provincial budgets are reported. The respondent noted that "government has also consistently changed the manner in which public accounts are reported, the scope of inclusion of entities for public reporting, and reduced the level of detail in public budgets, which have collectively, greatly obscured what is actually happening." In addition to this reporting concern, the budget changes for the municipal sector—both as a provincial department and in support for municipalities—occurred in the context of

Table 19.1. Population change in largest municipalities in Manitoba, 2011–2021.

LARGEST MUNICIPALITIES IN MANITOBA, BY POPULATION SIZE	POPULATION, 2021	CHANGE (%), 2011–2021
Winnipeg	749,607	13
Brandon	51,313	11
Steinbach	17,806	32
Winkler	13,747	29
Portage la Prairie	13,270	2
Thompson	13,035	-1
Selkirk	10,504	7
Morden	9,929	27
Total combined population of largest municipalities	879,211	13
Total provincial population	1,342,153	11
% of provincial population increase that occurred in largest municipalities		76

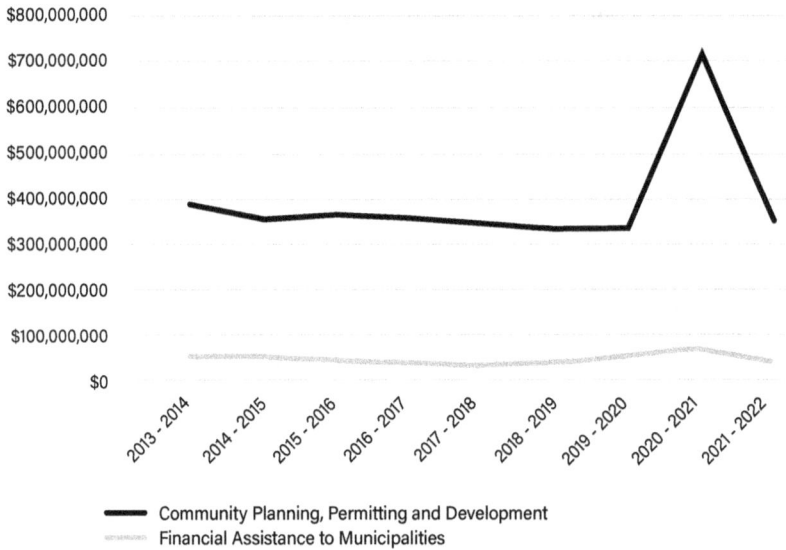

Figure 19.1. Budget appropriations to Municipal Relations, 2013–2022 (inflation adjusted).

Note: Federal flow-through COVID-19 funding, 2020-2021.

changes to the purpose of, and limitations imposed on, provincial funding. As one survey respondent explained, "Government has significantly reprofiled existing resources into other streams (e.g. redirecting staff budgets to multi-year consultant contracts instead of reducing expenditures)." As discussed below in the section on privatization and contracting out, this shift in how government activities are undertaken, such as through the use of private sector consultants, is not evident solely in year-to-year high-level budget changes. The next sections explore how employees perceive the presence of austerity measures and their impact, both on those supporting municipalities in the provincial government and those working in municipalities and nonprofits.

Overview of Austerity Measures Impacting the Municipal Sector

As municipalities are limited in their sources of revenue and dependent on provincial revenue sharing, the survey was open to provincial and municipal employees, as well as those in the nonprofit sector. Employees from

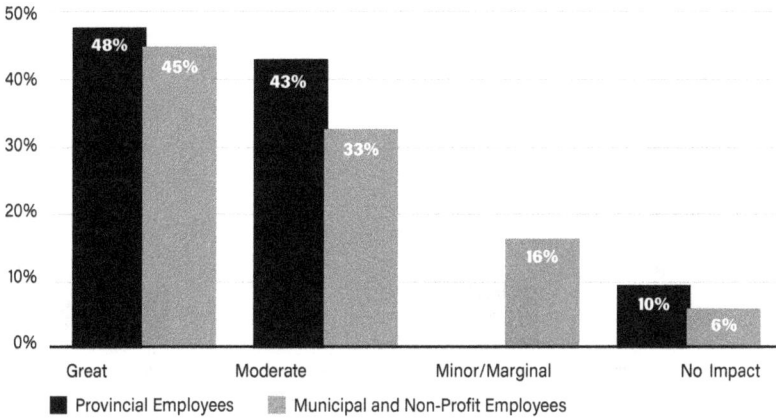

Figure 19.2. Survey responses: Impact of austerity on municipal and nonprofit employees.

nonprofits were included as they receive provincial or municipal funding and focus on community development. Of the seventy responses related to municipal services, 30 percent were provincial employees, 42 percent were municipal employees, and 10 percent worked for nonprofits or other agencies. Given the differing contexts for provincial and other types of employees, this chapter presents separate analyses by employer type. The majority of respondents felt that their work had been either greatly or moderately impacted by provincial austerity measures aimed at reducing expenditures and balancing the budget (Figure 19.2). This was more acute for provincial employees, as 91 percent felt their work had been greatly or moderately impacted by austerity measures, compared with 78 percent of municipal and other employees.

Participants were asked to compare austerity and expenditure restraint after the 2016 change in government from the New Democratic Party (NDP) to the Progressive Conservative (PC) Party. While the majority of both provincial and other employees felt that austerity measures had gotten more intense after the change in government, this was more substantial for provincial employees (Figure 19.3). Some municipal employees felt that measures had "relaxed" (7 percent) since the change in government, while no provincial employees agreed with this.

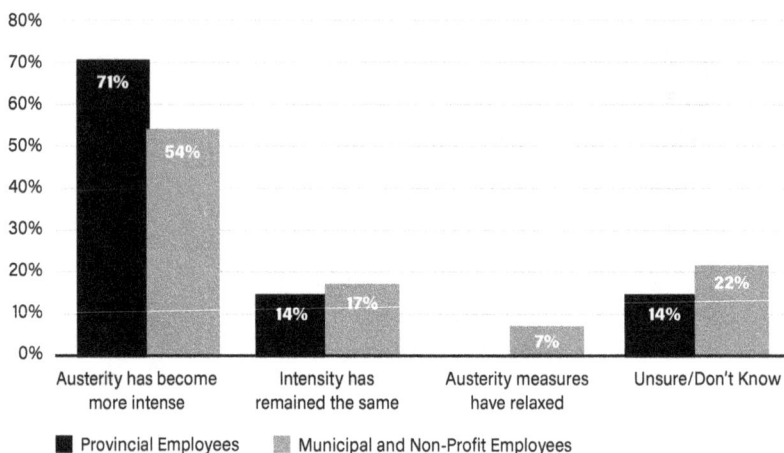

Figure 19.3. Survey responses: Perceived changes in expenditure between governments.

Austerity measures were seen as impacting diverse areas such as working conditions, job satisfaction, recruitment, and worker safety. Both types of respondents felt a negative impact on working conditions and the ability to recruit staff, while almost 40 percent of municipal and other employees saw worsened worker safety (Figure 19.4). As a result of austerity measures, 62 percent of provincial respondents and 61 percent of municipal employees reported they were considering jobs elsewhere or with other employers, while 19 percent of provincial respondents (4 percent of municipal/other) had left the public service. Overwhelmingly, both provincial (81 percent) and municipal respondents (76 percent) felt that due to austerity measures, they were being asked to provide the same or increased service with fewer resources.

Impact of Austerity on Work and Workers

Unfilled Positions and Workload Increases

With 90 percent of provincial employee respondents feeling that their work had been greatly or moderately impacted by austerity measures, there were broad concerns about workload intensification (81 percent of provincial respondents) and other changes to work (29 percent of

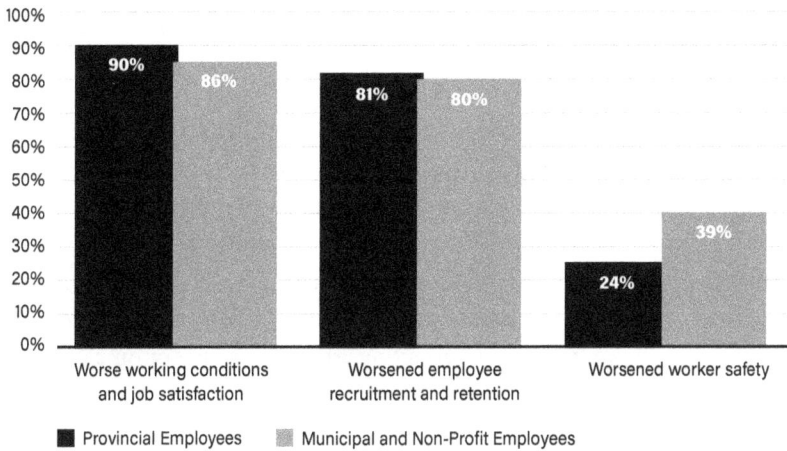

Figure 19.4. Survey responses: Impact of austerity measures on working conditions.

provincial respondents). Despite austerity measures, most provincial respondents felt that their work had not been scaled back (76 percent). A major concern was the impact of unfilled positions, leading to increased workloads and concerns about service quality. In 2022, the Department of Municipal Relations had over seventy-four unfilled F T E s, for a vacancy rate of 23 percent (Government of Manitoba 2022). Participants described being required to cover multiple positions, for long periods of time or permanently. For example, as one provincial employee explained, "I am . . . in an office that had [75 percent of its staff cut since] 2018, and the region I provide services to has expanded considerably."

In addition to workload increases, participants described other critical changes, including being responsible for work above their position grade or being forced to move departments when their position was eliminated. Municipal respondents also felt that their work had not been scaled back in response to austerity measures (67 percent) and pointed to similar issues with vacancies due to austerity measures, particularly related to difficulties filling positions, increased scope of work, or a lack of oversight from supervisors. As one respondent explained, "There are positions in my department that have gone unfilled for years while those duties are pushed onto other employees, contractors, rehired retired employees, or else just neglected until they become urgent."

The impact of unfilled vacancies can be long term, as they lead to the loss of institutional knowledge and gaps in training. As one municipal employee explained, budget cuts have knock-on effects on efficiency and the quality of work: "Budget cuts to municipal support payments during a global pandemic resulted in significant budget pressure on all city departments to cut non-essentials and find money through vacancy management. Struggles with talent retention in our department have resulted in reduced efficiency . . . more time spent correcting errors, constant training of new staff to replace departures, brain drain from departures resulting in a workforce with little to no experience."

Leaving positions unfilled as an austerity measure was a major concern across employees in both municipal and provincial sectors. While this strategy may offer immediate cost savings, the issues raised by survey participants point to long-term concerns about efficiency, work quality, and long-term sustainability.

Privatization and Contracting Out

The increasing role of the private sector—primarily the use of consultants for professional work—was highlighted as an issue by respondents in both sectors. Contracting out was a concern for about 30 percent of provincial respondents, all of whom described work such as reports, plans, policy work, and services for municipalities being outsourced to consultants. While fewer municipal and other respondents felt that more work has been contracted out (17 percent agree, and 17 percent unsure), there were similar themes between employees in the sectors. Both provincial and municipal employees noted concerns with the quality of work that has been outsourced, including process issues, insufficient results, and a reliance on the public service for source information. Overall, there were more concerns among provincial employees than municipal employees about outsourcing, but the two shared similar concerns about the quality of outsourced work, and more fundamentally about the role of the public sector in providing services.

Respondents also noted that contracting out can lead to problems with oversight and product quality and unnecessary projects, as well as negatively impacting provincial staff capacity. For example, as one public service employee noted, "Work that could be done in-house has been contracted out to consultants, with varying quality and success. This has limited potential for staff growth and opportunities to ensure quality control." For some employees, there was a similar concern about the role of the public sector and the limits to outsourcing for municipal services. One public sector employee noted, "Our function supports a public service that's not profitable and isn't meant to be profitable. It's meant to provide the public with useful service. When these types of services are contracted out, they are plagued with budget cuts and cost-cutting measures that destroy the public's satisfaction with the service provided." Others emphasized issues with the quality of outsourced work, with implications if it does not meet the needs of clients or for provincial interests. One public sector employee noted, "It has been my experience that the provincial government-subsidized private sector work product is of poor quality . . . must therefore be repeatedly amended or prematurely replaced to meet the needs of municipal clients and protect provincial interests."

Other participants explained that municipalities have been directed to use private sector consultants for work that was previously undertaken by the province, with these costs subsidized through provincial grants. One public sector employee noted that "provincial grants to municipal clients directed [the use of] private consultants to complete work previously completed by the Province [resulting] in much lower quality outputs that sometimes require the government to amend, repair, or replace." These questions about the quality and oversight of consultant work raises concerns about the long-term implications of widespread contracting out.

A critical issue with the contracting out of work in the municipal sector was seen as the possibility of conflicts of interest. For planning work, the majority of private sector firms work for both private and public sector clients, leading to questions about how regulatory and development roles are balanced (Linovski 2018). Respondents pointed to clear conflicts of interest from private sector outsourcing, with one stating, "We primarily function as a regulatory body that balances public and private interests. It would be a conflict of interest for private firms to administer our portfolio." Similarly, others felt that since government is responsible for protecting the public interest in areas such as land use planning and the protection of agricultural and natural resources, these services should not be contracted out.

Private Sector Efficiency: "Save a Nickel to Spend a Dollar"

The majority of provincial respondents (67 percent) felt that there were few efficiency gains from private sector outsourcing. Few provincial participants felt that the private sector would perform their organization's tasks in a more efficient manner (19 percent); those who did related this efficiency to more staff and administrative support in private sector firms.

Respondents' perceptions of the limits of private sector efficiency were tied to a low potential for profit (particularly in social and community services) and how that would impact the quality of work. Participants noted, "Nobody can provide municipalities the service we do for the small cost that our department charges [or] recovers." This means few opportunities to profit from the services provided, leading to concerns about how that would impact the quality of work as private sector firms aim to reduce costs. Several respondents referred to direct experience where private sector outsourcing did not result in lower long-term costs, with one participant referring to it as "saving a nickel to spend a dollar."

Municipal and other respondents similarly felt that there were few efficiency gains to be made through contracting out to the private sector (67 percent, with 24 percent unsure). For those that did feel that the private sector could be more efficient (8 percent of municipal or other respondents), this was tied to private firms providing services at a higher cost or being able to provide more staff. Respondents felt that the need for private sector profitability raised concerns about outsourcing. One public sector employee noted that "private companies need to make a profit so their goal is to extract as much money out of the government as possible while spending the least on the service so that they can pocket the rest."

Deferring work can result in higher costs in the long term, both in terms of staff time and due to inflation or delayed maintenance. As one financial manager noted, "A great deal of time is spent trying to identify where cuts can be made that will not impact service, safety, or resulting in significant increased future costs due to inflation and deterioration, when the work eventually has to be done." While outsourcing of government work has been motivated by perceived cost savings and efficiency, participants' direct experiences raise serious concerns about maintaining quality and protecting the public interest with this service model.

Changes in Nature of Work and Priorities

In addition to the impact of widespread vacancies and contracting out, provincial respondents pointed to other changes in their work. For example, reductions in support functions (such as human resources, IT, and finance) have led to a "slow creep of additional duties." Others note that in addition to vacancies, the geographic scope and number of municipal clients they are responsible for have increased significantly, leading to increased workloads.

There were also concerns about shifts related to political priorities, with one respondent noting a "dramatic increase in workload due to political priority initiatives in sector." In other cases, a respondent noted that politically sensitive work was transferred out of their branch. Several respondents also pointed to changes in how they interacted with the public or community, such as being moved from front-line community work to creating informational documents for senior management. As one policy analyst noted, "I went from interacting often with the public and funding recipients to [being] given very specific criteria in which I was allowed to communicate with the public. Anything outside of that required specific permission with using pre-drafted response."

Municipal sector respondents also pointed to the impact of funding priorities on their broader work context. For example, the prioritization of funding capital costs—without accompanying operational funding—can lead to long-term fiscal issues and limit the success of these projects. One City of Winnipeg employee noted that "the Province funds Transit and we no longer are funded properly so the City has to foot any overages or unexpected operating costs. The Federal and Provincial governments are eager to make capital purchases (i.e., purchase alternative fuel buses) however does not include funding to actually pay for storage of parts, employees to drive or maintain these vehicles. Nothing is completely thought through and unfortunately the people at the bottom suffer for it." While unfilled positions and year-to-year funding changes are easier to assess, these responses point to shifts in the context and substance of public sector work that may have significant impacts.

A Way Forward for Municipal Services

Despite the critical role that municipalities play in addressing the most pressing societal concerns, there is little evidence of provincial support to facilitate this. With limited funding and numerous unfilled positions, employees are asked to "do more with less," stretching the ability to maintain service quality and an efficient public service. Despite the promise of increased value for money through the contracting out of professional services, this has not been demonstrated in either the short or long term. In the short term, consultant costs can be higher than the cost of providing services in-house; and quality may not meet standards, requiring additional staff resources. Participants confirmed the long-term implications of the "hollowing out" of the public sector (Perl and White 2002), including limited staff capacity or expertise to evaluate the work of consultants, and ongoing concerns about the protection of the public interest. Overall, provincial austerity measures have had significant impacts on municipalities and those that provide services to them.

Participants provided numerous ideas about how services could be improved with sustainable and reliable provincial funding in diverse areas, including emergency services, transit, planning, poverty reduction, and environmental protection. While austerity measures may potentially provide immediate savings, the chronic underfunding of municipalities and municipal services has significant long-term costs, including in deferred maintenance, loss of internal capacity, and reduced service quality. Concerningly, the lack of sustainable funding means that critical issues remain unaddressed, as one respondent explained: "Implementing the Climate Action Plan and Community Energy Investment Roadmap would save the City money in the long term but requires significant investment now. If we support people experiencing houselessness, then they require fewer emergency services and may be able to contribute to the economy. We need to address the intergenerational impacts of colonization and trauma. Due to austerity measures, [we have] experienced decades of uncertainty and trauma, and that has been offloaded to low-income residents."

While austerity measures have been widely adopted, any potential cost savings must be evaluated in terms of the long-term impact on residents, communities, the environment, and the broader public interest.

Notes

1   In 2017, municipalities in Manitoba derived 43 percent of their income from property taxes, a rate similar to the national average of 46 percent (Kitchen, Slack, and Hachard 2019).

2   In 2023, the provincial government announced an increase in baseline grant funding to municipalities, ranging from a 14 percent increase to the City of Winnipeg to a 39 percent increase to the City of Brandon (Lambert 2023). The impact of these increases remains to be seen.

3   Funding to municipalities includes both general operating grants and strategic infrastructure funds which are earmarked for specific projects (Government of Manitoba 2021).

References

Blymke, Øystein. 1995. "Government Agencies and Consultancy—A Norwegian Perspective." In *Ethics and Consultancy: European Perspectives*, edited by Heidi Von Weltzien Hoivik and Andreas Føllesdal, 127–34. Dordrecht: Kluwer Academic Publishers.

Christensen, Tom, and Per Laegreid. 2001. "New Public Management: The Effects of Contractualism and Devolution on Political Control." *Public Management Review* 3 (1): 73–94. http://dx.doi.org/10.1080/14616670010009469.

Federation of Canadian Municipalities. 2020. Protecting Vital Municipal Services. https://fcm.ca/en/resources/protecting-vital-municipal-services.

Government of Manitoba. 2021. Manitoba Municipal Relations. *Annual Report, 2020–2021*. Winnipeg. https://www.gov.mb.ca/mr/annualreports/pubs/annual_report_2020_21.pdf.

———. 2022. Department of Municipal Relations. *2022 Committee of Supply, Department of Municipal Relations as at September 28, 2022 (Briefing Binder)*, 28 September. https://gov.mb.ca/asset_library/en/proactive/briefings/2022/mr-cos-binder-2022-redacted.pdf.

Kavanagh, Sean. 2021. "Province Tells City of Winnipeg It Must Explore Public-Private Partnership for Sewage Plant." CBC Manitoba, 17 May. https://www.cbc.ca/news/canada/manitoba/winnipeg-sewage-treatment-privatization-manitoba-government-1.6029460.

Kitchen, Harry, Enid Slack, and Tomas Hachard. 2019. *Property Taxes in Canada: Current Issues and Future Prospects*. Institute on Municipal Finance and Governance.

Lambert, Steve. 2023. "Manitoba Lifts Freeze on Municipal Grants." *Winnipeg Free Press*, 24 February.

Linovski, Orly. 2018. "Shifting Agendas: Private Consultants and Public Planning Policy." *Urban Affairs Review* 55 (6): 1666–1701. https://doi.org/10.1177/1078087417752475.

———. 2021. "Conflicting Interests: Professional Planning Practice in Publicly-Traded Firms." In *Professional Service Firms and Politics in a Global Era*, edited by Chris Hurl and Anne Vogelpohl, 295–319. London: Palgrave Macmillan.

MacKinnon, Shauna. 2021. *The Building Sustainable Communities Program after Two Years: Where Did the Money Go?* Winnipeg: Canadian Centre for Policy Alternatives–Manitoba. https://policyalternatives.ca/sites/default/files/uploads/publications/2021/06/BSC%20After%20Two%20Years%20-%20MacKinnon.pdf.

Perl, Anthony, and Donald J. White. 2002. "The Changing Role of Consultants in Canadian Policy Analysis." *Policy and Society* 21 (1): 49–73. https://doi.org/10.1016/S1449-4035(02)70003-9.

Saint-Martin, Denis. 1998. "The New Managerialism and the Policy Influence of Consultants in Government: An Historical-Institutionalist Analysis of Britain, Canada and France." *Governance* 11 (3): 319–56.

———. 2000. *Building the New Managerialist State: Consultants and the Politics of Public Sector Reform in Comparative Perspective.* Oxford: Oxford University Press.

Statistics Canada. 2022. "Population Growth in Canada's Rural Areas, 2016 to 2021." https://www12.statcan.gc.ca/census-recensement/2021/as-sa/98-200-x/2021002/98-200-x2021002-eng.cfm.

Thompson, David, Greg Flanagan, Diana Gibson, Laleah Sinclair, and Andy Thompson. 2014. *Funding a Better Future: Progressive Revenue Sources for Canada's Cities and Towns.* Canadian Union of Public Employees.

Chapter 20

AUSTERITY FROM THE PERSPECTIVE OF PUBLIC SECTOR WORKERS "BEHIND THE SCENES"

Shreya Ghimire, Karine Levasseur, and Andrea Rounce

Introduction

The public sector in Manitoba is diverse, but a common goal among public servants is to support the public interest. The survey respondents for this chapter are current or former public servants with the province of Manitoba, who have worked in the public sector between 2015 and 2022. For this chapter, respondents ($n = 86$) work(ed) in areas that we call administration departments, or those departments and organizations that serve government as a whole. Working in areas such as finance, government services, and the public service commission, as well as central units in large departments, these public servants work as senior managers, technical and content specialists, IT professionals, accountants, property managers, public policy analysts, and advisors; they work in administration and on projects that support the work undertaken by government. Their work takes place around the province, although the majority are geographically located in Winnipeg. While their labour happens mostly behind the scenes, it is essential to a well-functioning and account-able government.

When thinking about austerity in the Manitoba public sector since 2016, there are three points in time that highlight how austerity measures may have changed. First is the election of the Progressive Conservative (PC) government led by Premier Brian Pallister in 2016—a shift from the New Democratic Party (NDP) government which had been in power for sixteen years. A second important point is the transition from Premier Pallister to Premier Heather Stefanson in 2021. Last is the COVID-19 pandemic, which began in March 2020. When asked about how these different shifts impacted austerity in government, respondents were more likely to say that provincial austerity in their line of work became more intense with the election of the PC government (66 percent). The other two points in time coincide, making it more difficult to separate out austerity as a single variable. Instead, austerity must be viewed as interconnected with the pandemic. Some respondents said that austerity measures relaxed after the start of the pandemic, but most said that the intensity of provincial austerity remained the same (39 percent) or even became more intense (37 percent). The transition in premiers also took place during the pandemic, which means austerity measures taken by government were intercon-nected with the transfer and management of federal funds in support of the pandemic, healthcare system crises, and the transition from the most unpopular premier in the country (Pallister) to "new" leadership. Some respondents said that austerity measures relaxed under the new premier (22 percent), but most said that the intensity of provincial austerity remained the same (52 percent) or even became more intense (11 percent). This chapter acknowledges the importance of these transitions, noting that the impact of the pandemic cannot be fully separated out from the discussion of austerity. In essence, we assume that respondents (and we ourselves) see austerity through the lens of the pandemic, and vice versa.

The impact of the pandemic can be seen in expenditures and in staffing numbers for the Department of Finance, the Department of Government Services (a full department of its own a year prior to the survey), and the Public Service Commission. Despite government commitment to austerity measures, expenditures in all three of these departments increased signifi-cantly throughout the pandemic years. In some cases, the FTEs allocated to these departments also increased. However, pandemic-era spending increases occurred after three years of relatively flat expenditures (falling, if measured in inflation-adjusted dollars) and a decline in FTEs. In per capita inflation terms, expenditures decreased by 7.9 percent and FTEs fell by 5 percent from 2016/17 to 2019/20. Moreover, one of the challenges in assessing the expenditures and staffing levels for these administration departments is that we do not know how they flow throughout the departments. Given the influx of federal funds for pandemic supports, as well as the provincial monies allocated to pandemic supports, it makes sense that these departments would have a role to play in allocating the new emergency funds. Increases in expenditures and staffing during the pandemic years likely reflect these new temporary sources of revenue and emergency spending.

Austerity and Workplace Impacts

Individual Impacts

Austerity may impact different people in the public sector differently, depending in part on their employment roles and obligations. When asked about whether the Government of Manitoba's austerity measures aimed at reducing expenditures and balancing the budget impacted their work and that of their close coworkers (see Figure 20.1), nearly two-thirds (64 percent) of the respondents said that their work was greatly impacted.

When asked about whether their employment (generally) was impacted by the implemented austerity measures, 68 percent indicated that their workload has intensified or increased under Premiers Pallister and Stefanson's austerity measures (see Figure 20.2). One public sector employee in the Department of Finance said "morale has plummeted," while another employee observed that "one person is doing five people's jobs because government doesn't hire people."

Work scheduling was also an area impacted by austerity measures. Respondents indicated changes relating to the length and intensity of their work schedules, as well as staffing shortages that impacted their work. When asked about their work schedules, the most frequently reported changes were: an increased number of tasks (58 percent), shorter or missed breaks/meals (31 percent), being assigned longer shifts than desired (7 percent), and being assigned more shifts than desired (2 percent). Nearly

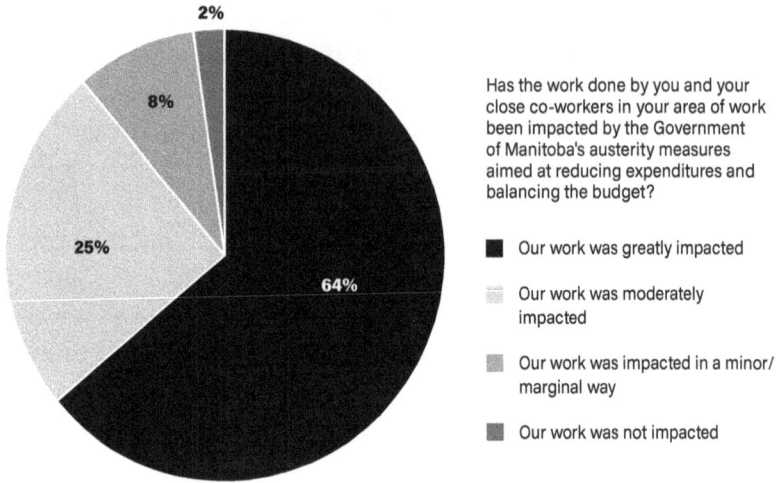

Figure 20.1. Survey responses: Impact of austerity on public sector workers.

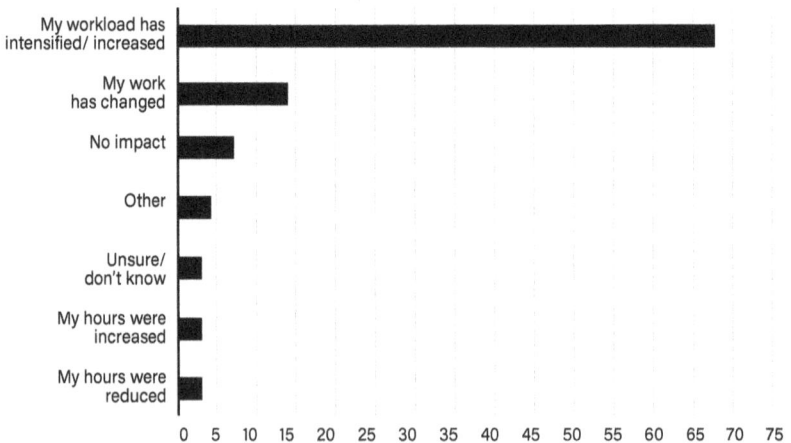

Figure 20.2. Survey responses: Impact of austerity on public sector employee workload.

two-thirds (64 percent) of respondents identified staffing shortages as a factor that impacted their work scheduling, and one-third (33 percent) identified more contract/casual staff being hired instead of permanent staff. Another significant issue reported by 37 percent of respondents was that employees faced other resource shortages due to reduced budgets or limiting spending to support people's work and tasks.

While it is evident from the data presented so far that austerity had a considerable impact on the working conditions of government employees, it is also important to assess whether and how these changes impacted individual workers' job satisfaction and commitment to their employers. We know that workplace morale has been impacted by austerity and by the COVID-19 pandemic overall, and that government workers are not exempt from these impacts.[1] This group of respondents was similar to others across government in that 88 percent reported that austerity measures implemented in their area of work made them less satisfied with their job. Turnover in government employment may be caused by retirements or by employees leaving for other reasons. When asked about the impact of austerity on their desire to stay with their public service employer, nearly three-quarters (72 percent) reported that it led them to consider jobs elsewhere or with other employers.

Broader Implications for Labour

Respondents were asked how austerity measures implemented in their areas of work impacted workers more broadly, in terms of their working conditions and job satisfaction, employee mental health, employee recruitment and retention, and worker safety. Not surprisingly, they outlined negative impacts for all of these factors.

A large proportion (88 percent) said that austerity measures implemented in their area of work led to worse working conditions and job satisfaction. Nearly nine in ten (89 percent) reported that austerity measures led to worse employee mental health. The same proportion (89 percent) said that austerity measures led to worse employee recruitment and retention. Many respondents highlighted the impact that austerity conditions and the resulting culture change in the public sector have had on themselves and their colleagues, including less interest in their work, low morale overall, and feeling underappreciated. One public sector employee stated, "There is a definite impact on staff mental health. Staff that have spent years willing to assist as required, even outside their duties, are now talking about union action and/or leaving the job." Others referred to the loss of FTEs; the increase in work that had to be done but was not fulfilling; a decrease in the number of hours staff are allocated, which leads to more work for their managers; and the inexperience of new staff, meaning that more work is required from the more experienced staff. Retirements not only impact the amount of work the remaining staff must do but also mean a loss in institutional memory.

Some respondents mentioned that sick time is high among staff, burnout and mental health stressors are common, job-related injuries have increased, and the culture created within the public service due to austerity measures causes a great deal of stress for people. In a class of workers like the respondents surveyed for this chapter, it seems likely that these impacts can be understood as workplace health and safety issues. Circumstances worsened with COVID-19, as this public sector employee noted: "If you were unlucky enough to get COVID, like me, you run out of sick time really quickly and end up not getting paid at all. They tried to make it sound like we were being taken care of over COVID, but if you had two days of sick time and were sick for a week or more, you had nothing." Another public sector employee expressed a different take on the impact of COVID-19, saying, "We hoped we'd get COVID so that we could have some time off."

Many respondents elaborated on the issues around recruitment and retention. Many said that they were considering other employment. Others emphasized the impacts that austerity has had on recruitment—particularly during a pandemic. Many said that contractors were being hired rather than permanent public servants, and that many more students and term employees were being hired for temporary work—often with such low salaries that new recruits would not find them attractive. One public sector employee in the Department of Finance noted that "the wage freeze resulted in hiring challenges as wages are less competitive." Respondents said that students and temporary employees were being asked to do work that normally would be done by permanent staff. Others said that many staff were in acting positions since no new hires were being allowed.

Privatization and Contracting: Hollowing Out the Public Sector

In addition to changing working conditions, privatization and contracting out represent other approaches to austerity. Privatization involves the selling of partially or wholly government-owned enterprises. Comparatively, contracting removes the delivery of a public good from the hands of public servants and finances a third-party agent to deliver said public good. Contracting involves some form of financing to the third-party delivery agent, often with specific predefined deliverables. Besides financing, contracting also controls performance of the third-party delivery agent (Scott 2003). Contracting has been used extensively in Canada since the height of public sector reforms in the 1990s to rely on third-party delivery agents such as private companies and nongovernmental organizations to deliver vital programs and services to Canadians (Phillips and Levasseur 2004). To what extent did Manitoba rely on these two approaches under the PC governments led by Premiers Pallister and Stefanson?

When asked whether work in their area was being privatized or contracted out to private companies or other nongovernmental organizations, nearly 43 percent answered "yes" compared to nearly 42 percent who answered "no." Almost 16 percent said they were unsure or did not know. How do we interpret these answers when nearly the same percentage of respondents say "yes" and "no"?

It is important to keep in mind exactly what these respondents do. As described, many of these respondents do not, generally, provide direct goods or services to the public. Rather, they spend their working hours reviewing financial data, reviewing policy options prepared by front-line departments, providing financial/human resources management for the whole of government, and providing advice to Cabinet. The responses also highlight two groups with different experiences: employees in Government Services had experienced a lot of contracting out, whereas other employees saw much less. Of the 43 percent who specified that there was more privatization or contracting, a larger proportion of Government Services workers (63 percent) specified that they saw privatization and contracting out.

The PC government contracted out parts of the big picture thinking to private companies. One example of this contracting out involved the contracting of KPMG to study public-private partnerships (P3) with

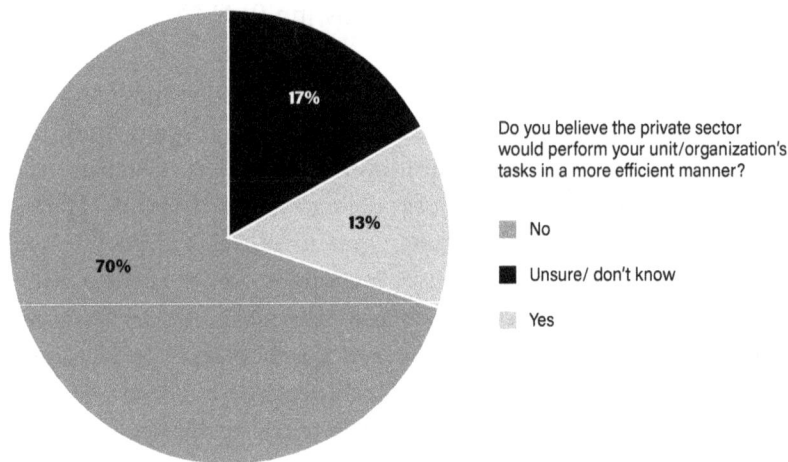

Figure 20.3. Survey responses: Perceived public and private sector efficiencies.

the goal of addressing the need to build new schools in the province (Government of Manitoba 2017). The PC government opted to employ a for-profit firm, instead of public servants, to develop and lead stakeholder consultations, conduct risk assessment workshops, and assess whether the P3 model or another model is a good fit to repair the infrastructure needs of schools. KPMG and PricewaterhouseCoopers Canada (PwC) were also hired to facilitate the centralization of procurement in the Government Services division. The hiring of consultants to do the big-picture thinking on these and other files means that public servants who have built considerable institutional memory are not doing this kind of work. These are illustrative examples, but not exhaustive. During this time, the government contracted KPMG and other consultants to provide programmatic, policy, and governance advice across different government areas, as noted elsewhere in this volume.

Austerity is underpinned by the assumptions that the public sector is bloated and that approaches such as privatization and contracting produce greater efficiency. When asked whether the private sector could perform their organizational tasks more efficiently, respondents overwhelmingly said "no." As illustrated in Figure 20.3, 70 percent said the private sector would not perform their tasks more efficiently.

Respondents who said the private sector would not yield greater efficiency questioned the trade-off between efficiency and other values such as equity and effectiveness. The public sector is often rooted in competing values, so when efficiency gains are made, it is generally at the expense of another value such as equity (Fernandez-Gutierrez and Van de Walle 2017). Moreover, making gains via efficiency could impose greater risks if vendors are not properly managed. While a small proportion of the respondents agree that there are some inefficiencies in government, many noted even if the private sector can be efficient in certain areas such as IT, realizing these gains requires a viable public sector to manage and supervise vendors.

Cost Savings, Value for Money, and the "Austerity Delusion"

Results from respondents present overall mixed opinions on the effects of austerity measures on cost savings for the public sector in the short term. When asked if austerity measures implemented in their area of work saved the public sector money within one to two years of their implementation, 38 percent of respondents selected "no." Furthermore, nearly 19 percent believed that the measures created savings for their area of work but transferred costs to other areas of the public sector. Nearly 12 percent believed the measures did create cost savings in their area and in the public sector as a whole. The relationship between austerity measures and overall cost savings for the public sector in the short term is thus, at best, ambiguous.

However, when asked if they believed austerity measures implemented in their area of work would save the public sector money in the long term, 59 percent responded "no." Nearly 12 percent of respondents believed that the measures would create long-term savings for their area but transfer costs to other areas of the public sector, and only 4 percent believed austerity measures would create savings for both their area and the public sector as a whole.

The results suggest that austerity measures are an uncertain strategy for cost savings in the short term and, to a majority of respondents, an infeasible one in the long term. Economist Paul Krugman (2015a, 2015b), political economist Mark Blyth (2013), and others refer to the disconnect between the promise of austerity for greater cost savings and its lacklustre outcomes as an example of the "austerity delusion" at work. When thinking about cost savings in the long term, responses from this group of public servants highlight the austerity delusion by pointing to how particular austerity measures led to the accumulation of costs over time. Some of these examples include how savings found in one area led to increased costs in others, as well as reflections on how initiatives to cut bureaucratic "red tape" resulted in greater amounts of time and work for public servants (and thus costs in terms of labour output). One public sector noted that spending reductions spurred a vicious cycle of "community need deficit," in which "the cuts to services only pushed more people into low-income or to situations requiring support from public services. The public need is higher which means we will eventually need to invest in services again, possibly privatizing or contracting out services, costing more in the long run."

Supplementing this is a consideration of the cost of *risks* to which the public sector becomes vulnerable as a result of austerity measures. Here, respondents referred to the risks of data security breaches due to spending reductions, as well as the increased risk of the public sector facing legal/civil action. As one public sector employee in Labour, Consumer Protection and Government Services noted, "God forbid we have a 'Grenfell' event in one of our public assets. It will be very bad for Manitoba. Any sort of legal (civil) action by victims will be at the cost of the taxpayers, the politicians. We are in a place of significant risk." The reference to the 2017 Grenfell Tower fire in London, UK, is powerful as it underlines the severity of consequences that can occur due to lax government oversight (Halliday 2023). From a cost-savings perspective, the risk of a similar disastrous event involving a Manitoba public asset illustrates how short-term savings could bear much greater long-term costs. Moreover, respondents' concerns about the consequences of financial risks are supported by the findings of the Auditor General's 2022 public accounts report which found that financial reporting errors have increased across government departments (Hoye 2022). While financial errors may not seem so consequential at first glance, the auditor general warned, "there may be decisions that are being made on incorrect or incomplete information" (Hoye 2022).

The theme of austerity savings as a delusion presents itself again in respondents' perspectives on whether austerity measures within their internal-facing departments have translated into greater value for money for Manitobans. Value for money refers to the ability for governments to provide additional or higher quality services in a cost-effective way. It is

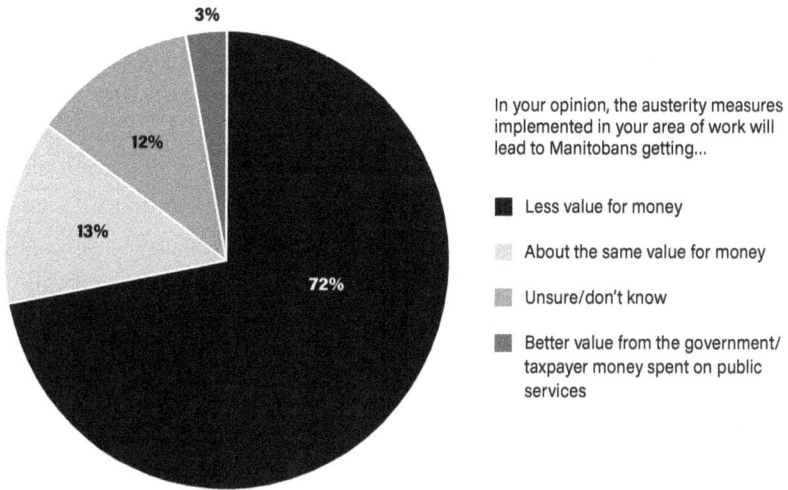

In your opinion, the austerity measures implemented in your area of work will lead to Manitobans getting...

■ Less value for money

▨ About the same value for money

▨ Unsure/don't know

▨ Better value from the government/ taxpayer money spent on public services

Figure 20.4. Survey responses: Austerity and value for money in the public sector.

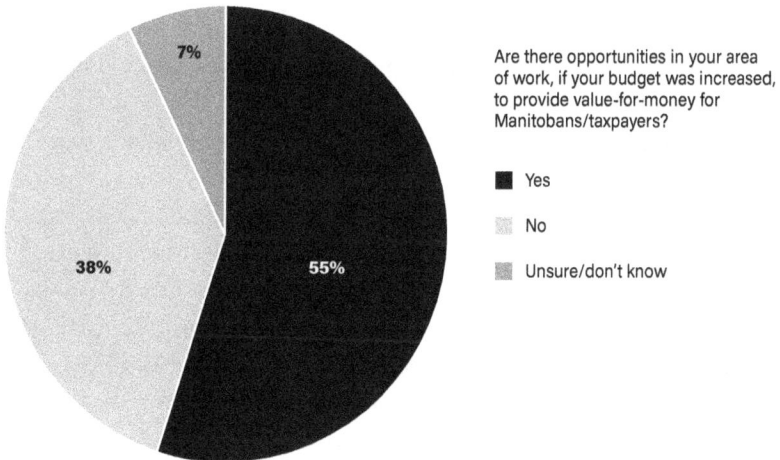

Are there opportunities in your area of work, if your budget was increased, to provide value-for-money for Manitobans/taxpayers?

■ Yes

▨ No

▨ Unsure/don't know

Figure 20.5. Survey responses: Opportunities to provide improved value in the public sector.

often presented by pro-austerity voices as a key outcome that austerity can deliver on. Illustrated in Figure 20.4, a significant 72 percent of respondents believed that austerity measures in their area of work will lead to less value for money for Manitobans as taxpayers.

On the other side of the value for money coin, this group of public servants provided ample examples of non-austerity options in their area of work that *could* increase cost effectiveness and lead to greater value for money to Manitobans. As Figure 20.5 illustrates, 55 percent of respondents believed that with an increased budget, there were opportunities in their line of work to provide value for money to Manitobans as both recipients of government services and taxpayers supplying government revenue. This result is interesting given that budget increases are antithetical to an austerity agenda.

Respondents commented on the value for money benefits that could be achieved by using an increased budget to hire more full-time, permanent staff and to better compensate full-time employees. These included fewer errors, better oversight (especially of private contractors), improved response times, and the ability to engage in long-term planning to help governments make more effective investments. Other respondents commented on how more resources would facilitate better working conditions, which would lead to better public services. One respondent noted how increased budgets would allow for IT updates which could increase value for money by introducing new efficiencies.

The responses from these public sector workers suggest that the austerity measures implemented in their areas of work do not result in cost savings in the long term and lack a strong value for money rationale. Moreover, non-austerity options for providing Manitobans with greater value for money are being presented by workers who have expertise in these issues—given their work in areas such as finance and treasury. Concerningly, however, in the current "culture of austerity" (Evans and Fanelli 2018, 8), their voices risk being erased as governments privilege external consultants for government advice over their own internal experts.

Conclusion

In sum, the effects of austerity are understood by this group of employees along three main themes: (1) austerity measures leading to worsening morale, working conditions, and job satisfaction; (2) concerns that auster-ity measures such as privatization and contracting are being used to hollow out even the internal-facing core functions of the public sector; and (3) looking to the future, austerity strategies not leading to cost savings or value for money in the long run.

The responses from this particular group of public sector workers indi-cate that austerity has effectively seeped through all layers of the Manitoba public sector, impacting not only the service providers and public-facing aspects of the public sector, but also (to a lesser, but still very important, extent) the policy advisors and public servants, who work for and provide support to our political representatives in government and Cabinet and manage the core infrastructure of government. Though statistics indicate that these Administration Departments have, on the whole, fared better than front-line services in terms of receiving more resources and full-time employees after the onset of the COVID-19 pandemic, further research is needed to determine whether or not these spending increases were a short-term response to the pandemic, what the increased spending was allocated toward, and how much of the increased spending was a direct result of federal, as opposed to provincial, allocation. However, what we do know is that, despite their essential day-to-day role supporting the provincial government, these workers have not been exempt from the effects of austerity measures. Importantly, it appears that these workers are also questioning the rationale of austerity as a means of providing cost savings and value for money to Manitobans. The benefits of austerity may in fact be a mirage: something that appears real at first glance, but on further and closer examination, vanishes into thin air.

Notes

1   See Sanders (2022) and Engage MB (2022).

References

Blyth, Mark. 2013. "The Austerity Delusion: Why a Bad Idea Won Over the West." *Foreign Affairs* 92 (3): 41–56. https://www.jstor.org/stable/23526835.

Engage M B. 2022. *Winter 2022 Employee Perspectives Survey Manitoba Government Report on Overall Results.* Accessed 15 March. https://www.gov.mb.ca/asset_library/en/proactive/20222023/employee-perspectives-survey-results-winter-2022.pdf.

Evans, Bryan, and Carlo Fanelli. 2018. "The Permanent Unequal Union: Canada's Provinces and Territories in an Era of Neoliberalism." Introduction to *The Public Sector in an Age of Austerity,* edited by Carlo Fanelli and Bryan Evans, 3–22. Kingston: McGill-Queen's University Press. https://www.jstor.org/stable/j.ctv39x4vq.4.

Fernandez-Gutierrez, Marcos, and Steven Van de Walle. 2017. "Equity or Efficiency? Explaining Public Officials' Values." *Public Administration Review* 79 (1): 25–34.

Government of Manitoba. 2017. "Manitoba Selects K P M G L L P to Study Public-Private Partnership Framework for New Schools." News Release, 2 August. https://news.gov.mb.ca/news/index.html?item=41941.

Halliday, Josh. 2023. "Gove Admits 'Faulty' Guidance Partly to Blame for Grenfell Fire." *The Guardian,* 29 January. https://www.theguardian.com/uk-news/2023/jan/29/gove-admits-faulty-guidance-partly-to-blame-for-grenfell-fire.

Hoye, Bryce. 2022. "Financial Reporting Errors Increasing Across Manitoba Government Departments: Auditor General." *Winnipeg Free Press*, 22 December. https://www.cbc.ca/news/canada/manitoba/government-financial-errors-auditor-general-report-1.6695159.

Krugman, Paul. 2015a. "The Case for Cuts Was a Lie. Why Does Britain Still Believe It? The Austerity Delusion." *The Guardian,* 29 April. http://www.theguardian.com/business/ng-interactive/2015/apr/29/the-austerity-delusion.

———. 2015b. "The Expansionary Austerity Zombie." *New York Times.* https://archive.nytimes.com/krugman.blogs.nytimes.com/2015/11/20/the-expansionary-austerity-zombie/.

Phillips, Susan, and Karine Levasseur. 2004. "The Snakes and Ladders of Accountability: Contradictions between Contracting and Collaboration for Canada's Voluntary Sector." *Canadian Public Administration* 47 (4): 451–74.

Sanders, Carol. 2022. "Public Service Employees' Satisfaction on Decline: Survey." *Winnipeg Free Press*, 13 June. https://www.winnipegfreepress.com/breakingnews/2022/06/13/public-service-employees-satisfaction-on-decline-survey.

Scott, Katherine. 2003. *Funding Matters: The Impact of Canada's New Funding Regime on Non-profit and Voluntary Organizations.* Ottawa: Canadian Council on Social Development.

CONCLUSION

Jesse Hajer, Ian Hudson, and Jennifer Keith

This volume examines the impact of the Manitoba Government's austerity agenda on public services across twenty-one unique areas of government from 2016 to 2022. It encompasses a wide range of public service areas in order to capture the full scope of provincial government activity, including health, education, and other services that enhance the quality of life, sustain healthy communities, and support a prosperous economy. Building upon the foundational analysis in the introduction, this conclusion evaluates the extent to which the changes to these service areas accord with or contradict our definition of austerity. This definition revolves less around balancing budgets or cutting expenses, although it can involve both of those things. It is more about cuts to areas in which the government provides protections for citizens; cuts that, in direct or indirect ways, often increase costs or reduce opportunities for profit by the private sector. The protective role occurs when government shields citizens from the negative consequences of a purely market outcome—for example, when it provides free health and education, prevents environmental damage, offers low-income housing, or provides subsidized childcare or income to those out of work. When these are cut back, it has the effect of reducing the resources available to people outside of their market income. The real logic of austerity is the use of the government budget to redistribute resources toward the private for profit sector and the wealth holding class (Evans and Fanelli 2018; Evans et al. 2023; Whiteside et al. 2021).

As part of this analysis, we have developed three categories of austerity and classified each of the twenty-one areas of public service investigated. The first is *classic austerity*, which includes areas with both spending cuts and staffing cuts along with an increase in privatization. The definition of austerity used here would predict that cuts would fall more heavily on protective spending—areas such as social assistance, housing, and labour. The second, *transformational austerity without spending reductions*, would be more common, according to our definition, in areas that are less connected with the protective role of the state; two examples would be justice and economic development. Finally, we need to account for the unique time period that we examined with a third category: *classic austerity with pandemic reversal*. There were a few areas in which spending increases were mandatory during the pandemic; health is the obvious example. In these areas, we would also still expect an increase in privatization along with the increases in pandemic spending.

These categories are primarily based on two quantitative metrics: inflation-adjusted actual expenditure per Manitoban, and full-time equivalent (FTE) staffing complement.[1] Tables 21.1 and 21.2 present the data for these two metrics in the twenty-one areas examined.

Classifying Program and Policy Areas vis-à-vis Austerity

Classic Austerity, Start to Finish

In some areas, the austerity observed between fiscal years 2016/17 and 2021/22 fits the broad definition of austerity that revolves around spending reductions (including reductions in expenditures and staff), contracting out, and a transformation of operations and policy to benefit private for-profit corporations (including their management and shareholders). Areas falling into this category included Post-Secondary Education (PSE), Adult Learning and Literacy, Immigration, Income Assistance and Disability Supports, Child Welfare Services, Gender Equity and Violence Prevention, Arts, Culture and Sports, Crown corporations, Labour and Consumer Protection, Transportation and Infrastructure, and Municipal Relations.

With the possible exception of Transportation and Infrastructure and Municipal Relations, all of these are areas that we have described as protective. Even municipalities, which allocate funds to areas that are not protective, such as infrastructure, still provide many essential protective services that are often undermined by provincial funding cuts such as affordable housing, immigrant settlement programs, and public health initiatives.

These cuts to protective programs negatively impacted Manitoba families in three distinct, but interrelated ways. First, in many of these cases, the

Table 21.1. Total actual expenditure per Manitoban (inflation adjusted) by program or policy area, 2016–2022.

CHAPTER	PROGRAM/POLICY	2016/17	2019/20	2021/22	% CHANGE, 2016/17 TO 2019/20	% CHANGE, 2016/17 TO 2021/22
1	Childcare	$144	$151	$183	5	27.4
	Childcare (net of federal funding)	$144	$140	$120	-2.5	-16.5
2	K-12 education and schools	$1,235	$1,144	$1,339	-7.4	8.4
	Additional funding by school divisions	$1,947	$1,843	$1,940	-5.3	-0.4
3	Post-Secondary Education total	$625	$567	$551	-9.4	-11.9
	Grants to universities and colleges only	$571	$519	$510	-9	-10.7
4	Adult Learning and Literacy	$26	$19	$19	-25.2	-27.8
5	Immigration	$7.21	$9.10	$3.03	26.2	-58
	Immigration (net of federal funding)	$7.21	$5.31	$3.03	-26.4	-58

CHAPTER	PROGRAM/POLICY	2016/17	2019/20	2021/22	% CHANGE, 2016/17 TO 2019/20	% CHANGE, 2016/17 TO 2021/22
6	Healthcare	$4,952	$4,701	$5,028	-5.1	1.6
7	Environment and Natural Resources	$139	$232	$165	67	19.2
8	Justice	$487	$499	$517	2.4	6.1
9	Income assistance and disability supports[a]	$936	$914	$862	-2.4	-7.9
10	Child Welfare	$457	$445[b]	$385	-2.7[c]	-15.8
11	Housing (provincial grant to Manitoba Housing and Renewal Corporation minus corporate surplus)	$81	$73	$93	-9.5	15.5
12	Status of Women Secretariat	$11.49	$11.22	$10.55	-2.4	-8.2
13	Arts, Culture and Sport	$80	$155	$66	94.4	-16.7

CHAPTER	PROGRAM/POLICY	2016/17	2019/20	2021/22	% CHANGE, 2016/17 TO 2019/20	% CHANGE, 2016/17 TO 2021/22
14	Economic Development and Agriculture	$269	$264	$313	-1.8	16.3
	Agriculture	$141	$142	$118	0.5	-16.7
	Economic Development	$128	$122	$195	-4.4	52.8
15	Crown corporations (Manitoba Hydro, Manitoba Public Insurance, Manitoba Liquor and Lotteries)	n/a	n/a	n/a	n/a	n/a
16	Transportation and Infrastructure	$219	$158	$145	-28	-33.8
	Labour and Consumer Protection	$22.26	$20.41	$16.95	-8.3	-23.9
17	Labour	$12.06	$10.94	$8.69	-9.3	-28
	Consumer Protection	$10.20	$9.47	$8.26	-7.1	-19
18	Indigenous Reconciliation and Northern Relations	$23.46[d]	$21.17	$27.45	-9.8	17

CHAPTER	PROGRAM/POLICY	2016/17	2019/20	2021/22	% CHANGE, 2016/17 TO 2019/20	% CHANGE, 2016/17 TO 2021/22
19	Municipal Relations	$367	$291	$289	-20.7	-21.3
	Administrative services	$183	$168	$461	-7.8	152.4
	Finance	$40	$37	$113	-6.8	181.1
20	Government Services	$124	$113	$323	-9	159.5
	Public Service Commission	$18	$18	$25	-2.1	40.2

a The data series for Income Assistance and Disability Supports include Rural and Northern Child and Family Services administration done directly by the province (not done by agencies) due to its integration with other Family Services programs until 2021/22. This spending accounted for approximately $9 million in 2021/22, equal to approximately 1 percent of the Income Assistance and Disability Supports expenditure that year.

b Data for 2018/19 used due to data limitations for 2019/20. See the online data set on the Austerity in Manitoba project website (Hajer 2023) for details.

c Data for 2018/19 used due to data limitations for 2019/20. See the online data set on the Austerity in Manitoba project website (Hajer 2023) for details.

d Data for 2015/16 used due to lack of comparable data for 2016/17.

Table 21.2. Full-time equivalent positions in Manitoba, by program or policy area, 2016–2022.

CHAPTER	PROGRAM / POLICY AREA	2016/17	2019/20	2021/22	% CHANGE, 2016/17 TO 2019/20	% CHANGE, 2016/17 TO 2021/22
1	Childcare	69.9	71	96	1.6	37.3
2	K-12 Education and schools (civil service)	368.9	331.9	317.4	-10	-14
	School division staffing	26319.9	26785.9	27508.9	1.8	4.5
3	Post-Secondary Education (civil service)	136	127	121	-6.6	-11
4	Adult Learning and Literacy	n/a	n/a	n/a	n/a	n/a
5	Immigration	73	72	53	-1.4	-27.4
6	Health (civil service)	775.35	719.45	765.45	-7.2	-1.3
7	Environment and Natural Resources	1236	910	918	-26	-26

CHAPTER	PROGRAM / POLICY AREA	2016/17	2019/20	2021/22	% CHANGE, 2016/17 TO 2019/20	% CHANGE, 2016/17 TO 2021/22
8	Justice	3225	3160.7	3217.9	-2	-0.2
9	Income assistance and disability supports[a]	1521.05	1439.75	1305.9	-5.3	-14.1
10	Child Welfare[b]	400.4	385.2	407.5	-3.8	1.8
11	Housing[c]	372	318	240	-14.5	-35.5
12	Status of Women Secretariat	17	12	12	-29.4	-29.4
13	Arts, Culture and Sport	203.8	157.6	153.6	-22.7	-24.6
14	Agriculture and Economic Development	760.8	803.7	749.9	5.6	-1.4
	Agriculture	393	365	380.5	-7.1	-3.2
	Economic Development	367.8	438.7	369.4	19.3	0.4

CHAPTER	PROGRAM / POLICY AREA	2016/17	2019/20	2021/22	% CHANGE, 2016/17 TO 2019/20	% CHANGE, 2016/17 TO 2021/22
15	Crown corporations	n/a	n/a	n/a	n/a	n/a
	Manitoba Hydro (MH) and Efficiency Manitoba	6411	5393	5035	-15.9	-21.5
	Manitoba Public Insurance (MPI)[d]	1922.9	1809	1879	-5.9	-2.3
	Manitoba Liquor and Lotteries (MBLL)[e]	3222[f]	3205	2959	-0.5	-8.2
16	Transportation and Infrastructure	1937.2	1960.3	1820.3	1.2	-6
17	Labour and Consumer Protection	300.6	267.2	263.7	-11.1	-12.3
18	Indigenous Reconciliation	91.0[g]	81	90	-11	-1.1
19	Municipal Relations	293.9	273	280	-7.1	-4.7

CHAPTER	PROGRAM / POLICY AREA	2016/17	2019/20	2021/22	% CHANGE, 2016/17 TO 2019/20	% CHANGE, 2016/17 TO 2021/22
20	Administrative services	1572.6	1493.6	1816.9	-5	15.5
	Finance	541	499.3	513.8	-7.7	-5
	Government services	722.6	716.8	913.8	-0.8	26.5
	Public Service Commission	309	277.5	389.3	-10.2	26

a Rural and Northern Child and Family Services staff, which were integrated with Regional Social Services delivering Employment and Income Assistance (EIA) services until 2020/21, are included in 2021/22 data for consistency and comparability with earlier years.

b Due to lack of published data, Rural and Northern Child and Family Services FTEs are not included in these totals. An estimated adjustment for the transfer of Family Reconciliation Services to Justice is also accounted for in this data.

c Due to lack of published FTE data, this data series was generated based on administrative records and provided by Manitoba Government and General Employees' Union (MGEU) upon request. The values represent MGEU member counts, as opposed to total employee counts or FTEs.

d FTE data for MPI represents filled FTEs, i.e., FTEs with employees in the positions.

e Data for MBLL represents Total Employees (including full-time, part-time, and casual), due to lack of published FTE data.

f Data for 2017/18 used due to lack of comparable data for 2016/17.

g Data for 2015/16 used due to lack of comparable data for 2016/17.

result was an increase in household out-of-pocket spending or a decrease in household income. For example, cuts to PSE meant that students paid higher tuition (see also Evans et al. 2023). Cuts to Arts, Culture and Sports can also be framed in this way. While many of the one-time, big-ticket items, such as the $47.5 million related to the stadium for the Winnipeg Blue Bombers, can probably be classified as "luxury" spending that subsidizes the relatively affluent sports fan, the core of the arts and sport programming, which has suffered absolute cuts in funding and staff, is to subsidize sports and culture programming to Manitobans. Organizations funded by the province had to cut staff and deal with more precarious funding. Affluent Manitobans will still be able to afford the increased arts and sports fees, but families that are more income constrained may not.

Second, in areas such as Adult Education, Immigration, Status of Women, and Child Welfare Services, decreased funding compromised government services available to low-income and at-risk members of society, eliminating crucial, and free, services that contributed to their meagre resources. For example, in Child Welfare, workers cautioned that these austerity measures intensified inequality and eroded progress in reversing the highly racialized nature of the child welfare system. The impact on children and families was devastating, cutting off some of the province's most vulnerable citizens from equal access to opportunities, and doing nothing to fix an oppressive system.

Third, austerity redistributed resources from households to businesses. In the example of income assistance and disability supports, reduced funding not only decreases the ability of highly vulnerable populations to access the benefits and services they need to meet their basic needs. Between 2016 and 2022, deeply insufficient income supports for food and nonhousing necessities continued to leave people in grinding, debilitating poverty. It can also reduce wages for an increasingly desperate labour force, an obvious redistribution of income from workers to firms. Similar redistributive consequences resulted from the cuts to Labour and Consumer Protection, which made it increasingly difficult to perform the duties of both areas, crucial in ensuring that Manitoba workers, consumers, and renters received protection from violations of labour, consumer, and rent regulations. Changes to the policy environment in the labour market also showed a consistent shift in favour of business and against workers:

the minimum wage was frozen for several years, dropping to the second lowest in the country; and new legislation like Bill 7, passed in 2016, made forming unions more difficult. Workers Compensation refunded employer premiums while reducing support for injured workers and the capacity to proactively respond to worker safety concerns. Respondents also raised concerns with rent controls being weakly enforced, with landlords consistently bypassing rent controls and receiving exemptions in a majority of cases (for a more comprehensive account of the connection between austerity and Canada's labour force, see Evans et al. 2023).

In addition to decreased funding in these areas, austerity transformed how services were delivered from public sector control toward an increased role for the private sector. Child Welfare saw the growth of third-party, for-profit service providers and the increased use of contract and casual staff. Much of the work that used to be completed by public service workers was contracted out to private companies in both Transportation and Infrastructure and Municipal Relations. The Crown corporations married large staffing cuts, particularly at Manitoba Hydro (MH), with increased use of the private sector. MH sold off Manitoba Hydro International, its profitable consulting arm, and saw maintenance work contracted out. Manitoba opted for a fully privatized model of cannabis retail, rather than the more public model of liquor stores. All three Crowns saw staff positions contracted out, sometimes with disastrously expensive results, as was the case with the IT system overhaul at Manitoba Public Insurance (MPI) known as Project Nova.

In all these areas, staff spoke of increased workloads, worsening mental health, reduced service to the public, and frequently, concern for the very existence of their mandate. As one respondent commented, "The government austerity since 2016 has been a disaster. . . . It will take years to rebuild the coordination and collaborative nature of the sector."

Transformational Austerity without Spending Reductions

The second category includes departments that did not show a clear pattern of spending contraction but saw significant transformational changes in line with the core objectives of austerity, to the benefit of private, for-profit corporations (Evans et al. 2023; Evans and Fanelli 2018;

Whiteside et al. 2021). Departments falling into this category include Childcare, Environment and Natural Resources, and Justice.

Two of these three categories, Childcare and Environment and Natural Resources, fit the category of protective areas that, under our definition, would be subject to outright cuts. In Childcare, civil service staffing and expenditures increased from 2016/17 to 2021/22. The increase, however, was resourced exclusively by an increase in federal transfers as part of the Liberal government's national childcare plan. When looking at provincial spending net of federal transfers for childcare, inflation-adjusted spending per capita fell by 16.5 percent over the period. The increase in spending in Environment and Natural Resources was similarly misleading. Although the real per capita budget increased by 19 percent between 2016/17 and 2021/22, this increase is difficult to interpret because of large one-time expenses related to capitalizing trusts and endowments as a way of funding environmental or conservation measures, an example of the extensive contracting out that has occurred. FTEs tell a different story, with declines of 26 percent during this period.

This leaves Justice as the sole area with an unequivocal budget increase, although its staffing numbers did fall. On one hand, some portions of Justice could conceivably be classified as protective in that they provide Manitobans on the margins with rehabilitation services. This would include programs such as restorative justice, and programs for people to be successful and safe outside justice institutions. These areas saw cuts. For example, the John Howard and Elizabeth Fry Societies' budgets were cut by 20 percent in 2017. On the other hand, a growing carceral state that solves its deep-rooted issues of racism, colonialism, and inequality by locking up its citizens is not protective.

What is clear is that these three areas saw a transformation in how their services were delivered from public to private. Childcare saw a significant push to support private and for-profit models, while the proven nonprofit centre-based model was starved of funding. In Environment and Natural Resources, a growing number of services, such as the campground permit, hunting, and fishing licence system, were contracted out. In Justice, programs that were previously offered in-house were, in the words of one respondent, "contracted out to the private sector, resulting in higher costs and supply issues."

In all three areas, cost containment has put serious pressure on workers and the services they deliver. For example, in Environment and Natural Resources, it created a concerning inability to offer the crucial environmental protection services, like licensing water systems. The staffing declines have stretched workers to such an extent that, at a time of genuine and undeniable climate crisis, they report that the environment and natural resources in Manitoba are not being adequately protected. In both Childcare and Justice, staff report wage freezes, increasing workloads, overtime, and precarious work situations that make it difficult to recruit and retain staff. The situation is sufficiently dire that Justice workers spoke of growing absences due to mental health issues and a system in "crisis."

Classic Austerity with Pandemic Expenditure Reversal

The third category includes areas of government that experienced austerity from fiscal years 2016/17 to 2019/20, but by 2021/22 saw reversals in expenditure trends, ending up with greater expenditures than before the pandemic (Table 21.3). Departments falling into this category include K–12 Education, Health, Housing, Agriculture and Economic Development, Indigenous Reconciliation, and Administrative Departments. We need to make two important distinctions in this category. The first, as with the other categories, is between the protective expenditures that are often cut under austerity, and other spending that often escapes the chopping block or even increase. The second division is between those areas in which the spending increases were caused by the pandemic and those in which spending increases were independent of the pandemic.

Turning first to those areas in which spending decreases were reversed because of the pandemic, Health is the obvious area, but Administrative departments also followed this pattern. In Health, real provincial spending per Manitoban fell by 5.1 percent between 2016/17 and 2019/20. Spending related to COVID-19 reversed this trend, resulting in a 1.6 percent increase between 2016/17 and 2021/22. This spending increase, however, should not hide the fact that between 2016 and 2021, Manitoba's healthcare system fell further behind other provinces in Canada by almost any measure—whether it was overall spending per person, physicians per 100,000 people, or wait times for surgery (see also Evans et al. 2023, 151).

Administration, which includes Finance, Government Services (procurement, asset/capital management, IT services, etc.), and the Public Service Commission, saw expenditure and staffing cuts made prior to COVID-19 reversed during the pandemic. The primary source of this increase was due to pandemic-related procurement, along with a centralization of procurement and other corporate services under Government Services, and the delivery of pandemic relief benefits being paid out to households and businesses through administrative departments. In the absence of the pandemic, it seems likely that these two areas would have continued the pre-2019 austerity regime, making them little different from the areas that suffered from classic austerity from start to finish.

Also, like the areas of classic austerity, many services, from air ambulances to surgery deals with U.S. clinics, were privatized. Further, the combination of privatization and an inadequate increase in spending to address the demands of the pandemic put considerable pressure on public service workers. Staffing shortages in many crucial positions, from nurses to healthcare aides, meant overwhelming overtime and impossible caseloads, leading many to leave the profession, further increasing the burden on those that remained. While there was talk across the country about a healthcare system in crisis during this period, in Manitoba there was even more cause for concern.

Other spending increases cannot be explained obviously by the demands of the pandemic. Many of these areas could be classified as being part of the protective role of the state, and therefore, we would predict subject to austerity cuts: K–12 Education, Housing, and Indigenous Reconciliation. For most of the period between 2016 and 2022, real spending per Manitoban on K–12 Education was below 2016 levels. In addition, the province enforced austerity on the school divisions by legislating a 2 percent cap on school division tax increases. However, in 2021, arbitrated wage settlements with teachers, some including a cost-of-living provision that matched inflation, required a large funding infusion to cover these costs. In Housing, pre-pandemic declines were reversed by significant increases during the pandemic years, resulting in a full recovery to 2016/17 levels and a 15.5 percent increase beyond those levels by 2021/22. However, the money for this came from federal transfers, not from provincial spending. From 2015/16 to 2019/2020, real provincial spending per

Manitoban on Indigenous Reconciliation and Northern Relations dropped by approximately 10 percent. The department, however, saw growth in the pandemic period, and by 2021/22 spending was 17 percent higher than 2015/16 levels.

These three areas (at least since the pandemic) escaped austerity when we would have predicted they would be subject to cuts. In Education this can be explained by an imposed wage settlement, and in Housing, by an increase in dedicated transfers to the province. Indigenous Relations is the only exception. Under our definition, this department would be subject to cuts, but it avoided them, at least after the pandemic. Despite this reversal, the department received a failing grade on their reconciliation report card, and staff reported an inability to visit communities and deliver programs and services. As with the other areas, there was an increase in involvement by the private sector, decreased morale among workers, and compromised delivery of services.

In Housing, the austerity agenda has included the decline in staffing, increasing reliance on the private sector management of social housing, and some high-profile sell-offs of social housing stock. Survey results demonstrate that the stagnant funding for Education (other than the increase for wage settlements) has compromised the quality of education provided to students and has hit more vulnerable students, who need more support, the hardest.

The remaining area that received a funding bump during the pandemic was Agriculture and Economic Development. This funding increase was not caused by the pandemic, but this is also not a protective area that we would predict would be subject to austerity measures. Although FTEs fell, expenditures ended up 15 percent higher in inflation-adjusted per capita terms in 2021/22 compared to 2016/17. Given that these two departments primarily support and advance the interests of private corporations, this increase is not necessarily at odds with a definition of austerity focused on increasing the relative power of business over workers. Reinforcing this point, there was a crucial change in emphasis away from a Community Economic Development and labour partnership approach in economic development toward a focus solely on the interests of business.

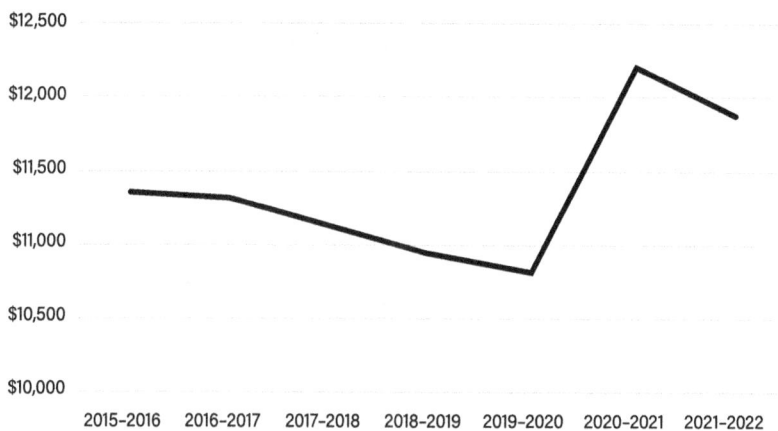

Figure 21.1. Total actual expenditure per Manitoban (inflation adjusted).

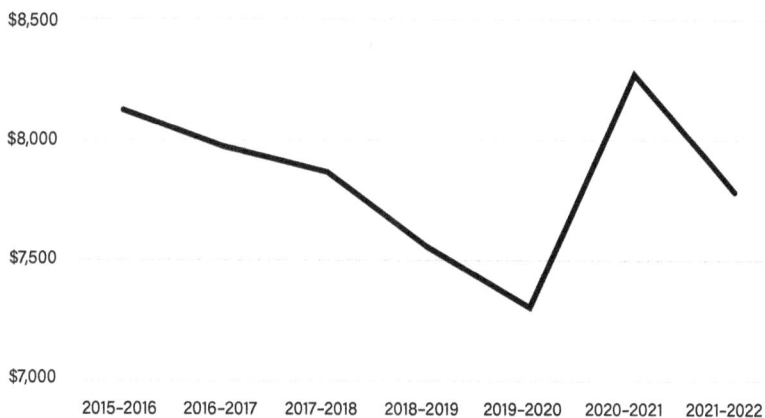

Figure 21.2. Own-source expenditure (total expenditure minus federal transfers) per Manitoban (inflation adjusted).

Table 21.3. Change in per capita spending in Manitoba during the COVID-19 pandemic by area of spending (inflation adjusted) 2021/22 versus 2019/20.

AREA OF SPENDING	YEAR-OVER-YEAR INCREASE (2021/22 COMPARED TO 2019/20) ($)
Health	327.74
Government Services (primarily procurement)	209.58
K–12 education (pandemic supports and arbitrated teacher wage settlement)	194.73
Finance (primarily pandemic-related cash benefits for households and businesses)	75.36
Economic Development (business and investment supports)	73.11
Other	176.88
Total	1,057.40

Total Expenditures

As shown in Figure 21.1, total inflation-adjusted per capita expenditures fit the profile of our third category, with expenditure austerity from 2016/17 to 2019/20 and a pandemic reversal. Table 21.3 shows the top five areas contributing to the $1,057 per capita increase in spending that took place over the pandemic years. As expected, increases in Health spending are the largest contributor, while increases in Government Services spending are the second largest, due primarily to increases in pandemic-era centralized procurement. Pandemic-related increases to K–12 education and a wage settlement with teachers, along with cash and other pandemic-related supports for households and businesses through Finance and Economic Development departments, drive the remaining three top areas of increased spending. Spending in these five areas account for 83 percent of the increased spending over this period.

It is important to note, however, that the increase in total provincial government expenditures was buoyed by growing federal transfers during the pandemic period. Figure 21.2 presents data on own-source provincial government expenditures (total expenditures minus federal transfers), adjusted for inflation, on a per capita basis. As can be seen, the pandemic did lead to a large increase in 2020/21, more than enough to offset the cuts since 2015/16, but by 2021/22, the provincial contribution to spending based on this measure had fallen to below 2015/16 levels.

Conclusion

Austerity only unambiguously came to Manitoba under the PC government elected in 2016, if one adopts a definition that is more nuanced than either balancing budgets or decreasing spending; one that includes public service reform and other initiatives to redistribute resources to the benefit of the private for-profit sector. Pre-pandemic spending followed a clear deficit and expenditure-cutting version of austerity. Overall spending contracted sharply on a real per-person basis, and few departments were spared. However, as Figure 21.1 shows, after 2019/20 real spending per Manitoban rose higher than when the PCs took power. Some of this spending, particularly in Health, is easily explained by the pandemic, although this increased spending did not keep Manitoba from falling further behind other provinces on almost any meaningful measure and was insufficient to address the demands that the pandemic placed on the medical system. The increased spending during the pandemic was also heavily supported by a large increase in federal transfers. If we net out federal transfers, provincial government spending on an inflation-adjusted per capita basis was lower in 2021/22 than when the PCs were elected in 2016.

In other areas with growth, spending increases were mostly due to dedicated federal funding for new initiatives (this was the case with Childcare and Housing) or in areas not associated with the protective role of the state (Justice and Agriculture and Economic Development)—that is, not associated with the definition of austerity under discussion. Indigenous Relations is the only exception to austerity. Even here, spending increases were not close to sufficient to even begin to correct for the historical underspending in this area. A theory of austerity that hinges on stripping nonwork income and services from citizens, and transforming the public sector to facilitate profits for the private sector, fits the PC record particularly well.

The PC austerity regime devastated the public service in Manitoba. Those responsible for maintaining public services in the face of reduced staffing, greater contracting out, and increased interventionist PC micro-managing expressed repeatedly that their ability to do their jobs was compromised, their stress levels increased, and their job satisfaction fell. Respondents to the survey frequently lamented that the profession that they had chosen and trained for, to which they had dedicated their careers, had become a source of anger, frustration, and resentment under the austerity regime. For many, these personal consequences were sufficiently disastrous that they were considering leaving their profession or had already done so. The cuts to funding and staff were so severe that many not only feared for their ability to continue to deliver crucial services but, in some cases, claimed that the system was in crisis.

Notes

1   The one exception is Chapter 15 covering Manitoba Hydro (MH), Manitoba Public Insurance (MPI), and Manitoba Liquor and Lotteries (MBLL).

References

Evans, Bryan, and Carlo Fanelli. 2018. Introduction to *The Public Sector in an Age of Austerity: Perspectives from Canada's Provinces and Territories*, edited by Bryan M. Evans and Carlo Fanelli. Kingston: McGill-Queen's University Press.

Evans, Bryan, Carlo Fanelli, Leo Panitch, and Donald Swartz. 2023. *From Consent to Coercion: The Continuing Assault on Labour*. Toronto: University of Toronto Press.

Hajer, Jesse. 2023. "Austerity in Manitoba." Manitoba Research Alliance, 29 August. https://mra-mb.ca/austerity-in-manitoba/.

Whiteside, Heather, Stephen McBride, and Bryan Evans. 2021. *Varieties of Austerity*. Bristol: Bristol University Press.

EPILOGUE

Jesse Hajer

I think the average Manitoban right now is looking at their family budget and they're making tough choices because of inflation about tightening the belt.... I think Manitobans should expect that their provincial government is going to be going through the same hard work so that we can deliver responsible government for you.—Premier Wab Kinew (Lambert 2024)

They seem to want to be responsive to any group that comes along and says, "We're experiencing economic hardship," or "We're entitled to more benefits than this."... So how they respond to the claims on the public purse and achieve a balanced budget by 2027 is hard to see at this point.—Paul Thomas (Lambert 2024)

On 3 October 2023, the New Democratic Party (NDP) of Manitoba led by Wab Kinew defeated the incumbent Progressive Conservatives (PCs) led by Premier Heather Stefanson, who had faced an uphill battle since first taking over from her deeply unpopular predecessor. Premier Pallister, seen as representing the rural right wing of the PC party, governed from a standard conservative playbook of lower taxes, smaller government, and policies benefiting corporations and the wealthy. The PCs initially managed to implement their austerity agenda without significant political blowback, remaining comfortably ahead of the NDP in the polls from 2017 to 2020 (Rollason 2024). With an unpopular COVID-19 pandemic response, including initially doubling down on austerity in all nonhealth areas of government (Hajer and Fernandez 2021), public favour toward the PCs began to deteriorate, with the NDP overtaking the PCs in the polls by the end of 2020; by June 2021, 47 percent of Manitobans polled indicated they would vote for the NDP compared to 29 percent for the PCs (Rollason 2024; Probe Research 2021). During this period, Brian Pallister dropped to the lowest approval rating of any premier, a position he would maintain until his eventual resignation in September 2021 (Angus Reid Institute 2024). A change in leader initially did little to alter public opinion of the PCs, with the NDP maintaining a sizable polling advantage both province-wide and especially in Winnipeg, and Stefanson taking over Pallister's position of least popular premier in Canada, with even lower approval ratings, for the duration of her tenure (Angus Reid Institute 2024; Rollason 2024).

In a concerted attempt to rehabilitate the public standing of the PC party, Premier Stefanson, representative of the relatively more socially progressive urban wing of the PCs, diverged from her predecessor's approach on multiple fronts. On 18 August 2021, the first day of her leadership campaign, she pledged to withdraw her government's bill that would have eliminated school boards and their ability to levy taxes (Kavanagh 2021). During the campaign she also committed to delay further property tax cuts, saying she would prioritize investments in healthcare instead (Lett 2021). Where Pallister often appeared to be in conflict with Indigenous leaders and governments—leaving office under a cloud of criticism relating to comments suggesting that colonization was undertaken with good intentions toward First Nations (Kives 2021)—Stefanson's first Speech from the Throne placed a heavy emphasis on reconciliation with Indigenous communities and signalled a reset of the relationship with the provincial government (CBC News 2021). A month after assuming the premiership, she rescinded the PCs' controversial wage freeze legislation that restricted public sector entities to wage increases of 0 percent in years one and two, and 0.75 percent increases in years three and four, despite the province having successfully defended the constitutionality of the legislation in court on appeal (Canadian Press 2021). Her first budget, released in the spring of 2022, also de-emphasized tax cuts and deficit reduction in its core messaging relative to previous PC budgets, with no new tax cuts and a proposed 5.6 percent increase in budgeted expenditures, well in excess of previous increases budgeted by the PCs under Pallister. The 2022/23 fiscal year also included two sets of broad-based payments to Manitobans totalling $287 million in spending, including carbon tax relief cheques, announced to assist with the rising cost of living (Manitoba 2022;

Bergen 2023). In the summer of 2022 Stefanson also announced a break with the PC minimum wage policy (Manitoba 2024c), leading to the minimum wage increasing by $3.35 per hour between September 2022 and October 2023, moving Manitoba from second-lowest to third-highest minimum wage among provinces (Employment and Social Development Canada 2024). Budget 2023 put forward a large increase in budgeted expenditures of 13.5 percent.[1] By June of 2023, three months before the fixed date provincial election, public opinion polling showed that Stefanson's efforts had pulled the PCs back into a tie with the NDP at 41 percent, the first time they had not been trailing the NDP since the fall of 2020 (Probe Research 2023).

Despite these progressive divergences, there are several important qualifications on the PCs' policy and fiscal shift under Stefanson that raise questions regarding the authenticity of the change. With respect to labour relations, despite the rescinding of the wage freeze legislation, bargaining directives to restrict wage increases led to several high-profile and prolonged public sector strikes, including at the University of Manitoba, Manitoba Hydro, Manitoba Liquor and Lotteries, and Manitoba Public Insurance (King 2023). The size of the public service also fell by 1.5 percent by March of 2023 relative to two years prior, reaching a new low after years of significant reductions.[2] Relations with First Nations also reached a new level of antagonism, with the provincial government deciding not to search a landfill for the remains of murdered and missing Indigenous women that were believed to be at the site, leading the Assembly of Manitoba Chiefs to call for the premier's resignation (Assembly of Manitoba Chiefs 2023). Stefanson's hard line with First Nations and public sector workers became a central plank in the PCs' reelection strategy, with campaign advertisements promoting her ability to defend the public purse despite special interest group pressure (Kives 2023e, 2023c).

With respect to fiscal policy, actual spending in 2022/23 did increase by 5.6 percent in Premier Stefanson's first full fiscal year in power, but this was well below the abnormally high inflation rate of 7.8 percent over this period.[3] High inflation and strong economic growth boosted revenues by 11.6 percent, leading to a surplus on the fiscal year of $373 million instead of the projected deficit of $548 million, a nearly $1 billion shift.[4] The surplus was made public days before election day, allowing the opposition parties to position the PCs as unwilling to invest in failing public services

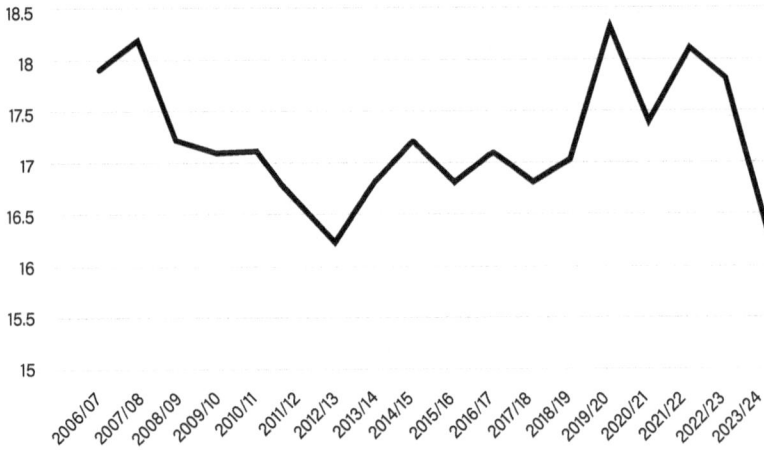

Figure 22.1. Manitoba own-source revenues (total revenues minus federal government transfers) as a proportion of GDP.

or support Manitobans who were struggling with the rising cost of living (Froese 2023). Budget 2023, an election year budget, not only increased spending massively but also cut income tax revenue by nearly $500 million, benefiting high-income earners the most (CCPA–MB 2023b). These tax cuts have brought Manitoba's own-source revenues (total revenues minus federal transfers) as a proportion of GDP to record lows (see Figure 22.1). Despite these tax cuts risking a structural deficit, the PCs committed to cut an additional $1.2 billion in taxes and to balance the budget by 2025 in their reelection campaign, foreshadowing an era of deep expenditure cuts should the PCs be reelected (Hajer 2023a; CBC News 2023a).

The NDP, facing a resurgent PC party, put forward a cautious and fiscally conservative election platform. On the expenditure side, commitments focused almost exclusively on healthcare, spotlighting PC service cuts, wait times, and wage freezes and linking ongoing morale, recruitment, and retention challenges to the PC government's healthcare transformation strategy (CCPA–MB 2023a; Gowriluk 2023). In a clear attempt to associate himself with the political success of former premier Gary Doer while distancing himself from the less popular premier Greg Selinger, NDP leader

Wab Kinew made several commitments: he would keep the Budget 2023 PC income tax cuts and the 50 percent property tax rebate for residential properties and farmers (although he would claw it back from "billionaires"); he would not raise the provincial sales tax; and he would balance the budget in his first term (Manitoba NDP 2023; Kives 2023b). To reinforce this message, the NDP also committed to further tax cuts in the form of a temporary suspension of the gas tax, and secured a public commitment from Doer to be a volunteer advisor to Kinew on trade issues (Da Silva 2023). While the PCs were seen to be fighting an uphill battle against their own record on healthcare and ended up with twelve fewer seats (34 versus 22) in the legislature, the parties were only separated by 3.4 percent in the popular vote, suggesting that the election was closer than one would have expected two years prior.

The newly elected NDP government was immediately faced with the fiscal reality left by the outgoing PCs. As was later detailed in a report undertaken by the accounting firm MNP, the PC government took a number of accounting and spending decisions "of high budgetary risk" (MNP 2024, 1) after tabling the 2023 Budget. These decisions included: implementing large tax cuts, projecting large hydro profits in the face of drought conditions, and pursuing unbudgeted new expenditures of $200 million in healthcare staffing and $1.4 billion in capital expenditures over and above large increases already in Budget 2023. By December 2023 the projected deficit had increased by $1.25 billion (Hajer 2023b; Manitoba 2024b), with the deficit eventually being booked at $1.97 billion compared to the original $363 million estimated in Budget 2023 (Manitoba 2024a). This deficit is all the more remarkable given federal transfers remaining well above historic norms and having returned to near-pandemic highs (see Figure 22.2).

Despite the election being framed as NDP spending versus PC tax cuts (Brodbeck 2023b), the NDP quickly pivoted to an austerity narrative. Projects initiated by the PCs were scaled back or delayed, including personal care homes (Kives 2023d), social housing commitments (Annable 2024), and school construction (Kives 2023a), as well as the NDP's promised hydro rate freeze (CBC News 2023b). Despite the premier acknowledging that the PCs had left them with a structural deficit (Brodbeck 2023a), a campaign by labour and community groups to get the NDP to reconsider its commitments to tax cuts (Lefebvre 2023) gained little traction, with the

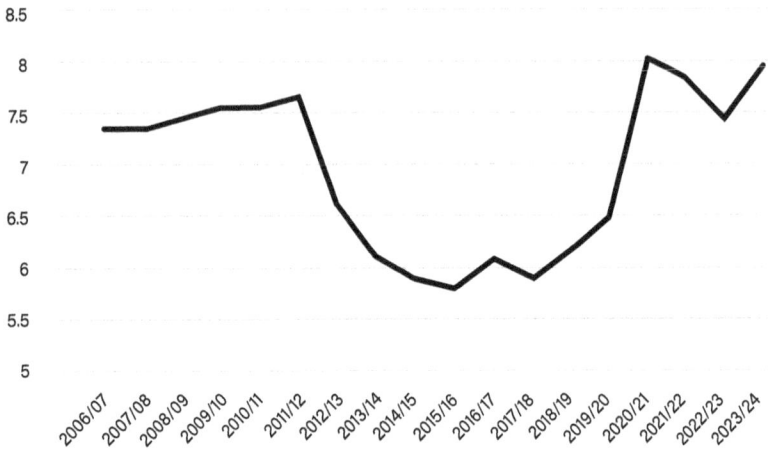

Figure 22.2. Federal government transfers to Manitoba as a proportion of GDP.

NDP making it clear that it was the expenditure side that was going to be adjusted to balance the budget. In response to confirmation of the nearly $2 billion deficit realized in 2023/24, Premier Kinew signalled that belt tightening was on the way (Lambert 2024).

Despite these post-election measures, as of fall 2024, there is no clear evidence of meaningful austerity at a government-wide level. When the massively enlarged deficit projection was released in December 2023, the government committed to a follow-up mid-year fiscal report with changes in response to the large deficit and expenditure management strategies, but the result left the projected deficit unchanged (Manitoba 2024b). Budget 2024, the Kinew-led NDP's first budget, included an expenditure increase of 10.3 percent relative to Budget 2023 and a $796 million dollar deficit. The budget also introduced some modest revenue measures by converting the PCs' property tax credit to a flat rate and scaling back some of the tax cuts for high-income earners, projected to generate $148 million in annual revenues when they fully take effect, equivalent to approximately 30 percent of the Budget 2023 income tax cuts or 10 percent of PC tax cuts implemented since 2016 (Hajer 2024). Public service employment levels also increased in 2024 (Public Service Commission 2024). As summarized in the quote from public administration scholar Paul Thomas at the beginning of this chapter, despite talking the talk of austerity, the government continues to respond with spending initiatives in response to pressing issues of the day, including a generous settlement with healthcare workers to avoid a strike (CBC News 2024). The government also reversed industrial austerity measures targeting labour unions, reinstating card check certification and tabling anti-scab legislation (Chang 2024; Da Silva 2024).

The NDP government, however, has not shied away from its commitment to balance in its first term, despite potential headwinds including: the depth of the 2023/24 deficit, particularly given record federal transfers and relatively solid economic growth;[5] a structural deficit arising from tax cuts paired with public sector compensation agreements providing large wage increases; the risk of federal transfers being reduced with a change in government; and economic risks associated with a Trump presidency, specifically new trade barriers for Manitoba exporters. While a deficit of nearly $2 billion in 2023/24 is a daunting figure, much was attributed to anomalous, one-time factors, including a drought-driven hydro revenue deficit of $810 million and the settlement of long-standing lawsuits against the government adding as much as $693 million. This left a $468 million deficit to overcome, an amount smaller than the yearly deficits run between 2011/12 and 2018/19. With inflation and record population growth driving up government revenues (and costs), managing this deficit could have been considered easier than during the last decade, all other things being equal, relying on steady economic growth to balancing the budget without deep expenditure cuts.

More recent developments however increasingly seem to be pushing a balanced budget without deep cuts out of reach. Budget 2025 projected a much larger than budgeted deficit for 2024/25 ($1.24 billion versus $796 million) and tabled a $794 million deficit for 2025/26 (Government of Manitoba 2025). It is clear, at a minimum, that attempting to balance the budget in the next two years without tax increases as committed to in the election will necessarily preclude sustaining any significant investments in repairing public services or mounting a meaningful government response to growing inequality and social challenges.

The Kinew NDP's commitment to maintaining the large PC tax cuts has created an inevitable trade-off between reducing deficits and investing in public services. As noted in the introduction and conclusion to this volume, the austerity implemented by the PCs was broad-based and multifaceted; but with respect to total expenditures, it focused on reprioritizing and constraining expenditures as opposed to overall cuts in dollar value terms, with more ambitious action on restructuring the state and labour relations. This still led to significant reductions in inflation-adjusted per capita terms, compromising service quality, but did not match some of the more extreme historical episodes of austerity such as the federal government cuts in the 1990s. This is the type of conservative fiscal policy that the Kinew-led NDP will likely pursue.

It is clear that Kinew views himself as a "third-way" social democrat in the mould of Gary Doer, who in turn was consciously modelled on Tony Blair and New Labour in the UK, as well as Bill Clinton and the fiscally conservative "New Democrats" in the United States. This "progressive neoliberalism" (Fraser 2017) or "social-liberal" (Camfield 2018, 106) approach did not exacerbate neoliberalism but it did not provide any alternative either. It amounted to a pro-business, corporate takeover of established political parties of the centre-left, accepting free market capitalism and its associated inequalities, while narrowing their social justice focus to poverty alleviation and diversity, equity, and inclusion initiatives (Evans et al. 2023). With is focus on electoral gains and survival, NDP leaders in Canada have been complicit in this transition (Camfield 2013, 218), as have social democratic parties more broadly (Evans 2014). This "austerity light" governance (Himelfarb 2024, 82), emphasizing balanced budgets and deficit reduction, has overseen skyrocketing inequality and growing economic precarity, fuelling the rise of right-wing anti-establishment populist nationalism, political polarization, misinformation and conspiracy theories, and emboldened white supremacist and anti-immigrant movements.

Following the reelection of Donald Trump, some long-standing proponents of progressive neoliberalism are questioning its ability to address the pressing political challenges of our time, suggesting a more radical, populist left-wing alternative may be necessary (Guastella 2024). This would require increasing taxes for the well-off, reining in corporate power, and using the borrowing capacity of the state to expand and create new Crown enterprises and universal public services. Unfortunately, this path to a genuinely inclusive and just Manitoba is not compatible with the self-imposed fiscal restraints and "third-way" governance philosophy of the current Manitoba NDP.

Notes

1   Author's calculations based on Government of Manitoba (2023).

2   Author's calculations based on Public Service Commission (2024).

3   Authors calculations based on Government of Manitoba (2024d) and Statistics Canada (2024a).

4   Originally the surplus was reported as $240 million in the 2022/23 public accounts but was revised upwards to $373 million in the 2023/24 public accounts released in September of 2024 (Government of Manitoba 2024a).

5   Real GDP growth in Manitoba averaged 2.4 percent between 2021 and 2023; the average growth rate between 1982 and 2019 was 2.1 percent. Author's calculations based on Statistics Canada (2024b).

References

Angus Reid Institute. 2024. "Archive." https://angusreid.org/archive/.

Annable, Kristin. 2024. "Manitoba NDP Scaling Back Former PC Government's 700-Unit Social Housing Pledge." CBC Manitoba, 16 January. https://www.cbc.ca/news/canada/manitoba/housing-ndp-promise-units-1.7081121.

Assembly of Manitoba Chiefs. 2023. "AMC Chiefs-in-Assembly Call for the Resignation of Manitoba's PC Party Leader." Assembly of Manitoba Chiefs, 18 August. https://manitobachiefs.com/press_releases/amc-chiefs-in-assembly-call-for-the-resignation-of-manitobas-pc-party-leader/.

Bergen, Rachel. 2023. "Manitoba Government to Hand Out Cheques to Help with Rising Food, Fuel Costs." CBC Manitoba, 26 January. https://www.cbc.ca/news/canada/manitoba/manitoba-financial-assistance-cheques-affordability-1.6726754.

Brodbeck, Tom. 2023a. "Strap In for Financial Turbulence if Premier Right about Deficit." *Winnipeg Free Press*, 14 December. https://www.winnipegfreepress.com/local/2023/12/14/strap-in-for-financial-turbulence-if-premier-right-about-deficit.

———. 2023b. "Tax Cuts vs. Restoring Services: Choice between Tories, NDP Stark." *Winnipeg Free Press*, 18 September. https://www.winnipegfreepress.com/local/2023/09/18/tax-cuts-vs-restoring-services-choice-between-tories-ndp-stark.

Camfield, David. 2013. "Labour's Response to the Crisis and the Future of Working Class Politics." In *From Crisis to Austerity: Neoliberalism, Organized Labour, and the Canadian State*, edited by Tim Fowler. Ottawa: Red Quill Books.

———. 2018. "Manitoba: Fiscal Policy and the Public Sector under 'Today's NDP.'" In *The Public Sector in an Age of Austerity: Perspectives from Canada's Provinces and Territories*, edited by Bryan M. Evans and Carlo Fanelli. Kingston: McGill-Queen's University Press.

Canadian Press. 2021. "Heather Stefanson Undoes Another Initiative of Her Predecessor, Plans to Repeal Wage-Freeze Bill." CBC Manitoba, 24 November. https://www.cbc.ca/news/canada/manitoba/manitoba-wage-freeze-bill-1.6260671.

CBC News. 2021. "Indigenous Leaders Express Hope for Renewed Relationship after Manitoba Throne Speech." CBC Manitoba, 24 November. https://www.cbc.ca/news/canada/manitoba/manitoba-throne-speech-indigenous-leaders-1.6260262.

———. 2023a. "Manitoba PCs Promise to Lower Income Taxes over Next 4 Years." CBC Manitoba, 5 September. https://www.cbc.ca/news/canada/manitoba/manitoba-progressive-conservatives-income-tax-cut-1.6957085.

———. 2023b. "Promised Manitoba Hydro Rate Freeze Might Be Delayed as Deficit at Utility Looms: Minister." CBC Manitoba, 24 November. https://www.cbc.ca/news/canada/manitoba/manitoba-hydro-drought-hydroelectric-freeze-1.7039403.

———. 2024. "New Health-Care Contract Will Lift Wages 27% over 4 Years, Unions Say." CBC Manitoba, 18 October. https://www.cbc.ca/news/canada/manitoba/manitoba-health-care-contract-cupe-1.7356366.

CCPA–MB (Canadian Centre for Policy Alternatives–Manitoba). 2023a. "Health Care Dominates First Post-Pandemic Manitoba Election." 26 September. https://www.policyalternatives.ca/news-research/health-care-dominates-first-post-pandemic-manitoba-election/.

———. 2023b. "More of Budget 2023 Tax Changes Go to Manitoba's Richest 10% than Bottom 50% Combined." *Policy Fix* (blog). Winnipeg: Canadian Centre for Policy Alternatives–Manitoba. 10 March. https://policyfix.ca/2023/03/10/more-of-budget-2023-tax-changes-go-to-manitobas-richest-10-than-bottom-50-combined/.

Chang, Arturo. 2024. "Manitoba Bill Banning Replacement Workers Now Prevents Employees from Crossing Picket Lines." CBC Manitoba, 31 October. https://www.cbc.ca/news/canada/manitoba/manitoba-omnibus-bill-replacement-workers-legislature-1.7368669.

Da Silva, Danielle. 2023. "Former Premier Doer Pledges to Work with Kinew's NDP." *Winnipeg Free Press*, 12 September. https://www.winnipegfreepress.com/breakingnews/2023/09/12/former-premier-doer-pledges-to-work-with-kinews-ndp.

———. 2024. "Kinew Touts Biggest Labour Law Changes 'in a Generation.'" *Winnipeg Free Press*, 19 March. https://www.winnipegfreepress.com/featured/2024/03/19/kinew-touts-biggest-labour-law-changes-in-a-generation.

Employment and Social Development Canada. 2024. "Historical Minimum Wage Rates in Canada." Open Government Portal, 21 November. https://open.canada.ca/data/en/dataset/390ee890-59bb-4f34-a37c-9732781ef8a0.

Evans, Bryan. 2014. "Social Democracy in a New Age of Austerity." In *Orchestrating Austerity: Impacts and Resistance*, edited by Stephen McBride and Donna Baines, 79–90. Halifax: Fernwood Publishing.

Evans, Bryan, Carlo Fanelli, Leo Panitch, and Donald Swartz. 2023. *From Consent to Coercion: The Continuing Assault on Labour*. 4th edition. Toronto: University of Toronto Press.

Fraser, Nancy. 2017. "The End of Progressive Neoliberalism." *Dissent Magazine*, 2 January. https://www.dissentmagazine.org/online_articles/progressive-neoliberalism-reactionary-populism-nancy-fraser/.

Froese, Ian. 2023. "Manitoba Posts $270M Surplus for 2022–23 Fiscal Year." CBC Manitoba, 29 September. https://www.cbc.ca/news/canada/manitoba/government-budget-surplus-2022-1.6982737.

Government of Manitoba. 2022. "Manitoba Families Most in Need to Benefit from $87-Million 'Family Affordability Package.'" News Release, 31 August. https://news.gov.mb.ca/news/index.html?item=56181&posted=2022-08-31.

———. 2023. *Historic Help for Manitobans: Budget 2023*. Manitoba. www.gov.mb.ca/asset_library/en/budget2023/budget-2023.pdf.

———. 2024a. "Annual Reports and Public Accounts." Government Finances. 2024. https://www.gov.mb.ca/government/finances/annualreports-publicaccounts.html.

———. 2024b. "Fiscal Updates." Government Finances. 2024. https://www.gov.mb.ca/government/finances/fiscalupdates.html.

———. 2024c. "Manitoba Government Announces Plan to Increase Minimum Wage to $15 by October 2023." News Release, 18 August. https://news.gov.mb.ca/news/?archive=&item=55959.

———. 2024d. "Provincial Annual Report and Public Accounts Archive." Government Finances. https://www.gov.mb.ca/government/finances/financial-reports-archive.html.

———. 2025. "Budget 2025." Province of Manitoba. 25 March. https://www.gov.mb.ca/budget2025/index.html.

Gowriluk, Caitlyn. 2023. "Manitoba NDP Bet Big on Health Care, Rode Wave of Discontent with Tories on Way to Victory." CBC Manitoba, 4 October. https://www.cbc.ca/news/canada/manitoba/2023-election-analysis-kinew-stefanson-1.6986075.

Guastella, Dustin. 2024. "We Can Do Better than Bidenism." *Jacobin*, 19 November. https://jacobin.com/2024/11/biden-economic-policy-inflation-welfare.

Hajer, Jesse. 2023a. "PC Tax Cut Claims Don't Add up." *Winnipeg Free Press*, 2 October. https://www.winnipegfreepress.com/opinion/analysis/2023/10/02/pc-tax-cut-claims-dont-add-up.

———. 2023b. "Tax Cuts True Threat to Manitoba's Finances." *Winnipeg Free Press*, 18 December. https://www.winnipegfreepress.com/opinion/analysis/2023/12/18/tax-cuts-true-threat-to-manitobas-finances.

———. 2024. "NDP Budget Starts Reversing PC Handouts for the Rich." *Winnipeg Free Press*, 18 April. https://www.winnipegfreepress.com/opinion/analysis/2024/04/18/ndp-budget-starts-reversing-pc-handouts-for-the-rich.

Hajer, Jesse, and Lynne Fernandez. 2021. *COVID-19, Austerity and an Alternative Social and Economic Policy Path for Manitoba*. Winnipeg: Canadian Centre for Policy Alternatives–Manitoba. https://www.policyalternatives.ca/publications/reports/covid-19-austerity-and-alternative-social-and-economic-policy-path-manitoba.

Himelfarb, Alex. 2024. *Breaking Free of Neoliberalism: Canada's Challenge*. Toronto: James Lorimer and Company.

Kavanagh, Sean. 2021. "End of Manitoba's Controversial Education Reform Bill Could Come in Several Ways: Political Scientist." CBC Manitoba, 21 August. https://www.cbc.ca/news/canada/manitoba/bill-64-education-manitoba-1.6148218.

King, Adam. 2023. "A Strike Surge in Manitoba Is Challenging Wage Repression." *Jacobin*, 1 October. https://jacobin.com/2023/10/manitoba-government-workers-strike-surge-wage-repression.

Kives, Bartley. 2021. "3 Strikes and You're Outed: Brian Pallister Makes Another Inflammatory Comment about Indigenous Relations." CBC Manitoba, 10 July. https://www.cbc.ca/news/canada/manitoba/pallister-comments-future-leadership-1.6096506.

———. 2023a. "Manitoba May Abandon PC Plan to Build Schools Using P3s." CBC Manitoba, 26 December. https://www.cbc.ca/news/canada/manitoba/p3-schools-manitoba-not-happening-1.7069394.

———. 2023b. "Manitoba NDP Promises to Follow in PC Footsteps on Property Tax Rebate if Elected." CBC Manitoba, 9 August. https://www.cbc.ca/news/canada/manitoba/ndp-kinew-financial-promises-1.6931503.

———. 2023c. "Manitoba Public Service Union Ridicules Premier's 'Draw the Line' Video." CBC Manitoba, 29 August. https://www.cbc.ca/news/canada/manitoba/stefanson-video-mgeu-response-1.6951274.

———. 2023d. "NDP Government Puts Manitoba Health-Care Projects on Hold." CBC Manitoba, 19 December. https://www.cbc.ca/news/canada/manitoba/manitoba-health-care-projects-postponed-1.7064172.

———. 2023e. "PCs Make Opposition to Landfill Search a Central Facet of Campaign as Manitoba Election Day Nears." CBC Manitoba, 25 September. https://www.cbc.ca/news/canada/manitoba/landfill-search-manitoba-pcs-election-1.6976993.

Lambert, Steve. 2024. "Manitoba's NDP Government Faces Fiscal Crunch during 1st Year in Office." CBC Manitoba, 2 September. https://www.cbc.ca/news/canada/manitoba/manitoba-ndp-government-2024-budget-1.7311230.

Lefebvre, Charles. 2023. "'Economic Circumstances Have Changed': Manitoba Unions Call on NDP to Reverse Provincial Tax Cuts to Fulfill Election Promises." CTV News Winnipeg, 13 December. https://winnipeg.ctvnews.ca/economic-circum-stances-have-changed-manitoba-unions-call-on-ndp-to-reverse-provincial-tax-cuts-to-fulfill-election-promises-1.6685945.

Lett, Dan. 2021. "Premiers-in-Waiting Break Silence: Stefanson or Glover Will Become the First Woman to Lead Manitoba's Government; the Six-Week Campaign Has Been a Quiet Affair Short on Specifics." *Winnipeg Free Press*, 27 October. https://www.winnipegfreepress.com/breakingnews/2021/10/27/premiers-in-waiting-break-silence.

Manitoba NDP. 2023. "Fiscal Framework." 21 September. https://www.mbndp.ca/fiscal_framework.

MNP. 2024. *Post-Election Financial Accountability Review*.

https://www.gov.mb.ca/asset_library/en/proactive/20232024/post-election-finan-cial-accountability-review-022124.pdf.

Probe Research. 2021. "NDP Lead Widens Further in Manitoba." Polls. 18 June. https://probe-research.com/polls/ndp-lead-widens-further-manitoba.

———. 2023. "NDP, PCs Head into Pre-election Period in a Dead Heat (June 2023 Provincial Voting Intentions)." Polls. 21 June. https://probe-research.com/polls/ndp-pcs-head-pre-election-period-dead-heat-june-2023-provincial-voting-intentions.

Public Service Commission. 2024. *Public Service Commission Annual Report*. https://www.manitoba.ca/csc/publications/annrpt/index.html.

Rollason, Kevin. 2024. "Manitoba NDP More Popular Now than on Election Day: Poll." *Winnipeg Free Press*, 13 June. https://www.winnipegfreepress.com/breakingnews/2024/06/13/ndp-more-popular-now-than-on-election-day-poll.

Statistics Canada. 2024a. "Table 18-10-0004-01: Consumer Price Index, Monthly, Not Seasonally Adjusted." Data. 19 November. https://www150.statcan.gc.ca/t1/tbl1/en/tv.action?pid=1810000401.

———. 2024b. "Table 36-10-0222-01: Gross Domestic Product, Expenditure-Based, Provincial and Territorial, Annual." Data. 7 November. https://www150.statcan.gc.ca/t1/tbl1/en/tv.action?pid=3610022201.

INDEX

www.ingramcontent.com/pod-product-compliance
Lightning Source LLC
Chambersburg PA
CBHW020453270326
41926CB00008B/581